# RESTLESS MIND
## *CURIOSITAS* & THE SCOPE OF INQUIRY IN
## ST. AUGUSTINE'S PSYCHOLOGY

# RESTLESS MIND
## CURIOSITAS & THE SCOPE OF INQUIRY IN
## ST. AUGUSTINE'S PSYCHOLOGY

*Joseph Torchia,* O.P.

MARQUETTE
UNIVERSITY

PRESS

MARQUETTE STUDIES IN PHILOSOPHY
NO. 83
ANDREW TALLON, SERIES EDITOR

LIBRARY OF CONGRESS CATALOGING-IN-PUBLICATION DATA

Torchia, N. Joseph (Natale Joseph), 1953-
 Restless mind : curiositas & the scope of inquiry in St. Augustine's psychology / by Joseph Torchia, O.P.
  pages cm. — (Marquette studies in philosophy ; No. 83)
 Includes bibliographical references and index.
 ISBN-13: 978-0-87462-719-0 (pbk. : alk. paper)
 ISBN-10: 0-87462-719-2 (pbk. : alk. paper)
 1. Augustine, Saint, Bishop of Hippo. 2. Curiosity. I. Title.
 BR65.A9T58 2013
 270.2092—dc23
                        2012049691

Printed at Brandt Doubleday, Davenport, IA, USA

Cover art: *St. Augustine in his cell*, 1490 (tempera on panel) Sandro Botticelli (1444/5-1510) Galleria degli Uffizi, Florence, Italy / The Bridgeman Art Library.

♾The paper used in this publication meets the minimum requirements of the American National Standard for Information Sciences—Permanence of Paper for Printed Library Materials, ANSI Z39.48-1992.

Association of American
University Presses

MARQUETTE UNIVERSITY PRESS
MILWAUKEE

The Association of Jesuit University Presses

# CONTENTS

IN MEMORY OF


ROBERT J. O'CONNELL, S.J.

(1925-1999)


AND


KURT J. PRITZL, O.P.

(1952-2011)


ANIMA UNA ET COR UNUM IN DEO

# PREFACE

In *The Dragons of Eden*, Carl Sagan made a somewhat jarring observation regarding his perception of St. Augustine's negative impact upon the western intellectual tradition:

In a time in some respects similar to our own, St. Augustine of Hippo, after a lusty and intellectually inventive young manhood, withdrew from the world of sense and intellect and advised others to do likewise: "There is another form of temptation, even more fraught with danger. This is the disease of curiosity." The time of Augustine's death, 430 A.D., marks the beginning of the Dark Ages in Europe.[1]

Whether Augustine was the spiritual father of a prolonged period of intellectual darkness (or how intellectually "dark" the Middle Ages actually were) is, of course, a matter of debate. In point of fact, however, Augustine not only considered curiosity a sin, but one of the primal vices responsible for drawing humans from the grasp of eternal truths toward the transitory and metaphysically impoverished world of sense experience. The question for us to ponder is why an inquiring and incisive thinker like Augustine, who committed himself wholeheartedly to attaining an understanding of the contents of his faith, should have developed such ambivalence toward the very inquisitiveness which prompts one to learn in the first place.

Augustine's negative attitude toward curiosity is certainly surprising, in view of his intellectual vibrance and the range of his speculative interests. And far from shunning the world of sense experience, he displays a healthy fascination with all aspects of the natural order.[2] Why, then, did Augustine place such a heavy emphasis on the role of curiosity as a pivotal factor in the soul's movement from God? In responding to this question, an initial observation is in order: Augustine's understanding of curiosity is by no means a monolithic one. It is as multi-faceted and multi-dimensional as any other aspect of his thought.

While Augustine's discussions of curiosity assume a pronounced moral tone (linking it as he does with a propensity toward sinfulness), this moral dimension is intimately connected with epistemological and metaphysical ones. In epistemological terms, Augustine deems curiosity a sin because it prompts us to pursue as objects of knowledge things which are either morally objectionable in themselves or which impede our spiritual progress by attaching us to mere images of authentic reality. Metaphysically speaking, this misplaced desire is intimately connected with our positioning in the scheme of creation. Curiosity is thus instrumental in precipitating the soul's movement from God in its loves and affections and defining its happiness in terms of mutable, corruptible reality.

This study, then, proceeds from the premise that an in-depth investigation of Augustine's diverse interpretations of curiosity offer a veritable *excursus* through the intriguing topography of his own distinctive world-view. This world-view was greatly shaped by the intense polemics in which he engaged throughout his prolonged career as a philosopher, theologian, and pastor. From this standpoint, an analysis of what Augustine says about the sin of curiosity provides something of a window through which we might penetrate various aspects of his thought, and thereby, even achieve what approximates a more systematic account of his intellectual outlook.[3]

The very fact that Augustine numbers curiosity among the principal vices imparts it with some significant anthropological implications. In Augustinian terms, however, any discussion of a Christian anthropology (encompassing theories of human nature and personhood) is ultimately a matter of psychology in its most literal sense (i.e., a study of the soul).[4] While the Christian Augustine strove for a balanced anthropology that upheld the "harmonious" union of soul and body (the spiritual and physical aspects of our humanness, respectively), he remained deeply committed to a spiritualistic model of human nature. From his earliest to his latest writings (even when he criticizes Platonic/Neoplatonic and Manichaean dualism), he still defined humans primarily in terms of souls which use bodies.[5] In this regard, Augustine's discussions of curiosity provide an ideal segue for examining his penetrating soundings of the depths of the inner life, that is, the life of the soul, or more precisely, the mind.

By virtue of his own experience, Augustine associated curiosity with the restlessness that dominated his pre-conversion life (and that he perceived as endemic in human existence and temporality in general). Undoubtedly, the most frequently quoted line from Augustine's vast *corpus* of writing is the one found at the very beginning of the *Confessiones* (I,1,1): "…our heart is restless until it rests in you." But the very currency of this quote can generate a misunderstanding. Students of Augustine tend to assume that he identified the notion of restlessness exclusively with the impulses of the heart. In actuality, however, Augustine could have easily substituted the word "minds" for "hearts" in this context. Indeed, Augustine was extremely preoccupied with the phenomenon of the restless mind and the multifarious intellectual endeavors it generates, for good or ill. More specifically, his psychology was attuned to that special brand of restlessness prompted by curiosity and the fundamental human desire to know.

Just as the Christian Augustine defines our humanness in terms of the soul and the body together (the inner and outer dimensions of the human being, respectively), he likewise posits a dual restlessness inherent in human nature that encompasses our affectivities and emotions (centered in the heart), and our intellectual desires (centered in the mind). Among Augustine's lasting contributions to the psychology of the self, I would venture, we must include his recognition of a deeply seated cognitive appetite, the impetus to our search for knowledge.

Augustine's analyses of curiosity, in effect, reveal a profound psychological discovery on his part, namely, that desire encompassing an intellectual component. While it is obvious that humans desire physical pleasure or sensual gratification, it is not so readily apparent that we can also be motivated by a cupidity of the mind. In a very real sense, Augustine did nothing less than solidify the connection between knowledge and cupidity that had already been crystallizing for a long time in the pagan and Christian traditions alike.

In this respect, however, the most salient feature of curiosity for Augustine does not lie in the mind's reliance upon images alone. It also encompasses the sheer desire to know (regardless of the objects of one's attention) and the visceral pleasure one derives from satisfying that craving. For this reason, Augustine's understanding of mind or intellect as an immaterial principle is crucial. Only the immaterialist thesis (that is, that we are more than bodily beings alone) allows him to view curiosity as more than a bodily desire. As an expression of mind and will working closely in conjunction (as a "rational will"), curiosity thus represents a drive that proceeds from a level of our humanness that transcends corporeal inclinations. If that is the case, it cannot be a mere outgrowth of instinct or biological drives alone. Rather, it reflects a general orientation of the self toward objects which define its relationship with God and neighbor alike.

But this study concerns more than Augustine's understanding of curiosity, its dynamics, and its effects.

It is multi-dimensional in scope and coverage. In broad terms, it is about the notion of curiosity itself, and the ways in which this notion has been understood in the western intellectual tradition. In this larger framework, Augustine makes a significant contribution toward the interpretation of curiosity in a critical manner, drawing upon what came before him and putting it to new and influential use in the interests of his own distinctive Christian vision. In this respect, Augustine's treatment of curiosity must be approached against the background of the various sources that contributed to the development of this notion in classical authors, in Scripture, and in the Fathers of the Church.

By the same token, this study is about more than the history of an idea. I also attempt to put Augustine in conversation with later currents of thought. In a 21st century context, his deliberations on the curious disposition have something significant to say about the nature and value of human inquiry. More specifically, they assume a surprising relevance for a contemporary rethinking of the meaning of *scientia* and its impact on the quality of our lives.

## ACKNOWLEDGMENTS & DEDICATION

The groundwork for this book took shape over the course of a sabbatical year (2007-2008), when I held the appointment of Visiting Scholar at the School of Philosophy at The Catholic University of America.

I acknowledge my deep gratitude to the late Rev. Kurt J. Pritzl, O.P. (then Dean of the School of Philosophy) for this appointment and the rich opportunities it offered for implementing this project from its inception. I am eternally grateful for his encouragement to bring it to fruition. Father Pritzl embodied the best of the Dominican ideal of *Contemplare et contemplata aliis tradere*. For me, he remains the model of that unique combination of priest, professor, scholar.

As I survey the course of my own intellectual journey, I must also acknowledge the contribution of the late Robert J. O'Connell, S.J., my perennial mentor for navigating the vast terrain of Augustinian thought. His influence manifests itself in everything I write, and I often hear the faint echo of his gentle but firm challenge: "Say it better!" Father O'Connell taught me much, but first and foremost, he imparted a sense of the joy of finding God in all things. It is to the memory of Kurt J. Pritzl, O.P. and to Robert J. O'Connell, S.J., then, that I respectfully dedicate this work. *Requiescat in pace.*

Priory of St. Thomas Aquinas
Providence College

## NOTES TO THE PREFACE

1. Carl Sagan, *The Dragons of Eden. Speculations on the Evolution of Human Intelligence* (New York: Random House, 1977), 236-237.
2. Augustine's early *De Ordine* (A.D. 11/386-3/387) exemplifies this world affirming fascination. Of particular interest in this connection is his extended discussion at *De Ordine* I,3 regarding the possible causes of the variations in the sound of running water through a drain. Another interesting testimony to his appreciation of the created universe is found in *Confessiones* VII,13 and its exaltation of the beauty and majesty of all aspects of nature.
3. The attempt to achieve a systematic presentation of Augustine's thought has been a perennial problem. In my book *Creatio ex nihilo and the Theology of St. Augustine: The Anti-Manichaean Polemic and Beyond* (New York: Peter Lang, 1999), I use Augustine's teaching on creation as an alternate referent for achieving such a systematic account. As I state in its *Preface* (ix-x), "we require a recurrent motif that enables us to discern certain salient features on the Augustinian landscape." From my standpoint, the doctrine of *creatio ex nihilo* provides one such motif. But I think that the topic of *curiositas* and its intimate connection with Augustine's triadic interpretation of iniquity can serve as another (at least to the extent that it brings to the fore the variety of Augustine's polemic endeavors, allowing us to assess his evolution as a thinker over his entire career).
4. In my book *Exploring Personhood. An Introduction to the Philosophy of Human Nature* (Lanham: Rowman and Littlefield Publishers, 2008), *Chapter 4* ("St. Augustine: A Harmonious Union") focuses on Augustine's anthropology and his ongoing emphasis on the primacy of the soul over the body, even as he attempts to harmonize the relationship between soul and body in achieving a theory of human persons as psychosomatic unities.

5. Cf., *De Quantitate Animae* 13,22; 34,77; *De Genesi contra Manichaeos* II,7(9); *De Genesi ad Litteram* VI,12(22).

# INTRODUCTION

Augustine's critical stance toward curiosity and its diverse expressions is particularly prominent in those works encompassing the period spanning his conversion to Christianity (c. A.D. 386) and the middle of his life (c. A.D. 397-400). From the composition of the Cassiciacum dialogues to the emergence of the *Confessiones*, his great spiritual autobiography, he consistently condemned "allurements of the eyes" (*illecebra oculorum*), whose chief attraction lies in their novel or unusual nature, rather than in their conduciveness to the good and happy life.[1] Long after his conversion (in both intellectual and moral terms), Augustine found himself driven by a curiosity for things of the world and the variety of experience it offered.

## THE PROBLEM DEFINED

On a personal level, the close connection between curiosity and carnal desire in the young Augustine's experience insured that his attachment to the world and its goods would only intensify. The cultural milieu in which he moved (with its lavish spectacles, eroticism, and violent exhibitions) provided a continual lure (which in his reckoning, at least,) could only draw him further from God.

Augustine, then, discerned the marked presence of curiosity in his life, and this disposition assumed a pivotal role (indeed, something of a driving force) in shaping the character of his spiritual journey. But "personal experience" is a broad category that encompasses all of the encounters and influences that were instrumental in forging his outlook. Accordingly, we must pay special attention to the variety and impact of Augustine's intellectual sources in coming to terms with the highly fluid character of curiosity in his writings.

In previous studies of this topic, I confined my analysis of Augustine's sources of curiosity to Plotinus and Neoplatonism.[2] But in the interim, I have come to see that we cannot limit those influences to the

Neoplatonic tradition alone. Rather, an examination of Augustine's discussions of curiosity and its various manifestations suggest his reliance upon a plethora of sources: classical Greek and Latin, patristic, and scriptural. And even if his primary influence for certain aspects of his treatment of curiosity point to a Plotinian influence, we must still be attuned to the influences that had shaped Plotinus's own understanding of this notion, or more precisely, the notion of a restlessly active nature.[3]

But as this study will show, any instability that curiosity exhibits in Augustine is not attributable to him alone. Rather, the notion he inherited from his predecessors (in the broadest possible sense) was already deeply imbued with a fertility (and frequently, an ambiguity) of meaning. This is one of the reasons why an investigation of Augustine's overall treatment of curiosity offers such a fascinating prospect. For, given his own intellectual imagination and penchant for creative adaptation and synthesis, he was undoubtedly struck by its rich potential for fresh applications. Likewise, such diverse applications at least partially reflect Augustine's uneasiness with this notion. He frequently seems uncertain about its full import, groping for an adequate explanation of its role in shaping the soul's life and destiny.

## CONCEPTUAL/LINGUISTIC DIMENSIONS OF CURIOSITY

We confront, then, an inevitable difficulty in attempting an investigation of Augustinian curiosity (*curiositas*), or alternatively, "the lust of the eyes" (*concupiscentia oculorum*). But this difficulty is only compounded when we attempt to investigate curiosity along broader historical lines. As Neil Kenny has queried, 'is it the history of a 'concept'...or of a set of words, or of some extra-conceptual and extra-linguistic reality, such as 'desire'?"[4] The problem is one of clarification, a clarification not easily achieved, in light of the many meanings that have accrued to curiosity in the western tradition. From this perspective, Augustine is by no means alone in developing something of a "patchwork" of connotations surrounding the notion, from inquisitiveness, to an excessive desire for novel (but trivial) information, to a meddlesomeness, to an aimless restlessness, to an officious preoccupation with everyday matters, to a presumptuous impiety. Augustinian curiosity represents an encoding of all these connotations and more.

In this vein, we much broach some guiding questions.

When Augustine writes of curiosity as a sin or vice, to what is he referring? Is he (following Kenny's lead) designating a concept, a linguistic category, or some hybrid encompassing both conceptual and linguistic dimensions? In historical terms, is he describing exactly the *same thing* or *same experience* that his predecessors and contemporaries understood by this notion? By the same token, will our assessments of Augustinian curiosity inevitably be shaped by modern and contemporary interpretations? For that matter, do Augustine's interpretations of curiosity have anything relevant to say to a 21st century audience? Each of these questions, of course, must be addressed in their appropriate context as this investigation unfolds. But at the outset, some preliminary observations are in order.

First and foremost, we must recognize the fact that curiosity is (and apparently always was) heavily laden with meanings. Accordingly, the 21st century interpreter of Augustine's treatment of this notion will bring to bear considerable hermeneutical baggage that represents the slow accretion of various interpretative judgments over the centuries. In this respect, what we now understand by the term "curiosity" (and how we judge its value) is as much a legacy of the past as it is of our own cultural setting. Here, Kenny's distinction between curiosity as a concept, as a linguistic expression, and as an extra-linguistic reality is most thought-provoking. Curiosity (perhaps more than many other notions we take for granted in our day-to-day discourse) is inextricably bound up with its etymological underpinnings. This is an important consideration in coming to terms with its significance in ancient and medieval sources (including Augustine himself).

Augustine's discussions of curiosity bear the imprint of its rather checkered history, and thereby, reveal the creativity of a thinker steeped in the literary heritage of antiquity, in both the secular and ecclesiastical spheres. By the same token, the variety of interpretations which he applied to curiosity reflect the expansion and evolution of his own philosophical, theological, and polemical interests. This evolving understanding of curiosity was very much shaped by his own requirements as a thinker and his creative adaptation of diverse sources (pagan and Judeo-Christian alike).

## A CONTEMPORARY ISSUE

In this writer's estimation, then, we must approach Augustine's indictments of curiosity within the framework of conceptual history. In
that broader setting, we not only come to appreciate its intellectual
moorings in past thinkers, but its contemporary relevance as well. As
we will see, curiosity received decidedly "bad press" in both classical
antiquity and the Christian patristic era. In numerous representatives
of those traditions, we find the suggestion that curiosity constitutes a
somewhat dangerous tendency that can easily lead one into forbidden
areas of investigation. For pagans and Christians alike, there was a
shared assumption that some intellectual pursuits and the desire that
motivates them are morally objectionable.

While curiosity continued to be viewed with disdain (or more drastically, condemned as a vice) throughout the Middle Ages, it was greatly rehabilitated in the modern era, when the desire to know for its own
sake was extolled as one of the noblest virtues. Still, curiosity retained
its ambiguous status, as a trait that can be viewed as good or bad, depending upon the context in which the desire to know emerges, or the
excessiveness with which it finds expression. But if curiosity is deemed
blameworthy, wherein lies its deficiency? Does it proceed from the
very activity in question, or in the attitude of the one engaging in it? In
Augustinian terms, curiosity encompasses both the activity itself and
the accompanying attitude of those in its grasp.

We frequently encounter, in fact, a blurring of the distinction in
Augustine's writings between the intellectual pursuit in question and
the moral quality of one's curious desire to know. On the one hand,
Augustine might not view pursuits like astrology or natural science
as wrong *per se*. For him, the fault lies in the practitioners' excessive
preoccupation with empty images, the antithesis of a commitment to
genuine truth and wisdom. On the other hand, however, Augustine
would condemn intellectual pursuits themselves that have no useful
purpose, other than the satisfaction of a vain desire to know (e.g., what
Augustine terms a "perverted science" engaged in for no better reason
than a fascination with what is merely unusual or even grotesque).

In a very real sense, Augustinian curiosity underscores a certain tension in western thinking between an exaltation of the quest for knowledge and a condemnation of the visceral desire to know as frivolous
or even impious. The fact that these attitudes toward cognitive desire

are not easily reconcilable bespeaks a deeply rooted bias transcending ideological and religious outlooks. The perennial suspicion of curiosity in the West reveals a concern as to where it might lead, or even a fear over the pitfalls of overstepping the bounds of human inquiry. Roger Shattuck assesses this tendency in these terms:

> Carefully considered in their complete versions, the ancient stories of Adam and Eve, of Prometheus and Pandora, of Psyche and Cupid, and even of the genie in the jar appear to give more credence to limits than to liberation, to the dangers of unauthorized knowledge than to its rewards. Ignorance may not be bliss, but the observation of prudent restrictions on knowledge might have prevented the fate of Orpheus, of Icarus, and of Lot's wife.[5]

Paradoxically, however, the persistent view of curiosity as something objectionable (or potentially so) presupposes an intellectual support system that makes a value-based distinction between "legitimate" pursuits of knowledge (directed toward what are viewed as worthy objects of investigation) and counterfeit claims to knowledge (e.g., "pseudo-science") that simply do not measure up to rigorous epistemological standards of truth, objectivity, and verifiability.[6] The standards, of course, can change markedly over the centuries and from one perspective to another. Accordingly, we must attune ourselves to the extent to which a given thinker's interpretation of curiosity (whether it be positive or negative) reflects that thinker's own outlook and value judgments.

## METHODOLOGY AND OVERVIEW

This book comprises three parts: **Part I**, "The Sources of Augustinian *Curiositas*" (**Chapters 1-3**), **Part II**, "*Curiositas* and the Soul's Journey" (**Chapters 4-6**), and **Part III**, "*Curiositas* and the Earthly City" (**Chapters 7-9**).

The "Assessment" sections at the end of Chapters 3, 6, and 9 have a dual function: they summarize what has been covered in that part of the book, and provide segues to what immediately follows. In this way, they serve as bridges from one line of discussion to another.

The **Conclusion** and the **Epilogue** round out the study, placing Augustine in contact with contemporary issues and currents of thought.

**Part I** investigates the philosophical and theological roots of Augustine's treatment of this notion. More specifically, I explore his possible inspirations in both the Greek tradition (**Chapter** [1]: *Classical Greek Origins*) and Latin tradition (**Chapter** [2]: *Classical Latin Origins*) of classical antiquity, as well as in the Bible and the Fathers of the Church (**Chapter** [3]: *Scriptural and Patristic Sources*). In my estimation, **Part I** can stand on its own as a conceptual history of curiosity in its most seminal manifestations in the western tradition.

While this history does not purport to be comprehensive in its scope and coverage (as perhaps no conceptual history of this rather unwieldy topic can honestly claim to be), it does offer the reader a liberal overview of pertinent texts from a wide range of authors and viewpoints. For the larger purposes of this study, such an overview hopefully provides a useful touchstone for assessing Augustine's contribution to this concept and for delineating the influences that might have been operative in his own Christian interpretation. As we have observed, *curiositas* had acquired a plethora of meanings by the time that Augustine began his speculative endeavors. From this standpoint, I wish to approach Augustine not only as a notable representative of the patristic era, but as an influential western thinker whose treatment of curiosity was anchored in a vibrant intellectual tradition (embracing pagan and Judeo-Christian sources), even as it reflects his creative originality.

**Part II** provides a thematic investigation of the significance of curiosity in Augustine's psychology. This investigation unfolds with a sensitivity to the various contexts in which Augustinian curiosity assumes a salient role, with an attention to its moral, epistemological, and metaphysical dimensions. **Chapter** 4 (*Curiositas in Augustine's Moral Triad*) traces the evolution of Augustine's interpretation of curiosity as the "lust of the eyes" and the triadic schematization of iniquity (in terms of pride, curiosity, and carnal concupiscence) in which that interpretation gradually took shape. **Chapter** 5 (*Peregrinatio Animae*) grounds this interpretation in Augustine's account of his spiritual journey in the *Confessiones*. A careful reading of that penetrating document of the inner life shows us why Augustine perceived his curious attraction to worldly allurements as a pivotal factor in his prolonged and circuitous journey to God. This self-assessment finds its most salient expression in the incisive examination of conscience that dominates the tenth book of the *Confessiones*, where he reflects on the persistence of *curiositas* in his post-conversion experience.

**Chapter** [6] (*Curiositas and the Plotinian Hypothesis*) fuses Augustine's depiction of *curiositas* as one of the primal vices with his appropriation of the fall motif he appropriated from Neoplatonism, along with Plotinus' theory of the motives for the soul's gravitation toward temporality. In this connection, we must be alert to what is uniquely Christian in Augustine's negative attitude toward curiosity, and what represents an adaptation of ideas drawn from secular wisdom. Augustine was firm in his conviction of a consonance between Judeo-Christian Revelation and what he derived from the "books of the Platonists". This conviction allowed him to interpret what he found in Scripture and in patristic writing from a Neoplatonic perspective. In so doing, he also drew upon the broader legacy of the classical tradition and the diverse meanings it imparted to the inquisitive spirit.

When viewed through a Neoplatonic, and more specifically, a Plotinian "lens," Augustine's discussions of curiosity assume significant anthropological implications. This is particularly apparent in his account of the soul's subjection to the cares inherent in temporal involvement. This consideration provides a segue to **Part III**, and its investigation of Augustine's interpretation of the dynamics of curiosity in an existential context, that is, in the "Earthly City". **Chapter** 7 (*In Imago Dei*) lays the groundwork for this interpretation, against the background of Augustine's analysis of the constitution of human nature as developed in the *De Trinitate*. In that work, Augustine makes a distinction between a higher contemplative function of the mind directed toward eternal truths and a lower active (or "sciential") function directed toward the outer world of sense experience and its mutable images. In *De Trinitate* XII, Augustine examines the soul as created in God's image in connection with the drama of Original Sin and the biblical account of the expulsion of Adam and Eve from a pre-lapsarian condition. This exegetical exercise provides Augustine with an opportunity to investigate the effects of sin (including the sin of curiosity) upon the proper ordering of humans in the scheme of creation.

Augustine's emphasis on the tension between the active and contemplative orientations of the mind are addressed in more concrete terms in **Chapter** 8 (*The Curiositas of Pagans*). In the *De Civitate Dei* (the textual focus of this chapter), Augustine analyzes those "faults of the mind" that provide the roots of iniquity. If, as Augustine assumes, curiosity is a sin and a key motive for human "fallenness," then its effects are most evident in a secular environment that stands opposed to the value system of the Christian Gospel. Curiosity assumes a key polemical role in Augustine's overall indictment of the magic, superstition, idolatry, and spectacles prominent in pagan culture.

But Augustine by no means confined the human susceptibility to the negative effects of curiosity to pagans alone. Indeed, he considered pagans and Christians alike as suffering under the penal condition of Original Sin. In **Chapter** 9 (*The Curiositas of Christians*), I address his diagnosis of the ills plaguing his own Christian community, as a mixed body of saints and sinners immersed in a world largely shaped by a pagan value system. While Augustine could laud the intellectual heritage of classical antiquity, he also offered his brethren guidelines for sound intellectual inquiry in a manner consistent with a Christian vision of truth. From Augustine's perspective, such inquiry presupposes a distinction between what is essential to human beings en route to their supernatural destiny and what is merely superfluous or even detrimental to the achievement of that end.

It is interesting to observe that some of Augustine's most powerful statements regarding the pursuit of true knowledge emerge in the context of his pastoral writing. In this context, he reveals the intimate relationship between the way of the mind and the way of the heart in his own intellectual journey. In the final analysis, however, Augustine conceives the pursuit of truth in theocentric terms. In other words, he considers all attempts at achieving knowledge on a naturalistic level as subordinate to the knowledge of eternal truths that ultimately proceed from the higher light of Divine Wisdom. This is why Augustine would reject the suggestion that scientific inquiry is a value-neutral endeavor.

From an Augustinian perspective, scientific inquiry must be guided by those transcendental values which reflect a universal moral order and the inherent goodness of creation. For this reason, scientific investigation and the curiosity which spurs it cannot provide their own justification, independently of considerations of a common good. I address this issue in my **Conclusion** (*Augustine, Curiositas, and Scientific Values*), which links the Augustinian polemic against curiosity with a discussion of the ends of science itself.

Does Augustine's polemic say anything significant to a contemporary audience about the parameters and possible limits of the scientific enterprise? This question is especially compelling at a time when many uncritically view science as paradigmatic of knowledge, and scientific progress as the ultimate justification for research on every level. From my standpoint, what Augustine says along these lines is most relevant. Accordingly, I craft what I characterize as an "Augustinian ethic" of scientific inquiry rooted in his moral, metaphysical, and epistemological presuppositions about the foundations of truth, knowledge, and the human good.

Augustine's critique of an unrestrained curiosity (which can rationalize any investigation whatsoever in order to satisfy its sheer appetitiveness), does not automatically put him at odds with the scientific enterprise as a means to achieving truth. Rather, that critique merely discloses that Augustine places a higher premium on attaining wisdom than the analysis of nature and the gathering of empirical data. In this respect, Augustine can find kindred spirits in those contemporary thinkers who have rediscovered the appeal of contemplative or meditative ways of knowing, above and beyond what the empirical sciences yield. The **Epilogue** (*Augustine in a New Voice*) attempts to put Augustine in conversation with that outlook, drawing upon Martin Heidegger's extended commentaries on Augustine's interpretation of curiosity as the "lust of the eyes."

In my estimation, Heidegger allows Augustine to speak to us in a manner attuned to the exigencies of life in a world often more enamoured with technology and its benefits than with the toil and risks of genuine thinking. But however the message is articulated, the sentiments are unmistakably Augustinian. At base, Augustine issues us a powerful "wake-up" call: a challenge to be humble enough to recognize the mystery of things; a capacity to gaze in wonder at creation; and an acceptance that there are some things that must always elude our complete understanding.

## NOTES TO THE INTRODUCTION

1. Cf., *De Quantitate Animae* 19(33), for an illustration of this viewpoint in the early Augustine and *Confessiones* X,34(55), for its presence in his examination of conscience at mid-life.
2. "*Curiositas* in the Early Philosophical Writings of Saint Augustine," *Augustinian Studies* XIX (1988): 111-119; "Curiosity," *Saint Augustine through the Ages: An Encyclopedia*. Edited by Allan D. Fitzgerald, O.S.A. (Grand Rapids, Michigan: William B. Eerdmans, 1999): 259b-261a;

"Plotinian *Tolma* and the Fall of the Soul in the Early Philosophy of Saint Augustine," *Dissertation Abstracts International* 48, issue #4 (1987), Fordham University.

3. I qualify my characterization of curiosity here as a "restlessly active nature", since that is the way in which Plotinus would have construed what we designate by the broad term "curiosity".

4. Neil Kenny, *Curiosity in Early Modern Europe Word Histories* (Weisbaden: Harrassowitz Verlag, 1998), 17.

5. Roger Shattuck, *Forbidden Knowledge* (New York: St. Martin's Press, 1996), 23.

6. In the religious sphere, a parallel distinction might be made between what is appropriate for human investigation and what lies beyond our claim to know. In the classical tradition, the aspiration to know what exceeds the parameters of our knowledge is tantamount to *hubris* and impiety.

# PART I

# THE SOURCES OF AUGUSTINIAN *CURIOSITAS*

# CHAPTER I

# CLASSICAL GREEK ORIGINS

What is the meaning of the word "curiosity"? According to the *Oxford English Dictionary*, its most fundamental set of meanings pertain to its significance "as a personal attribute."[1] But an attribute of what? An adequate response to this question, it seems, requires a consideration of the term's adjectival form. The *Oxford English Dictionary* further informs us that "to be curious" (as a subjective quality) entails the following traits (among others):

> …bestowing care…careful; studious, attentive; anxious; concerned; solicitous; fastidious or particular regarding details; skillful; clever; desirous of seeing or knowing; eager to learn; no right to know, or what does not concern one, prying; devoting attention to occult art.[2]

This catalogue of meanings carries over into the substantive "curiosity," a term encompassing all the characteristics associated with the "curious" disposition. The rich import of these English words points to their etymological roots in the Latin and Greek languages.

## ETYMOLOGICAL ROOTS

An examination of the Latin origins of our English word "curiosity" reveals an intriguing linkage between the noun *cura*, the adjective *curiosus*, and the noun *curiositas*.[3] In this respect, the substantive *curiositas* (an apparent neologism coined by Cicero) seems to have been derived from the adjective *curiosus*, which found its source in *cura*, with its connotations of care, concern, anxiety, and diligence.[4] Initially, however, there was nothing especially pejorative about the cluster of meanings associated with *curiosus* (or its corresponding adverb *curiose*) and *cura*.

If *curiositas* eventually assumed a negative import, it largely proceeded from its etymological derivations. Accordingly, any pejorative connotations associated with *curiosus, curiose,* and *cura* were transmitted to *curiositas* as well. In this respect, *curiositas* fulfilled the much needed terminological role of expressing a passion for knowledge, but one characterized by all the meanings (both positive and negative) that *curiosus* came to acquire. As Neil Kenny suggests, "in classical antiquity *curiositas*…seems to have been exclusively associated with a desire for knowledge (and) almost always denoted excessive desire."[5] But an excessive desire for knowledge also encompassed an impious aspiration to teachings and insights beyond the appropriate parameters of human investigation.

In this chapter and the one which follows, we assess the diverse meanings inherent in *curiositas* and its root words, with a special focus upon those pejorative connotations that assumed a prominence in classical authors. But these connotations were not the product of the Latin tradition alone. They also point to the influence of parallel terms in the Greek language. In this context, a broad survey of writings serves as a means of illustrating the wide-ranging significance of Greek and Latin vocabulary alike. This chapter, then, considers the relevant Greek sources; the next chapter considers the relevant Latin ones.

## A BROAD LITERARY SURVEY

In point of fact, the Latin word *curiositas* (along with its adjectival and adverbial variants) incorporates the assorted connotations of two Greek words: *periergos* and *polupragmon* (and their corresponding substantives *periergia* and *polupragmosune*). *Curiosus* (and by extension, *curiositas*) acquired this wide-ranging significance from those Greek counterparts.[6] On the one hand, this Greek terminology generally designates an excessiveness of speech or manner that manifests itself as a fastidious, officious, or meddlesome nature. On the other hand, these words assume an epistemological connotation of a zealous (or more precisely, an over-zealous) pursuit of knowledge or a rash inquisitiveness. We begin with an examination of some salient usages of *periergia*-language.[7]

While *periergia* can rightfully be translated as "curiosity," such a rendering must be appreciated in light of a broader set of meanings. From this standpoint, the notion of intellectual desire is closely associated with various ideas expressive of a preoccupation (either ordinate or inordinate) with oneself, with the affairs of others, or with the world at large. There is indeed a rather fine line between exercising a concern and the application of one's mind to careful inquiry. In this connection, *periergia* provides something of a generic term for an intellectual acuity or a mental agility conducive to learning and challenging investigations.[9] Julian, for example, highlights the capacity of riddles to inspire us to engage in diligent study of hidden truths in the interests of improving our intelligence.[10] Lucius likewise links such intellectual activity with a desire for that kind of adventure that prompts us toward exciting and even hazardous ventures.[11]

But one discerns a certain ambivalence in ancient Greek literature toward an excessiveness in intellectual endeavors consistent with a disdain for excess on any level and the correlative exaltation of balance and moderation in promoting the realization of the good life.[12] Accordingly, *periergia*-language offers a convenient vehicle for indicting counterfeit claims to genuine knowledge. In this vein, Hippocrates critiques those superfluous pursuits of knowledge that bestow no advantage on their objects of investigation, which are motivated by a selfish desire for personal gain, or which are antithetical to a search for wisdom that is free of needless elaboration and outward show.[13]

What applies to the intellectual life is applicable to human existence as a whole. Indeed, Greek literature offers ample examples of a rather dim view of extravagance in appearance or dress, pleasurable activities, speech, and even religious rites.[14] In each instance, excessiveness finds its mode of expression in *periergia*-language. By implication, such language provides a means of contrasting what is objectionably elaborate with what enhances human character, especially through the proper exercise of rationality. In the words of Epictetus, "learn who you are, and then, in the light of that knowledge, adorn yourself."[15] From this standpoint, we are not only mortal animals, but rational ones. Accordingly, those who exemplify the *periergic*-attitude oppose the life of virtue as well.

Theophrastus, in fact, isolates the *periergos* as a specific character type given to an officiousness promoting an over-assumption of responsibility, in word or deed.[16] Officious individuals, in short, fail to deliver on their promises, precisely because they exceed their ability to do so. We discern a marked utilitarian bias in this particular motif that rejects what is considered unnecessary or futile in a given context.

This emphasis on what is useful over what is not prompts a general condemnation of idle or futile pursuits, or those things better left alone.[17]

But such moral judgments also presuppose some ideal of order and standards for guiding fitting or decent behavior. In this vein, *periergia*-language can connote a presumption that challenges accepted norms of piety.[18] Socially speaking, this terminology can likewise designate an overstepping of bounds that infringes upon the interests of others. Accordingly, *periergia*-language suggests a tendency toward troublemaking or meddlesomeness.[19] In this respect, these connotations dovetail with those inherent in *polupragmon*-language.

The most literal translation of *polupragmon* is its most expressive one: *busy about many things* (or, for the substantive *polupragmosune*, *busyness about many things*). On the surface, this notion is by no means blameworthy. Rather, it might well be considered laudatory to engage actively in a variety of tasks (or, in contemporary parlance, "to multitask"). But what immediately stands out in a perusal of relevant sources is the assumption that this kind of behavior invariably yields ill consequences. Meddlers are equated with troublemakers, intriguers, and busybodies preoccupied with plotting and usurping rights.[20] While such meddling can occur in many areas of life, *polupragmon*-language has a special affinity for the description of inquisitive forays into the realm of knowledge, including those that intrude into peoples' private affairs. In this respect, *polupragmon*-language can be conveniently coupled with *periergia*-language.[21]

This is not to say that the inquisitive spirit is always condemned. On the contrary, Polybius stresses that the ability to negotiate crises proceeds from that study of history and inquiry in general that provides entertainment for the mind.[22] In this context, *polupragmon*-language is equated with a healthy intellectual curiosity that contributes to an expansion of human horizons.[23] By the same token, Polybius offers the caveat that inquiries drawn from books pose no hazard for us, so long as the appropriate documents and libraries are readily accessible.[24] But unrestricted inquisitiveness is also perceived as immoral. In this respect, Pausanias recounts the tale of the irreverent man who entered a religious shrine for no other reason than to satisfy his bold inquisitiveness and thereafter suffered for his presumption.[25]

## THE PHILOSOPHICAL LEGACY

The richness of meaning inherent in *periergia*-language and *polupragmon*-language finds a special applicability in Hellenic philosophy and its Hellenistic offshoots. In this respect, an adequate survey of the possible sources and inspirations of Augustinian *curiositas* must not only address its Plotinian background, but the Platonic, Aristotelian, and Middle Platonic forerunners of the Neoplatonic tradition as well. While these discussions display a clear ethical and epistemological import (consistent with what we encounter in the literary tradition), the vocabulary under scrutiny eventually assumes a distinct metaphysical significance in Plotinus' *Enneads*. For this reason, classical philosophy offers a crucial medium for analyses of the negative implications of the notion of curiosity. These analyses would provide Augustine with a series of compelling precedents in his own interpretations of that notion.

## PLATO AND ARISTOTLE

In a philosophical context, *polupragmon*-language provides the terminological vehicle for describing the proverbial "busybody." The image of the busybody is a key component of Plato's (c. 429-347 B.C.) portrayal of Socrates' (469-399 B.C.) mission and his defense of the philosophical way of life. The dual indictment directed against Socrates (i.e., impiety and corrupting the youth of Athens) carries an implicit charge that Socrates failed to mind his own business, both in infringing upon the prerogative of parents to educate their children in the values of the *polis* and in setting up "new gods" of reasoning that were perceived as threats to the *status quo*.

According to the charge delineated in Plato's *Apology*, Socrates' characterization as a busybody is intimately connected with the assumption that he was committed to the practice of natural science, like those Sophists who manipulated truth and language in their own egocentric interests.[26] In point of fact, however, Socrates himself readily acknowledged his penchant for interfering with the affairs of other people and challenging their uncritical presuppositions. This constituted the essence of Socrates' perception of his philosophical mission and the task it imposed upon him, namely, questioning those who professed to know what they did not know, and then, leading them to a recognition of their own ignorance.[27]

In a very real sense, Socrates' ideal of wisdom dictates that the wise person is one who performs his or her own work, and thereby, refrains from meddling in areas beyond one's ken. This position finds expression in the early Socratic dialogues and their portrayal of Socrates in action. But Plato's most philosophically sophisticated use of *polupragmon*-language is found in the *Republic* and its attempt to define what constitutes the just state. Plato's analysis of the underpinnings of justice is intimately bound up with his tripartite schematization of both the *polis* and human nature.

What holds true for humans holds true for the *polis* as well. In Platonic terms, the division of human nature into its rational, spirited, and appetitive parts finds its political counterpart in the division of states into philosopher-kings, guardians, and workers, respectively. In both cases, justice is defined as the principle of "doing one's own business," or conversely, "not being a busybody."[28] This principle is wholly consistent with the classical Hellenic ideal of justice (*diké*) and the accompanying ideal of order (*taxis*). Both ideals encourage the allocation of things and people to their appropriate roles and functions in the cosmos. By extension, these ideals complement the Greek understanding of piety or holiness (*eusebeia*) as a reverence or respect for what is held most dear in the *polis*. Among these values is the implicit dictum that we should not overstep the bounds of our social position or role before humans and gods alike. To do so renders one guilty of the crime of impiety (*asebeia*) and the *hubris* that prompts such presumptuous behavior in the first place.

These sentiments must be understood in the context of fourth century (B.C.) political developments and the growing sense of the evils of imperialism in the face of the Peloponnesian War and its aftermath. As Viktor Ehrenberg observes, "Athenian imperialism was the main result of Athenian πολυπραγμοσύνη, or...πολυπραγμοσύνη was the psychological basis of Athenian imperialism."[29] Thus, Plato's emphasis upon the importance of "doing one's own business" is by no means a call to detach oneself from public life altogether, or an endorsement of a passive indifference to political concerns. Rather, it reflects the Socratic conviction that citizens should perform the tasks for which they are best equipped, because they possess the requisite knowledge that allows for proficiency in a given endeavor. Still, the fact remains that "doing one's own business" can easily become an exercise in egotistical self-promotion, if the practitioner does not act with a sense of the common good of the *polis* as a whole.

In the final analysis, any political division is comprised of individual human beings. From this standpoint, the various strata of the *polis* will function properly as long as their members observe the norms of proper order. In this way, Plato endorses the principle "embodied in child, woman, slave, free, artisan, ruler, and ruled, that each performed his one task as one man and was not a versatile busybody" (καὶ οὐκ ἐπολθπραγμόνει).[30] But if Plato defines justice as the principle of everyone doing his own business, then such a single-minded attentiveness to one's task is the *sine qua non* of excellence in the polity as a whole (even in the absence of the other virtues).

> A thing, then, that in its contribution to the excellence of a state vies with and rivals its wisdom, its soberness, its bravery, is this principle of everyone in it doing his own task. And is it not justice the name you would have to give to the principle that rivals these as conducing to the virtue of state?[31]

By the same token, the underlying presupposition that the just state is comprised of those "doing their own business" serves as a means of defining what constitutes injustice and the evil of a state. From Plato's standpoint, the seemingly innocuous vice of being a busybody has the potential to undermine and ultimately destroy the commonwealth.

> One who is by nature an artisan...tries to enter into the class of counselors and guardians, for which he is not fitted, and these interchange their tools and their honors, or when the same man undertakes all these functions at once, then....you too believe that this kind of substitution and meddlesomeness (μεταβολὴν καὶ πολυπραγμοσύνην) is the ruin of a state.[32]

Yet, Plato's major concern does not so much lie in external displays of people adhering to their own business, but rather, in the internal dispositions of the soul that motivate them. Indeed, one might well perform an assigned task in life, but still be driven by a turbulent spirit that disrupts the delicate balance of the soul's tripartite structure. Because Plato espouses a psychology that is essentially a soul-centered one, then, his indictment of meddlesomeness on any level looks to the harmonization of the parts of the soul in the individual.

> Justice in the true sense concerns oneself, and the things of one-
> self—it means a man must not suffer the principles in his soul
> to do each the work of some other and interfere and meddle
> (πολυπραγμονεῖν πρὸς ἄλληλα) with one another, but that
> he should dispose well of what in the true sense of the word is prop-
> erly his own.[33]

By the same token, Plato draws upon the political analogue of a rebel-
lion to describe the turmoil that besets a soul divided by the encroachment of one task upon another. In this respect, injustice is defined
as "a kind of civil war of these principles, their meddlesomeness and
interference (πολυπραγμοσύνην καὶ ἀλλοτριοπραγμοσύνην)
with one another's functions, and the revolt of one part against the
whole of the soul."[34]

While Plato indicts the tendency toward busyness with many things
in upholding justice for all levels of society, Aristotle (384-322 B.C.)
does so with a specific focus upon promoting the efficiency of leaders.
In this respect, Aristotle perceives a greater advantage for the state if
administrators confined themselves to one major task alone. "Every
task is better attended to," he maintains, "if the attention is directed to
one thing only than if it is busy with many" (καὶ βέλτιον ἕκαστον
ἔργον τυγχάνει τῆς ἐπιμελείας μονοπραγματούσης ἢ
πολυπραγματούσης).[35] His emphasis upon single-mindedness assumes an implicit epistemological significance. For, the concentration
of one's efforts on a solitary pursuit provides something of an analogue
for the dynamics of knowledge (and the immutable foundations it
presupposes), as understood by both thinkers. In Plato and Aristotle
alike, knowledge consists in the mind's discernment of universal form,
and the ability to analyze a given thing in terms of its fundamental
causes. This, of course, also presupposes an ability to recognize those
extraneous or superfluous features of a given truth (that is, what is not
essential to the definition of the reality in question). In this connection, Plato and Aristotle also employ *periergia*-language in stipulating
what is germane to genuine knowledge and what is not.

In the *Statesman*, Plato defines the proper goal of dialectical inquiry as the pursuit of true reality (and the corresponding awareness of
what is tendentious to the issue). In this context, Plato considers the
impatience of those engaged in extended talk about matters like weav-
ing, the turning of the universe, and the sophistic debate about the
existence of non-being.

We felt that they were too long, and we reproached ourselves for all of them, fearing that our talk was not only long, but irrelevant (δείσαντες μὴ περίεργα ἅμα καὶ μακρὰ λέγοιμεν).[36]

From Plato's standpoint, perceptions of the quality of a discussion should not be based upon considerations of whether it is tedious, or excessively verbose, or boring. Rather, the guiding standard must be what is most fitting for improving one's dialectical skills in expressing the truth (that is, what is the case). In other words, it lies in an ability to discern what is appropriate to the business at hand and what otherwise detracts from this lofty end.

Aristotle exhibits a similar grasp of the criteria of knowledge, but with a more pronounced interest in the causal analysis inherent in natural philosophy and scientific pursuits in general. As he stresses in his *Metaphysics*, the earliest philosophers pursued science for the sake of knowledge, and not necessarily for the sake of utility.[37] In this respect, he finds a common ground between natural philosophy and medicine, since practitioners of both endeavors isolate the causes of health and disease. While Aristotle recognizes the differences between these sciences, he acknowledges that "those physicians who have subtle and inquiring minds (γὰρ ἰατρῶν ὅσοι κομψοὶ ἢ περίεργοι) have something to say to natural science."[38]

Aristotle's causal emphasis shapes his scientific approach to human nature as well. In his treatise *On Rhetoric*, he contends that human action must be interpreted in light of seven fundamental causes (i.e., chance, nature, compulsion, habit, reasoning, anger, and appetite). In Aristotelian terms, only these causes provide viable bases for human motivations. Accordingly, he deems it superfluous (περίεργον) to base distinctions regarding a given act upon such considerations as age or moral character.[39]

For Aristotle and Plato, as we have seen, the very preoccupation with extraneous matters attests to that busyness with many things that undermines the single-minded pursuit of genuine knowledge. Indeed, the image of the "busybody" becomes their recurrent touchstone in upholding a cosmic vision of reality, the state, and the individual. In each case, the proper allocation of individual tasks and concerns is crucial for the sake of a greater good.

## PLUTARCH OF CHAERONEA

In light of a teleological ideal of order (*taxis*), the busybody motif is easily identified with the disruption of the harmonious functioning of a system or community. This ideal presupposes that delicate part-to-whole relationship central to the cosmic consciousness of the ancient Greek outlook. The very failure to mind one's own business (that is, to be a busybody) has serious repercussions, precisely because it involves an intrusion into others' affairs (whether they be humans or gods) that leads one into uncharted waters or forbidden terrain. This particular motif occupies center stage in the moral piety of Plutarch, whose essay "On Being a Busybody" (Περί Πολυπραγμοσύνης) represents a veritable compendium of classical Greek presuppositions about the dangers that accompany the excessively meddlesome disposition.[40]

In approaching this particular essay, an immediate admonition is in order. It is all too easy to translate Plutarch's references to *polupragmosune* simply as "curiosity," that is, as a desire to learn or to know. But this is precisely where the ambiguity inherent in this term makes a crucial difference in our understanding of its full significance. Indeed, a translation of *polupragmosune* exclusively as "curiosity" in this context misses something vital about its meaning for Plutarch. This author (like other ancient Greek authors we have already considered) believes that the very desire to learn about the minutiae of people's lives bespeaks an intrusiveness that observes no limits.

For this reason, Plutarch numbers the all too human tendency of *polupragmosune* among those injurious maladies or diseases of the mind that pose a genuine threat to our moral well-being. In this case, the malady in question encompasses "a desire to learn the troubles of others."[41] But what prompts this unhealthy disposition? Plutarch ultimately roots it in a dissatisfaction with what already lies within oneself, and a corresponding preoccupation with others' concerns. Accordingly, the busybody's scope of attention is not confined to one particular social group or class of individuals, but extends to everyone without discrimination.

After Plutarch diagnoses this psychic illness, he proposes a cure. Interestingly, however, he does not present a blanket condemnation of *polupragmosune* in all its forms. Rather, he encourages a refinement of inquisitiveness that will allow the soul to focus upon subject matter that befits its nature.[42] In point of fact, however, one driven by a zeal for meddling (τὸ περίεργον) into base things (like a maggot's attachment to rotten meat) might well be wholly unconcerned with nobler pursuits of the intellect.[43]

On one level, then, Plutarch links *polupragmosune* with an interest in things in general. But he lends it a special affinity with a perverse delight in calamities and the tragic aspects of life. In this respect, he defines *polupragmosune* as a "passion for finding out whatever is hidden and concealed" ("Εστι γὰρ ἡ πολυπραγμοσύνη φιλοπευστία τῶν ἐν ἀποκρύπτει καὶ λανθανόντων).[44] The assumption here is that only evil things prompt one toward concealment; good things need not be hidden. Because the busybody desires to investigate troubles, Plutarch perceives an element of malignancy in this drive that displays a kinship with both envy and spitefulness: while envy prompts a certain pain at someone's good fortune, the malignancy of *polupragmosune* takes delight in the evil that befalls others.[45]

In practical terms, however, there is still a rather fine line between the malady that Plutarch describes (which he roots in a vicious nature) and a normal solicitousness toward the welfare of people. In this connection, he contrasts the morally blameworthy busybody with the inquisitive physician. While the physician's investigations are good so long as they are not directed toward frivolous ends (like exchanging gossip about the patient's infirmities), the busybody's searches are concerned with nothing more than revealing personal matters.[46] The pitfall inherent in this latter form of behavior is that its preoccupation with the interests of others only diminishes one's own interests in the long run.

As the precise moralist that he is, Plutarch provides an intriguing survey of the detrimental effects of *polupragmosune* on the basis of a series of analogues with other vices: like adultery, *polupragmosune* entails a search after secret things, hidden from public view; like evil speech, it prompts a desire to reveal the information that one so earnestly pursues; like incontinence, it reflects an attitude of utter folly and ignorance.[47] Accordingly, this particular vice generates a nettling paradox: the very desire to know impedes its fulfillment, since people are reluctant to say or do anything in the presence of a busybody.[48] By the same token, Plutarch bemoans the fact that busybodies (by virtue of their incessant absorption in peoples' privacy) deprive themselves of the good that life has to offer.[49] Instead, they become fixated with just the opposite, frequently haunting those places that display monstrosities or grotesque features of nature.[50]

If *polupragmosune* constitutes a vice, it requires a long cultivation. Conversely, it can only be neutralized and overcome by the practice of self-control. As Plutarch teaches, "it is by habituation that the disease has come to increase, advancing...little by little."[51] In this respect, his very emphasis upon the dangers of giving free rein to this tendency (and thereby, wedding oneself to its practice) attests to his recognition that the disease of *polupragmosune* represents a distortion of a healthy desire that is part and parcel of our rational nature.

Like a sharp cutting edge, this positive "curiosity for learning" (τὸ πολύπραγμον τοῦ φιλομαθοῦς) can easily become dulled by a fascination with trivial or unseemly things.[52] In the final analysis, the very capacity to refine our desire for knowledge (and to resist a culpable *polupragmosune*) presupposes a rationality that is the proper guide of human behavior. Yet even here, Plutarch discerns a potential pitfall. For him, the very acquiescence to one's curious appetites (including those that are wholly legitimate) can open us to their misuse. "When one nourishes his curiosity...until he renders it vigorous and violent," he warns, "he is no longer able to master it easily, since it is borne, by force of habit, to forbidden things."[53]

From an ethical standpoint, Plutarch's indictment of an objectionable inquisitiveness accentuates the importance of moderation in human desires (even good ones) and the role of reason in guiding our appetites to appropriate ends. In this respect, "On Being a Busybody" assumes a practical tone, geared as it is to a diagnostic assessment of a moral malaise and a strategy for undermining its influence in a concrete moral context. A later generation of Platonism would impart a deeper metaphysical significance to the *polupragmatic* tendency that draws upon the very kind of behavior that Plutarch so effectively treats in this particular treatise.

## PLOTINUS

It is fitting that we conclude this survey of classical Greek sources with Plotinus (A.D. 204-270), the prime exponent of that somewhat eclectic blend of Platonism, Aristotelianism, and Stoicism (along with various other philosophical/religious currents of late antique thought) designated as Neoplatonism. On the one hand, Plotinus himself could draw upon the manifold meanings which had accrued to *polupragmon*-language in Hellenic and Hellenistic writing. On the other hand, Plotinus' *Enneads* served as an important conduit for the transmission of these insights to the Christian intellectual world, and most significantly, to St. Augustine (through his reading of the *libri platonicorum*).[54]

We will return to this vital inspiration of Augustine's understanding of *curiositas* when we explicitly address the question of his creative adaptation of Plotinus for his own purposes. For the moment, however, let us address the mainlines of Plotinus' usages of *polupragmon*-language, with a special focus on the metaphysical import it assumes in his psychological theory. This brief look at Plotinus, then, is a preview of what will be treated in greater detail in the second part of this book.

The *locus classicus* of Plotinus' references to *polupragmon*-language is found in *Ennead* III.7(45).11, in his rich account of the temporalization of Soul (the third hypostasis in his intelligible universe, following the One and *Nous* or Intellect, respectively). That account reflects a marked distinction between contemplation and action. While contemplation and action encompass two different modes of being, however, they also exhibit a certain coextensiveness, whereby the active life reflects certain traces or vestiges of the contemplative, albeit in a diminished way.

In Plotinian terms, contemplation constitutes the quiet life, that is, whole and unbounded, and focused upon eternal and immutable truth.[55] By implication, however, the quiet life of contemplation provides an important touchstone for Plotinus' definition of time. In his quasi-mythical rendering, "there was a restlessly active nature" (φύσεως δὲ πολυπράγμονος) which desired self-determination and autonomy, and sought more than it already possessed.[56] For Plotinus, the movement generated by this turbulent spirit constitutes time's origin, or more precisely, the temporalization of Soul. In a manner consistent with Platonic teaching, Plotinus thus defines time as "an image of eternity," that is, an imitation of the being of the intelligible world motivated by a desire for an increase in its own range of interests.[57]

In figurative terms, Plotinus describes the life of the temporalized Soul as a spreading out of its powers. But such a movement represents a squandering of those powers which results in a distention or "weaker extension," comparable to a seed's diminishing and loss of its internal unity in the very process of growth.[58] The fragmenting of being that accompanies temporality is reflected in a corresponding fragmenting of thought that allows for a distinction between "before" and "after" in relation to an ordered succession of events.

As a result of its temporalization, Soul assumes an intermediate position between the higher life of *Nous* or Intellect and the sense perception of material realities. Accordingly, Soul's activity at this level is the discursive reasoning that proceeds from premises to conclusions. By virtue of this rational activity, however, Soul cannot confine its cogitive life to self-contemplation alone, but must observe "what is outside it and busying itself (πολυπραγμονεῖν) with it."[59] Plotinus extends this inquietude to the objects of reasoning as well.

Indeed, objects of reasoning reflect everything that is antithetical to the peace and stability of the noetic world, that is, an inquietude and fussiness.[60] In this respect, Soul's preoccupation with temporal affairs (and the reasoning process through which it finds expression) presupposes a focus on the partial rather than a single-minded concentration on one thing alone. Plotinus specifies that the very desire to apprehend the part is inquisitiveness (περίεργον), "as if a man were to look at himself and if it is not for some purpose, it is futile."[61]

In psychic terms, Plotinus' reference to the "part" is a way of designating the purview of individual souls, those extensions of the life of the hypostasis Soul into the temporal realm, and ultimately, the governing principles of material bodies. From this standpoint, Plotinus interprets the fall of souls as a loss of an awareness of their divine origins after an over-excessive immersion in temporal affairs and a subjection to bodily influences. Once again, Plotinus draws upon *polupragmon*-language in describing the characteristics of fallen souls.

> They change from the whole to being a part and belonging to themselves, and…when a soul does this for a long time…and does not look towards the intelligible, it…is isolated and weak and fusses (πολυπραγμονεῖ)…caring for things outside…and sinks deep into the individual part.[62]

For Plotinus, however, dialectic and discursive reasoning have definite limits. In keeping with the general thrust of his vision of reality (which presupposes the complementary movements of an outward emanation [*proodos*] of all things from the One, and a return [*epistrophé*] of everything to its ultimate source), he sees the goal of dialectic as an ascending movement from the turbulence, multiplicity, and fragmentation of the sense world to the peace, unity, and wholeness of the contemplative life of the intelligible world.

> It stops wandering about the world of sense and settles down in the world of intellect and there it occupies itself…and then, keeping quiet… busies itself (πολυπραγμονοῦσα) no more, but contemplates, having arrived at unity.[63]

In strictly epistemological terms, however, the very nature of knowing presupposes a multiplicity and diversity that reflects the dichotomy between the knower and what is known that is mark of a lower level of understanding. Plotinus extends this dichotomization to self-reflection as well: even here, the knower must objectify the self, and in so doing, duplicate the self in the very act of knowing it.[64] This kind of division contrasts sharply with the contemplative activity of the One, which surpasses any such epistemological distinctions. In this regard, Plotinus pointedly states that the One "will not need to make a fuss about itself" (πολυπραγμονεῖν ἑαυτό).[65] Accordingly, the epistemological dividing line between what is higher and lower in Plotinus' scheme can be viewed as a faultline between stability and peace on the one hand, and restlessness and increasing turmoil on the other.

> For altogether blessed beings it is alone enough to stay still in themselves and be what they are; restless activity (τὸ δὲ πολυπραγμονεῖν) is unsafe for those who…violently move themselves.[66]

In Plotinus' usage, *polupragmon*-language (and on a somewhat limited basis, *periergia*-language), assume a decidedly negative import, expressing the motives for the descent of Soul into temporality, or a focus upon the images derived from sense experience. These connotations (which filtered into the Latin term *curiositas*) would assume a prominence in Christian patristic accounts of the origins of sin (most notably, in the accounts of Augustine). In this connection, the image of the "busybody" defined by classical authors becomes symbolic of a restlessness which stands in opposition to a refinement of human thought and reasoning in pursuit of truths which reflect the highest goals of intellectual striving.

In the various philosophical contexts in which it is employed, the busybody motif highlights a desire to know what is none of one's appropriate concern. But implicit in this character-type, there is also an intrusiveness into people's lives and interests. In Plato and his Neoplatonic successor Plotinus, this negative dimension of inquisitiveness become the veritable paradigm of moral and metaphysical disorder. But as this survey has shown, the classical Greek tradition did not condemn inquisitiveness *per se*. Indeed, this was the same tradition that produced the critical spirit of philosophy and that love of wisdom which drove it to such great heights of expression. Socrates' teaching that "the unexamined life is not worth living" and Aristotle's dictum that "all humans desire to know by their very nature" bespeaks an exaltation of the very quest for knowledge. When the Greeks censure the intellectual appetite, then, it is only when it exceeds the parameters of good behavior, as defined within a larger social and cosmic framework. This tension between a positive and a negative inquisitiveness is evident in classical Latin authors as well, who translated the diverse connotations surrounding *periergia*-language and *polupragmon*-language into a whole new idiom.

### NOTES TO CHAPTER I

1. *The Oxford English Dictionary*, Second Edition. Volume IV. (Oxford: Clarendon Press, 1989), 144a-b. In addition to this primary meaning, the **OED** also delineates "curiosity" as a "quality of things" (144b) and "a matter or thing that has this quality" (144b-144c). For the present purposes, I confine my analysis to the notion of "curiosity" as "a personal attribute."
2. *The Oxford English Dictionary*, 144c-145a.
3. For excellent studies of the history of "curiosity" (both etymological and conceptual), see Andre Cabassut, "Curiosité," *Dictionnaire de Spiritualité*, Tome II, pt. 2 (Paris: Beauchesne, 1953), 2654b-26661a; André Labhardt, "*Curiositas*. Notes sur l'histoire d'un mot et d'une notion," *Museum Helveticum* 17(1960): 206-224; Neil Kenny, *Curiosity in Early Modern Europe Word Histories* (Weisbaden: Harrassowitz Verlag, 1988); Richard Newhauser, "Towards a History of Human Curiosity: A Prolegomenon to its Medieval Phase," *Deutsche Vierteljahrsschrift für Literaturwissenschaft und Geistesgeschichte* 56(1982): 559-575.
4. Neil Kenny, *Curiosity in Early Modern Europe Word Histories*, 33; Newhauser, "Towards a History of Human Curiosity: A Prolegomenon to its Medieval Phase," 563, n. 10. Cf., André Labhardt, "*Curiositas*. Notes sur l'histoire d'un mot et d'une notion," 208: "Le latin pouvait se passer d'un substantif dérivé de *curiosus* et se satisfaire de *cura*, aux acceptions multiples et qui designe en particulier le soin apporté à une recherche,

scientifique ou non. Il aurait pu aussi créer un dérivé *curiositas* affecté de tous les sens de *cura*, mais de valeur virtuelle, par opposition à la valeur actuelle de *cura*." Also consider the assessment of André Cabassut, in his *Dictionnaire de Spiritualité* article ("*Curiosité*," 2654b): "Le terme latin *curiositas* est un dérivé assez tardif de *curiosus*, adjectif de *cura*=soin, sauci, application. *Curiosus*, dans le latin classique, surtout chez Cicéron, a d'abord le sens général de soigneux, appliqué, studieux, avec parfois une nuance péjorative: soigneux à l'excès, minutieux. Il a ensuite le sens particulier de 'qui recherche avec soin', 'avide de connaître', 'curieux', et il se prend alors soit en bonne, soit en mauvaise part. C'est ce sens particulier de *curiosus* que se rattache le sens du mot *curiositas*, lequel désigne soit une qualité, soit un défaut."

5. Neil Kenny, *Curiosity in Early Modern Europe Word Histories*, 36.

6. André Labhardt, "*Curiositas*," 207: "*Curiosus* possede toutes les résonances que font pressentir les termes grecs correspondants."

7. I use the phrase "*periergia*-language" as a broad category encompassing all the forms of Greek terminology usually (but not exclusively) translated as "curious," "curiously," "to be curious," or "curiosity" (i.e., adjectival, adverbial, verbal, and substantive forms, respectively). Similarly, I employ the phrase "*polupragmon*-language" as a broad category encompassing all forms of corresponding Greek terminology. This section draws freely upon terminology from a wide variety of writings. My discussion of these references, however, is conceptual and thematic in orientation, rather than geared toward the historical development of the words under scrutiny. Accordingly, I refer to these authors without any strict adherence to chronological ordering. But for the reader's convenience, I now list them in their (approximate) chronological order: Herodotus (historian), c.490-c.425B.C.; Hippocrates (physician), 469-399B.C.; Thucydides (historian), 460-400B.C.; Aristophanes (poet of Old Attic Comedy), c.460-c.386B.C.; Isocrates (Athenian orator), 436-338B.C.; Xenophon (historian, philosopher), c.430-?B.C.; Aeschines (orator), c.397-c.322B.C.; Demosthenes (orator), 384-322B.C.; Theophrastus (associate/successor of Aristotle), 372/1-288/7B.C.; Menander (writer of New Comedy), 344-292/B.C.; Polybius (historian), c.200-c.118B.C.; Dionysius of Halicarnassus (critic, historian, rhetorician), fl.30-8B.C.; Plutarch (philosopher, biographer), A.D. (before)50-(after)120; Epictetus (Stoic), A.D.(mid)1st-2ndc.; Pausanias (periegetic writer), fl.A.D.c.150; Lucianus (writer of comic prose dialogue), A.D.c.120; Libanus (rhetorician), A.D.314-c.393; Julian, Emperor (writer of panegyrics, polemics, theology, satire), A.D.331-363.

8. Polybius, *Historia* xviii.51(1-3): "...he himself did not in the least go out of his way to concern himself with the affairs of Italy" (αὐτὸς περιεργάζεσθαι).

9. Lucian, *Alexander the False Prophet* 4: "In understanding, quick-wittedness, and penetration he was beyond everyone else; and activity of mind,

readiness to learn (περίεργον καὶ εὐμαθὲς), natural aptitude for studies—all these qualities were his."

10. Julian (Emperor), *Oration* VII, 217c (To the Cynic Heracleios): "...the
more paradoxical and prodigious the riddle the more it seems to warn us
not to believe simply the bare words but to study diligently the hidden
truth" (ἀλλὰ τὰ λεληθότα περιεργάζεσθαι).

11. Lucian, *Verae historiae* I,5: "...setting out from the Pillars of Hercules and
heading for the western ocean with a fair wind, I went voyaging. The motive and purpose of my journey lay in my intellectual activity and desire for
adventure" (περιεργία καὶ πραγμάτων).

12. Julian (Emperor), *Oration* IV, 130d (*Hymn to King Helios. Dedicated to
Sallust*): "I was considered to be over-curious about these matters and to
pay too much attention to them" (ἐδόκουν τε περιεργότερον ἔχειν
πρὸς αὐτὰ καὶ πολυπράγμων τις εἶναι).

13. Hippocrates, *Decorum* 1: "Most kinds of wisdom...have manifestly
come into being as superfluities (αἱ γὰρ πολλαὶ πρὸς περιεργίην
φαίνονται γεγενημέναι) which confer no advantage upon the objects
that they discuss." In referring to the wisdom that is opposite to what is
motivated by a love of gain and unseemliness, Hippocrates (*Decorum* 3)
exalts "no studied preparation and no over-elaboration" (οἷς οὐ διδακτὴ
κατασκευή, οὐδε περιεργίη). Hippocrates likewise advises the physician (*Decorum* 7) to avoid gossip and to "do none at all of these things
in a way that savours of fuss or of show" (ποιεῖν δὲ κάρταμηδεν
περιέργως αὐτῶν, μηδὲ μετὰ φαντασίης). Similarly, Hippocrates'
*Precepts* (X) counsel the physician to "avoid adopting, in order to gain a
patient, luxurious headgear and elaborate (περίεργος) perfume." Cf.,
Libanus, *Orations* II,53: "What is the point of this unnecessary fuss"
(τί οὖν αὐτοις ἡ περίεργια βούλεται)? and Isocrates, *Oration to
Philip* 98: "...you would rightly think it senseless and gratuitous in me to
tell you the story of your own deeds" (δικαίως ἂν ἀνόητος ἅμα καὶ
περίεργος εἶναι δοκοίην).

14. Cf., Dionysius of Halicarnassus, *Lysias* 14: "...Lysias aimed at vulgarity and
laboured expression in his speeches (τῶν φορτικῶν καὶ περιέργων),
and sought artificiality rather than realism"; Lucian, *Letter to Nigrinus* 13:
"His other vulgarities they turned into jest...the overall extravagance of
his life" (τὸ περίεργον ἢ τῆς διαιτης); *Letter to Nigrinus* 15, for a
reference to one "who has unreservedly committed his soul to pleasure and
fond of extravagant fare" (φίλος μὲν περίεργον τραπεζῶν); Plutarch,
*Lives* (Alexander), II,5-6: "...all the women imitated the practices of the
Edinian and the Thracian women from whom 'threskeueon' came to be
applied to the celebration of extravagant and superstitious ceremonies"
(περιέργους ἱερουργίαις); Arrianus, *Discourses of Epictetus* III,1(1)
for a reference to "a young student of rhetoric whose hair was...too elabo-
rately (περιεργότερον) dressed."

15. Arrianus, *Discourses of Epictetus* III,1(25).
16. Theophrastus, *Characters* 13. Cf., Aeschines, *Against Ctesiphon* 229: "…when a man fashioned from bitter and contrived words (πικρῶν καὶ περιέργων) takes his stand on simplicity and action, who could bear it?"
17. Aristophanes, *The Ecclesiazusae* 220: "And would it not have saved/The Athenian city had she let alone/Things that worked well, nor idly soughts things new" (εἰ μή τι καινὸν ἄλλο περιεργάζετο)? Cf., Isocrates, *Oration to Antidosis* 117: "…this is the first requisite of good strategy, and if one makes any mistake about this, the result is inevitably a war which is to no purpose" (περίεργον εἶναι); Herodotus, *Historiae* II,15: "…it was but a useless thought that they were the oldest nation on earth" (τί περιεργάζοντο δοκέοντες πρῶτοι ἀνθρώπων γεγονέναι).
18. Xenophon, *Memorabilia* I,III(1), where Socrates advised others to heed the injunction of the Delphic priestess to follow the customs of the state, in the interests of pious behavior: "…to take any other course he considered presumption and folly" (τοὺς δὲ ἄλλως πως ποιοῦντας περιέργους καὶ ματαίους ἐνόμιζεν εἶναι).
19. Demosthenes, *Against Aristogeiton* II,15: "…in the case of these mischief-makers (τῶν περιεργαζομένων), who annoy everyone alike and pretend to be superior to the rest"; Lucian, *Icaromenippus* 21: "I have often thought of moving as far away as possible to a place where I might escape their meddling tongues" (ἵν᾽ αὐτῶν τὴν περίεργον ἂν γλῶτταν διέφυγον); Menander, *Samia* 85: "There's not a thing…that escapes this man./He's quick to know what's going on./A meddler, he" (ἔστι γὰρ περίεργος).
20. Aristophanes, *Plutus* 913: "So being a busybody is beneficence" (εὐεργετεῖν οὖν ἐστι τὸ πολυπραγμονεῖν)? Cf.,. Isocrates, *Oration to Antidosis* XV,230: "…if it be true that cleverness in speech results in plotting against other people's property, we should expect all able speakers to be intriguers and sycophants" (πολυπράγμονας καὶ συκοφάντας); *Oration to Antidosis.* XV,237: "But I can show you the names of our trouble-makers (πολυπράγμονας) and the men liable to the charges these people apply to the sophists"; Xenophon, *Anabasis* V.1(5): "…while engaged in some intrigue (πολυπραγμονῶν) he was killed." In addition, such language conveys the notion of troubling oneself or not minding one's own business. Cf., Polybius, *Historia* XVIII.51(1-3): "…he requested them not to trouble themselves at all about Asiatic affairs" (μηδὲν αὐτοὺς πολυπραγμονεῖν); Herodotus, *Historiae* III,15(5-6):. "…had he but been wise enough to mind his own business" (ἔι δὲ καὶ ἡ πιστήθη μὴ πολυπρηγμονέειν).
21. Arrianus, *Discourses of Epictetus* III,1(21): "Are you so inquisitive, O Socrates, and meddlesome" (οὕτως περίεργος, εἶ, ὦ Σώκρατες, καὶ πολυπράγμων)? Cf., Aristophanes, *Birds* 471: "That's because

you're naturally ignorant and uninquisitive (ἀμαθής γὰρ ἔφυς κοὺ πολυπράγμων), and you haven't thumbed your Aesop."

22. Polybius, *Historiae* V,75(6): "...we can gain this experience from study of history and inquiry while enjoying honourable repose and procuring entertainment for our minds" (ἐκ τῆς ἱστορίας καὶ πολυπραγμοσύνης περιποιεῖσθαι τὴν τοιαύτην ἐμπειρίαν); *Historiae* IX,15(7): "...it is difficult to tell the hour of the night, unless one is familiar with the signs of the Zodiac knowledge of which it is quite easy to gain by studying the constellations" (τὰ φαινόμενα πεπολυπραγμονηκόσιν).

23. Polybius, *Historiae* III,38(2-3): "...part of Europe is up to now unknown to us, and will remain so unless the curiosity of explorers lead to some discoveries" (ἐὰν μή τι μετὰ ταῦτα πολυπραγμονοῦντες ἱστορήσωμεν); *Historiae* IX,1(4): "...such as we find in Ephorus, attracts the curious and lovers of recondite lore" (τόν δὲ πολυπράγμονα).

24. Polybius, *Historiae* XII,27(4): "Inquiries from books may be made without any danger or hardship, provided only that one takes care" (ὅτι τὰ μὲν ἐκ τῶν βυβλίων δύναται πολυπραγμονεῖσθαι χωρὶς κινδύνου καὶ κακοπαθείας).

25. Pausanias, *Description of Greece* X,32(17): "...a profane man entered the shrine to satisfy his rash inquisitiveness" (πολυπραγμοσύνης τε καὶ τόλμης).

26. Plato, *Apology* 19b: "Let us take up from the beginning the question, what the accusation is in which Miletus trusted when he brought this suit against me. What did those who aroused the prejudice say to arouse it? I must read their sworn statement as if they were plaintiffs: 'Socrates is a criminal and a busybody (ἀδικεῖ καὶ περιεργάζεται), investigating the things beneath the earth and in the heavens and making the weaker argument stronger and teaching others these same things.'" Cf., *Laws* VII,821a: "We commonly assert that men ought not to enquire concerning the greatest god and about the universe, nor busy themselves in searching out their causes (οὔτε πολυπραγμονεῖν τὰς αἰτίας ἐρευνῶντας), since it is actually impious to do so."

27. *Apology* 19c: "Perhaps it may seem strange that I go about and interfere in other people's affairs (περιιὼν καὶ. πολυπραγμονῶ) to give this advice in private, but do not venture to come before your assembly and advise the state."

28. Plato, *Republic* IV,x(433a-b): "...each one man must perform one social service in the state for which his nature was best adapted and that to do one's own business and not to be a busybody is justice (καὶ μὴν ὅτι γε τὸ τὰ αὑτοῦ πράττειν καὶ μὴ πολυπραγμονεῖν δικαιοσύνη ἐστί) this, then appears to be justice, this principle of doing one's own business" (ἡ δικαιοσύνη εἶναι, τὸ τὰ αὑτοῦ πράττειν).

29. Viktor Ehrenberg, "*Polypragmosyne*: A Study in Greek Politics," *The Journal of Hellenic Studies* 67(1947): 47. Thucydides' Corinthian speech

(I,70) contrasts the characters and dispositions of the Spartans and Athenians on the basis of the Athenian proclivity for the active life (and its pitfalls): "An Athenian is always an innovator, quick to form a resolution and quick at carrying it out...Athenian daring will outrun its own resources...against their better judgment.... always abroad, for they think that the farther they go the more they will get...they prefer hardship and activity to peace and quiet...by nature incapable of either living a quiet life...or of allowing anyone else to do so."

30. *Republic* IV,x(433d).
31. *Republic* IV,x(433d).
32. *Republic* IV,x(434b). Cf., *Republic* VIII,vii(552a): "In such a state the citizens are busybodies (τὸ πολυπραγμονεῖν) and jacks-of-all-trades, farmers, financiers and soldiers all in one."
33. *Republic* IV,xvii(443d).
34. *Republic* IV,xviii(444b).
35. Aristotle, *Politics* IV,xii,4(1299b).
36. Plato, *Statesman* 286c.
37. Aristotle, *Metaphysics* I,ii(982b).
38. Aristotle, *On Respiration* XXI(480b27,27).
39. Aristotle, *Rhetoric* I,x.9(1369a): "But it is superfluous (περίεργον) to establish further distinctions of men's acts based upon age, moral habits, or anything else."
40. This essay is listed as No. 36 in all editions of Plutarch's *Moralia*.
41. *Moralia* 1(515d).
42. *Moralia* 5(517c-d). Among these investigations, Plutarch includes the study of celestial and terrestrial things.
43. *Moralia* 5(517e).
44. *Moralia* 6(518c).
45. *Moralia* 6(518c): "Since, then, it is the searching out of troubles that the busybody desires (κακῶν οὖν ἱστορίας ὁ πολυπράγμων ὀρεγόμενος), he is possessed by the affliction called 'malignancy,' brother to envy and spite."
46. *Moralia* 7(518d-e).
47. *Moralia* 8(519b); 9(519c-d); 9(519e).
48. *Moralia* 9(519d).
49. *Moralia* 9(519f).
50. *Moralia* 10(520c).
51. *Moralia* 11(520d).
52. *Moralia* 11(520f): "For as eagles and lions draw in their claws when they walk so that they may not wear off the sharpness of the tips, so, if we consider that curiosity for learning (τὸ πολύπραγμον τοῦ φιλομαθοῦς) has also a sharp and keen edge, let us not waste or blunt it upon matters of no value."
53. *Moralia* 15(522e).

54. St. Augustine, *Confessiones* VII,9(13), where Augustine recounts his encounter with "certain books of the Platonists" that had been translated from Greek into Latin.

55. *Ennead* III.7(45).11,3-5.

56. *Ennead* III.7(45).11,14.

57. *Ennead* III.7(45).11,47.

58. *Ennead* III.7(45).11,23-27.

59. *Ennead* V.3(49).3,18.

60. *Ennead* VI.3(44).23,1-5: "And the movement which is in sense-objects comes in from another and shakes and drives and wakes and pushes the things which have a share in it, so that they do not sleep and are not in sameness; in order that they may be held together by this inquietude and this sort of fussiness which is an image of life" (ἵνα δὴ τῇ μὴ ἡσυχίᾳ καὶ οἷον πολυπραγμονήσει ταύτῃ εἰδώλῳ συνέχηται ζωῆς).

61. *Ennead* IV,4(28).25. Cf., *Ennead* IV.4(28).6, where Plotinus muses that it is daring "to be busy" with speculations regarding such lofty questions as the "memories" of the pscyhic principles of celestial bodies, and ultimately, the "memories of Zeus himself."

62. *Ennead* IV.8(6).4,10-22.

63. *Ennead* I.3(20).4,9-19.

64. *Ennead* V.3(49).10.

65. *Ennead* V.3(49).10,46.

66. *Ennead* III.2(47).1,42.

# CHAPTER 2

## CLASSICAL LATIN ORIGINS

When classical Latin authors wished to describe the desire to know, they could find some illuminating referents in the catalogue of meanings surrounding *periergia*-language and *polupragmon*-language. The notion of a fastidious attention to detail (on any level), coupled with a restless zeal for action easily translated into the idea of a diligent concern or care (*cura*). *Cura*, in fact, provided the etymological root of the adjective *curiosus* (and the adverb *curiose*). In the Latin tradition, we observe a phenomenon similar to what we encounter in the Greek: a transition from an emphasis upon a carefulness in general terms to an exclusive focus upon this particular trait in an epistemological context.

Just as *periergia*-language and *polupragmon*-language were not necessarily confined to discussions of inquisitiveness, the same holds true for *curiosus/curiose*. In Neil Kenny's assessment, "*cura* did not in itself denote any quest for knowledge," while the inquisitive disposition was "often absent from the senses of *curiosus* and especially the adverb *curiose*."[1] At a certain point, however, *curiosus/curiose* became inextricably linked with the notion of a cognitive appetite. As suggested in the last chapter, this trend came to fruition with the coining of a new word for expressing that brand of desire that we now take for granted in our intellectual life, that is, "curiosity" (*curiositas*). *Curiositas*, then, incorporated all the connotations of *curiosus/curiose*, with a specific applicability to the desire for knowledge. Let us now consider the evolution of the concept of inquisitiveness in classical Latin authors, with an attunement to their influence by Greek sources.[2]

## FROM *CURIOSUS* TO *CURIOSITAS*

Apparently, the earliest extant reference to the curious disposition among classical Latin authors is found in Plautus, who provides an intriguing play on the words *curiosam, curio,* and *cura.* In Plautus' *The Aulularia,* the character Euclio worries that "the lamb is too curious" (that is, *curiosam*); but Megadorus (misinterpreting Euclio's distress), inquires how a lamb could be a priest (that is, a *curio*); Euclio, in turn, attempts to conceal his initial reference to the lamb as a *curiosam* by stressing that he merely implied that the lamb was careworn (that is, *cura*).3

A more explicit link between care and inquisitiveness is found in Varro's *De Lingua Latina,* and its illuminating etymological analysis of relevant terminology. In this context, Varro unites what he designates as three etymologically distinct sets of words (i.e., *cura, curare, curiosus; cor, recordari;* and *cura, curio*).

> *Curare* 'to care for, look after' is said from *cura* 'care, attention.' *Cura,* because it *cor urat* 'burns the heart'; *curiosus* 'inquisitive,' because such a person indulges in *cura* beyond the proper measure. The *curiae* 'halls,' where the senate *curat* 'looks after' the interests of the state, and also there where there is the *cura* 'care' of the state sacrifices; from these, the *curiones* 'priests of the *curiae*.'[4]

Cicero continued to attach the notion of inquisitiveness to *curiosus.* In so doing, however, his writings provide something of a nodal point in the classical Latin understanding of the curious disposition.[5] Indeed, he came to utilize the adjective *curiosus* and the adverb *curiose* far more often than his predecessors.[6] But the importance of his contribution here is not merely based on a frequency of usage. On the one hand, he imparts a more explicit epistemological connotation to this terminology. On the other hand, he demonstrates the extent to which the Latin tradition (following Greek precedents) closely intertwined the ideas of inquisitiveness with the ideas of "care" and "concern" derived from *cura.* This crucial linkage (which stands in continuity with classical Greek usages of *periergia*-language and *polupragmon*-language) is evident in several texts which employ *curiosus* in expressing the character of being precise, discriminating, diligent, or inquiring.[7] But in all of these references, Cicero adopts a rather positive attitude toward inquisitiveness (or at least a neutral one). By no means does he invest *curiosus* with a blameworthy character.

But Cicero's description of the various expressions of the curious disposition is but one side of this coin. In an isolated passage, Cicero also substantivates this behavioral trait by means of a new word specifying the curious desire itself, or more precisely, *curiositas*. This nonce word (as Labhardt describes it) represents a synthesis of all the connotations inherent in *curiosus* and *curiose*.[8] In his *Epistle to Atticus*, Cicero introduces the term along these lines:

> I learned a dozen times as much about affairs from your letter as from his talk…and you have made me wild with inquisitiveness…my curiosity is insatiable (*in curiositate* ὀξύπεινος).[9]

But this initial reference to *curiositas* in Cicero by no means insured its widespread adoption. In point of fact, it all but seems to vanish from the literary landscape until its reappearance and popularization some two centuries later in Apuleius.[10] In the interim, however, we observe an interesting shift in the manifold connotations already attached to *curiosus/curiose* by classical Latin authors. After Cicero, this terminology assumes an increasingly pejorative import, in a manner consistent with what we saw in its Greek counterparts.

In the immediate aftermath of Cicero, the curious desire was linked with a fascination with the unusual or occult. The poetry of Catullus and Horace suggest that such an attraction is associated with the practice of sorcery and witchcraft. For Catullus, expressions of human affection exceed anything that "the curious shall count up" (*pernumerare curiosi possint*) or "an evil bewitch" (*mala fascinare lingua*).[11] Horace, on the other hand, indicates that curiosity opens one to manipulative practices affecting nature and human life alike.

> I can make wax dolls feel, as you yourself are aware thanks to your curiosity; I can draw down the moon from the sky by my incantations, rouse to life the dead…and brew potions that induce desire.[12]

But classical Latin discussions of the curious trait are also attuned to a more concrete moral context. In this connection, the Stoic moralist Seneca decries those superfluous or extraneous concerns which distract from what is essential to human existence and conducive to the realization of happiness. "Do not be inquisitive" (*ne fueris curiosus*),

Seneca enjoins, since one preoccupied with malicious gossip "is responsible for his own disquietude" (*ne ipse inquietat*).[13] This indictment of the inquiring attitude, however, has a more specific target in Seneca's writings, namely, those intellectual pursuits which serve no useful purpose in relation to the common good. Even when Seneca does not rely upon the term *curiosus*, his message is clear: he consistently condemns the desire "to know more than is sufficient" (*plus scire velle quam sit satis*) as intemperance, the vice of those who put superfluous things on a par with useful ones.[14]

Such rhetoric suggests a distinct anti-intellectual bias strongly at odds with Seneca's own powerful intellectual gifts. Accordingly, his indictment of the "useless furniture of learning" must be placed in proper perspective.[15] If he exhibits a bias, it is not toward learning *per se*, but toward counterfeit claims to learning so extravagant that they are far removed from the practicalities of life. For Seneca, the devotees of these arts "know more about careful speaking than about careful living" (*ut diligentius loqui scirent quam vivere*).[16] Regardless of its sophistication, the argumentation of these individuals displays a major failing. "They might have discovered the essentials," Seneca laments, "had they not sought the superfluous also (*nisi et supervacua quaesissent*)...in quibbling about words."[17]

Quintilian continued in this vein, drawing an explicit parallel between the Greek *periergia* and the Latin *curiosus*. In both terms, he finds a means of distinguishing a mere pedant from a real scholar, and superstition from genuine religion.[18] His objection here is directed toward a carefulness above and beyond what is necessary in these contexts. Quintilian (like Seneca) thus imparts a blameworthy significance to *curiosus* that harkens back to the negative valuations attached to *periergia*-language and *polupragmon*-language by Greek authors. In this respect, Richard Newhauser argues that key Greek terminology "had taken on almost from their genesis an essential character of going intemperately beyond a just measure."[19] Late antique writers thus found in *curiosus* a convenient means of expressing this notion of excessiveness.

In certain situations, of course, such carefulness or precision is mandatory, especially when truth is at stake, and a proper clarification of the issues requires a detailed or elaborate investigation.[20] But scholarly or religious pursuits (while good in themselves) still should not adopt extreme behavior that only diminishes their efficacy.[21] In this regard, *curiosus* likewise assumes the connotation of meddlesomeness so prominent in Greek usages of *polupragmon*-language. Suetonius, in fact, uses the adjective to describe those attributes associated with eavesdroppers and spies.[22] But like the Greek tradition, the Latin tradition would view meddlesomeness as encompassing human and divine affairs alike. The understanding of curiosity as a presumptious interference with affairs beyond our appropriate ken became a dominant feature of late antique Latin literature, especially in the highly influential writings of Apuleius.

## APULEIUS OF MADAURA

Apuleius was born at Madaura in the middle of the second century of the Christian era. His extensive travels took him to Carthage, Athens, Egypt, and Rome. If it were not for his authorship of Latin romance literature, Apuleius might well have been known chiefly as an exponent of Middle Platonic philosophy. But his enduring claim to fame lies in his writing of the sole extant novel of Latin classicism, *The Golden Ass* or *Metamorphoses*.[23] This particular work insured that he would enjoy a more pervasive influence, and one which assumes a special relevance for the history of *curiositas*. Indeed, that term reemerges in the *Metamorphoses*, after a long literary hiatus following its initial appearance as a nonce word in Cicero.

Apuleius, in effect, provides nothing less than the conduit through which the diverse meanings and connotations surrounding the notion of curiosity (along with what is derived from the Greek tradition) would be transmitted to Christian patristic writing. But while Apuleius is recognized as the author of the *Metamorphoses*, scholars debate its origins.[24] This debate proceeds from Apuleius' own prologue to the *Metamorphoses*, in which he states that this work represents a version of a Greek tale (*fabulam Graecanicam incipimus*).[25] In this connection, the work shares certain key themes and motifs in common with an epitome entitled *Lucius or the Ass* (an apparent condensed version of a lost Greek story (Μεταμορφώσεις).

According to the 9th century Patriarch Photius (Bibl. Cod. 129, Migne), the author of that lost Greek text was Lucius of Patrae.[26] A shorter edition of this work (the one entitled *Lucius or the Ass*) is included in the works of Lucian. As one commentator observes, scholarly

controversy centers on the question as to what portions of Apuleius'
*Metamorphoses* are traceable to the lost Greek story (specifically those
portions not found in *Lucius or the Ass*).[27]

Both Apuleius' *Metamorphoses* and *Lucius or the Ass* provide a window into the late antique conviction that unregulated curiosity can
only carry detrimental effects.

More significantly, both works utilize the motif of a transformation of a human being into an animal as a consequence of such un-
bridled inquisitiveness. Likewise, both incorporate an account of their
respective protagonists' rescue through divine assistance. But that is
where the resemblances end. In Apuleius' work, we find a markedly expanded version of the story, including a parallel tale about Cupid and
*Psyche* (drawing upon the traditional legend of these two characters).
Apuleius, however, inserts his account firmly in a Middle Platonic
context, in a manner reminiscent of Plutarch's essay "On Being a
Busybody" and its depiction of the foibles of the *polupragmosune*.[28]
Furthermore, curiosity assumes a pronounced religious character as a
sacrilegious impiety tantamount to overstepping the bounds between
the divine and human spheres of interest.[29]

## APULEIUS' *METAMORPHOSES*

In the *Metamorphoses*, the narrator (Lucius) informs the reader that he
was beset with an eagerness to find out the strange features of Thessaly
(known far and wide as the source of magical arts).[30] Lucius' inquisitiveness sets the tone for his method of investigation. "I studied each
feature with care" (*curiose singula considerabam*), he acknowledges.[31] In
this respect, however, he immediately perceives the vast disparity between reality and appearances. Everything in this strange setting had
undergone change into a wholly different form, by means of incanta-
tion. Lucius, however, qualifies his attitude toward this environment
by means of a distinction between a blameworthy inquisitiveness and
a laudatory appetite for knowing.

> I am not inquisitive, but am the type which like to know about
> everything, or at least about most things (*impertite sermone non
> quidem curiosum, sed qui uelim scire uel cuncta uel certe plurima*).[32]

But can he successfully detach his curiosity from his cognitive desires
in general, especially when they prompt him toward certain areas of

investigation? In this connection, he readily admits his susceptibility to a curiosity for the arts of magic, even when this exacts a heavy penalty.

> I was already disposed to curiosity, and as soon as I heard mention of the art of magic which I had always prayed for (*ego curiosus alioquin, ut primum artis magicae semper optatum nomen audiui*), so far from taking precautions against Pamphile, I was eager without compulsion to undergo such schooling willingly, and to pay a heavy price for it.[33]

As subsequent events confirm, he is indeed "impelled by habitual curiosity" (*ego familiaris curiositatis admonitus*).[34] Lucius, however, falls victim to his own folly. He becomes fascinated with the sorcery of his landlady and her ability to assume the form of a bird. But in his vain attempt to duplicate this transformation, he accidentally changes himself into an ass.[35] This metamorphosis leads to a series of bizarre encounters that culminate in Lucius' return to human form. The account of Lucius' rescue is laden with references to the cult of Isis. For, it is Isis herself who responds to his prayerful intercession for release.

Ironically, Lucius' initial bestial transformation only provided a means of intensifying (and satisfying) the curiosity that prompted it. Because people made no attempt to disguise their activities around an animal, he gained new access to knowledge. "Nowhere…was there any consolation for my pain-wracked existence," he bemoans, "except that my innate curiosity did something to restore me (*nisi quod ingenita mihi curiositate recreabar*), for no one took any account of my presence."[36]

The reader is confronted, then, with the portrait of one driven by a deeply ingrained inquisitiveness capable of drawing him to those things beyond his appropriate range of pursuits. This account dovetails with a story embedded in the principal narrative. In the tale of Cupid and *Psyche*, an unregulated inquisitiveness is likewise the cause of great upheaval. The victim of such rashness is *Psyche* (a clear personification of the soul), whose desire to penetrate religious mysteries is depicted in terms of a sacrilegious curiosity.[37]

*Psyche's* impiety first leads her to gaze upon her husband Cupid's human form (despite his admonitions). She eventually engages in a Pandora-like opening of a box, an act which subjects her to the "sleep of Hades" and complete unconsciousness. In a very real sense, *Psyche's*

plight provides a means of highlighting the dynamics of Lucius' down-
fall as well: in both cases, curiosity coincides with a rebellious spirit of
disobedience that remains oblivious to any advice or warnings against
the dangers of entering into prohibitive realms of knowledge. But
while *Psyche's* situation bespeaks an ongoing attraction to forbidden
knowledge, Lucius' transformation into an ass provides the impetus to
his eventual commitment to truth (and an acceptance of the appropriate parameters of what can be known).[38]

In the concluding Book XI, Apuleius describes Lucius as submit-
ting himself to a purification, and devoting himself to the service of
the one who secured his freedom.

After reaching Rome, Lucius has a dream about someone named
Asinius Marcellus; Marcellus in turn had dreamt that Osiris informed
him that "a man from Madauros who was quite poor was being sent to
him."[39] Lucius, then, represents none other than Apuleius himself, the
very same one "from Madauros" who now proclaims the insignificance
of his earlier learning and the negative consequences of such trivial
concerns.

> In the green years of youth, you tumbled on the slippery slope
> into slavish pleasures, and gained the ill-omened reward of
> your unhappy curiosity (*curiositate inprospere sinistrum praemium
> reportasti*).[40]

A new transformation has taken place. Lucius' former curiosity with
magical arts and the occult has been replaced by an ardent desire to be
initiated into the mysterious rites of the Isaic cult.[41] But this admission carries an admonition to the reader whose own curiosity might
well wish to penetrate this privileged knowledge.

> I would tell you if it were permitted to reveal them; you would
> be told if you were allowed to hear. But both your ears and my
> tongue would incur equal guilt; my tongue for its impious
> garrulity, and your ears for their rash curiosity (*sed parem nox-
> am contraherent aures et lingua, illae temerariae curiositatis*).[42]

From this standpoint, it would be wholly erroneous to view Apuleius'
*Metamorphoses* as a blanket condemnation of the desire for knowledge
in general. Rather, Apuleius offers the reader a compelling diagnosis of
the negative effects of a reckless desire to know on the part of those beset with this curious appetite (that is, Lucius and *Psyche*). But implicit

in such unrestricted desire is an attempt to know those things improper for humans to know (or even seek to know) at all. Accordingly, Lucius' initiation into the mysteries of Isis coincides with a radical reorienting of his quest for knowledge. In contrast to the debasement which follows his foray into the occult, his religious conversion results in a completion of his very nature as a human being.[43]

## APULEIUS' CONTRIBUTION

As a Middle Platonist philosopher in his own right, Apuleius could readily appreciate the difference between legitimate and blameworthy desires for knowledge. In the context of this tradition, a good expression of curiosity (that is, the desire to know what is worthy of our investigations) must be distinguished from a curiosity which preoccupies itself with spurious claims to knowledge. In his *Apology*, in fact, Apuleius explicitly endorses the goals of natural philosophy, in attempting to penetrate the causes of the physical universe. "Don't you think," Apuleius queries, "that philosophy is obligated to trace all these things…to pry into them (*philosophia haec omnia uestigare et inquirere*)?"[44] Conversely, Apuleius bemoans the fact that people often confuse philosophy with a preoccupation with magic. The implication is clear: the proper desire for knowledge is rooted in the love of wisdom and the pursuit of sublime truths, while curiosity in the vulgar sense pursues what is beneath our appropriate range of cognitive interests.

Apuleius offers a highly illuminating point of contact between pagan and Christian attitudes toward *curiositas*. In its wide-ranging usage, *curiositas* bears the bold imprint of all the connotations that accrued to the term by virtue of the hybridization of *periergia*-language and *polupragmon*-language in classical Greek sources. It also reflects the subsequent development of these sources by classical Latin writers in describing an excessive care, zeal, or inquisitiveness for knowledge on all levels.

But Apuleius himself lived and wrote in the Christian era. By this time, Christian patristic writers had begun their own deliberations on the scope and extent of a blameworthy cognitive desire. On one level, these deliberations reflect the literary and philosophical legacy of the Greek and Latin traditions. On a more fundamental level, patristic thinkers (encompassing both the Greek and Latin Fathers of the

Church) could also find their inspiration in Scripture. By extension, Augustine's understanding of *curiositas*, the "lust of the eyes" (*concupiscentia oculorum*), would also be grounded in this rich biblical and patristic background. It is this background that we now consider.

## NOTES TO CHAPTER 2

1. Neil Kenny, *Curiosity in Early Modern Europe Word Histories* (Weisbaden: Harrassowitz Verlag, 1988), 35.

2. I here list the wide-range of classical Latin authors considered in this chapter in approximate chronological order: Titus Maccius Plautus (comic playwright), c.205-184 B.C.; Terence (playwright), d. 159 B.C.; Marcus Terentius Varro (scholar, philologist, encyclopedist), 116-27 B.C.; Marcus Tullius Cicero (orator), A.D. 106-43; Catullus (poet), c.84-c.54 B.C.; Horace (poet and satirist), 65-8 B.C.; Seneca (Stoic philosopher), 4 B.C.-A.D. 65; Quintilian (advocate and rhetorician), A.D. 35-90's; Suetonius (biographer), b. c.A.D. 70-c.A.D. 130; Apuleius (writer, philosopher, orator), c.A.D. 125; Ambrosius Theodosius Macrobius (philosophical commentator and encyclopediast), b. (end of) A.D. 4th c.

3. Plautus, *The Aulularia*, 562-564: *Quo quidem agno satis scio magis curiosam nusquam esse ullam beluam. Volo ego ex te scire qui sit agnus curio. Quia ossa ac pellis totus est, ita cura macet.* Cf., Terence, *Eunuchus* 553, which echoes Plautus' interpretation of *curiosum*, but with a greater emphasis on its manifestation as a meddlesomeness worthy of a busybody: "To think of no busybody meeting me now to follow me all about and deafen and kill me with endless questions" (*sed neminemne curiosum intervenire nunc mihi qui me sequatur quoquo eam*).

4. Varro, *De Lingua Latina* VI,46: *Curare a cura dictum. Cura, quod cor urat; curiosus, quod hac praeter modum utitur. Recordari, rursus in cor revocare. Curiae, ubi senatus rempublicam curat, et illa ubi cura sacrorum publica; ab his curiones.* Cf., Varro's *De Re Rustica* II,3,5, which refers to "shepherds who have watched quite closely" (*curiosiores*), implicity conjoining the notions of careful attention with inquisitiveness.

5. Cf., Andre Labhardt, "*Curiositas*. Notes sur l'histoire d'un mot et d'une notion," 207: "Chez Cicéron, *curiosus* commence à se différéncier. Tântot l'accent repose sur le desir de connaître, qui peut aller jusqu' à l'indiscretion tantôt sur l'effort déployé dans une recherche quelconque, sans qu'il soit toujours aisé, ni même possible, dégager la nuance prépondérante. L'important est que *curiosus* (attesté 23 fois) et son adverbe (5 fois) sont toujours liés à un context impliquant une enquête, avec ou sans jugement de valeur..."

6. Neil Kenny, *Curiosity in Early Modern Europe Word Histories*, 35.

7. Cicero, *Tusculan Disputations* I,45,108: "Chryssippus collects a large number of other instances as suits his inquisitive way" (*Permulta alia colligit Chryssippus, ut est in omni historia curiosus*); *Orato pro Sestio* 9,22: "...the screen is not lasting, nor is it so thick that it cannot be seen through by inquisitive eyes" (*ut curiosus oculis perspici non possit*); *De Natura Deorum* I,35,97: "...not even the most diligent (*curiosissimi*) investigators could possibly collect information"; *Oratio pro Flacco* 70: "...let me be inquisitive" (*patere me esse curiosum*); *De Finibus Bonorum et Malorum* II,9,28: "...I can find...people less precise (*curiosus*)...than yourselves"; *Epistulae ad Familiares* 64 (III,1,1): "He is so sensible and...so inquisitive" (*curiosus*); 225 (IV,13,5): "...the more curious I am to probe" (*hoc sum ad investigandum curiosior*).

8. Andre Labhardt, "*Curiositas*. Notes sur l'histoire d'un mot et d'une notion," 209: "L'histoire de *curiositas* est singulière. Contrairement à *curiosus*, ce dérivé n'est pas attesté avant Cicéron, dans une lettre du 19 avril 59 à Atticus (2,12,2)."

9. Cicero, *Epistulae ad Atticum* II,12. In the remainder of the *Epistulae ad Atticum*, Cicero confines himself to the adjective *curiosus*, in describing a prying, inquisitive nature (IV,11; XV,26), or a careful, devoted interest (V,14).

10. Neil Kenny, *Curiosity in Early Modern Europe Word Histories*, 36l. Cf., A. Labhardt, "*Curiositas*. Notes sur l'histoire d'un mot et d'une notion," 216: "Quant a l' abstrait *curiositas* lui-même, nous avons vu plus haut que, après une apparition accidentelle dans une lettre de Cicéron, il avait été comme rayé du vocabulaire latin, jusqu' à Apulée qui l'accrédite définitivement dans la langue et prépare son entrée dans la littérature chrétienne."

11. Catullus, *Carmina* VII,11.

12. Horace, *Epodes* 17,77.

13. Seneca, *De Ira* III,xi,1.

14. Seneca, *Epistulae Morales ad Lucilium* 88,36.

15. Seneca, *Epistulae Morales ad Lucilium* 88,36.

16. Seneca, *Epistulae Morales ad Lucilium* 88,42-43. Cf., *Epistulae Morales ad Lucilium* 88,45, where Seneca derides the superfluous theories of liberal arts studies (*supervacuum studiorum liberalium*), while conceding that knowing useless things is better than knowing nothing at all.

17. Seneca, *Epistulae Morales ad Lucilium* 45,4-5.

18. Quintilian, *Institutiones Oratoriae* VIII,iii,55: *Est etiam quae periergia vocatur, supervacua, ut sic dixerim, operositas, ut a diligenti curiosus et religione superstitio distat. Atque, ut semel finiam, verbum omne quod neque intellectum adiuvat neque ornatum vitiosum dici potest.*

19. Richard Newhauser, "Towards a History of Human Curiosity: A Prolegomenon to its Medieval Phase," *Deutsche Vierteljahrsschrift für Literaturwissenschaft und Geistgeschichte* 56(1982): 572.

20. Quintilian, *Institutiones Oratoriae* VII,5,24: "This question is not…always raised before the commencement of the trial, like the elaborate deliberations of the praetor" (*qualia sunt praetorum curiosa consilia*). Cf., Suetonius, *Vespasian* 1,4: "…I have found no evidence whatever of this, in spite of rather careful investigation" (*satis curiose inquirem*).

21. Quintilian, *Institutiones Oratoriae* XI,3,143. Cf., *Institutiones Oratoriae* I,8,21, for a reference to *curiosus* in a positive sense: "…if the subject is familiar the careful investigator will often detect the fraud" (*nam in notioribus frequentissime deprehenduntur a curiosus*).

22. Suetonius, *Augustus* 27,3: "…noticing that Pinarius… was taking notes, he ordered that he be stabbed… thinking him an eavesdropper and a spy" (*curiosum ac speculatorum*).

23. For general background information on Apuleius' *Metamorphoses*, see P.G. Walsh, "The Rights and Wrongs of Curiosity (Plutarch to Augustine)," *Greece & Rome*, 2nd Ser., Vol. 35, No. 1 (Apr., 1988): 73-85. Walsh provides an excellent survey of the main themes of the work, and its relationship to the portrayal of the "busybody" in Plutarch. For biographical information on Apuleius, see Walsh's Introduction to his translation of *The Golden Ass* (Oxford: Clarendon Press, 1994), xi-xiv.

24. For scholars who address the question of the origins of Apuleius' *Metamorphoses*, see P.G. Walsh, "The Rights and Wrongs of Curiosity (Plutarch to Augustine)," 74-75.

25. P.G. Walsh, Introduction to his translation of *The Golden Ass*, xx; M.D. MacLeod, translation of *Lucius* or *The Ass* in *The Loeb Classical Library* (Cambridge, Mass.: Harvard University Press; London: William Heinemann Ltd., 1967), 47-48. According to H.J. Mason ("*Fabula Graecanica*: Apuleius and His Greek Sources," in *Aspects of Apuleius' Golden Ass*. A Collection of original papers edited by B.L. Hijmans, Jr. and R.Th. van der Paardt [Groningen: Bouma's Boekhuis B.V., 1978], 6), the phrase *fabula graecanica* must be construed with caution: "Apuleius' adaptation is part of a long tradition of Roman reworking of Greek themes. To criticize him for plagiarism is to miss the point of much of Roman literature and to misunderstand the nature of the creative process." In this respect, Mason pointedly challenges the common interpretation that *fabula graecanica* points to the derivation of *The Golden Ass* or *Metamorphoses* from the Greek *Metamorphoseis*.

26. M.D. MacLeod, translation of *Lucius or The Ass*, 47; P.G. Walsh, Introduction to his translation of *The Golden Ass*, xx. But the claim of Lucius of Patrae's authorship (as attested by Photius) is disputed by Ben Edwin Perry, *The Ancient Romances. A Literary-Historical Account of their Origins* (Berkeley and Los Angeles: University of California Press, 1967), 212.

27. Alexander Scobie, *Apuleius' Metamorphoses. Asinus Aureus* I. A Commentary (Meisenheim am Glan: Verlag Anton Hain, 1975), 2.

28. P.G. Walsh, "The Rights and Wrongs of Curiosity (Plutarch to Augustine)," 75: "Apuleius develops in a more philosophical and theological direction the theme of curiosity which he has taken over from the περιεργία of the Greek *Metamorphoses* and the πολυπραγμοσύνη of Plutarch." Cf., L.A. MacKay, "The Sin of the Golden Ass," *Arion* 4(1965), 477: "The moral of the story, a moral not at all surprising in a Second Century Platonist, is that power and wealth and all self-seeking are fatal to the soul…" Horst Rüdiger echoes these sentiments ("*Curiositas und Magie. Apuleius und Lucius als literarische Archetypen der Faust-Gestalt*," in *Wort und Text*. Festschrift für Fritz Schalk. Herausgegeben von H. Meier und Hans Schommodau [Frankfurt am Main: Vittorio Klosermann, 1963], 64), contrasting the entertainment value of *Lucius or the Ass* with the deeper significance of Apuleius' story: "Weit konsequenter als der Verfasser des Lukios hat Apuleius das Motiv der *curiositas* zum primum movens seiner Handlung gemacht. Im Lukios tritt es nur gelegentlich auf; es wirkt komisch und dient der Unterhaltung. Bei Apuleius steht es im Mittelpunkt und ist weit mehr als 'ein dramaturgisches Motiv,' 'ein Stuck Erzählungstechnik, ein literarischer Trick.'"

29. P.G. Walsh, "The Rights and Wrongs of Curiosity (Plutarch to Augustine)," 75, where he points out that if Lucius possesses a philosophical pedigree, "he should have been sufficiently schooled in moral philosophy to avoid the sins of sensuality and unholy curiosity…" But Alexander Scobie (Apuleius' *Metamorphoses*, 81) challenges the claim that Apuleius focuses upon the religious dimension of *curiositas*, arguing that "it is unbalanced to insist on the purely religious aspects of *curiositas* in the *Metamorphoses*." Accordingly, Scobie places the story in the genre of folklore. Elsewhere, Scobie (*Aspects of the Ancient Romance and its Heritage. Essays on Apuleius, Petronius, and the Greek Romances* [Meisenheim am Glan: Verlag Anton Hain, 1969], 76) challenges the scholarly trend which emphasizes the religious and philosophical aspects of curiosity in the story: "Apuleius demonstrates that misguided inquisitiveness is undesirable in that it brings torment to the person afflicted with it, and writes, not as a hostile social reformer, but as a sympathetic novelist who not only employs the theme for moral instruction, but also finds it structurally useful as a motivating device to explain his hero's actions…"

30. Apuleius, *Metamorphoses* II,1.

31. Apuleius, *Metamorphoses* II,1.

32. Apuleius, *Metamorphoses* I,2.

33. Apuleius, *Metamorphoses* II,6. Andre Labhardt ("*Curiositas*. Notes sur l'histoire d'un mot et d'une notion," *Museum Helveticum* 17 (1960): 215), emphasizes Lucius' desire "connaître les secrets de la magie." In this connection, Labhardt (215-216) also cites the work of Hans Joachim Mette ("*Curiositas*," Festschrift Bruno Schnell [München: C.H. Beck'sche Verlagsbuchhandlung, 1956], 227-235), who links Apuleius' account with

the hermetic tradition: "M. Mette souligne les rapports de cette conception de la curiosité avec le hermétisme de l'Asclepius (14) et du Discours de Momos à Hermès dans la Revélation d'Isis à son fils Horus. Cette derniere, notamment, montre la curiosité inquiète des hommes, qui force les secrets de la nature, pénètre jusque dans le ciel, pour recevoir le juste châtiment de sa démesure. M. Mette croit pouvoir affirmer l'origine diatribique de ce jugement négatif. Sans vouloir me prononcer sur ce point, je soulignerai avec lui que, chez Apulée, la notion de curiosité a reçu de la περιεργία grecque, peut-être travers l'hermétisme, une dimension nouvelle, à la fois philosophique et religieuse." Cf., Antonie Wlosak ("Zur Einheit der Metamorphosen des Apuleius," *Philologus* 113 (1969), 72), who likewise perceives an emphasis on the intellectual curiosity or thirst for knowledge of magic as central to Lucius' plight: "In der Darstellung des Lucius handelt es sich bei seiner *curiositas* um eine heftige, unfassende Wissbegierde. Es wird aber sehr rasch deutlich, dass dieser Wissendrang in eine ganz bestimmte Richtung geht; er ist aus auf Magie. Lucius vertritt also eine besondere gesteigerte Form menschlicher Wissbegierde."

34. Apuleius, *Metamorphoses* III,14.
35. According to J.L. Penwill ("Slavish Pleasures and Profitless Curiosity: Fall and Redemption in Apuleius' *Metamorphoses*," *Ramus: critical studies in Greek and Roman literature* IV (1975): 50), the transformation itself is not to be construed as a punishment or fall; the transformation is of a piece with the general traits he consistently exhibits: "...he constitutes a paradigm of man in a state not altogether dissimilar from the Christian concept of original sin...and it is from this state that he is relieved by his deliverance. The 'fall' in the *Metamorphoses* is not to be found in Lucius' transformation. Rather we should be looking for an account of why human beings in general and Lucius in particular display the characteristics that they do in Books 1-10."
36. Apuleius, *Metamorphoses* IX,13. In this connection, J.L. Penwill ("Slavish Pleasures and Profitless Curiosity: Fall and Redemption in Apuleius' *Metamorphoses*," 66) observes that *curiositas* does not necessarily amount to a character flaw on Lucius' part: "...the desire to know, which is what *curiositas* really is, is in itself no bad thing: indeed, without it there can be no discovery." According to S. Lancel ("*Curiositas* et preoccupations spirituelles chez Apulee," *Revue de l'histoire des religions* 160 (1961): 26-29), we must distinguish two senses of curiosity in the *Metamorphoses*, namely, "la *curiositas* des *mirabilia*" (that is, a desire for the knowledge of novelty) and "une autre curiosité beaucoup plus dangereuse" (that is, a curiosity with magic). Lancel contends (31) that Apuleius indicts the second expression of curiosity alone: "...elle est un sentiment d'impatience qui conduit à des initiatives sacrilèges accomplies suivant des techniques contraignantes, magiques pour tout dire. Nous avons vu tout à l'heure qu'une pente fatale pouvait y mener de la *curiositas* des *mirabilia*. Mais celle-ci

est différente de nature; elle est *nefaria* et des châtiments y sont attachés."
Carl C. Schlam ("The Curiosity of the Golden Ass," *The Classical Review*
64, no. 1 [October, 1968], 120b, n. 3), however, takes issue with Lancel's
distinction between a curiosity concerned with *mirabilia* and a curiosity
concerned with magic (and the claim that Apuleius only condemned the
latter expression of curiosity): "The distinction is useful, but I believe that
Apuleius places the whole range of curiosity in the same religious perspective." In the same article, Schlam affirms (125b) that "the treatment of
intellectual curiosity in the *Metamorphoses* is not one of simple condemnation. The pleasure of learning…of satisfying the desire for what is strange
and marvelous is never denied."

37. Apuleius, *Metamorphoses* V,6: "She must not through sacrilegious curios-
    ity tumble headlong from the lofty height of her happy fortune, and for-
    feit thereafter his embrace" (*neue se sacrilega curiositate de tanto fortunarum
    suggestu pessum deiciat*); V,23: "Psyche trained her gaze insatiably and with
    no little curiosity on these her husband's weapons" (*quae dum insatiabili
    animo Psyche, satis curiosa rimature atque pertractat, et mariti sui miratur
    arma*); VI,20: "…her mind was dominated by rash curiosity, in spite of her
    eagerness to see the end of her service" (*quanquam festinans obsequium ter-
    minare, mentem capiture temeraria curiositate et*). P.G. Walsh, Introduction
    to his translation of *The Golden Ass*, xli) contends that Apuleius inserts
    this parallel tale into the larger framework of Apuleius' *Metamorphoses* in
    a manner consistent with his Middle Platonist agenda: "In this adapta-
    tion of a traditional story, our author's Platonist preoccupations are es-
    pecially prominent; he has grafted on to his source the names of the pro-
    tagonists to indicate that *Psyche's* separation from, and ultimate reunion
    with, Cupid is an allegory for the soul's restless aspiration to attain the
    divine as Plato depicts it in his *Phaedrus*. Beyond this, it has been suggest-
    ed that the Platonist doctrine of the two Venuses, as first recounted…in
    the *Symposium* and reproduced by Apuleius in his *Apology*, is central to
    the story." In contrast, Robert Joly ("*Curiositas*," *L'Antiquité Classique* 30
    (1961): 34), minimizes the philosophical import of the work as a whole:
    "Quant a la *curiositas* du roman d'Apulée, notons-le, c'est une conception
    toute banale, elle n'est nulle part l'objet d'une élaboration quelque peu
    philosophique." In this respect, Joly dismisses Apuleius' interpretation of
    curiosity (43) as a vulgarization of a philosophical concept: "Apulée n'a fait
    qu'emprunter et vulgariser dans son roman une idée bien courante de sans
    temps."

38. J.L. Penwill ("Slavish Pleasures and Profitless Curiosity: Fall and
    Redemption in Apuleius' *Metamorphoses*," 76) characterizes the novel
    as a commentary on the soul's quest for life's meaning which becomes "a
    Platonist's personal account of how he finally escaped from the cave of
    delusion into the sunlight of reality."39. Apuleius, *Metamorphoses* XI,27.

40. Apuleius, *Metamorphoses* XI,15.

41. Apuleius, *Metamorphoses* XI,21.
42. Apuleius, *Metamorphoses* XI,23. Cf., G. Sandy, "Knowledge and Curiosity in Apuleius' *Metamorphoses*," *Latomus. Revue D'Etudes Latines* 31,1(1972): 183: "Thus the transformation is complete; he has come from the point of being one who was too curious to know what was forbidden and who suffered as a result to the point of warning future ages against similar inquisitiveness."
43. J.L. Penwill, "Slavish Pleasures and Profitless Curiosity: Fall and Redemption in Apuleius' *Metamorphoses*," *Ramus: critical studies in Greek and Roman literature* IV (1975): 71.
44. Apuleius, *Apology* II, 16. Cf. Macrobius (b. end of 4th c. [A.D.], *Saturnalia* I,11, 44-45, who likewise refers to a curiosity for "secret causes": *De Epicteto autem philosopho nobili, quod is quoque servus fuit, recentior est memoria quam ut possit inter oblitterata nesciri. Cuius etiam de se scripti duo versus feruntur, ex quibus aliud latenter intellegas, non omni modo dis exosos esse qui in hac vita cum aerumnarum varietate luctantur, sed esse archanas causas ad quas paucorum potuit pervenire curiositas.*

# CHAPTER 3

# SCRIPTURAL & PATRISTIC SOURCES

The Graeco-Roman intellectual tradition provides a significant reservoir of ideas and themes pertinent to the development of the notion of curiosity—not just as a concept in its own right, but more specifically, as the "sin of curiosity" so prominent in Augustine and other early Christian thinkers. Accordingly, Graeco-Roman sources provide key conduits to Augustine's diverse interpretations of curiosity, in the various contexts in which these interpretations emerge in his writings. But another significant current is rooted in the Judeo-Christian tradition. In respect to those sources which shaped Augustine's understanding of curiosity as the "lust of the eyes," this tradition (grounded in the teachings of Revelation) offered a set of influences operative in his own faith commitment.

An important qualification, then, is in order here. Any reference to the Judeo-Christian tradition in this context must presuppose a firm grounding in biblical ways of thinking. For this reason, we must first address scriptural treatments of curiosity. Indeed, these treatments (found largely in the Old Testament) provide the basis of patristic interpretations of curiosity as a morally blameworthy (i.e., sinful) inclination on our part. In this connection, however, we must also come to terms with two intermediary influences that bridge the gap between biblical and patristic attitudes toward this notion.

Philo Judaeus is one of these influences. In this intriguing Hellenistic commentator on the Pentateuch, we encounter a thinker who inserts biblical sentiments regarding the pursuit of knowledge squarely into a Middle Platonic context. By virtue of his thought-provoking exegesis (and the philosophical idiom in which it finds expression), Philo provided the Fathers of the Church with a highly fertile referent for exploring the nuances of the sin of curiosity. The second influence, in contrast, stands outside the mainstream of biblical Revelation. In a very real sense, the Hermeticist *corpus* provides a significant conduit of pagan teachings concerning curiosity that display a marked affinity with key Judeo-Christian presuppositions about the appropriate limits and character of human knowing. While these presuppositions are ultimately rooted in Old Testament and Jewish Hellenistic sources, they assume a fresh stimulus in the philosophical and theological deliberations of the Greek and Latin Fathers of the Church.

## SCRIPTURAL TRENDS

The Old Testament is rich in its references to a blameworthy desire for knowledge on the part of humans. In point of fact, however, the Septuagint contains relatively few explicit instances of the use of *periergia* and *polupragmon*-language. But despite this terminological paucity, we find a marked critique of the curious disposition for intellectual matters. A consideration of this critical attitude must begin with the Book of Genesis and the fall account presented in its initial chapters.

In the figure of the tree of the knowledge of good and evil, we have a veritable standard for distinguishing what is proper to human knowing from what is not. In Genesis ii, the reader is given a clear indication that this tree assumes a special significance among the trees of the Garden of Paradise. But this tree, we learn, is bound up with death.

> And the Lord God…commanded him saying, "Of every tree of paradise thou shalt eat, but of the tree of knowledge of good and evil thou shalt not eat. For in what day soever thou shalt eat of it, thou shalt die the death."[1]

The reason for this prohibition only becomes evident in Genesis iii, in connection with the serpent's temptation of Eve. In response to Eve's repetition of God's warning, the serpent offers these words of encouragement:

> You certainly will not die…God knows well that the moment you eat of it your eyes will be opened and you will be like gods who know what is good and what is bad.[2]

Accordingly, Genesis establishes a direct link between knowledge and divinity: to partake of the fruit of the tree of the knowledge of good and evil is to share in something reserved for the Divine alone, that is, the ability to distinguish between good and bad.[3] In this context, the attainment of knowledge (and the moral capacity it entails) is described in visual terms, as an opening of the eyes. Once Adam and Eve succumb to the serpent's temptation, the acquisition of knowledge carries the added dimension of self-awareness, and the dichotomy between knower and what is known that is the mark of knowledge on any level.

> Then the eyes of both of them were opened, and they realized that they were naked.[4]

But one must not be too quick to read this text exclusively in terms of an indictment of the human pursuit of knowledge *per se*. Indeed, we must understand the transgression of man and woman in the broader sense of an overstepping of the limits assigned to creatures, albeit the highest among creatures. As one commentator puts it, the transgression of creaturely limits amounts to a decision as to what is in one's own best interests, a choice for autonomy apart from a submission to the will of God.[5] From this standpoint, the very violation of God's command to refrain from eating of the tree of knowledge is tantamount to a usurpation of God's prerogative. The alienation which follows the transgression bespeaks a distancing of humans from nature and humans from God. By virtue of their "eye-opening" experience, man and woman are locked out of God's protective sphere.

In Genesis, then, we find the basis of a key Old Testament motif regarding the proper parameters of human knowing and the ultimate standard for knowledge in general. This motif is prominent in both the Psalms and in the Wisdom tradition. In those contexts, we find an implicit distinction between that cognition which reflects the all-embracing knowledge of God and those proud but feeble attempts at knowing on the part of humans. "How precious to me are your designs, O God," proclaims the Psalmist, "how vast the sum of them."[6] In the face of God's comprehensive care for every facet of the universe (including humans), the only reasonable conclusion is that such knowledge is wholly beyond our grasp.

> Lord, my heart is not proud;
> nor are my eyes haughty.

> I do not busy myself with great matters,
>    with things too sublime for me.[7]

But as we move into the sapiential literature, we encounter a more nuanced treatment of this theme. Indeed, Wisdom itself provides the crucial link between Divine knowledge and human investigations of the cosmos. In this respect, the Book of Wisdom offers what amounts to a natural theology in stressing the human capacity (under the guidance of Wisdom) to use a diversified knowledge of the cosmos as a means to God.

> For he gave me sound knowledge of existing things,
>    that I might know the organization of the
>    universe and the force of its elements,
> The beginning and the end and the midpoint of times,
>    the changes in the sun's course and the variations
>    of the seasons.
> Cycles of years, positions of the stars, natures of
>    animals, tempers of beasts,
> Powers of the winds and thoughts of men, uses of
>    plants and virtues of roots
> Such things as are hidden I learned, and such as are plain;
>    for Wisdom, the artificer of all, taught me.[8]

An intimate relationship exists between God and Wisdom. If God is the source of knowledge, Wisdom is the intermediary of that knowledge to humans, as "instructress in the understanding of God."[9] But human access to Wisdom carries a responsibility to subordinate oneself and one's intellectual endeavors to what is higher and more exalted. Accordingly, the positive attitude toward natural knowledge found in the Book of Wisdom is tempered by a more pessimistic outlook in the Book of Ecclesiastes. In Ecclesiastes, humans are almost placed on a par with animals.[10] For this reason, humans must recognize the limitations of their cognitive capacity.

> For what advantage has the wise man over the fool, or what advantage has the poor man in knowing how to conduct himself in life? What the eyes see is better than what the desires wonder after. This… is vanity and a chase after wind.[11]

The implication is clear: what humans aspire toward in their pursuits (above and beyond what they already possess) is no more than a vain exercise in futility. As Qoheleth concludes, "God made mankind straight, but men have had recourse to many calculations."[12] Yet such calculations only pale in comparison to the Wisdom of God, Who made all things. "However much man toils in searching," Qoheleth bemoans, "he does not find it out."[13]

In the Book of Ecclesiasticus, the maintenance of due respect for the limits of human knowing is closely connected with the cultivation of a spirit of humility in our dealings with God. Accordingly, Ben Sira enjoins us against seeking what is beyond human understanding.

> What is too sublime for you, seek not,
>> into things beyond your strength search not.
> What is committed to you, attend to;
>> for what is hidden is not your concern.
> With what is too much for you meddle not,
>> when shown things beyond human understanding.[14]

In this passage, the command "to meddle not" (μὴ περιεργάζου) with what exceeds our proper ken is tantamount to an affirmation of human finitude and the limits it imposes upon us and our activities. Finite beings cannot penetrate the Lord's wonders, no matter how hard we try.

> Whom has he made equal to describing his works, and who can probe his mighty deeds?[15]

The sapiential literature thus presents an ambiguity in its attitudes toward intellectual endeavors. On the one hand, it integrates the Graeco-Roman receptivity toward natural knowledge into the mainstream of Judaic religious belief; on the other hand, it highlights the perennial biblical condemnation of intellectual arrogance and the presumption that human knowledge can supplant Divine Wisdom.[16] While the value of intellectual inquiry is recognized, this never precludes a deep and abiding sense of the limits of human knowing and the vanity inherent in attempts to grasp those hidden truths reserved for God alone. Not only should such truths not be sought by humans; they simply cannot be grasped. From this standpoint, what is blameworthy is not the desire to know on the part of humans, but a desire to know without acknowledging God's ultimate sovereignty, in both moral and intellectual terms.[17]

## PHILO JUDAEUS

The encounter of Judaism with the broader Hellenistic culture decisively transformed the language through which it expressed some
of its basic religious presuppositions. The very translation of the Old
Testament into the Septuagint involved an interpretation of Hebraic
ways of thinking on the basis of vocabulary heavily laden with Greek
philosophical connotations. Likewise, the Wisdom literature introduced a distinctive Hellenistic mentality into the faith of the people of Israel. In this connection, the writings of Philo Judaeus (fl. 20
B.C.-A.D. 40) provide a crucial point of contact between biblical and
Hellenistic perspectives. As Henry Chadwick observed, Philo was
"fully hellenized, presenting a very Greek face to the world," even as he
was firm in his adherence to Mosaic law.[18]

But Philo by no means appropriated Greek philosophical teachings
in an uncritical manner. Instead, he drew upon them selectively, adapting these sources to accommodate his own fidelity to the scriptural
tradition. Accordingly, his use of Greek philosophy in his allegorical
interpretation of Genesis really resulted in a revision of the philosophical concepts, rather than in a reduction of biblical teaching to
a purely secularized interpretation.[19] Philo's discussions of curiosity
provide an intriguing illustration of this methodology in action. In
this connection, he offers what amounts to a Hellenistic reading of
Old Testament attitudes toward curiosity. In so doing, he incorporates
the varied meanings that had accrued to *periergia*-language and *polupragmon*-language throughout antiquity.

At the outset, some observations about the epistemological dimension of Philo's thought are in order. Indeed, his understanding of the
parameters of human knowing can serve as a something of a standard
for his wide-ranging assessment of the curious disposition. In Philonic
terms, the human intellect enjoys a kinship with God, by virtue of
its creation in the image of the Divine *Logos*.[20] For this reason, Philo
adopts a highly positive stance toward human knowing, assuming that
God endows humans with the ability to know higher truths by their
very nature. Any excessive preoccupation with the world of sense experience, however, reflects a diminishing of this nature.

In a manner consistent with his general receptivity to the Platonic
perspective, Philo adopts a dualistic account of our humanness that
highlights the tension between the life of the mind and the body,

between reasoning and sense experience. *Periergia*-language and *po-lupragmon*-language provide a means of expressing those orientations which detract from our proper contemplative focus and preoccupy the soul (or more precisely, the intellect) with what is extraneous to our rational nature. In keeping with its general literary usages, Philo uses this terminology in regard to what is excessively embellished in manner, decorum, or one's way of living. In this respect, he contrasts the wise man (exemplified by Moses) who shuns pleasures with those who exhibit that gradual improvement allowing them to enjoy simple pleasures while rejecting what is excessive and over-elaborate (δε περιεργον και περιττην).[21] By the same token, Philo views the life of temperance as one characterized by a simplicity and self-denial. Intemperance, by contrast, opens one to superfluity and extravagance (δὲ περίεργιαν καὶ πολυτέλειαν).[22]

Like the Stoic philosophers, Philo also assumes a critical stance in regard to a fastidious preoccupation with details in matters of learning. A special target of Philo's invective in this context is the hypercriticism of words, in lieu of a commitment to the cultivation of moral character.[23] Those who give themselves over to petty debates and conceptual hair-splitting lose sight of what is really essential in attaining happiness. From Philo's standpoint, the life of virtue is developed through the practice of a genuine philosophy "free from the pedantry of Greek wordiness" (ἡ δίχα περιεργίας Ἑλληνικῶν).[24]

Philo also uses this terminology in indicting the busyness and restlessness which undermine the discipline and focus of the life of wisdom.[25] Such traits are not only conducive to an intellectual diffuseness, but to a prying inquisitiveness as well. In this connection, Philo emphasizes the encroachment of the senses upon the life of the intellect.

> The eyes wide open to all things visible, even those which it is not right to look upon, meet with disaster. The ears welcome all sounds and are never satisfied; they are athirst all the time for particulars about other people's business (διψῶσαι δὲ ἀεὶ περιεργίας καὶ φιλοπραγμνοσύνης)…and go far and wide on these errands.[26]

Here, Philo conjoins *periergia* (as a curious interest in particulars) with *philopragmosunes* (φιλοπραγμνοσύνης), that is, the "love of busyness." In his reckoning, this combination poses a real threat to the quality of moral life. Elsewhere, he refers to the worthless individual whose life is no more than a prolonged "love of restlessness."[27]

But the real focus of Philo's critique is that "meddlesome curiosity" (πολυπράγμονος περιεργίας) which prompts an eagerness to penetrate the affairs of others.[28] The remedy for this brand of intrusiveness can only be found in that detachment which frees one from the frenetic concerns of the active life.

> They take the temple for their part as a general haven and safe refuge from the bustle and great turmoil of life (πολυπράγμονος καὶ ταρχωδεστάτου βίου)…and released from the cares whose yoke has been heavy upon them.[29]

Philo thus endorses the fundamental Platonic tension between the active and contemplative ways of living. While he does not necessarily depict the active way of life as evil he nonetheless subordinates it to the contemplative life of the intellect. In this respect, he recognizes the open-endedness of the cognitive appetite and its capacity to lead us into diverse areas of inquiry.

> Love of learning is by nature curious and inquisitive (ζητητικὸν καὶ περιεργόν)…prying into everything…an extraordinary appetite for all there is to be seen and heard…not content with what it finds in its own country.[30]

This very love of learning, however, carries a potential pitfall. When Philo speaks of one's "own country," his words must be understood as a reference to what is essential to human nature, that is, the soul and intellect rather than the body and the senses.

By the same token, Philo does not view every desire for knowledge as admissible. Indeed, he takes a rather dim view of an idle curiosity whose sole motivation is the desire to know.

> For what purpose…do you investigate the rhythmic movements and revolutions of the stars? Is it just to busy yourself in idle labour with what is there (ἆρ᾽ ἵνα αὐτὸ μονόν τὰ ἐκει περιεργάσῃ)? And what good can result from all that idle busying (καὶ τίς ἐκ τῆς τοσαύτης περιεργίας γένοιτ᾽ ἂν ὠφέλεια)?[31]

Philo, in effect, interprets knowledge (and the very desire for knowledge) in teleological terms. From this standpoint, knowledge assumes a distinct moral focus. Accordingly, any study of nature that does not contribute to the virtuous life is deemed as useless as trees which cannot bear fruit.[32]

But regardless of its motive (and our natural love of learning), Philo perceives a severe limitation in the human quest for knowledge rooted in our very finitude.

> Though curiosity…may give us the wish to force our way…we shall like blind men stumble over the obstacles before us…but…it is not truth but conjecture that is in our grasp.[33]

The failure to acknowledge our creaturely limits is most egregious in relation to that knowledge reserved for God alone. In this respect, Philo reflects that same uneasiness with human presumptuousness in the epistemological sphere that we encounter throughout the Old Testament. "Quit your meddling (περιεργίας) with heavenly concerns," he cautions us.[34]

Once again, Philo integrates the notion of vain curiosity with a meddlesomeness into things beyond our appropriate range of interests.

> Why do you venture to determine the indeterminate? And why are you so busy with what you ought to leave alone, the things above (τί δὲ πολυπραγμονεῖς ἃ μή σε δεῖ, τὰ μετέωρα)? And why do you extend even to the heavens your learned ingenuity?[35]

The implication in Philo's writings is that these forays into the realm of knowledge are ultimately futile enterprises on our part. This is especially so in regard to attempts to penetrate the ultimate causes of the universe. Such knowledge exceeds our capacity to grasp.

> The task argues a busy, restless curiosity too great for human ability (περιεργίας γὰρ καὶ φιλοπραγμοσύνης μείζονος ἢ κατὰ ἀνθρωπίνην δύναμιν τὸ ἔργον): marvel at all that has come into being, but as for the reasons…cease to busy yourself (μὴ πολυπραγμόνει).[36]

In this context, it is significant that Philo is a major exponent of the *via negativa* and its assumption that God's supreme transcendence places Him above the limits of human comprehension, at least in respect to His essence. If we are able to arrive at a knowledge of God's existence, Philo maintains that it can only be through the medium of the created universe, on the basis of what reasoning discloses. Any direct knowledge of God, however, he attributes to Divine inspiration or revelatory experience.[37] Accordingly, Philo's own hellenization contributes decisively to his understanding of the scope and extent of human knowing. For this reason, Chadwick perceives in Philo "a stage on the way to Hermetic tractates which express in the form of divine revelation a content derived from the commonplaces of popular philosophy."[38] We now turn to the Hermetic *corpus* as an additional touchstone for exploring late antique interpretations of curiosity, specifically in the theological sphere.

## HERMETICISM

As we have seen, the linkage of curiosity with an impious spirit of arrogance and a presumptiousness to exceed the parameters of human knowledge is a salient feature of Old Testament teaching. In the Middle Platonic commentaries of Philo Judaeus, this theme is closely intertwined with a philosophical discussion of the moral implications of curiosity and the busyness of human existence in general. This moral dimension will assume a prominent role in early Christian critiques of the curious disposition. But it also assumes a prominence in a perspective that would itself exert an influence on patristic writing. In Hermeticism, we find another important late antique source of interpretations of curiosity that parallels and complements what we encounter in both the classical and scriptural traditions.

Hermeticism (or alternately, Hermetism) derives its title from the Egyptian god Thoth, also known as Hermes Trismegistus ("the third greatest Hermes"). This collection of doctrines represents a rather eclectic blend of Greek philosophy, Egyptian and Near Eastern religious influences, and occultism, as expressed through a wide range of Greek writings composed between A.D. 100 and 300.[39] For early Fathers of the Church like Tertullian and Lactantius, Hermes Trismegistus assumed the character of a pagan prophet from the time of Moses who anticipated the coming of Christ. According to Reale, "what impressed them was the elevated theological and moral conceptions...encountered in some of the Hermetic writings."[40]

While these works include philosophical treatises, they do not provide a "philosophy" in the strict sense of the word.[41] Rather, they reflect the widespread religious yearning in late antiquity for salvific illumination. In this respect, the *Hermetica* exhibit a marked kinship with Gnosticism. Like their gnostic counterparts, the Hermeticists stress the need for a revelatory awareness of the soul's divine origins. Hermeticism offers that revelation through its teachings. But unlike

Gnosticism, it does not condemn matter and the material universe. In contrast to the Valentinians, for example, the Hermeticists do not attribute the world's creation to a rash act of audacity.[42] If they display a pessimistic attitude, it is directed toward the soul's embodiment, and the negative influence of sense experience and the passions on the soul's life and destiny.[43]

According to Garth Fowden, the monism endorsed by Hermeticist teachings (and its emphasis on the transcendence of the Divine nature) prompted a tendency toward a devaluing of the world and human existence consistent with a dualistic tendency.[44] For Fowden, Hermeticist treatises reflecting these monistic or dualistic perspectives simply cannot be placed in distinct, mutually exclusive categories. Instead, he contends that the *Hermetica* view successive levels of spiritual enlightenment as opening the way to successive levels of insights into the truth of God, world, and humanity.

From this standpoint, the knowledge of the world which might be good at initial stages of spiritual development is indicted as a sinful curiosity at knowing for the sake of knowing.[45] In this context, *periergia*-language designates an impiety that represents a violation of that philosophical piety directed toward a knowledge of the things of God. While the Hermeticist writings extol all types of knowledge focusing upon God's creative activity, they also equate a preoccupation with natural science (along with mathematics, astronomy, and music) with the sin of curiosity.[46] Salient Hermeticist critiques of the curious pursuit of natural knowledge are found in the *Kore Kosmou* and the *Asclepius*.

A notable feature of the *Kore Kosmou's* references to the moral drawbacks of curiosity lies in its characterization of inquisitiveness as an audacious daring (*tolma*). Indeed, it describes the very creation of humans as "a daring, this making man, with eyes inquisitive and talkative of tongue" (τολμηρὸν ἔργον ποιῆσαι τὸν ἄνθρωπον, περίεργον ὀφθαλμοῖς καὶ λάλον γλώσσῃ).[47] The author of this treatise closely connects this inquisitive and loquacious nature with a tendency to use all the senses (but principally inquisitive "eyes") as a means of expanding our overall grasp of the world at large, and by implication, gaining access to things of no concern to us.

But the *periergia* that is part and parcel of the human creation is not confined to the things of this world alone. The *Kore Kosmou* offers a dim prognosis of this wide-ranging desire for knowledge: humans will not only "daringly gaze upon the...mysteries" of nature, but will also "reach into mysteries beyond the earth."[48] In this context, the use of *tolma*-language underscores the fact that such epistemological ventures are indicative of an impiety regarding the limits imposed on human striving in relation to what is reserved for the divine.

> Men will seek out...the inner nature of the holy spaces which no foot may tread, and will chase after them...desiring to observe the nature of the motion of heaven.[49]

But this curious overstepping of bounds reveals a deeper turbulence that calls to mind Plotinus' reference to a "restlessly active nature" (*Ennead* III.4[45].11) and the inquietude that results in the generation of temporal process. In this connection, the *Kore Kosmou* combines the language of *periergia* and *tolma* in condemning an "overbusy daring" (περίεργονίτόλμαν) that is not content with remaining stationary, but engages in perpetual movement.[50] This orientation toward the kinetic and material world of sense experience (with all its diversity and variety) stands opposed to what should be our proper focus, namely, that which contributes to the salvation of the soul.[51]

From this standpoint, any pursuit of knowledge which does not contribute to this salvific end must be rejected. In this respect, the *Kore Kosmou* (and the Hermeticist *corpus* in general) indicts curiosity on two levels. On the one hand, these writings downgrade any pursuit of knowledge that is inferior to our appropriate spiritual end. On the other hand, these sources view those attempts to extend our knowledge toward what is above us in the order of reality as impious, precisely because such cognitive aspirations bespeak an unwillingness to observe our creaturely limitations.

The Latin *Asclepius* provides a more explicit discussion of the appropriate focus of human thought, specifically in the context of philosophical endeavors. Again, we find certain parallels with Plotinus' treatment of the Soul's distention in temporal preoccupations and the fragmentation of its noetic powers on a vast multiplicity of concerns. In the language of the *Asclepius*, rendering a proper account of divinity requires "a godlike concentration of consciousness" (*diuinitatis etenim ratio diuina sensus intentione noscenda*).[52] Only an integration and sharpening of one's cognitive faculties suffices for such a lofty investigation. But this level of attentiveness and the true understanding it yields is not easily attained. Accordingly, the sage issues a warning:

people are susceptible to deceit and rashly pursue what is no more than an image that "transforms the best of living things into a beastly nature" (*transformat optimum animal in naturam ferae moresque beluarum*).[53] This admonition presupposes a dichotomy between a genuine truth accessible through the mind and an inferior image rooted in the world of sense experience.

In broader terms, however, the *Asclepius* draws a sharp distinction between pursuits which promote immortality and the divinity inherent in human nature and a mortality reflected in those material attractions that draw the soul from its destiny. But those who confine their intellectual investigations to the "material part" confront an inevitable paradox. Indeed, the body and its material limitations can only impede the search for ultimate truth.

> Searching warily (*suspiciosa indagatione sectetur*) mankind hunts in things for variations…and… because the heavy and excessive vice of body slows him down, he cannot rightly discern the true causes of their nature.[54]

In this context, "searching warily" (that is, *suspiciosa indagatione*) assumes the connotation of a curiosity given over to opinion or conjectures, and the accompanying uncertainty of those inferior claims to knowledge.[55]

By implication, the *Asclepius* stresses the antithesis between that authentic philosophy that is the mark of true piety (allowing us to recognize divinity) and the pseudo-philosophy of the multitude that only distorts the truth.

The many make philosophy obscure in the multiplicity
of their reasoning (*multi etenim et eam multifaria
ratione confundunt*).[56]

Such a spurious claim to philosophy is tantamount to sophistry. For all their cleverness, sophists are alienated from the "true, pure and holy philosophy" (*vera, pura sanctaque philosophia*) that remains "unprofaned by relentlessly curious thinking" (*nulla animi inportuna curiositate uiolata philosophia*).[57]

## PATRISTIC REFERENTS

The Greek and Latin Fathers of the Church prior to (and contemporary with) St. Augustine treat the notion of curiosity in a manner

consistent with classical models and with a fidelity to scriptural ones
(along with the parallel treatments that emerge in Philo Judaeus and
Hermeticist sources). In this way, patristic references to curiosity as
an inquisitiveness or desire to know build upon the diverse connotations that had accrued to relevant Greek and Latin terminology over
the centuries. Accordingly, Greek and Latin Fathers alike use this terminology to express the notions of an excessive care or diligence; a
busyness with many things; a meddlesomeness; and a preoccupation
with magical arts.

Greek patristic writings employ *periergia*-language and *polupragmon*-language as a means of indicating an excessive concern with empty pursuits which pose a threat to Christian life. In this vein, Tatian
(a second century Apologist) polemicizes against the immorality of
Greek tragedy and the very need to fuss over (πολυπραγμνεῖν) the
details of mythical tales that offer no spiritual benefit.[58] Elsewhere,
Tatian decries the futile expenditure of effort by those who plagiarize
Mosaic teaching with "much vain labor" (πολλῇ περιεργίᾳ).[59] But
needless pursuits are intimately connected with a pomposity given
over to public displays. Accordingly, Clement of Alexandria also critiques the "vain ostentation" (πολυπραγμοσύνης) of senseless endeavors.[60] Clement likewise perceives a significant religious import in
such showiness and its accompanying attentiveness to trifles. For him,
these vain pursuits are fostered by "idle opinion" (περιεργασίας) and
an ignorance that gives rise to idolatrous rites.[61] Cyril of Jerusalem,
in contrast, later uses this same terminology in a liturgical context,
attributing an "idle curiosity" (περιεργὶα) to unworthy candidates
for baptism who seek to know those teachings accessible only to the
initiated.[62]

Other Greek Fathers build upon these themes. For Athanasius, *periergos* provides a means of highlighting the fact that the simplicity of
faith in the Lord's words is "better than an elaborate process of per-
suasion" (βελτίων ἐστὶ τῆς ἐκ περιεργίας πιθανολογίας).[63]
Gregory of Nyssa further uses *periergia*-language in contrasting the
graces of virtue with "alien adornments and curious (περιεργασίας)
devices."[64] His fellow Cappodocians, on the other hand, apply this terminology to the condemnation of officiousness and superfluity in sensual delights.[65] In this respect, however, the notion of excessiveness in
attention to detail or appearance can be subsumed under the broader
category of an excessive care (or alternatively, an excessive diligence).[66]

While *periergia*-language is prominent in expressing these notions, *po-lupragmon*-language assumes an especially salient role, most notably in expressing a busyness or intensity in searching for something.

Clement of Alexandria uses this terminology in precisely this man-ner, describing different manifestations of this restless tendency.[67] Other Greek Fathers echo these sentiments, with a more explicit use of *polupragmon*-language in regard to intrusive busybodies.[68] This lan-guage assumes a marked epistemological dimension, emphasizing an investigative zeal, for good or ill.[69] In this connection, *periergia*-lan-guage and *polupragmon*-language connote a curiosity in the strict sense of inquisitiveness.

In some instances, the Greek Fathers approach this inquiring atti-tude in a positive way. Eusebius, for example, praises the young Origen, who "busied himself" (πολυπραγμονεῖν) with deeper speculations into the meaning of Scripture.[70] Likewise, Clement of Alexandria dis-cerns in the "inquisitive king" (ὁ περίεργος βασιλεύς) Abimelec a representation of the wisdom that transcends the world.[71] In keeping with his favorable view of the philosophical enterprise and his con-viction in a Christian *gnosis*, Clement considers the universe a verita-ble "Athens" through the instruction received from Christ the Word. From this standpoint, however, Clement emphasizes that "in our cu-riosity" (πολυπραγμονοῦντας) we need no longer turn to the hu-man teaching exemplified in the secular wisdom of pagan Athens and the rest of Greece.[72]

Conversely, the Greek Fathers also follow classical and Hellenistic precedents in condemning that curiosity involving an overstepping of the well-defined limits of human striving and our appropriate range of concerns. Justin Martyr, for example, cites the example of those philos-ophers whose reliance on their natural reason led to their prosecution as "irreligious and meddling persons" (ἀσεβεις καὶ περίεργοι).[73] But if *periergia*-language assumes a pejorative connotation in Greek pa-tristic writing, it is chiefly in regard to the practice of magic and related activities. In this way, such terminology becomes a fertile, somewhat all purpose linguistic device for expressing occult practices, enchant-ments, magical arts, spells, superstition, and a broader category best described as "curious arts."[74] The language in these Christian sources is evocative of what we encountered in Apuleius' *Metamorphoses*, and the genre of pagan Hellenistic writing given over to a reaction against the dangers of dabbling with knowledge that takes us out of our cognitive depth, opening us to supernatural or naturalistic forces beyond our control. This is the central meaning of Latin counterpart terminology (i.e., *curiositas* and its adjectival or adverbial forms).

Tertullian is a key exponent of *curiositas* in this vein, especially in respect to challenging heretical tendencies and teachings. For him, the ultimate standard which defines the parameters of intellectual investigation is the Rule of Faith. Tertullian contrasts this fidelity to orthodox teaching with a restless curiosity which is the mark of heresy. Curiosity is to be given free rein, he advises, "as long as its form exists in proper order."[75] In this respect, Tertullian directs this admonition toward those curious seekers (*curiosus quaerens*) who are gifted with true knowledge.[76] For the rest, he stresses that ignorance is preferable to attaining knowledge of what one ought not to know.

Tertullian extends this restriction to that skill in Scripture encompassing the "curious art which must give way to faith" (*cedat curiositas fidei*) in the interests of salvation.[77] In this context, he finds an important scriptural touchstone in the injunction of Mt. 7:7: *Seek and you shall find*. But how far should the commitment to seeking extend? Tertullian perceives a danger in unrestricted intellectual pursuits in matters of faith. For, what might be taken by the faithful as an incentive for curious inquiries can be construed by heretics as a means of introducing unbelief.[78] Tertullian has specific heretical targets in mind here—those like Marcion and Valentinus, who first adhered to the faith until they were consumed by "their ever restless curiosity" (*inquietam semper eorum curiositatem*).[79] From this standpoint, he can only bemoan the fact that they did not use this same curiosity as a means of discerning the truth of Christian teaching. "Here alone," he complains, "the curiosity of human nature sleeps" (*humana curiositas torpescit*).[80]

Tertullian's critique of pagan culture extends to religion and philosophy alike. On the one hand, he discerns an eager "curiosity after superstitious observances" (*curiositas superstitiosa*) in the religious life of imperial Rome.[81] On the other hand, he indicts philosophers for their apparent plagiarization of Sacred Scripture, in the "inquisitiveness to investigate every manner of learning" (*curiositatem omnimodae litteraturae inspiciendae*).[82] In the philosophical sphere, Tertullian interprets the celebrated fall of Thales into a well (while gazing absentmindedly at the sky) as a commentary on those who devote their investigations to a futile end by encouraging a "foolish curiosity" (*stupidam curiositatem*) over the things of nature.[83]

In view of Tertullian's famous query "What has Athens to do with Jerusalem?," it is all too easy to caricature him as an anti-dialectical theologian.[84] But for someone of such impressive intellectual gifts, this was clearly not the case. In a manner consistent with biblical ways of thinking, Tertullian draws a sharp distinction between the "simplicity of truth" (*simplicitate veritatis*) and the curiosity that promotes spurious claims to knowledge.[85] In this respect, he perceives a link between the so-called "curious arts" and sin on its most primal level. The *Ad Marcionem* provides a case in point: here, Tertullian traces the curious art of astrology to the investigations of the fallen angels, those initial creaturely defectors from Divine fellowship.[86]

For Tertullian, then, curiosity has a rather broad reach, not only encompassing a flawed desire for knowledge, but also a wide range of pursuits prompting a deviation from authentic Christian teaching. His use of *curiositas* (and related terminology) clearly reflects a scriptural inspiration. But it also reflects some general patristic trends, which in turn exhibit a marked continuity with pagan sources we have encountered in earlier chapters. In P.G. Walsh's assessment, the Christian Fathers of the Church reveal a "conscious adaptation of current attitudes of the Greco-Roman philosophical schools to harmonize with the Hebraic teaching of the Bible."[87]

In a very real sense, Tertullian provides a key intermediary in this context between two prominent fellow North Africans: Apuleius of Madaura and Augustine of Hippo. In regard to Apuleius, Tertullian expands his indictment of an interest in magic and the occult in the *Metamorphoses* (*The Golden Ass*) to embrace the broader category of all curious arts that threaten a fidelity to Christian faith.[88]

In regard to Augustine, Tertullian bequeathes him a distinct suspicion of pagan philosophy. The glaring irony is that the Augustine who so enthusiastically appropriated the insights of secular thought for his own Christian purposes as a philosopher and theologian displayed such a wariness toward that same *curiositas* which might have drawn him to those sources.[89]

## ASSESSMENT OF PART I

St. Augustine's deliberations on the dynamics of curiosity and its implications (i.e., epistemological, moral, metaphysical) permeate his writings. These discussions are firmly grounded in his distinctive vision of reality and the place it accords human beings within the order of creation. But his crafting of his interpretation of the curious mind is very much in continuity with the literary, philosophical, and theological history of *curiositas* (and related terminology) in the classical Greek, classical Latin, scriptural, and patristic sources examined in the previous three chapters. I now assess these diverse sources with a view toward discerning their possible influence upon Augustine. This assessment is highly tentative; a more explicit consideration of influences arises in the course of our exploration of Augustine's understanding of the sin of *curiositas* in Part II of this study.

In surveying the vast range of treatments of curiosity that emerge in the classical, biblical, and patristic traditions, we discern some salient trends that suggest a hypothetical line of descent between these sources and Augustine. This hypothesis is necessarily sparse. Indeed, it can only be fleshed out in light of what Augustine himself contributes to the ongoing debate regarding the benefits and drawbacks of the desire for knowledge. Accordingly, I propose three branches of this line of descent, that is, moral, epistemological, and metaphysical.

The moral branch in question is the dominant one. As the previous three chapters have shown, the vast majority of sources under scrutiny on this topic address the blameworthiness (or potential blameworthiness) of the curious disposition. In this respect, however, the moral dimension of curiosity is closely aligned with an epistemological one. If curiosity is viewed as possessing a morally questionable status, it is only because it is evaluated in terms of a certain standard of knowledge. This standard presupposes a key distinction between genuine knowledge and its false claimants. On the basis of this distinction, we also find criteria for judging the moral quality of the very desire to know, and whether the goal of one's investigations is worthy of our cognitive efforts. For this reason, Augustine's interpretations of *curiositas* in these terms could find inspiration in the Fathers of the Church (especially Latin Fathers such as Tertullian and Ambrose) and their mediation of ideas derived from Scripture, the *Hermetica*, the Stoics, and most notably, Apuleius. In these sources, he had ready access to a polemical attitude toward magic and a preoccupation with sense images to the neglect of eternal truths.

The metaphysical branch here proposed complements the moral and epistemological ones, albeit with a more explicit focus on the relation between the inquisitive and restless dispositions and one's place in the overall scheme of reality. In this regard, Augustine could find a particularly compelling source of creative adaptation in Neoplatonism, and more specifically (although perhaps not exclusively) in the Neoplatonism of Plotinus. Indeed, the epistemological dimension of *curiositas* as a blameworthy desire assumes a more penetrating metaphysical import when interpreted as contributing to a displacement of one's proper station in a broader cosmic context. Once viewed from a Neoplatonic perspective, Augustinian *curiositas* becomes infused with a dynamic character as an impetus toward involvement in those temporal pursuits which impede our ability to discern truth and confine us to mere images of genuine reality.

Part II of this study will trace Augustine's discussions of *curiositas* as they develop in relation to his triadic interpretation of iniquity. At the outset, we consider the gradual emergence of Augustine's triad of vices (i.e., pride, curiosity, and carnal concupiscence) as a moral category in its own right, with a special focus upon the pivotal role of *curiositas* in this triadic schematization. But any consideration of how Augustine understands the sin of *curiositas* points to those diverse sources which influenced his deliberations, either explicitly or implicitly. In a very real sense, however, those implicit influences might well be the most significant, and indeed, the most pervasive.

Augustine's background as *grammaticus* and *rhetor* would have acquainted him with a vast array of classical and patristic literature that enriched his understanding of *curiositas*. This does not deny the pivotal importance that the *libri platonicorum* assumed in his post-conversion outlook. But any influence that these Neoplatonic writings exerted upon him in this vein would have been greatly enhanced by the manifold discussions surrounding *periergia*-language and *polupragmon*-language in the classical tradition, and which extended into the Christian tradition as well.

## NOTES TO CHAPTER 3

1. Gen. 2:15-17: *Dominus Deus…praecepitque ei dicens, "Ex omni ligno paradisi comede, de ligno autem scientiae boni et mali ne comedas. In quocumque enim die comederis ex eo, morte morieris."*
2. Gen. 3:4-5.
3. Cf., Gen. 3:22.

4. Gen. 3:7.

5. Terence Fretheim, *The New Interpreter's Bible*, Volume 1 (Nashville: Abingdon Press, 1994), 351a. Cf., Howard N. Wallace, "Tree of Knowledge and Tree of Life," *The Anchor Bible Dictionary*, Volume 6 (New York/ Toronto/Sydney/Auckland: Doubleday, 1992), 657b, who interprets the tree as a means to attaining a universal knowledge of the secrets of nature, and thus, an entry to imitating God's creative activity.

6. Ps. 139:17.

7. Ps. 131:1. Cf., Ps. 139:6: "Such knowledge is beyond me, far too lofty for me to reach."

8. Wis. 7:17-22.

9. Wis. 8:4.

10. Eccl. 3:19-21.

11. Eccl. 6:8-9.

12. Eccl. 7:29.

13. Eccl. 8:17.

14. Sir. 3:20-22.

15. Sir. 18:2.

16. For discussions of this dual emphasis in the Wisdom tradition, see Michael Kolarcik, S.J., "Introduction to the Book of Wisdom," in *The New Interpreter's Bible*, Volume V (Nashville: Abingdon Press, 1997), 506 (who stresses the author's welcoming attitude toward the insights of Greek and Hellenistic philosophy while recognizing "other voices in Scripture that warn of the folly of an arrogant commitment to one's own knowledge"), James L. Crenshaw, "Introduction to the Book of Sirach," in *The New Interpreter's Bible*, Volume V (Nashville: Abingdon Press, 1997), 663 (who points to Jewish leaders' acknowledgement of the significance of intellectual inquiry on the part of Jewish leaders, while imposing restrictions on endeavors involving speculations into the "unknown and unknowable"), and W. Gibley Towner, "Introduction to the Book of Ecclesiastes," in *The New Interpreter's Bible*, Volume V (Nashville: Abingdon Press, 1997), 306 (who contends that withholding knowledge of God's works lies within God's sovereign authority and provides a means of keeping humanity in awe and submission).

17. While the use of such motifs are not widespread in the Greek New Testament, they are nonetheless evident in several passages. Cf., Acts 19:19, where *periergia*-language designates the practice of sorcery: "A number who had practiced sorcery (περίεργα πραξάντων) brought their scrolls together and burned them publicly." Also see II Thessalonians 3:11, for an indictment of those who are idle: "We hear that some among you are idle. They are not busy; they are busybodies" (περιεργαζομένους). Cf., I Peter 4:15: "If you suffer, it should not be as a murderer or thief or any other kind of criminal, or even as a meddler" (ἢ ὡς ἀλλοτριεπίσκοπος).

18. H. Chadwick, "Philo," Part II, Chapter 8 of *The Cambridge History of Later Greek and Early Medieval Philosophy*, edited by A.H. Armstrong (Cambridge: Cambridge University Press, 1967), 137.

19. Paul Edwards, ed., *Encyclopedia of Philosophy*, Volume 6 (New York: Macmillan Publishing Co., Inc. & The Free Press; London: Collier Macmillan Publishers, 1972), s.v. "Philo Judaeus" by Harry A. Wolfson, 151b. Cf., H. Chadwick, "Philo," *The Cambridge History of Later Greek and Early Medieval Philosophy*, 155.

20. H. Chadwick, "Philo," *The Cambridge History of Later Greek and Early Medieval Philosophy*, 139.

21. *Legum Allegoria* III,48,140.

22. *De opificio mundi* 58,164.

23. *De Congressu Quaerendae Eruditionis Gratia* X,53.

24. *Quod Omnis Probus* XIII,88.

25. *In Flaccum* 5; *De Vita Mosis* IX,46.

26. *De Agricultura* VII,35.

27. *De Abrahamo* III,20.

28. *De Abrahamo* III,21.

29. *De Specialibus Legibus* I,12,69.

30. *De Migratione Abrahami* XXXIX,216.

31. *De Mutatione Nominum* X,72. Cf., *De Sobrietate* VII,32.

32. *De Mutatione Nominum* X,73.

33. *De Ebrietate* XLI,167.

34. *De Migratione Abrahami* XXXIV,187. Cf. *De Ebrietate* XXXIV,135, where Philo stipulates that those who violate the tabernacle and its contents or even look at them "with a curious eye" (ἢ διὰ περιεργίαν ὀφθαλῶν) will die, according to the ordinance of the law.

35. *De somniis* I,x,54.

36. *De Fuga et Inventione* XXIX,162.

37. According to Wolfson (*Encyclopedia of Philosophy*, Volume 6, s.v. "Philo Judaeus," 153b), the direct way of knowing God represents an alternate version of the indirect ways of attaining Divine knowledge, "flashed upon the mind suddenly and simultaneously by divine inspiration." Similarly, Chadwick ("Philo," *The Cambridge History of Later Greek and Early Medieval Philosophy*, 149) argues that "if God is to be known, it is because He makes Himself known by grace when He grants revelation in accordance with the capacities of the recipients."

38. H. Chadwick, "Philo," *The Cambridge History of Later Greek and Early Medieval Philosophy*, 156.

39. John Procopé, "Hermetism," *Routledge Encyclopedia of Philosophy*, Volume 4. Edited by Edward Craig (London and New York: Routledge, 1998), 395a. Procopé (396a) provides a helpful delineation of these diverse writings, dividing them into philosophical treatises (concerning God, world, and humans) and technical treatises (on subjects like astrology, alchemy,

and the occult). The philosophical treatises comprise the *Asclepius* or *Perfect Discourse* (in extant Latin translation); the *Corpus Hermeticum* proper, encompassing fourteen treatises translated into Latin by Ficino in the fifteenth century under the title *Poemandres*; and about twenty-nine extracts compiled in an anthology by John Stobaeus in the fifth century (that includes fr. 23 of the *Kore Kosmou*). According to Frances A. Yates ("Hermeticism," in *The Encyclopedia of Philosophy*, Vol. 3 [New York and London: MacMillan Publishing Co. and The Free Press, 1972], 490a), the myth of "Hermes Trismegistus" proceeded from the writings of an Egyptian seer or sage who lent great authority to the *Hermetica*.

40. Giovanni Reale, *A History of Ancient Philosophy* (Part IV. *The Schools of the Imperial Age*), Edited and translated from the Fifth Italian Edition by John R. Catan (Albany: State University of New York Press, 1990), 275. But Reale also points out (275) that modern research from the 18th century onward designates these writings as *pseudepigrapha* that were composed by various authors under the patronage of the Egyptian god. On the basis of 20th century scholarship, however, Reale recognizes that the most important of these writings reflect ideas of the Hellenistic age.

41. In this connection, Roelof van den Broeck argues ("Gnosticism and Hermetism in Antiquity: Two Roads to Salvation," *Gnosis and Hermeticism from Antiquity to Modern Times* [Albany, New York: State University of New York Press, 1998], 6) that while the Hermeticist texts cannot be completely explained apart from Greek philosophical traditions, they assume a distinctly religious thrust. In this vein, Procopé ("Hermetism," 396b) stresses that those writings are "documents of spirituality," rather than philosophy, representing the translations and output of native Egyptian religion cast in the language of Middle Platonism.

42. Here, van den Broeck ("Gnosticism and Hermetism in Antiquity: Two Roads to Salvation," 9) points out that "according to several gnostic systems, the first step in this downward development was the wish of Sophia to become equal to God by producing something on her own; as a result of Sophia's insolence, the soul…became incarcerated in the body." In contrast, the Hermeticist texts (according to van den Broeck, 10) are absent in claims that the cosmos is bad, or created by an evil demiurge.

43. R. van den Broeck, "Gnosticism and Hermetism in Antiquity: Two Roads to Salvation," 11.

44. Garth Fowden, *The Egyptian Hermes. A historical approach to the late pagan mind* (Cambridge, UK: Cambridge University Press, 1986), 102. Fowden (104) addresses this seeming contradiction in these terms: "If we are to take Hermetism seriously, we must give an account of it that assigns due weight to all these different levels of approach to the truth, rather than obscuring them so that they can be accomodated to some predetermined doctrinal scheme. And we should bear in mind too the possibility that the Hermetists deliberately formulated mutually contradictory statements

about God, in order to convey something of His transcendence and the comprehensiveness of His power, indescribable in the language of human reason."

45. Garth Fowden, *The Egyptian Hermes. A historical approach to the late pagan mind*, 103.

46. Garth Fowden, *The Egyptian Hermes. A historical approach to the late pagan mind*, 112

47. *Kore Kosmou* 25 (NF IV, Fr. 23, 44, 23-24). Jan Assmann ("*Periergia*: Egyptian reactions to Greek Curiosity," in Erich S. Gruen, ed., *Cultural Borrowings and Ethnic Appropriations in Antiquity* [Stuttgart: Franz Steiner Verlag, 2005], 39) interprets Hermeticist commentary on curiosity as indicative of "the confrontation between the Egyptian image of the Greeks and the Greek apprehension of that image." In the *Kore Kosmou*, he further discerns (39) the central text for conveying this Egyptian attitude toward the Greeks: "It is tempting to see in these descriptions a reflection of the Egyptian experience of having served for centuries as the object of Greek Egyptology and of having been exposed to the Greek thirst for knowledge."

48. *Kore Kosmou* 25 (NF IV, Fr. 23, 44, 3-4).

49. *Kore Kosmou* 26 (NF IV, Fr. 23, 45, 14-15). We find a significant overlapping between the *Kore Kosmou's* treatment of an audacious striving for privileged knowledge and the myth of Sophia's fall in Valentinian Gnosticism. While the myth assumes various versions, its key message is that Sophia aspired to penetrate the mystery of the Godhead, or alternately, to imitate the Father's creative work. According to Irenaeus (*Adversus Haereses* I, 2, 2), however, Sophia's transgression lay in a curious desire to investigate the Father's nature, and thereby, to grasp his greatness.

50. *Kore Kosmou* 15 (NF IV, Fr. 23, 24, 2-6).

51. Garth Fowden, *The Egyptian Hermes. A historical approach to the late pagan mind*, 113. Here, Fowden contends that "for the Hermetist no product of human intellectual investigation (not even knowledge of God) was an end in itself," but must be directed toward a release from the world for the sake of the soul's salvation.

52. *Asclepius* 3 (NF II, 298, 20-299, 2).

53. Asclepius 7 (NF II, 303, 23-304,1).

54. *Asclepius* 11 (NF II, 310, 6-10).

55. Brian P. Copehaver's translation of the phrase *suspiciosa indagatione* (*Hermetica. The Greek Corpus Hermeticum and the Latin Asclepius* [Cambridge, UK: Cambridge University Press, 2000], 225) draws on NF II, 368, n. 105, which renders the phrase as "scrute avec une inquiète curiosité," pointing out that *suspiciosa* "peut signifier aussi: 'une curiosité qui se contente d'opinions, de conjectures non sûrement fondées' suspicio impliquant une forte proportion d'incertitude."

56. *Asclepius* 12 (NF II, 311, 11-24). Cf. Seneca, *Ep.* 95.47 (which equates knowledge of the divine with piety) and Cicero, *On the Nature of the Gods* 2.61. 153 (which roots piety in the knowledge of the gods).

57. *Asclepius* 14 (NF II, 312, 16-313,1). In this context, Assmann ("*Periergia*: Egyptian reactions to Greek Curiosity," 40) agains discerns an Egyptian cultural commentary upon the scientific mindset of the Greeks and the depiction of such empirical interests as an "importunate curiosity."

58. *Oratio ad Graecos* 24.

59. *Oratio ad Graecos* 40.

60. *Pedagogus* 2, 12, 125 (PG 8: 549a). Cf., *Pedagogus* 3, 2, 8 (PG 8: 565a), which uses *periergos* in respect to what is overdetailed.

61. *Protrepticus* 10, 99, 1.

62. *Protocatechesis* 4 (PG 33: 341a).

63. *orationes tres adversus Arianos* 3.1 (PG 26: 324a).

64. *homiliae in orationem dominicam* 3 (PG 44: 1149a).

65. Gregory Nazianzenus, *Ep.* 14 (PG 37: 48a): "...oppose the officiousness and dishonesty of the man" (τῇ περιεργίᾳ καὶ ἀγνωμοσύνῃ τοῦ ἀνδρὸς); *Ep.* 47 (PG 37: 96c): "...you are being worried by some sophistical officiousness" (περιεργιας); Basil of Caesarea, *regulae fusius tractate* 20.3 (PG 31: 973a), for reference to a "rareness or abundance" (βρωμάτων καὶ περιεργιᾳ). Cf., Gregory Thaumaturgus, *Origenem oratio panegyrica* 11 (PG 10: 1084a), which cites the "officious anxieties of life" (τὸν βίον πολυπραγμοσύνης); John Chrysostum, *Homilies on John* II, 6 (PG 59: 32d), which links an excessive concern about one's mode of expression (περιεργία) with sophistry; XVI, 2 (PG 59: 104d), which mocks the attempt to persuade by flattery and "ill-timed officiousness" (ἀκαίρου περιεργίας).

66. John Chrysostum, *Homilies on St. John* XXIV, 2 (PG 59: 146a), which characterizes Christ's teaching in obscure terms (i.e., through parables) as a means of rendering His hearers more "active and zealous" (περιεργότερον) in raising questions; *hom.* 14.3 in I Tim. (PG 62: 574c): "...it is firmly retained with all care and diligence" (περιεργασίας).

67. Clement of Alexandria, *Protrepticus* 10, 106,5: "He who seeks after God is busy about his own salvation" (πολυπραγμονεῖ σωτηρίαν); *Stromateis* I, 14,3 (PG 8: 760b): "We really must be concerned with the origin of the universe" (τὴν γένεσιν τοῦ κόσμου πολυπραγμονῆσαι); I, 3, 24 (PG 8: 713b): "...the Greeks...called those who spend too much time on a single object sages or sophists" (περὶ ότιοῦν πολυπράγμονας); *Pedagogus* II, 1,2 (PG 8: 380b): "There are those who reject simplicity of diet...in a frantic search (πολυπραγμονούντων) for expensive menus." Cf., Hippolytus of Rome, *refutatio omnium haeresium sive philosophoumena* VI.3 (PG 16: 3207a): "...after repeated intrigues (πολυπραγμονῶν), he...failed to accomplish his desire"; Gregory Nanzianzus, *orationes* 28.9

(PG 36: 37a): "He who is eagerly pursuing (πολυπραγμονῶν) the nature of the Self-existent."

68. Basil of Caesarea, *Ep.* 114 (PG 32: 528b): "In attempting...this, I cannot fairly be blamed as a busybody" (δικαίως πολυπράγμονος); John Chrysostum, *hom.* 49.5 in Mt. (PG 58: 501c): "...to many I seem over-minute in busying myself about these things" (ταῦτα περιεργαζόμενος); Cyril of Jerusalem, *Protocatechesis* 3 (PG 33: 736b): "We read...of a busybody (ἐπολυπραγμονησέ) who one day decided to investigate a wedding-feast."

69. Other Fathers use *polupragmon*-language in the sense of a careful investigation or busy search: Athanasius, *apologia (secunda contra Arianos)* 5 (PG 25: 257a): "...after we understood what they had written, we made diligent enquiry" (πολυπραγμονήσαντες); Basil of Caesarea, *De Judicio Dei* 2 (PG 31: 656a): "...after a long time in this state of indecision...I was still busily searching for the cause" (τὴν αἰτίαν ἣν εἶπον πολυπραγμονῶν).

70. *The Ecclesiastical History* VI, 2,9.

71. *Pedagogus* I, 5,21 (PG 8: 276a).

72. *Protrepticus* 11 (PG 8: 224a). Cf., *Stromata* I, 1, 6 (PG 8: 692d), where Clement contrasts the proper attitude of those consecrated to Christ with those so preoccupied with worldly things as they would examine the buildings of cities "out of curiosity" (περιεργίας).

73. II *Apology* 10 (PG 6: 460c).

74. Such usages are especially prominent in Eusebius' histories: *The Ecclesiastical History* IV, 7,9: "These did not, like Basilides, desire to transmit the magic of Simon secretly, but openly...speaking almost with awe of their magical ceremonies (περιεργίαν)...love charms...dreams...and of other similar performances"; *Life of Constantine* 3.57 (PG 20: 1124b): "...they witnessed the...uncleanness concealed beneath...the objects of their worship...either the bones of dead men or dry skulls...adorned by the arts of magicians" (περιεργίαις); *Life of Constantine* 2.45 (PG 20: 1021b), which refers to a law which "provided that no one should erect images, or practice divination and other...foolish arts (ταῖς ἄλλαις περιεργίαις), or offer sacrifice." Cf., Sozomenus, *historia ecclesiastica* V, 5,15 (PG 67: 1260b): "Alaphion...was possessed...and neither the pagans nor the Jews...by any incantations and enchantments (ἐπῳδαῖς καὶ περιεργίαις), deliver him"; Origen, *Contra Celsum* 2, 51 (PG 11: 877b): "...it is a corollary...of magic and sorcery...by evil daemons...enchanted by elaborate spells (περιέργοις) ...that wonders done by divine power must also exist"; Irenaeus, *adversus haereses* I, 23,4 (PG 7: 673a): "...the mystic priests...practice magical arts... exorcisms and incantations...and...other curious arts" (*alia perierga*).

75. *De Praescriptionibus Adversus Haereticos* xiv (PL 2: 27a): *Caeterum, manente forma ejus in suo ordine, quantum libet quaerens et tractes, et omnem libidinem curiositatis effundas;*

76. *De Praescriptionibus Adversus Haereticos* xiv (PL 2: 27b).

77. *De Praescriptionibus Adversus Haereticos* xiv (PL 2: 27b).

78. *De Praescriptionibus Adversus Haereticos* viii, 1 (PL 2: 21a).

79. *De Praescriptionibus Adversus Haereticos* xxx (PL 2: 42a). Cf., Ambrose, *Hexaemeron* I, 2, 7 (PL 14: 125d), who warns against being led astray by "vain opinions" (*vanis abducamur opinionibus*) that attribute inadequate first principles to the governance of the universe. Also see Minucius Felix, *Octavius* X, 5, which ironically depicts the pagan critique of the Christian God as "a troublesome, restless, shameless and interfering being" (*inquietum, inpudenter etiam curiosum*) who has a hand in everything that is done.

80. *Apologeticus* 1 (PL 1: 265a). Elsewhere, Tertullian questions (*Apologeticus* 5, PL 1: 296-297a) why pagans who exhibit a "curiosity for exploring all things" (*curiositatem omnium explorator*) enact anti-Christian laws in their impiety. Cf., *Ad Nationes* I,1 (PL 1: 559b-c), where Tertullian bemoans the fact that those who criticize Christianity in ignorance of its teachings do not allow themselves suspicions which may be true, the "only instance in which human curiosity grows torpid" (*hic tantum curiositas humana torpescit*). Cf., Arnobius, *Disputationes Adversus Gentes* II, 57 (PL 5: 900a), who contends that the conflicting opinions of arguments could be resolved if "human curiosity could reach any certainty" (*si certum aliquid tenere curiositas posset humana*).

81. *Apologeticus* 25 (PL 1: 429-430a).

82. *Ad Nationes* II, 2 (PL 1: 588b).

83. *Ad Nationes* II, 4 (PL 1: 591c-592a).

84. *De Praescriptionibus Adversus Haereticos* vii.

85. *Ad Marcionem* II, 21 (PL 2: 309c-310a).

86. *De Idolatria* ix (PL 1: 671a). Cf., *De cultu feminarum* I, 2 (PL 1: 1305c-1306a), where Tertullian roots feminine ostentation in "several not well revealed arts and every curiosity" (*artes plerasque non bene revelatas et omnem curiositatem*), including the interpretation of the stars.

87. P.G. Walsh, "The Rights and Wrongs of Curiosity (Plutarch to Augustine)," *Greece and Rome*, 2nd Ser., Vol. 35, No. 1 (Apr., 1988), 80.

88. But while acknowledging this broad scope of Tertullian's critique, P.G. Walsh ("The Rights and Wrongs of Curiosity," 81) also stresses that "the most prominent group to which the label of pernicious *curiositas* is attached by him, are the contemporary schools."

89. In this connection, P.G. Walsh ("The Rights and Wrongs of Curiosity," 81) argues that "this radically anti-philosophical stance...becomes a commonplace in the writings of fourth-century Christians in the West, but it is in Augustine, another African, where we find such condemnations most frequently associated with *curiositas*." Cf., the remarks of Andre Labhardt

("*Curiositas.* Notes sur l'histoire d'un mot et d'une notion," *Museum Helveticum* 17[1960]: 224), who highlights the thread linking Apuleius, Tertullian, and Augustine: "Sur les traces de son compatriote africain, mais non sans s'inspirer premierement de saint Paul, Tertullien fait éclater avec vigeur l'opposition curiosité—foi, avec une pointe incisive contre l'occultisme sous toutes ses formes, l'hérésie et même la théologie spéculative. Chez saint Augustin enfin—car entre Tertullian et lui, aucun Père latin n'a abordé le problème de la curiosité intellectuelle d'une maniere systématique—on retrouve les points acquis par ses prédécesseurs, mais les rapports entre la science et la philosophie, d'une part, et la foi chrétienne, de l'autre, sont soumis à un nouvel examen, qui aboutit au refus de toute curiosité, c'est-à-dire de toute aspiration à une science désinteressée, non ordonnée à la fin dernière de l'homme, qui est le salut."

# PART II

# *CURIOSITAS* AND
# THE SOUL'S JOURNEY

# CHAPTER 4

## *CURIOSITAS* IN AUGUSTINE'S MORAL TRIAD

Augustine does not treat curiosity in complete isolation, as if it operates independently of other desires in our range of affectivities. Rather, he includes it in a closely interrelated triad of vices. Augustine found the scriptural inspiration for this triad in I Jn. 2:14-16, and its condemnation of the lust of the flesh (*concupiscentia carnis*), the lust of the eyes (*concupiscentia oculorum*), and the ambition of the world (*ambitio saeculi*). This "triple concupiscence" provided what amounted to his key for resolving the problems that drove his early intellectual struggles: "Whence comes evil?" and "Whence comes iniquity?"

After grappling with the origin of moral evil for a number of years, Augustine would eventually coordinate this "triple concupiscence" with the sins of carnal concupiscence, curiosity, and pride, respectively. In this triadic schematization, pride (*superbia*) was identified with the Johannine ambition of the world, curiosity (*curiositas*) with the Johannine lust of the eyes, and carnal concupiscence with the Johannine lust of the flesh.

This investigation uses Augustine's triadic interpretation of iniquity as an initial touchstone for assessing his treatment of curiosity (as well as related terminology and concepts), from his earliest to his latest works. An examination of the various expressions of this disposition offers an illuminating referent for coming to terms with Augustine's ongoing evolution as a thinker. Thus, even if the triadic schematization is not central to this study, we must be attuned to its presence and shifting roles in Augustine's psychological deliberations.

Augustine's understanding of curiosity reflects an ongoing development. He continually expanded the parameters of the term (or more precisely, the notion the term expresses), using it in various contexts and adapting it for a variety of purposes. A conservative list of these contexts should include a critique of Manichaeism (along with a polemic against the limitations of natural science and an indictment of materialism, sensism, and corporeal conceptions of the Divine nature), an account of the soul's distention in time; an exaltation of the contemplative life over one given over to action and temporal involvements; an investigation of the human intellect as image of God (in the context of his trinitarian theology); and a polemic against pagan superstition and immorality.

## THE GENESIS OF TRIADIC SCHEMATIZATION

The triad of pride, curiosity, and carnal concupiscence offered Augustine a means of delineating scriptural teachings on the causes of iniquity which he gradually synthesized with ideas, motifs, and images drawn from the secular tradition. While Neoplatonism exerted the pivotal influence on his outlook, Augustine also drew upon a host of literary, philosophical, and theological sources. In this respect, his triadic schematization grew out of a process of creative adaptation and refinement. This conceptual evolution is traceable to those writings which he wrote between his baptism in A.D. 386 and the completion of the *Confessiones* (c. A.D. 400).

This chapter analyzes that process from Augustine's earliest works until the point in his career (just preceding the composition of the *Confessiones*) in which he forged a full-fledged triadic interpretation of primal sin. This triadic schematization is fully operative in four key works: the *De Genesi contra Manichaeos* (A.D. 389), the *De Musica* (A.D. 387-389), the *De Vera Religione* (A.D. c. 390/1), and the *De libero arbitrio*, Book II (A.D. c. 391-395).[1] (Augustine fully exploits this triadic schematization in his *Confessiones*, his penetrating account of the soul's movement from God, and its gradual ascent toward its *Summum Bonum*.) The present chapter, then, provides something of a scaffolding or framework within which we will investigate the various dimensions of Augustine's understanding of the sin of *curiositas* in Chapters 5 through 9. But before we embark upon that investigation, we must address an overarching question (in fact, the dominant question of this chapter): *Why does Augustine deem curiositas one of the primal vices?*

## AUGUSTINE'S EARLY WRITINGS

Augustine's earliest writings do not employ the triad as a formal organizing principle in its own right. In those works, we encounter initial manifestations of his ongoing struggle to come to terms with the problem of evil. Augustine's focus lies in those irrational tendencies within human nature that threaten our moral life and the realization of genuine happiness. For this reason, he stresses the importance of a detachment from the seductive and deceptive character of temporal and corporeal images. Indeed, the entire world of sense experience is depicted as an obstacle to truth. At this early juncture, Augustine endorses the Stoic equation of happiness with the exercise of reasoning and the rational control of desires.[2] This Stoic dimension reveals itself in his seeming aversion to fleeting goods liable to involuntary loss.[3]

The Cassiciacum dialogues (composed in A.D. 386), define iniquity chiefly in terms of cupidity (*cupiditas*) or blameworthy desire, the core of a cluster of vices that include individual sins pointing to the triadic components (or their variants).[4] From the very outset of his intellectual project, pride (along with vain glory, audacity, and the desire for popular acclaim) is defined as the preeminent sin and the greatest obstacle to the soul's conversion.[5] When Augustine isolates cupidity, passion, and sensuality as impediments to the good life, he anticipates the all-embracing character of carnal concupiscence. His critique of idle interests that enervate the mind anticipate the sin of curiosity. Accordingly, he stresses the urgency of supplanting carnal lusts and material attachments by the love of wisdom which enables us to rise above excessiveness of all kinds.[6] Everything that once yielded sensual pleasure (including visual spectacles) must be renounced for the sake of conversion.[7] Augustine's *De Ordine* provides a particularly illuminating touchstone for exploring his contrast between legitimate intellectual endeavors (instrumental in the pursuit of wisdom) and the mind's application to what amounts to mere "curiosities," that is, no more than objects of passing fascination.[8]

These initial suggestions of the blameworthiness of curiosity are evocative of the classical and patristic sources at Augustine's disposal. In a manner consistent with the Latin tradition, Augustine perceives the "cares" (*curae*) bound up with temporal involvements and sensual attachments as lying at the heart of the curious disposition. Augustine considers conversion itself as nothing less than a release from the "heavy burdens of daily cares."[9] From this standpoint, the ones most vulnerable to deceit are those who are curious about perishable things, who desire transitory power, or who are awe-struck by meaningless prodigies.[10] From Augustine's standpoint, in fact, even rash forays into areas of learning are conducive to a proliferation of cares, a naive credulity, and an inordinate scepticism.[11]

By the same token, the early Augustine displays a fidelity to late antique and patristic indictments of the seductiveness or "trickery of images" which "weigh down" the soul, drawing it from God.[12] Such language bears the imprint of writers like Apuleius and Tertullian. In Augustinian terms, the soul's surrender to such counterfeit reality is closely linked with all the characteristics of a life dominated by vanity and the desire for self-aggrandizement: vileness (*sordes*), fear (*timor*), grief (*maeror*), and cupidity (*cupiditas*).[13]

From Augustine's Christian Neoplatonic perspective, the temporal world is but an image of the really and truly real. Augustine describes this orientation toward temporality as a "pouring over" (*excurrere*) that severely dilutes its powers. In a manner reminiscent of *polupragmon*-language in various Greek sources (both pagan and Christian), Augustine depicts this distention as a turn toward the manifold, "because its nature forces it to seek everywhere what is one," like the aimless meandering of a beggar.[14] His specific target lies in those pursuits whose chief appeal lies in the fact that they are unusual or extraordinary, rather than truly useful to us as rational agents.[15] Augustine thus exhibits the same ambivalence toward frivolous or fastidious pursuits that is so prominent in Stoicism.

> To employ the sense of smell and taste in the dainty appraisal of food, to know how to tell in what lake a fish was hooked or from what vintage a wine was made ...while appearing to enlarge the soul, merely shrivels the mind.[16]

Paradoxically, such interests diminish the soul because they plunge it into a "weaker extension" of its powers (to use the terminology of Plotinus' *Ennead* III.7[45].11). For Augustine, pride and curiosity display a kinship, prompting the soul to "swell" outward (Cf., Eccl. 10:9-14) into the temporal manifold, and thereby, expend its innermost good.

In the first book of the *De libero arbitrio* (A.D. 388), Augustine further refines his early definition of sin in terms of cupidity (*cupiditas*), linking it with passion (*libido*), the "ruling factor in every kind of wrongdoing."[17] Metaphysically and epistemologically, cupidity and passion are conducive to a movement from God and true being and a corresponding inclination toward sinfulness and non-being. While the life of reasoning constitutes the basis of the soul's proper order, it plunges into disorder under the domination of desire.[18]

In keeping with Augustine's understanding of *ordo*, desire directs the soul toward what is "lower" in the scale of creation. In this way, the initial book of the *De libero arbitrio* attempts something of a systematization of the interpretation of sin found in the Cassiciacum dialogues. In its broadest terms, Augustine defines sin as a turning or aversion from what is immutable and stable to what is mutable and unstable.[19]

In volitional terms, desire is part and parcel of the dynamics of love. In this respect, Augustine differentiates between the good will and the evil will, based on the objects of one's love or affection. While the object of the good will is eternal and immutable Truth, the evil will focuses upon temporal concerns and material goods, to the neglect of the higher things of the intellect.[20] The evil use of the will entails a disruption of the soul's proper mid-rank between God and corporeal natures.[21] In this way, it surrenders itself to what it should rightfully govern in the larger *ordo* of creation.

The conflict between the good and evil expressions of will is further highlighted in the *De Moribus Ecclesiase Catholicae et de Moribus Manichaeorum* (hereafter referred to as "*De Moribus*"). In the *De Moribus* (A.D. 387-388), cupidity stands opposed to love (*caritas*). More precisely, cupidity constitutes lust, an inordinate attachment to lower goods of a temporal/corporeal nature. But the tension between love and lust also assumes a metaphysical import as a dichotomy between being and non-being. Since God is the highest Good and source of being, He is also the highest object of the soul's love. While the love of God amounts to a clinging (*inhaerere*) to the *Summum Bonum*, the lust for temporal/corporeal ends consists in a turning or aversion from God.[22] As Augustine affirms, "the farther the mind departs from God in lust after what is below Him, the more it is filled with mere folly."[23]

Any assumption that the soul is on equal footing with the Divine nature reveals a proud desire or audacity to be God-like.[24] But implicit in this appetite, Augustine discerns an overlapping of vanity and curiosity. On the one hand, pride prompts a desire for popular renown that underscores a spirit of self-reliance at odds with a submission to

Divine authority. On the other hand, pride encourages the quest for a scientific knowledge that rests upon "certain corporeal images conceived by the mind and called natural science."[25]

Augustine's language represents an indictment of materialism, and its naive assumption that matter alone exists. This critique provides the occasion for Augustine's first explicit discussion of the blameworthiness of curiosity. Once again, we see his close intertwining of curiosity and pride.

> There are some individuals who suppose themselves to be engaged in a great enterprise when they busy themselves with intense and eager curiosity exploring that universal mass of matter we call the world. Such pride is engendered in them…they imagine themselves dwelling in the very heaven they so often discuss.[26]

Augustine's remarks here are wholly consistent with the spirit of his ongoing anti-Manichaean polemic that extends from the composition of the *De Moribus* (A.D. 389-400) until the completion of the *Contra Faustum* (c. A.D. 398-400).[27]

In this succinct passage, we can discern some of the key aspects of that polemic. First, it implicitly challenges the Manichaeans' emphasis on the primacy of reason over authority in investigating the truth. But more explicitly, it highlights their rejection of incorporeal, immaterial reality (and thus, the assumption that nothing but matter exists). The Manichaeans reduced God Himself to the corporeal, attempting to grasp Him on the basis of vain images alone.[28] In support of this position, Augustine's reference to St. John's first epistle presages his full schematization of iniquity in terms of the triple concupiscence of flesh, eyes, and ambition.[29] On the basis of the Johannine admonition against excessive love of the world, Augustine enjoins his readers (in a Stoic manner) to approach material goods with the "moderation of a user rather than the passion of a lover."[30]

## THE TRIAD *QUA* TRIAD

Augustine's *De Genesi contra Manichaeos* (hereafter referred to as "*De Genesi*"), signals his entry into the final phase of his struggle to isolate the sources of iniquity. Earlier definitions of sin in terms of *cupiditas* and *libido* now crystallize into the formal triad of pride, curiosity, and carnal concupiscence. The *De Genesi* provides a highly structured analysis of iniquity in terms of its moral, metaphysical and epistemological implications.

Augustine's *Retractations* (I,9,1) tell us that the *De Genesi* represents a defense of the Old Testament against Manichaean attacks. But implicit in this defense is a discussion of scriptural teachings regarding the origins of primal sin.[31] In this connection, *De Genesi* I,23(40) provides Augustine's first reference to the triad *qua* triad. On the basis of his hierarchical model of creation (and the soul's mid-rank position between God and corporeal reality), humans are designated as caretakers in charge of living things. The triad of cattle (*pecora*), serpents (*serpenta*), and birds (*aves*) provides Augustine's scriptural symbols of the primal sins of carnal concupiscence, curiosity, and pride, respectively.

> Men are given to carnal concupiscence like cattle and obscured by dark curiosity like serpents, and carried away with pride like birds.[32]

The symbolic force of Augustine's parallels is apparent: appetitive bovine creatures symbolize carnality; cunning serpents symbolize curiosity, with its connotations of deceit and meddlesomeness; birds symbolize a soaring pride. Those subject to such sins assume the character of their symbolic counterparts. Augustine expands upon this triadic interpretation in *De Genesi* II, focusing on the serpent's triple condemnation in Genesis_3:14: "*It crawls on its breast, and slithers on its belly, eats earth.*"

According to the allegorical method of exegesis Augustine freely employs in this work, breast (*pectus*) and belly (*venter*) signify pride and carnal desire, respectively.[33] But in the punishment to "eat earth all the days of your life," Augustine perceives a "third kind of temptation, which is curiosity."[34] Here, he plays on his earlier depiction of the curious disposition in serpentine terms:

> For one who eats earth penetrates things deep and dark, but nonetheless temporal and earthly.[35]

Augustine now has the basis of a fully formulated triadic interpretation of iniquity. Earlier deliberations on the roots of moral evil coalesce into a tightly integrated unit.

> He does not deceive anyone except the proud, who arrogate to themselves that which is not proper to them, mistakenly believing that what belongs to God and to the human soul are of one nature;

or those implicated in carnal desires...or the curious (*curiosus*), who
relish earthly things and investigate spiritual questions with earthly
eyes.[36]

In keeping with scriptural teaching, Augustine posits pride as the
source of iniquity, and by implication, the principal vice. In broader
ontological terms, sin amounts to the soul's forfeiture of its proper
mid-rank between the Divine nature (what is "above") and the totality
of corporeal nature (what is "below") that it should rightfully govern.[37]
Pride thus prompts a refusal to exist "under God" (*sub Deo*) in an attitude of humble submission.

In addition to pride, carnality and curiosity contribute to the soul's
condemnation to mortality.[39] The soul's embodiment and openness to
the input of sense experience create difficulties for discerning truth. It
becomes burdened by doubts and daily cares.[40] Such a characterization of the soul/body relationship, of course, must be understood in
terms of Augustine's broader conception of cosmic and moral order.
In this respect, sin undermines the perfection that gives humans their
claim to creation in God's own image. According to Augustine's exegesis, this special dignity is reflected in an upright posture that signifies
the soul's kinship with eternity, its spiritual dwelling place.[41] The soul's
"spiritual delight" consists in its ability to rise above earthly desires.[42]
Conversely, the soul is drawn downward by the "weight" (*pondus*) of its
sins to its most appropriate *locus* in creation.[43]

The quantitative metaphor of "weight" serves Augustine well in delineating the dynamics of the soul's movement from God. If the soul
can be said to be pulled "down," it does so by its desires. Drawing on
Aristotle's natural philosophy, Augustine creatively adapts the teaching that each body tends to its proper place in the interests of his own
moral theory.[44] In this way, he identifies the soul's "weight" with the
object of its love. In broader metaphysical terms, the "weight" of love
establishes the soul's position in relation to God or lesser things.

## CURIOSITY AND TEMPORALITY

Augustine's *De Musica* brought to completion a planned series of writings on the liberal arts. *De Musica* VI assumes a special relevance for
his triadic understanding of iniquity. In that final book, Augustine refines some key themes already introduced in the *De Genesi*. The *De*

*Musica*, however, relates the full triadic schematization of iniquity (which emerged in the *De Genesi*) to the "triple lust" of St. John's first epistle. Most notably, Augustine depicts the soul's gravitation toward corporeal enticements as a moral and metaphysical disordering that forfeits its proper mid-rank between God and lesser things.[45]

Augustine's *De Musica* also continues in the vein of the *De Moribus* and the *De libero arbitrio*, treating love as the chief expression of free will. In eudaimonistic terms, the soul moves toward objects that it discerns as good, and thus, desirable. In this respect, the soul's delight provides its standard or norm of moral living.[46] For Augustine, however, the soul's true good consists in its delight in a joy in the higher things of eternity, "where there is no time, because there is no change."[47] Time, on the other hand, constitutes an image of eternity, encompassing the harmonious succession of all things (both terrestrial and celestial) that Augustine describes metaphorically as the "poem of the universe."[48] This universal order provides a place for all, "sewn into the order according to our merits."[49] When disorder manifests itself, then, it proceeds from voluntary sin, not God. But even sinners can be considered participants in a larger *ordo* within which we act as free agents, for good or ill.[50]

In Augustine's reckoning, the soul's proper delight in the higher things of eternity renders it free of disturbance by inferior things.[51] Sin is thus bound up with an orientation toward the active life, in mind and body. Accordingly, sin or moral evil not only encompasses what we freely do, but also what we suffer as the consequence of our defective choices.

Augustine roots the soul's aversion from eternal Truth in both pride and curiosity. If the sin of pride (the "beginning of all sin," in scriptural terms) can be defined as a species of love, then it encompasses the "general love of action," prompting the soul's affective separation from God.[52] Pride reveals an arrogant reliance on self that represents the very antithesis of an attitude of subservience to our Creator.

> The soul lapses by pride into certain actions of its own power, and neglecting universal law has fallen into doing certain things private to itself, and this is called turning from God.[53]

More literally, this "turning from God" constitutes a "standing apart from God" (*apostatare a Deo*) by which the soul seeks to exist by and through itself in a God-like manner. In this connection, he draws on

Ecclesiasticus (10:9-14) as the *locus classicus* of scriptural teaching on pride as the root of sin.

> And so it is rightly written in Holy Scripture: 'The beginning of man's pride is to fall from God' and 'The beginning of all sin is pride.' What pride is could not have been better shown than where it is said: 'What does earth and ashes take pride in, since in its own life it spews forth its inmost things? For since the soul is nothing through itself…whatever it is is from God.[54]

As the primal sin that generates a "general love of action," pride is the root of the soul's curiosity as well. In Augustine's analysis of curiosity in *De Musica* VI, this disposition is operative in three affective movements: *first*, the love of acting on bodily passions (and a burdening with cares); *secondly*, the love of operating on bodies (with an attendant restlessness); *third*, the love of vain knowledge (that binds the soul to temporal concerns).[55] The soul's attention in the body's direction poses a special challenge, precisely because it is drawn into manifold endeavors that distort its vision of truth. In this way, curiosity commits the soul to a private sphere of interests, to the neglect of universal law.[56] For this reason, Augustine characterizes curiosity as a natural "enemy of peace." This is consistent with his understanding of sin as an option for what is partial and circumscribed over a commitment to the whole of things. Sin in triadic terms (that is, as pride, curiosity, and carnal concupiscence) constitutes an appropriation of a good proper to oneself alone, in place of a willing participation in the good common to all. The *De Musica's* detailed treatment of the dynamics of sin finds its counterpart in a discussion of the process of conversion. The soul's outward movement from God is transposed into a movement away from carnal delights and a return to the cultivation of the inner life. If sin is a turning from God (*excurrere*), then conversion involves an inward turning back (*recurrere*) from the world. In the mathematical language of the *De Musica*, carnal delight gives way to a renewal of delight in the "numbers" of reason.[57] In the final analysis, conversion consists in a drastic change in the quality of the soul's love, in a manner consistent with its proper order.

Disordered love, however, is tantamount to the unregulated desire which finds expression in the triad of pride, curiosity, and carnal concupiscence. Augustine now explicitly coordinates these vices with the "triple lust" of I Jn. 2:14-16:

> Do not love this world, because all things in the world are concupis-
> cence of the flesh, concupiscence of the eyes, and secular ambition.[58]

Augustine easily identifies the Johannine sin of fleshly concupiscence
with carnal pleasure and the sin of secular ambition or pride with the
love of vain honors and praises. What remains to be defined is that
rather nebulous form of lust, the "concupiscence of the eyes."

Augustine will fully delineate this "ocular" variety of concupiscence
in the *Confessiones*. But the *De Musica* moves decisively in this direction, linking the Johannine "concupiscence of the eyes" with curiosity, the sin responsible for "exploring…things touching the body from
without."[59] Accordingly, Augustine views curiosity as a species of the
general love of action which the *De Musica* associates with pride. More
precisely, curiosity prompts a lust for the whole range of experience
connected with temporal existence.

Augustine attributes a profound metaphysical significance to the
Johannine indictment of the "love for the world" (and its lustful expressions). The sinful soul surrenders the integrity of the inner life for
the distention of temporality and a reliance upon fleeting images for
knowledge. Together, cognitive and carnal appetites subject the soul
to those things which it should rightfully govern and use for the realization of its true good. More specifically, the general love of action
(prompted by pride) and the love of operating on bodies (prompted
by curiosity) expand the soul's range of interests into the outermost
reaches of creation.[60]

## THE RULE OF PERFECT RELIGION

By the time he completed the *De Musica*, Augustine had fully formulated a triadic interpretation of the sources of iniquity that was
firmly grounded in the "triple concupiscence" of I Jn. 2:14-16. The *De
Vera Religione*, however, provides his most incisive treatment of the
triad in his pre-*Confessiones* writings. At the very outset of this work,
Augustine affirms that salvation is found only in the religion which
worships one God alone, acknowledging Him as supreme Creator.
This observes the "rule of perfect religion," that is, to serve the Creator
rather than the creature and to resist vanity in our thoughts.[61]

Augustine recognized the complementarity between the admonitions of I Jn. 2:14-16 and the prescription of the "rule of perfect

religion." In its exegetical survey of the pervasiveness of iniquity, the *De Vera Religione* provides its own catalogue of warnings against prominent vices.[62] But the "triple concupiscence" delineated in St. John's first epistle offers a succinct formula covering every expression of disordered love. In this context, sin constitutes a proud motivation to power (*superbia*), a carnal attachment to pleasures (*concupiscentia carnis*), or the superstitious reliance upon groundless phantasms and fascination with temporal affairs (*curiositas*). Augustine refers each triadic member to a specific category of sinners.

> Three classes of men are thus distinguished; for lust of the flesh means those who love the lower pleasures, lust of the eyes means the curious, and ambition of this world denotes the proud.[63]

In each case, disordered love is correlative with a disordering of priorities, whereby what is last in the hierarchy of creation assumes a primacy in the soul's esteem.[64] In the case of curiosity, the soul becomes so engrossed in visible forms that it is rendered all but oblivious to the grasp of eternal truths. In Augustine's reckoning, the very quest for such semblances of true being is no more than a futile search for "shadowy phantasms," or more radically, a loss of oneself in the "vanity of the vain."[65]

Augustine perceives an idolatrous dimension in any such violation of the "rule of perfect religion." In the case of curiosity, the soul succumbs to a "worship of phantasms," falling prey to a variety of enticements rooted in sense experience.[66] Augustine takes the Johannine admonition to "keep yourself free from images" in the most literal terms, but with an attunement to its deeper epistemological and metaphysical implications.[67] His conception of images as mere semblances of the really and truly real sets the tone for his critical stance toward the soul's temporal orientation. It also accounts for his depiction of the phantasmal in such stark, adversarial terms.

> Setting further away from these primal objects we embrace our phantasms. When we return to seek Truth phantasms meet us in the way and will not allow us to pass on, attacking us like brigands with dangerous pitfalls.[68]

Overall, Augustine's triadic interpretation of iniquity offers a versatile device for sounding out this tension between the pursuit of Truth (and abiding reality) and the soul's attraction to the transitory objects of the outer world. In each instance, he describes sin as a movement from true being to various manifestations of non-being.[69] Just as he closely aligns the motivations of pride and curiosity, Augustine discerns a rather intimate connection between the sins of carnality and curiosity. Both primal vices are instrumental in directing the soul's attention to groundless phantasms. "Vain and perishable curiosity," however, assumes a distinctive character as an inordinate desire for knowledge of temporal matters.[70] Once again, the tension between a commitment to true reality and an attraction to images is apparent.

> Let us find food and drink for our minds; for they are weary and parched with the hunger and thirst of vain curiosity, and desire in vain to be refreshed and satisfied with silly phantasms, as unreal as painted banquets.[71]

Augustine puts the triad to additional use in analyzing the plight of sinful humanity as a whole. The soul's love of lesser things amounts to a servitude to a three-fold desire: the carnal desire for pleasure; the proud desire for excelling; and the curious desire for novel spectacles.[72] His indictment of the curious attraction to spectacles puts him in direct continuity with the sentiments of his North African predecessor, Tertullian. In broader terms, it hearkens back to the general ambivalence toward the spectacular (especially in a visual sense) that weaves its way through the patristic and classical Latin traditions. In the *De Vera Religione*, Augustine links the lure of the *spectaculi* with the sheer exhilaration of knowing.

> All curiosity with regard to spectacles aims at nothing else than the joy of knowing things. What, then, is more wonderful and beautiful than truth?[73]

Indeed, the spectator reveals the implicit drive to grasp true reality that underscores our search for God as the ultimate Ground of Truth, the genuine goal of the restless heart and mind. Even the spectator of trickery or stunts wants the "real thing," and appreciates the difference between truth and deception.[74]

Christ's example provides Augustine's counterpoint to a life dominated by the lust for the world. As humans succumb to the triad of lusts, Christ transforms these world-oriented drives. In the life of Jesus, pride, curiosity, and carnal desire were supplanted by humility, single-mindedness, and piety, respectively.[75] Christ thus reconciles the tension between the inner and outer man. Again, the triad provides Augustine's interpretative key. In and through Christ, the soul frees itself of its servitude to the lusts which seek contentment in the emptiness of images.

> Curiosity seeks nothing but knowledge, which cannot be certain knowledge unless it be of eternal things; pride seeks nothing but power, but power is attained only by the perfect soul which is submissive to God; bodily pleasure seeks nothing but rest, and there is no rest save where there is no poverty and no corruption.[76]

## THE *COMMUNE* AND THE *PROPRIUM*

Augustine consistently affirms that genuine happiness is not grounded upon the vagaries of temporal existence, but only upon an immutable source of the good. He fully develops this theme in the second book of the *De libero arbitrio*. In this context, Augustine again depicts moral evil as the will's turning from an eternal, changeless Good to temporal, mutable ones. This aversion, we have seen, constitutes a defective movement toward the privation of non-being. In this respect, Augustine identifies our *Summum Bonum* with Truth and Wisdom itself: Truth and Wisdom (i.e., Christ, the second Person of the Trinity) are interchangeable with our highest Good (i.e., God the Father, the first Person of the Trinity).[77]

Augustine characterizes the will itself as an "intermediate" good. Since the will has the capacity to shift its allegiance from the immutable Good common to all to goods proper to itself alone, Augustine characterizes it as an "intermediate" good.

> When it turns away from the changeless good common to all, and turns toward a good of its own, or to an external or lower good then the will sins.[78]

According to a key distinction in Augustine's moral theory, the will sins by appropriating things as its own possession or "property" (*proprium*) in lieu of its commitment to that Good common to all (*commune*).[79] Once again, Augustine puts the triad to work, interpreting this distinction in terms of the "triple concupiscence" of pride, curiosity, and carnal concupiscence.

> It turns toward a good of its own whenever it wants to be its own master; to an external good, when it is eager to know the personal affairs of others, or whatever is none of its business; to a lower good,

> when it loves the pleasures of the body. Thus, a man who becomes
> proud, curious, and sensuous is delivered over to another kind of
> life, which, in comparison with the higher life, is death.[80]

The foregoing quote highlights the fundamental difference between
the sins of pride and curiosity. Pride is oriented toward the self and its
unabashed aggrandizement. In willing a "good of its own," the proud
soul opts for a part of creation over a commitment to an all-embracing Good.[81] Curiosity, on the other hand, moves the soul toward "external goods," in seeking to know what does not specifically concern
it. Augustine's depiction of curiosity in such terms is reminiscent of
the meaning inherent in the Greek *polupragmosune*, one of the major
sources of *curiositas*-language in the Latin tradition. This interpretation of curiosity as a meddlesome intrusion into the affairs of others
is reinforced by the notion of sin as a choice of the *proprium* over the
*commune*.

Like pride and curiosity, carnal concupiscence inspires a desire for
what is partial and circumscribed. Carnal desire, however, assumes
a special relevance to those pleasures proper to the body (that is, to
"lower goods" of a corporeal nature). Only the soul free of an inordinate attachment to personal, external, or lower goods is able to cling to
that universal Good which simply cannot be lost involuntarily.

## THE SIGNIFICANCE OF *CURIOSITAS*

Augustine's selection of *curiositas* as one of the three primal sins tells
us as much about him (and his intellectual presuppositions regarding
true knowledge) as it does about the significance of *curiositas* itself. On
the one hand, an adequate grasp of the meanings he attaches to cognitive desire demands an attunement to the different contexts in which
he discusses its blameworthy character. (His anti-Manichaean polemic provides a case in point.) On the other hand, we must be sensitive
to the influences that were operative in his designation of *curiositas* as
one of the chief sins.

First and foremost, Augustine was influenced by Scripture in his
emphasis upon the moral import of curiosity. In both I Jn. 2:14-16
(and its condemnation of the "lust of the eyes") and in I Cor. 4:18
("*Look not on things seen…*"), he found warnings against the visual experience of the world that serves as a metaphor for curiosity in general.

These scriptural pronouncements are consistent with the philosophical notion that vision provides an analogue for knowing in its broadest sense.[82] Likewise, they suggest a distinction between this-worldly concerns and a higher spiritual orientation. This distinction is conducive to a synthesis of scriptural and Neoplatonic insights.

In Augustine's earliest discussions of curiosity, we find a condemnation of materialism and sensism that assumes a central role in his extended anti-Manichaean polemic. In this respect, he was especially critical of the materialist assumption that matter alone exists. The *De Moribus'* critique of the scientific enterprise as an outgrowth of curiosity anticipates the *Confessiones'* later reaction against that "perverse" science which attempts to penetrate the "secrets of nature" for no reason other than the desire to know.[83] From this standpoint, the "lust of the eyes" specified by the Johannine text prompts the soul to focus upon what are no more than semblances of the really real.

Augustine adheres to the Neoplatonic distinction between the genuine knowledge of stable, abiding truths and counterfeit claims to knowledge based on the mutable things of sense experience. The fact that Augustine can make such a distinction puts him at odds with an epistemology confined exclusively to the data of sense experience. In a very real sense, however, the Manichaeans' epistemology was also consistent with a broader metaphysical vision. Accordingly, their inability to recognize the existence of incorporeal reality shaped their understanding of the natures of God and the soul alike.

In Augustine's account of the dynamics of moral evil, curiosity and pride work closely together in inciting the soul's interest in a "vain knowledge" of images.[84] For this reason, he considers the scientific enterprise (at least as he understood *scientia*) as symptomatic of an intellectual arrogance that focuses exclusively upon the material world.[85] By confining itself to images (thereby placing empirical limits on our range of knowing), the soul is "deceived into thinking that matter alone exists."[86]

Augustine's critique of natural science, then, is intimately linked with his polemical interests. This link is evident in his interpretation of the condemnation of the serpent ("obscured by dark curiosity"), his scriptural symbol of the curious disposition.[87] In Augustine's exegesis, the serpent's punishment to "eat earth" refers to curiosity and its inclination to penetrate temporal matters.[88] The physical proximity of serpents to ground-level makes them the ideal model of those whose grasp of being is distorted by a dependence upon spatio-temporal images.

While Augustine clearly has a proverbial bone to pick with his Manichaean opponents, his polemic is directed against all who rely upon images and phantasms for their knowledge. In Augustine's rendering, the curious soul delights in the lowest things, and thereby, subjects itself to manifold deceptions. His pointed characterization of curiosity as a form of emptiness or vanity is particularly telling: "vain and perishable" curiosity can only lead the soul to metaphysical impoverishment.[89]

But the sin of curiosity involves more than a passive reliance upon images. It also assumes an active interpretative role in casting spiritual realities in a material and temporal mould. In Augustine's language, the curious soul investigates spiritual questions "with earthly eyes." In this respect, the Manichaeans' error was rooted in their assumption that God's nature coincides exactly with its corporeal depiction.

By the same token, a preoccupation with temporal images can prompt a direct involvement in temporal activities. In this way, the "lust of the eyes" assumes a dynamic connotation as a restlessness for the active life of temporality. The *De Musica*, in fact, roots curiosity in those sensible numbers which generate the "love of vainest knowledge" in attending to bodily life.[90] By virtue of this attentiveness toward the outer man, the curious soul incurs countless burdens. Augustine's etymological analysis of *curiositas* underscores this very point. Like other Latin commentators on this topic, he traces the term *curiositas* to the care (*cura*) which proceeds from the soul's involvement in dissipating temporal endeavors.[91]

Augustine's ongoing emphasis upon the kinship of curiosity and pride is especially pronounced in the *De Musica*. If curiosity is oriented toward the acquisition of worldly experience, then this desire ultimately stems from the pride which generates a general love of action. But pride also shapes the soul's relation to other souls. The love of action thus engenders a desire to dominate, not merely in brute physical terms, but by such manipulative tactics as persuasive speech.[92] As an ambitious rhetor in his own right, the young Augustine was intimately acquainted with this latter tendency. His poignant account of such failings and the moral obstacles he negotiated enroute to conversion comes fully to the fore in the *Confessiones*. I address the role of curiosity in Augustine's circuitous *peregrinatio* in the next chapter.

NOTES TO CHAPTER 4

1. This chapter builds upon my analysis of the development of Augustine's triadic schematization in my dissertation "Plotinian *Tolma* and the Fall of the Soul in the Early Philosophy of St. Augustine" (Fordham University, 1987), Chapters VI and VII.

2. I consider the Stoic dimension in the early thought of Augustine in several of my writings: *Creatio ex nihilo and The Theology of St. Augustine. The Anti-Manichaean Polemic and Beyond* (New York: Peter Lang Publishers, Inc.,1999); "The Significance of the Moral Concept of Virtue in Saint Augustine's Ethics," *The Modern Schoolman* LXVIII(November, 1990): 1-17; entry in *Saint Augustine through the Ages: an Encyclopedia*. Allan D. Fitzgerald, O.S.A., General Editor. (Grand Rapids, Michigan: William B. Eerdmans, 1999): "Stoics, Stoicism," 816b-820a.

3. Cf., *De Beata Vita* II,11; IV,4.

4. The early Augustine cites such clusters of vices in *De Beata Vita* IV,4 (luxuries, power, pride, and what he broadly designates as "other things of this kind") and in *De Ordine* II,8,25 (wantonness, gluttony, excessive care,bodily adornment, silly games, sloth, jealousy,detraction, envy, ambition, and the desire for praise).

5. Cf., *De Beata Vita* I,3; *Contra Academicos* II,8(21); *De Quantitate Animae* 34,78.

6. *Soliloquia* I,13(23); *De Ordine* I,8(24).

7. *Contra Academicos* II,2(6).

8. In this vein, Augustine speculates (*De Ordine* I,8[26])why something like the spectacle of a cockfight can distract one from higher study.

9. *Contra Academicos* II,2(3).

10. *De Ordine* II,9(27).

11. *De Ordine* II,5(17).

12. *De Beata Vita* IV,33.

13. *De Beata Vita* IV,33.

14. *De Ordine* I,2(3).

15. *De Quantitate Animae* 19,33.

16. *De Quantitate Animae* 19,33. Cf., *De Ordine* II,12(37),where Augustine criticizes spurious claimants to scientific investigation because the subject matter of their inquiry is so ill-defined and multi-faceted that it generates more cares than truth-value.

17. *De libero arbitrio* I,3(8); I,4(9).

18. *De libero arbitrio* I,10(20).

19. *De libero arbitrio* I,16(35).

20. *De libero arbitrio* I,13(28); I,16(34).

21. *De libero arbitrio* I,11(22). Augustine's catalogic bent is again apparent in his detailed enumerations of the negative effects of passion on the soul (*De libero arbitrio* I,11[22]), torn in all directions by fear, desire, anxiety,

empty delights, torment over loss, pain for an injury suffered, or the urge to avenge it. In the same passage, Augustine designates passion as the core of a plethora of vices, from the central sin of pride to greed, sensuality, ambition, envy, sloth, obstinacy, and distress over subjection.

22. *De Moribus* I,11(18).

23. *De Moribus* I,12(20).

24. *De Moribus* I,12(20).

25. *De Moribus* II,21(38).

26. *De Moribus* I,21(38): PL 32,1327: *Sunt enim...magnum aliquid se agere putant, si universam istam corporis molem, quam mundum nuncupamis; curiosissime intentissimeque perquirant. Unde tanta etiam superbia gignitur ut in ipso coelo, de quo saepe disputant.*

27. More specifically, Augustine's anti-Manichaean polemic spans the years A.D. 388-401, and encompasses the following works: *De Moribus* (388), *De libero arbitrio* (Book I, 388; Books II-III, 391-395), *De Genesi contra Manichaeos* (389), *De Vera Religione* (c. 391), *De duabus animabus contra Manichaeos* (392), *Acta contra Fortunatum Manichaeum* (392), *De Genesi ad litteram imperfectus liber* (393), *Contra Faustum Manichaeum* (398-400), *Contra Felicem Manichaeum* (398), *De Natura Boni Contra Manichaeos* (399), *Contra Secundinum Manichaeum* (399), *De Genesi ad litteram* (405-post-420).

28. *De Moribus* I,21(38). Manichaeism (founded by Mani, A.D. 216-277) was a rather eclectic blend of Persian Zoroastrianism, Christianity, and Buddhism, with a radically dualistic emphasis. In this respect, Manichaeism can be viewed as a late expression of the gnostic outlook that assumed such a prominent role in the religious experience of late antiquity. This gnostic dimension is not only evident in Manichaeism's stark dualism, but also in its exclusivistic understanding of salvation. From this standpoint, salvation was reserved for those in possession of an enlightened awareness of the means to liberating the soul from its embodiment. In a manner consistent with its radical dualism, Manichaeism took an extremely dim view of the body and bodily existence. In broader cosmic terms, the Manichaeans believed that the universe and the soul's very presence in the body were the result of a great primordial conflict between the principles of Good (or Light) and Evil (or Darkness), in which the particles of Light became imprisoned in the opacity of matter. In Manichaean terms, matter (*Hyle*) constitutes the embodiment of Evil itself. For an historical treatment of Manichaeism and its spread in the ancient world and beyond, see S. Lieu, *Manichaeism in the Later Roman Empire and Medieval China* (Manchester, NH: Manchester University Press, 1985). For Manichaean doctrine, see F. Decret, *Mani et la tradition manichéene* (Maitres spirituels, Paris, 1974).

29. *De Moribus* I,21(39). This claim, I recognize, has been the focus of some debate. While Olivier du Roy (*L'Intelligence de la foi en la Trinité selon saint Augustin. Genese de sa theologie trinitaire jusqu'en 391* [Paris, 1966], 344,

n. 1) maintained that the triad is already at work in *De Moribus* I,37-38, Robert J. O'Connell (*St. Augustine's Early Theory of Man, A.D. 386-391* [Cambridge, Mass.: The Belknap Press, 1968], 175) was more sceptical about its emergence at this early juncture in Augustine's writings. I tend to favor O'Connell's cautious stance here, in view of the fact that the triadic schematization clearly becomes fully organizational only in the *De Genesi contra Manichaeos* (composed after the *De Moribus*).

30. *De Moribus* I,21(39).

31. The *De Genesi* exhibits Augustine's thoroughgoing use of the allegorical method of exegesis to which he had been introduced by the preaching of Ambrose, Bishop of Milan. Accordingly, Augustine seeks a "spiritual" grasp of the figures, enigmas, and allegories which obscure or hide those truths embedded within the text. In the polemical spirit in which he composed the *De Genesi*, this exegesis is directed against the "carnal-minded" Manichaeans who could not rise above corporeal images in their depictions of God and God's creative activity.

32. *De Genesi* I,23(40): PL 34,192: *homines, vel carnali concupiscentiae dediti sicut pecora, vel tenebrosa curiositate obscurati quasi serpentes, vel elati superbia quasi aves.*

33. *De Genesi* II,17(26).

34. *De Genesi* II,18(27): PL 34,210: *vel certe genus tertium tentationis his verbis figuratur, quod est curiositas.*

35. *De Genesi* II,18(27): PL 34,210: *Terram enim qui manducat, profunda et tenebrosa penetrat, et tamen temporalis atque terrena.*

36. *De Genesi* II,26(40): PL 34,217: *Non enim decipit, nisi aut superbos, qui sibi arrogantes quod non sunt, cito credunt quod summi Dei et animae humanae una ea natura sit; aut desideriis carnalibus implicatos...curiosos, qui terrena sapiunt, et spiritualia terreno oculo inquirunt.*

37. According to Augustine's vision of universal *ordo*, the properly ordered soul must submit itself to what is above it and the governance of what is below it. As so ordered, it directs itself to God (i.e., what is ontologically "higher" or "before" it) and remains detached from corporeal desires that are "lower" or "behind" it (*De Genesi* II,9[12]). In this same passage, Augustine expounds upon the soul's position in the hierarchy of creation by means of an exegesis of references to the "trees planted in the middle of paradise": *first*, the "tree of life" (which he interprets as the intelligence whereby the soul understands its properly ordained mid-rank status among existent things); *secondly*, the "tree of differentiation between good and evil" (which Augustine interprets as the soul's mid-rank itself.

38. For Augustine, this proud rebelliousness on the part of souls entails an overstepping of the bounds of their middle station (*medietate*) which subjects them to God and places them over corporeal natures. Sin is defined as a desire for autonomy, in that it takes inordinate delight in its own powers, without reference to God. In keeping with scriptural teaching (and the

lessons of his own moral experience), Augustine affirms the centrality of the sin of pride (*superbia*), the "beginning of all sin." Drawing upon the imagery of Ecclesiasticus (10:9-14), the *De Genesi* (II,9[12]; 15[22]) further describes the soul's willful movement as a "swelling with pride" (*intumescit superbia*). This "swelling" metaphor provides a key motif in Augustine's subsequent discussions of the negative effects of *superbia*. But its use in his writings is traceable to the *De Quantitate Animae* (19,33), where the soul's intellectual expansion is characterized as a tumorous growth. Such imagery is consistently shaped by the teaching of Ecclesiasticus and its depiction of the proud soul as torn asunder, "projecting its innermost good" (*per superbia projecerat intima sua*) on the manifold of temporal concerns (*De Genesi* II,15[22]). Augustine further characterizes the soul's pride in terms of the biblical sin of idolatry, with a craving to be the equal of God. In this respect, *De Genesi* II,5(6) explicitly identifies pride with an apostasy or "standing apart from God" (*apostatare a Deo*), an expansive, outward movement in which it turns from what is highest toward what is lowest in the hierarchy of creation. Accordingly, sin (proceeding from pride) obscures the soul's vision of eternal Truth in the darkness of falsehood.

39. In reference to its pre-lapsarian status, the *De Genesi* II,3[4]; 4[5]) describes the soul as an invisible, spiritual creature, symbolized by the greenery of the fields, sustained by an "inner fountain" that is its conduit of Truth, not in a discursive sense, but on a higher contemplative level.

40. *De Genesi* II,20(30).

41. *De Genesi* I,17(28).

42. *De Genesi* II,9(12).

43. *De Genesi* II,22(34).

44. For a discussion of Augustine's interpretation of this Aristotelian motif, see my "'*Pondus meum amor meus* ': The Significance of the 'Weight' Metaphor in St. Augustine's Early Philosophical Writings," *Augustinian Studies* XXI (1990): 163-176. For a discussion of Augustine's understanding of the order of creation, see my "The Significance of *Ordo* in St. Augustine's Moral Theory," in *Collectanea Augustiniana III* (New York: Peter Lang Publishing, Inc, 1991), 321-335.

45. *De Musica* VI,11(29).

46. *De Musica* VI,11(29).

47. *De Musica* VI,11(29).

48. *De Musica* VI,11(29).

49. *De Musica* VI,11(30).

50. *De Musica* VI,11(30).

51. *De Musica* VI,11(29).

52. *De Musica* VI,13(40).

53. *De Musica* VI,16(53): PL 32,1190: *superbia labi animam ad actiones quasdam potestatis suae, et universali lege neglecta in agenda quaedam privata cecidisse, quod dicitur apostatare a Deo.*

54. *De Musica* VI,13(40): PL 32,1184-1185: *Recte itaque scriptum est in sanc-*
    *tis Libris:* Initium superbiae hominis apostatare de Deo; et Initium omnis pec-
    cati superbia. *Non potuit autem melius demonstrati quid sit superbia, quam*
    *in eo quod ibi dictum est:* Quid superbit terra et cinis, quoniam in vita sua
    projecit intima sua? *(Eccli. X,14,15,9,10). Cum enim anima per seipsam nihil*
    *sit...quidquid autem illi esse est, a Deo sit;* The above quote likewise refers
    us back to the *De Genesi* II,6: both passages utilize the common images of
    projection, "spewing forth," or "swelling" (*projecit intima sua*). In seeking au-
    tonomy in imitation of God, the soul expands outward into the manifold
    of temporality. Accordingly, "swelling with pride" constitutes an expansion
    into the outermost range of being (*extima*). The "tumor" analogy of the
    *De Quantitate Animae* (19,33) is most apt: like a malignant growth, the
    soul's enlargement has purely negative effects. Apart from God, the soul is
    nothing; it becomes empty (*inanescere*), expending its innermost good (*in-*
    *tima*). As Augustine argues (*De Musica* VI,13[40]), "to puff with pride is
    to go forth to the outermost...giving up the inmost things, that is, putting
    yourself away from God, not in the span of places, but in affect of mind"
    (PL 32,1185: *Quare superbia intumescere, hoc illi est in extima progredi...id*
    *est, longe a se facere Deum, non locorum spatia, sed mentis affectu*).
55. *De Musica* VI,13(39).
56. *De Musica* VI,14(48): PL 32,1188: *Attentio namque animae ad corporis*
    *partem inquieta negotia contrahit, et universali lege neglecta privati cujusdam*
    *operis amor...*
57. *De Musica* VI,11(33).
58. *De Musica* VI,16(51).
59. *De Musica* VI,14(44); VI,14(48): PL 32,1188: *Quaemobrem neque in*
    *voluptate carnali, neque in honoribus et laudibus hominum, neque in eorum*
    *exploratione quae forinsecus corpus attingunt...*
60. *De Musica* VI,13(40).
61. *De Vera Religione* 10(19). From the very beginning of the *De Vera Religione*
    (3[3]; 4[6]; 5[8]), Augustine links scriptural teachings with insights de-
    rived from Platonism and Neoplatonism. On the basis of a fictional dia-
    logue with Plato, Augustine affirms the accessibility of truth to the human
    mind. From this standpoint, lust and the mind's dependence upon imag-
    es pose the greatest impediments to the pursuit of truth. For Augustine,
    however, Platonism merely points the way to a philosophical path to wis-
    dom that will be brought to completion in the Christian faith, as "the most
    secure and certain way of salvation" (*De Vera Religione* 10[19]).
62. *De Vera Religione* 3(4).
63. *De Vera Religione* 38(70): CC XXXII,233: *Hoc modo tria illa notata sunt,*
    *nam concupiscentia carnis uoluptatis infimae amatores significat, concupiscen-*
    *tia oculorum curiosus, ambitio saeculi superbos.*
64. *De Vera Religione* 20(40); 21(41).
65. *De Vera Religione* 14(27); 21(41); 40(76).

66. *De Vera Religione* 38(69).

67. I Jn. 5:21.

68. *De Vera Religione* 49(95): CC XXXII,249: *ab eis recendentes amplexamur nostra phantasmata. Nam redeuntibus nobis ad inuestigandam ueritatem ipsa in itinere occurrent et nos transire non sinunt nullis uiribus, sed magnis insidiis latrocinantia…*

69. *De Vera Religione* 41(78); 45(84).

70. *De Vera Religione* 49(94); 52(101).

71. *De Vera Religione* 51(100): CC XXXII,252: *pascamus animum atque potemus uanae curiositatis fame ac siti fessum et aestuantem et inanibus phantasmatibus tamquam pictis epulis frustra refici satiarique cupientem. Hoc uere liberali et ingenuo ludo salubriter erudiamur.*

72. *De Vera Religione* 38(69).

73. *De Vera Religione* 49(94): CC XXXII,248: *Iam uero cuncta spectacula et omnis illa quae appellatur curiositas quid aliud quaerit quam de rerum cognitione laetitiam?*

74. At *De Vera Religion* 49(94), Augustine cites the example of people watching a juggler, enjoying the performance as long as his deceptiveness is not readily apparent; once they "see through" the trickery of the stunt, however, they take pride in their own resistance to such deception.

75. *De Vera Religione* 38(71).

76. *De Vera Religione* 52(101).

77. *De libero arbitrio* II,13(36).

78. *De libero arbitrio* II,19(53): CC XXIX,272: *Voluntas autem auersa ab incommutabili et communi bono et conuersa ad proprium bonum aut ad exterius aut ad inferius, peccat.*

79. Augustine's extensive discussion of this key distinction is found in *De libero arbitrio* II,7(15)-13(37). Since Truth is not the exclusive property of any single individual, its fullness can be enjoyed by all. According to the *Oxford Latin Dictionary* (Oxford: Clarendon Press, 1982], 369-370; 1495-1496), the adjective *commune* pertains to things held in joint possession by two or more parties, or which belong to and affect everyone; *proprium* encompasses what pertains exclusively to oneself or one's own property, personal possession, or private interest (i.e., what is proper, appropriate, or suitable to a individual or group). For a more extended discussion of the *commune/proprium* distinction in Augustine, see my "The *Commune/Proprium* Distinction in Saint Augustine's Moral Theory," *Studia Patristica* XXII: 356-363. Papers of the 1987 Oxford Patristics Conference. Edited by Elizabeth Livingstone. Leuven: Peeters Press, 1989.

80. *De libero arbitrio* II,19(53): CC XXIX,272: *Ad proprium conuertitur, cum suae potestatis uult esse, ad exterius, cum aliorum propria uel quaecumque ad se non pertinent cognoscere studet, ad inferius cum uoluptatem corporis diligit. Atque ita homo superbus et curiosus et lasciuus effectus excipitur ab alia uita, quae in comparatione superioris uitae mors est;*

81. This option for the soul's own good is consistent with a desire for self-mastery. Cf., *De Moribus* I,12(20) and *De Musica* VI,16(53), with its reference to the proud soul's lapse into "certain actions of its own power," that is, private actions in defiance of the dictates of universal law.

82. I refer here to the basic model of knowing that runs through classical Greek philosophy. This model is clearly operative in Plato's *Republic* (VI-VII), where the ascent to knowledge is described in terms of visual experience, and knowledge in general is analogous to "taking a look at" a reality beyond the self, that is, the Form (*eidos*) on which knowledge depends.

83. Cf., *De Moribus* I,21(38); *Confessiones* X,35(55).

84. *De Moribus* I,21(38).

85. *De Moribus* I,21(38).

86. *De Moribus* I,21(38). In the *De Moribus* (I,21[38]), Augustine considers interpretations of the Divine nature in corporeal terms as an implication of this assumption. From this standpoint, God is depicted in terms of the images derived from sense experience.

87. *De Genesi* I,23(40).

88. *De Genesi* II,18(27).

89. *De Vera Religione* 52(101).

90. *De Musica* VI,13(39); 11(29).

91. *De Musica* VI,14(48); 13(39).

92. *De Musica* VI,13(40)-(41).

# CHAPTER 5

## PEREGRINATIO ANIMAE

Around the turn of the fifth century (A.D. c. 397-400),
Augustine wrote his monumental spiritual autobiography,
the *Confessiones*. From this midlife perspective, he sur-
veyed his pilgrimage on both an intellectual and a moral
level. In intellectual terms, we learn about the prolonged
search for genuine wisdom which took him down a number of paths
(including his nine year association with Manichaeism and his foray into
scepticism). This quest culminated in his introduction to Neoplatonism
and the expansion of his metaphysical and epistemological horizons that
this philosophy precipitated in his outlook. In moral terms, we follow
Augustine in his struggle to accept the Christian way of life, even after
he accepted it on purely intellectual grounds.

In the *Confessiones*, Augustine exploits the triad of pride, curiosity,
and carnal concupiscence in a thoroughgoing manner in assessing the
ebb and flow of his journey toward God, a *peregrinatio* of heart and
mind punctuated by an ongoing series of turns from His Creator in
favor of the world and its manifold delights. He skillfully analyzes this
*excursus* in terms of the operation of these three primal vices. In this
respect, the Augustine of the *Confessiones* drew upon the triadic interpretation of iniquity that crystallized and solidified in the writings
examined in the preceding chapter.

> These are the chief kinds of iniquity, and they spring forth from lust
> for power, of the eyes, or of sensuality, whether from one of these, or
> two, or all three together.[1]

By the time he composed the *Confessiones*, then, the triad had become
a standard feature of Augustine's delineation of the sources and motives of iniquity. The *Confessiones*, however, take this triadic interpretation in bold new directions in forging a comprehensive definition of

iniquity in the context of Augustine's own existential situation (and by implication, the experience of everyman).

In this connection, the primal sin of *curiositas* (which Augustine now readily identifies with the *concupiscentia oculorum* of I Jn. 2:14-16) provides a crucial nexus between the drive for personal exaltation rooted in pride and the desire for sensual gratification inherent in carnal concupiscence. On the one hand, the soul's curious interest in worldly matters carries with it a certain self-absorption consistent with pride; on the other hand, *curiositas* assumes a distinct experiential focus not only encompassing what is sensually appealing (the mark of carnal concupiscence) but the whole panoply of temporal and corporeal involvement.

The *Confessiones* provide Augustine's definitive response to the problems which plagued him over the course of his rather circuitous journey: *first*, "Whence comes evil?" and *secondly*, "Whence comes iniquity?" He found the solutions to these problems in the triad (that is, in the triad as a whole or in its individual components or combinations of those components). Pride, curiosity, and carnal concupiscence all constitute a perversion of the will which results in a misuse of the goods of creation. In this respect, the triad assumes a broader metaphysical significance as a source of disorder within the hierarchy of creation that undermines the soul's proper mid-rank between God and corporeal natures. In a very real sense, the *Confessiones* not only subject Augustine's life (from his infancy to his moral conversion) to a triadic interpretation, but the history of the human race as well. This chapter examines this hermeneutic, with a special attentiveness to the role of curiosity in Augustine's deliberations.

## FROM INFANCY TO ADOLESCENCE

Augustine's conviction in the pervasiveness of sinfulness in the human condition graphically manifests itself in the opening book of the *Confessiones* and its deliberation on the "sins" of his infancy. "How," he queries, "did I sin at that age?"[2] The very question underscores an assumption that shapes and defines his understanding of human fallibility and our susceptibility to moral error at each and every stage of our lives. In this respect, Augustine deems no one (not even the newborn), as "clean of sin," or more precisely, the legacy of Adam's sin.[3]

In the apparent selfishness, jealousy, and obstinacy he has observed in the very young, Augustine finds a sobering commentary on the flaws of humans in general. If his own life encompasses the experience of everyman in microcosm, then the tendencies of children point toward and anticipate those of adults.

> Is this boyish innocence? It is not…for these are the practices that pass from tutors and teachers…to governors and kings, and to money and estates and slaves. These very things pass on, as older years come in their turn, just as heavier punishments succeed the birch rod.[4]

Augustine's early encounters with classical learning provide his initial touchstone for exploring the dynamics of curiosity in his own *psyche*. As in his previous deliberations on the sources of moral error, curiosity works closely in conjunction with pride, "the beginning of all sin" and the core of the triad. Indeed, his youthful desire for dominance at childhood games is only nurtured by his attraction to the fabulous— both on a literary and a theatrical level. In this regard, he discerns a clear coextensiveness between the "games" of children and adults.

> I loved to win proud victories in our contests, and to have my ears tickled by false stories, so that they would itch all the more intensely for them, with the same kind of curiosity glittering more and more in my eyes for shows, the games of grown-up men.[5]

Implicit in this critical assessment of his growing fascination with spectacle, we discern the same epistemological dichotomies which Augustine consistently employed in his earlier moral discussions: *truth vs. falsehood; reality vs. images; being vs. non-being.*

As observed in the previous chapter, however, such dichotomies assume moral and metaphysical connotations that also enter into Augustine's understanding of the nature of *curiositas* and its effects. At this juncture, he draws an additional distinction between studies which are useful and those which are wholly superfluous.

> As a boy I sinned when I preferred these inane tales to more useful studies…when…"One and one are two, and two and two are four" was for me a hateful chant, while the wooden horse full of armed men, the burning of Troy, and Creusa's ghost were most sweet but empty spectacles.[6]

In broader terms, Augustine depicts his inner conflict as a tension between the one and the many, that is, between the unity of all things (including the self) in God and the multiplicity of cares and preoccupations that are part and parcel of an increasing absorption in the world. In recounting the deeds of his sixteenth year, he boldly outlines for the reader the "carnal corruptions" of his soul.[7] From the vantage point of the critical commentator on his own past, Augustine depicts this period in clear Neoplatonic terms as given over to a disordered expenditure of the self upon the manifold of temporal pursuits and corporeal desires, "tossed about and spilt out" in his own fornications.[8]

In the concrete setting of his life experience, these candid reflections focus upon Augustine's year of idleness in Tagaste after an interruption of his studies. This timeframe provides the context for his famous "theft of pairs" episode and its role as a paradigm for the sinful disposition.[9] When he informs us that what he loved in that theft was the act of theft itself, he highlights what he considers the essence of moral evil on all levels: an irrational drive for non-being that runs counter to the realization of our true good.

> Foul was the evil, and I loved it. I loved to go down to death. I loved my fault, not that for which I did the fault, but I loved my fault itself.[10]

Augustine's emphasis on his savoring of the very experience of sin points toward the triadic analysis of iniquity undergirding the *Confessiones* as a whole. By the same token, it anticipates his later claim that he was "in love with love" itself.[11] In this connection, his confession that he could do evil without purpose (that is, for the sake of evil itself) dovetails with his contention that all sin is no more than a vicarious experience which seeks an imitation of genuine reality. But this recognition of the emptiness of sinfulness presupposes an understanding of the *ordo* of creation in which all things are considered good because they are created by God. Accordingly, sin constitutes a desertion of the best and highest goods (identified with God) in favor of the lower goods in which we take delight.[12]

Augustine's treatment of the dynamics of sin thus relies heavily upon a metaphysical theory of privation, whereby moral wrongdoing (like evil in general) is viewed as a diminishing of the created goodness of God. This presupposition is operative in his analysis of the motivation for wrongdoing and a detailed compendium of vices reminiscent of the cataloging of sins in his earliest writings.[13] In each instance, Augustine depicts the sin in question as a paltry imitation of God or some aspect of Divine activity. In this plethora of vices, however, he also isolates two of the triadic members—pride and curiosity. Interestingly, he imparts an intellectualist dimension to both vices (in keeping with his reflections on his early student days). Pride imitates a "loftiness of mind" before the God Who is highest in all things.[14] Curiosity, however, "pretends to be a desire for knowledge, while you know all things in the highest degree."[15]

For Augustine, curiosity constitutes a mere pretense for knowledge precisely because it focuses the soul's attention on what is ontologically impoverished. But this sin is not confined to Augustine alone. His remarks point to the extended anti-Manichaean polemic that assumes such a prominent feature of the *Confessiones*. Indeed, his commentary on the theft of pairs and the other sins of his youth might well be construed as anticipating his critique of the arrogance and flawed epistemology of the Manichaeans in relegating God Himself to a corporeal level.

> In a perverse way, all men imitate you who put themselves far from you, and rise up in rebellion against you. Even by such imitation of you they prove that you are the creator of all nature, and that... there is no place where they can depart entirely from you.[16]

## IN SEARCH OF TRUTH

Augustine's confession of his deeds during his student days at Carthage finds vivid expression in the graphic metaphor he uses to describe his insatiable appetite for carnal gratification. His soul, he relates, was eager to be "scratched by the things of sense."[17] While this image is usually interpreted in terms of sexual lust, Augustine's focus is really the totality of worldly experience. In this context, he again condemns the vicariousness inherent in spectacles and in his own tendency to exalt what is no more than illusory pleasure.

> Why is it that a man likes to grieve over doleful and tragic events which he would not want to happen to himself? The spectator likes to experience grief at such scenes, and this very sorrow is a pleasure to him. What is this but a pitiable folly?[18]

At this juncture, however, Augustine is not only concerned with the pitfalls posed by spectacles themselves or the allurement of fanciful tales. He also recognizes his own susceptibility to intellectual error, a weakness rooted in his passionate commitment to the pursuit of truth. How far would this curiosity lead him away from God?

> Upon what great evils did I waste myself, and what a sacrilegious desire for knowledge did I pursue, so that it might bring me, a deserter from you, down into the depths of apostasy and into the deceitful service of demons![19]

In this seemingly healthy cognitive appetite (which opens up the possibility of knowledge), Augustine discerns the beginning of his subsequent gravitation to Manichaeism and the allure of its teachings for his restless intellect. But this critique of his curious attraction to erroneous teachings must be balanced against his abiding passion for the philosophical way of life. In Cicero's *Hortensius* (which he read in his late teens), Augustine found a work which he claimed did nothing less than turn his affections to God with new purposes and desires.[20]

The *Hortensius*, in fact, would ignite Augustine's interest in the pursuit of wisdom, thereby serving as a crucial stimulus in his lifelong search for God and things Divine. In what amounts to a Christian adaptation of the Platonic notion of *eros*, Augustine describes himself as "burning with desire" to flee earthly things and soar to God.[21] Such sentiments are revealing, because they highlight his ongoing receptivity to secular wisdom in pursuit of an ultimate Divine Wisdom.[22] But in broader soteriological terms, Augustine could also view his philosophical inspiration by Cicero in terms of an admonition to seek a more genuine claim to truth. From this standpoint, secular wisdom (no matter how profound) can only be a means to a greater end for Christians.[23] Accordingly, Augustine still laments that the *Hortensius* made no reference to Christ. In a roundabout way, then, he was driven back to Scripture, a *corpus* of writings he had consistently derided for its literary shallowness, his "swelling pride turned away from its humble style."[24]

But Augustine's early inability to penetrate the deeper meaning of Scripture reflected a naive literalism that confined him to the surface appearances of things. This literalism was only intensified in his gravitation to Manichaeism and its depiction of all things (including God) in terms of corporeal images.[25] This epistemological limitation

(whereby he could not rise above the corporeal) extended to his understanding of evil as well. How could he know that evil is a privation
of the good if he could only see bodies and phantasms?[26] Augustine
viewed his eager embrace of the fiction of Manichaeism as consistent
with his pursuit of a vacuous fame and popularity. "We were seduced,"
Augustine acknowledges, "and…seduced others openly by the so-
called liberal arts and secretly in the name of a false religion."[27] In this
connection, Augustine's critique of the liberal arts focuses specifically
on the art of rhetoric, as a skill directed toward the inculcation of a
spirit of deceit in his students. Fittingly, his attachment to a spurious
religious outlook finds its parallel in all the counterfeit claims to truth
that now dominate his life.

In a very real sense, however, Augustine's search for truth (however
questionable the avenues it pursued) reflected the same fragmentation
that he discerned in temporal existence as a whole. On the one hand,
this fragmentation manifests itself in the mutability inherent in the
beauty arousing the soul's many appetites. If change is the veritable
"law of their being," then the comings and goings of beautiful things
can only inspire a relentless desire to pursue them.

> These things go where they were going so that they may cease to
> be, and thus they rend the soul asunder with pestilent desires. For
> the soul wishes to be and it loves to find rest in things that it loves.
> But in such things there is no place where it may find rest, for they
> do not endure.[28]

From this standpoint, the metaphysical instability that accompanies
mutable reality prompts a parallel instability in the soul's range of
loves. In a Neoplatonic variation of the *commune/proprium* distinction
that Augustine discusses extensively in the *De libero arbitrio* (II,7,ff.),
he depicts those governed by fleshly interests as fixed on the partial,
to the exclusion of an appreciation of the whole to which the parts
contribute.[29]

Augustine's deliberation on his attraction to creaturely beauty is an
outgrowth of his larger investigation of the dynamics of love. By his
own admission, this is no easy task, in the face of that "mighty deep"
that is man, the creature whose "hairs are easier to count than his affections and the movements of his heart."[30] At this stage in his life's
journey, those affectivities assumed an exclusive materialistic character.
As such, they prevented his acceptance of the possibility of spiritual

reality, even in respect to the Divine nature. In this regard, Augustine's early acquaintance with Aristotle's *Categories* only reinforced these presuppositions. Since he assumed that anything which exists falls under the ten predicates, he concluded that God's attributes were in God as in a subject, and thus, distinguishable from his nature.[31]

After he became disenchanted with Manichaean teachings, Augustine turned to the doctrines of the philosophers. But while their doctrines concerning the natural world seemed more probable than those taught by the Manichaeans, Augustine also lamented that the philosophers did not recognize the source of their wisdom.[32] In point of fact, he roots that failure in the same triad of pride, curiosity, carnal concupiscence which dominates his own moral struggles. In this connection, Augustine's characterization of the sins of the philosophers is reminiscent of the imagery of the *De Genesi contra Manichaeos* (I,23[40]) and its identification of each triadic member with a specific kind of animal.

> They do not slay their own prideful boasts (like fowls of the air) or their selfish curiosity (like the fishes of the sea), by which they wander along the hidden paths of the deep or their carnal indulgence (which is like the beasts of the field).[33]

Augustine's indictment of the "selfish curiosity" of the philosophers resonates with his critique of his own preoccupation with the external world. He initially found an attractive alternative in philosophy because it displayed such a skill at disclosing truths concerning the natural world (in comparison with the fanciful, unfounded claims of the Manichaeans).[34] In this respect, God is not found by those too proud to acknowledge the efficacy of their Creator, "not even if they could number with curious skill the stars and sands, and measure the constellations, and plot the courses of the planets."[35] Accordingly, the philosophers (like the Manichaeans) succumb to a fatal flaw. By virtue of a vanity that cannot recognize *God as God*, they violate the rule of perfect religion, serving the creature rather than the Creator.[36] In a very real sense, however, Augustine was implicitly commenting on his own struggles with the limitations of an epistemology which only allowed him to conceive of God in terms of an "vast corporeal mass," leading to his assumption that something without a body did not exist.[37]

In the imperial city of Milan (where his worldly aspirations reached their peak), Augustine's life would take a radical turn after the Catholic bishop Ambrose introduced him to the allegorial method of scriptural interpretation. This method provided Augustine's key to an appreciation of the sophistication of Scripture, in contrast to his early disdain of what he perceived as the naivete of biblical teaching. In this way, it allowed him to grasp the deeper significance embedded in the letter of the text.[38] In the face of Ambrose's contribution to Augustine's new spiritual awareness, an episode occurs which Augustine came to view as nothing less than an admonition from God.

After observing a drunken beggar in the street, he compares the beggar's temporary (but satisfying) enjoyment with his own futile search for happiness "by many a troubled twist and turn."[39] The incident magnified his growing awareness of the emptiness of his own ambitions. Once again, he discerns the disparity between his immersion in a counterfeit reality and his desire for genuine truth.

> It was not true joy that he possessed, but by my ambitious plans I sought one much more false. Certain it was that he was in high humor, while I was troubled; he was free from care, while I was full of fear.[40]

Augustine's words underscore the restlessness which accompanies his world-oriented *excursus*. The multiple cares (*curae*) which now beset him (in contrast to the beggar's freedom from such trouble) run to the very heart of the curious disposition. We have seen how the term *cura* provided the etymological root of *curiositas*-language in the Latin tradition. Augustine fully exploits this connotation. The recognition of his restlessness only affirms the depth of his need for the serenity of union with God. At the very outset of the *Confessiones*, Augustine memorably proclaims that "our heart is restless until it rests in you."[41] At this juncture of his extended self-scrutiny, however, the restlessness of his heart finds its cognitive counterpart in a restless mind which finds no peace in its absorption in the natural world. But the immediate focus of Augustine's analysis of the dynamics of *curiositas* is not himself but his friend Alypius.

Augustine describes how Alypius (a native of Augustine's own hometown of Tagaste, who had been his student at Carthage) had freed himself from his attraction to the spectacles of the circus.[42] But after he was taken by friends (against his will) to gladiatorial combats, he became intoxicated with the frenzy of the crowd. Augustine skillfully uses this experience as a means of demonstrating the extent to which we cannot detach our minds from our bodily experience. Alypius, in contrast, assumed that he "will be absent, though present," as if the mind can be completely divorced from bodily influences, as the dualists claim.[43] In one of the most graphic scenarios of the *Confessiones*, Augustine depicts Alypius as having closed his eyes, not anticipating the alluring power of the crowd's exaltation in the violent display before him.

> For when one man fell in the combat, a mighty roar went up from the entire crowd and struck him with such force that he was overcome by curiosity.[44]

In this case, curiosity is aroused by external stimuli. But once the mind is so aroused, it gives itself over to what the senses absorb, even before the will's own aversion, no matter how horrible the subject matter. In fact, the very horror may well heighten the pull of the curious attraction.

> As he saw that blood, he drank in savageness…fixed his sight on it, and drank in madness without knowing it. He took delight in that evil struggle, and he became drunk on blood and pleasure. He was no longer the man who entered there, but only one of the crowd that he had joined, and a true comrade of those who brought him there.[45]

This language reminds us of Augustine's earlier description of the collective delight he and his friends took in raiding the pear orchard. Once again, he emphasizes the corporate character of sin. In this instance, the appeal of the ampitheater provides the ideal test case for exploring the depths of the curious urge and its capacity to move our entire being toward an absorption in worldly concerns. When Augustine says that Alypius "was not longer the man who had entered there," his message is all too clear: *curiositas*, like other expressions of unregulated desire, result in nothing less than a loss of self, a forfeiture of one's very identity in pursuit of transitory, extraneous pleasures. In this respect, Alypius' craving for new experiences emerges in another context, when Augustine relates his friend's desire for marriage, not out of lust, but simply out of curiosity.[46] In this curiosity, Augustine perceives a paradoxical attraction to the very subservience under which Augustine himself now struggles. From his standpoint, Alypius' curiosity initiates something of a causal chain culminating in the soul's bondage to its own desires.

> A mind free from that bondage wondered at my servitude, and
> from that wonder it passed into a desire to experience it. Next he
> might go on to the experience itself, and then perhaps he would fall
> into that very slavery at which he wondered.[47]

Augustine's reflections on Alypius' travails prompts a preliminary examination of conscience which anticipates the extended self-scrutiny
that emerges in *Confessiones* X. At this point, he surveys his progress
from the age of nineteen, when he acquired his zeal for the philosophical way of life and resolved to abandon the vain concerns which now
ensnare him. At present, he is torn between a desire to cleave to God
and an attachment to those things he considers antithetical to the pursuit of abiding truth. In this connection, he is still driven by ambition
and a proud self-reliance that deceives him into thinking that even
continence lies within his powers.[48]

## INIQUITY DEFINED

As Augustine entered early adulthood (*inventus*, that is, 20-40 years
of age), he discerned his ongoing absorption in vain things.[49] But this
preoccupation drew upon the thoroughgoing materialism with which
he struggled throughout his life. While he believed in the incorrupt-
ibility, inviolability, and immutability of God, he was burdened by
his inability to conceive the substantiality of anything not accessible
through the senses (including God and the soul). In a particularly poignant moment, Augustine confesses that "my heart cried out violently
against all my phantasms…and I tried to beat off the throng of unclean images."[50]

   As noted above, Augustine's materialism also shaped his positivis-
tic understanding of evil. But any definition of evil that he formulated in this materialistic mindset only reflected his understanding of
the cause of evil. In this respect, one of the major implications (and
benefits, from the young Augustine's standpoint) of the Manichaean
theodicy was a refusal to root evil in the operation of the will itself. By
attributing its cause to the encroachment of *Hyle* (the embodiment of
evil), the Manichaeans conveniently exculpated humans from any real
wrongdoing.

   Augustine's rejection of Manichaeism was intimately connected
with his growing conviction that "when I willed a thing or refused to

will it that it was I alone who willed or refused to will."[51] In the face of this conviction, Augustine would drastically redirect his investigation of evil from a search for its overarching cause to a search for the source of the evil will itself. For all practical purposes, this amounts to asking "Whence comes iniquity?"

Early in the *Confessiones*, as we have seen, Augustine found the primal expressions of iniquity in the triad of pride, curiosity, and carnal concupiscence.[52] But these sins are themselves rooted in the will's negative movement. Augustine's recognition of the volitional roots of his own sin presupposes his appreciation of the goodness of creation as a whole. His ability to do so was largely the result of what he came to interpret as the decisive admonition from God, one of those "inner goads" which prompted him toward the truth.[53] His introduction to Neoplatonism opened him to a vision of reality he would find highly consonant with scriptural teachings.[54]

On the basis of his reading of the "books of the Platonists" (*libri platonicorum*), Augustine discovered a metaphysics which committed him to the incorporeality of God and the soul. In this scheme, evil cannot be a substantial reality in its own right; it is no more than a privation or deficiency of the good which God creates. From this standpoint, God constitutes the highest standard of being and goodness Who creates mutable realities capable of suffering corruption, even though they are fundamentally good. As Augustine affirms, "I saw... that you have made all things good, and...there are no substances... you have not made."[55] In this case, he can ultimately trace the cause of evil to iniquity, the manifestation of the evil will.

> I asked "What is iniquity?" and I found that it is not a substance. It is perversity of will, twisted away from the supreme substance, yourself, O God, and towards lower things, and casting away its innermost good, and swelling beyond itself.[56]

Augustine's definition of iniquity (representing an amalgam of insights drawn from Ecclesiasticus 10:9-14 and Neoplatonic teaching) is significant on two levels.[57] First, it frees God from any causal responsibility for moral evil by localizing its origin in the movement of the will. Secondly, Augustine defines sinfulness on its most primal level in terms of an aversion or turning from the higher immutable goodness of God to lower mutable goods (rather than from absolute goodness to absolute evil, as the Manichaeans taught). Building upon

the imagery of Ecclesiasticus 10:9-14, he further depicts iniquity as
the soul's distention beyond its proper limits, that is, its properly ordained order between God and lesser realities. In a manner consistent with the "weight" (*pondus*) metaphor operative in earlier discussions of the soul's affectivities, he now describes his movement from
God as a downward plunge "into the midst of those lower things"
under the weight of carnal custom.[58] But lower things are not evil
*per se*. According to the theodicy he derived from the "books of the
Platonists," such things must be understood in terms of the larger order of creation in which they contribute to the goodness and completion of the whole.

> From the heights of heaven down to the depths of the earth, from
> the beginning to the end of time, from the angel even to the worm,
> from the first movement up to the last, you seated, each in its proper
> place, all varieties of good things.[59]

By shifting the responsibility for iniquity to the human will, Augustine
thus upholds the goodness of creation. But the human will is itself a
part of the created goodness of God. The paradox (indeed, the unsettling surd in the order of creation) lies in the fact that the will can
either opt for the good or reject it. Accordingly, lust in all its forms
(exemplified by the triad of sins) constitutes a profound misuse of the
will, and by extension, a misuse of the goods to which it commits itself.
In surveying his own experience (and the grip of carnal custom upon
his range of choices), Augustine perceives himself as enslaved in a servitude to the very things he loves.

> Lust is made out of a perverse will, and when lust is served, it be-
> come habit, and when habit is not resisted, it becomes necessity. By
> such links, joined to one another...a harsh bondage held me fast.[60]

As he approached the point of his moral conversion to Christianity,
Augustine discerned in himself a conflict of wills: an old carnal will
and a new spiritual one (a variation of the Pauline distinction between
the inner man of the spirit and the outer man of the flesh).[61] But this
conflict by no means ceased following his conversion. After recounting the dramatic series of events which consummated in his complete
commitment to the Catholic faith, Augustine undertakes an elaborate
examination of conscience in light of the triad of pride, curiosity, and
carnal concupiscence.

## A TRIADIC EXAMINATION OF CONSCIENCE

The tenth book of Augustine's *Confessiones* provides something of a critical commentary on his very attempt at confession. In so doing, he offers the reader what amounts to a probing example of his *exercitatio animi* technique, that is, an exercising of the mind's own powers by applying it to probing questions worthy of its efforts. By extension, he challenges us to embark on this noble endeavor in which we all have such a personal stake. From Augustine's Christian Neoplatonic perspective, the attainment of a greater level of self-knowledge is crucial if we are to come to terms with the ground of our own being. Indeed, self-knowledge opens us to a knowledge of God and those immutable standards of truth by which we understand in the midst of the changing things of bodily existence.[62] But on a deeper level, this inward turning attunes us to the truth about ourselves which only God discerns with clarity.[63] In this connection, Augustine seeks to expose those "dark areas" within his soul in which even his own capacities remain hidden to himself, unless revealed by some experience.[64]

In moral terms, the interiorization which confession presupposes allows us to transcend the mutable world of the soul's lusts and grasp the incorporeal reality which invests our strivings with intelligibility, meaning, and value. The fact that the first part of *Confessiones* X is dominated by Augustine's deliberations on memory, then, is not surprising.[65] Indeed, any attempt to bridge the gap between the corporeal and the incorporeal, the visible and the invisible, the mutable and the immutable can only proceed from an analysis of the memory whereby we pass from the mere images of things to an apprehension of true reality, and ultimately, to a knowledge of God.

The scope of memory's "fields and spacious palaces" is immense.[66] Among its contents, Augustine discerns the images of things implanted by old habits.[67] Accordingly, he embarks upon an elaborate self-examination in terms of what he now recognizes as the chief expressions of iniquity, namely, the concupiscence of the flesh and eyes, and the ambition of the world.[68] Each member of this triad of sins finds its counterpart in a virtue: in the concupiscence of the flesh, he finds the antithesis of the love of God and neighbor; in the concupiscence of the eyes (curiosity), he finds a spurious claim to genuine wisdom; in the ambition of the world, he finds the opponent of a humble submission to the Divine will.

Just as the inner and outer dimensions of human existence are close-ly related and complementary, so too are virtue and vice part and par-cel of our fundamental orientation to the good. In this respect, the "triple lust" of carnal concupiscence, curiosity, and proud ambition are no more than unregulated expressions of what might otherwise be viewed as healthy human desires. This is particularly the case in regard to curiosity, the lust of the eyes. How does one draw a moral line be-tween the drive for knowledge that is so vital to human fulfillment and the distortion of that drive into a frivolous concern with matters of no real cognitive significance? This blurring of the distinction between vice and virtue is evident in carnal concupiscence and pride as well. And therein lies the ambiguity and paradox of the sinful disposition.

If one overlooks this anomalous character of sin, then Augustine's ensuing self-examination seems overly harsh in its quickness to cen-sure what often appear as normal human tendencies. But at this point in his spiritual journey, he is acutely aware of the pervasiveness of sin in his life and how easily the most virtuous conduct can give way to vicious acts in the absence of moderation and restraint. In this vein, Augustine's order of procedure is significant. He begins with an as-sessment of the presence of carnal concupiscence and concludes with a survey of the persistence of pride in his moral outlook. The sin of curiosity provides the crucial link between these two vices.

Augustine thus begins with the sin in his life that assumes the most wide-ranging and pervasive character. In carnal concupiscence, he finds all the excessive desire for things connected with bodily existence, and more specifically, the lust for pleasures of the body (the outer dimen-sion of the human being). What is noteworthy in this analysis (as it is in his analysis of the other triadic sins) is Augustine's focus on the blameworthiness of ordinary conduct. It is clear that his conversion and sense of his spiritual progress have considerably "raised the stakes" in his own moral expectations. If he seems unduly self-critical here, it is because he now views his life (and the depth of his sinfulness) not only through the lens of the convert, but from the distance of nearly fifteen years of life as a Christian.

In keeping with this self-critical perspective, Augustine addresses his desire for food and drink.

Are not eating and drinking indispensable for the promotion of life? The very goodness of these activities underscores how easily he can slip into an excessiveness for the very things he requires for his own

well-being. Augustine's own experience discloses that fasting itself can
open him to a special "snare of concupiscence" in the very pleasure he
takes in eating and drinking after a period of strict self-denial. Therein
lies a moral pitfall proceeding from a deceptive attempt to legitimize
what is no more than indulgence in the interests of health.

> Since good health is the reason for eating and drinking, a dangerous
> pleasure makes herself my companion. Often it becomes a matter of
> doubt whether it is the care needed by the body that seeks help or
> a deceitful desire for pleasure that demands service…and…under
> pretense of health it may disguise a pursuit of pleasure.[69]

It would be erroneous to assume that Augustine condemns each and
every bodily pleasure in the manner of the puritanical Manichaean.
As his remarks indicate, his focus here lies in that "dangerous pleasure" which entails a forfeiture of the mean between excess and defect
defining the virtuous life. In this respect, Augustine upholds his ongoing understanding of sin as a pretense or counterfeit version of true
reality. Each of the primal sins, as we have seen, presuppose some imitative claim to the good, the true, and the beautiful. In this instance,
Augustine is concerned with a specific expression of the lust of the
flesh, namely, the sin of gluttony which "creeps upon your servant."[70]
But he extends this tendency to the sense of hearing, when it gives rise
to those entangling "delights of the ear" (*voluptates aurium*).[71]

The fact that Augustine's critique of auditory pleasures focuses
principally on his enjoyment of liturgical music might well suggest an
excessive scrupulosity on his part. But as the *Confessiones* reveal, the
sense of hearing had assumed an important role in his conversion experience. He was drawn back to the study of Scripture, we recall, by
the preaching of Ambrose. And his conversion was consummated after
he heard the child's repeated chant of *Tolle lege, tolle lege!*" Accordingly,
Augustine invests a great significance in what the ears disclose.

Along with vision, hearing provides access to the external world,
and conversely, a means of receiving sensory input from the surrounding environment, along with all the delights we derive from that experience. Once again, however, Augustine must confront a paradox in a
sensual pleasure that can so quickly fluctuate between virtue and vice.

> This sensual pleasure…often leads me astray, when sense does not
> accompany reason in such wise as to follow patiently after it, but…
> even tries to run ahead and lead reason on.[72]

On the one hand, Augustine is reluctant to indict the sacred music which is such an exalted source of Divine praise and spiritual edification. On the other hand, he recognizes a moral pitfall in his own tendency to be "moved more by the singing than by what is sung."[73]

In Augustinian terms, the essence of concupiscence lies in an intemperate enjoyment of what is fundamentally good. Accordingly, Augustine finds himself wavering between "the danger of sensual pleasure and wholesome experience."[74] This instability is particularly apparent on the level of visual experience. If concupiscence arises on the basis of what we see, then, the "concupiscence of the eyes" can be interpreted on both a literal and a metaphorical level. In literal terms, we derive pleasure from the objects of vision themselves. This is part and parcel of the sensual delight we derive through all the senses. From this standpoint, the eyes and vision become conduits of carnal pleasure. In metaphorical terms, however, the "lust of the eyes" pertains to the specific primal vice of curiosity, the inordinate desire for knowledge and the acquisition of novel experiences.

But herein lies the difficulty in neatly distinguishing the concupiscence of the flesh from curiosity (*curiositas*) or the concupiscence of the eyes (*concupiscentia oculororum*). Indeed, things which yield visual pleasure for their very beauty or novelty are also conducive to our curious attraction to them. Accordingly, Augustine observes that the soul takes delight in "fair and varied forms and bright and beauteous colors."[75] He considers these natural things good because they were so created by God. But he also recognizes other visual attractions which are the products of human technology, encompassing all the implements and artifacts of civilization.[76]

By fixing their attention on the delights of the outer world (and pursuing what is external to the innermost self), humans "inwardly" forsake their focus on the Creator responsible for all things (including humans capable of exercising their own creative powers).[77] In so doing, they establish a new criterion of value, based on sensual appeal rather than that supreme Cause which is ultimately responsible for the existence of everything. But if they acquire their norm of valuation from external beauties, they also forfeit a norm for their *proper use*. In contrast to the attractions of nature, things of human making thus exceed the parameters of moderation and purpose.[78] This is where Augustine's analysis of the concupiscential dimension of vision both coincides with and differs from curiosity, the lust of the eyes.

> In addition to the concupiscence of the flesh present in delight in all the senses and in every pleasure... by reason of those same bodily senses, there is present in the soul a certain vain and curious desire, cloaked over with the title of knowledge and science, not to take pleasure in the flesh but to acquire new experiences through the flesh.[79]

At this point, Augustine explicitly defines the sin of *curiositas* in terms of the prescriptions of I Jn. 2:16.

> Since this is rooted in the appetite for knowledge, and since the eyes are the princely senses, it is called in God's Scriptures concupiscence of the eyes.[80]

Vision, in effect, serves as a compelling metaphor for knowing. By extension, the lust of the eyes refers to an inordinate desire for the acquisition of knowledge. In broader terms, however, Augustine also applies the phrase "lust of the eyes" to all sense experience.

> The function of sight, in which the eyes hold primacy, even the other senses appropriate in an analogous way when they investigate any object of knowledge.[81]

If *curiositas* prompted us to aesthetically pleasant things alone, it would not exhibit any substantive moral difference from *concupiscentia carnis*. But Augustine's interpretation of *curiositas* as an appetite for worldly experience in general considerably expands its coverage.

While carnal desire seeks things that are sensually attractive, curiosity might seek the very opposite. "What pleasure is there," Augustine asks, "in looking at a mangled corpse that causes you to shudder?"[82] In this context, he isolates an ambiguity endemic in human desire that underscores the instability inherent in our creatureliness (and more specifically, in our fallenness and susceptibility to sin). His words call to mind the revulsion people might feel in watching a graphic horror film, even as they find themselves drawn to watch. This is what Augustine pointedly characterizes as a "morbid curiosity" that goads one to those "monstrous sights" exhibited in side-shows.[83]

But in Augustine's probing analysis, such "morbid curiosity" finds its most pronounced outlet in scientific activities whose motivation is rooted in no more than a vain desire to know. Earlier in the *Confessiones*, he found this brand of desire a major incentive in his own movement toward Manichaeism and its promises of a rational understanding of natural processes and celestial movements. At this juncture, however, his indictment of scientific curiosity extends to those distorted expressions of science by which "men proceed to search out the secrets of nature, things beyond our end, to know which profits us nothing, and of which men desire nothing but the knowing."[84]

While the Manichaeans are the immediate candidates for Augustine's invective, he perceives such vain curiosity at work in the magical arts as well.[85] In this respect, it also manifests itself in a religious context, when people desire signs and miracles on the part of God in order to satisfy their experiential craving. This, in fact, is the very form of curiosity which Augustine still discerns in himself, even after he has been freed from attachments to the theater and astronomical inquiry, and even as he detests sacrilegious rites.[86] Accordingly, his persistent desire for signs from God attests to the ongoing moral danger posed by the lust of the eyes. In this connection, he readily acknowledges the variety of ways in which his curiosity continues to be aroused, through such commonplace lures as idle conversation, the excitement of observing a hunt, and the sight of natural phenomena.[87] While these experiences are not evil, their very impact on the soul creates an inner turbulence conducive to distraction from prayer and contemplation.

> Who can number in how many trivial and contemptible things our curiosity is daily tempted, and how often we fall![88]

The pervasiveness of curiosity in Augustine's daily activities renders a single-minded devotion to God extremely difficult to maintain. But he also perceives a threat to such single-mindedness in the final sin he addresses in his examination of conscience. In this respect, Augustine considers pride (the scriptural "beginning of all sin") as his most challenging vice. He finds this particular sin the most resistant to self-examination, precisely because of his fundamental need for praise.

The fact that praise accompanies a good moral life presents Augustine with a rather acute dilemma: while he can evaluate his success at curbing his carnal and curious lusts, he cannot imagine life completely devoid of praise. "Must we not live an evil life," he queries, "that no one can know us without detesting us?"[88] He likewise confesses his susceptibility to false humility, presumption, and self-centeredness.

Paradoxically, however, Augustine's ongoing struggles with the sin of pride coincides with a recognition of his utter dependence upon God. He poignantly recounts his movement from encounters with the external world through the instrumentality of the senses to an entry into the very recesses of his memory.[89] By means of this interiorization process, Augustine came to the realization that he could grasp nothing whatsoever without God. Indeed, his very capacity to investigate the things of sense experience and the depths of his sinfulness attest to his utter dependence upon God for knowledge and being.

In epistemological terms, Augustine finds that he could discern nothing in the absence of that abiding Divine Light that illumines his mind; in deeper metaphysical terms, he confronts the stark truth that he himself is not God, and that none of the things he perceives through the senses are God.[90] In this regard, he contrasts himself with those who proudly seek God by their learning and turn to the false mediator who deludes the proud.[91] Once again, we see the intimate link in Augustine's moral deliberations between pride and an inquisitive curiosity which leads us away from our Creator. For his part, then, he considers the "sickness of my sins" by means of the triple concupiscence.[92] In his infirmity, only God can offer the healing that his soul requires through that true Mediator (i.e., Christ) who provides the ultimate model of humility.

### CURIOSITAS AND AUGUSTINE'S PEREGRINATIO

Augustine's discussions of the sin of curiosity in the context of his spiritual pilgrimage invests his analysis of this vice with a certain poignancy and credibility. He conveys the impression that he knows of what he speaks. In point of fact, however, the importance of curiosity in this account of his *excursus* can easily be overlooked in the face of his more pronounced emphasis on the sins of pride and carnal concupiscence in his moral development. But a careful reading of the first ten books of the *Confessiones* discloses that curiosity provides Augustine's continual stimulus for entry into the external world of sense experience on various levels. From this standpoint, the "lust of the eyes" is instrumental in both his carnal attachments and in his proud exaltation of self over God and others.

It is no overstatement, then, to assert that the sin of *curiositas* is intimately linked with Augustine's pilgrimage of mind and heart. This constitutes more than an extended journey. In Augustine's recounting, it amounts to a quest exhibiting a haunting sense of his goal or final end at every step of the way. For this reason, Augustine viewed his life in eudaimonistic terms, as a movement to God with an implicit awareness of that *Summum Bonum* in all our strivings. Accordingly, Augustine depicts the primal sins of carnal concupiscence, curiosity, and pride as lustful distortions of what might well be virtuous behavior, if it were subjected to the governance of the rational will.

If Augustine understands sinfulness in general as a pretense or imitation of a genuine good, then curiosity assumes a special character as the pleasure one derives from the experience of sinning itself. In this regard, he closely aligns *curiositas* with vanity on two levels: *first*, it prompts the soul into a vain search for knowledge in what is lower in the order of creation by relying on our cognitive powers to the neglect of God; *secondly*, it naturally tends toward the emptiness or *vanitas* of mere images of the really and truly real.

But the meaning of curiosity also overlaps with that of carnal concupiscence, even as those vices exhibit significant differences. Both derive pleasure through the instrumentality of the senses. But while carnal concupiscence takes delight in the sheer enjoyment of corporeal things, curiosity encompasses the pleasure derived from the experience of the external world. In this connection, vision provides Augustine's metaphor for describing this experiential desire specifically as a desire for knowledge.

Early in the *Confessiones*, Augustine directs his criticism toward what he perceives as superfluous learning. This stance is consistent with the general Stoic ambivalence toward intellectual pursuits exceeding the parameters of moderation and usefulness. Augustine's critique is revealing, in light of his own literary bent. His training as a rhetorician steeped him in a knowledge of the Latin classics. Such a grounding could have easily attuned him to the overall hostility toward excessive inquisitiveness that looms so large in that tradition. In broader terms, the influence of Greek authors upon Latin ones afforded Augustine a window to ongoing pagan indictments of excessively florid or lurid writing, along with scholarly endeavors characterized by a fastidiousness or pedantry, rather than an abiding commitment to truth and the inculcation of wisdom.

This outlook shapes Augustine's attitude toward secular philosophy as well. While Augustine is highly receptive to secular wisdom (in contrast to other Fathers of the Church), the *Confessiones* disclose his tendency to distinguish good philosophy (i.e., what he found in Cicero and the *libri platonicorum*) from its counterfeit competitors. In this respect, Tertullian and Ambrose might have imparted to Augustine a suspicion of pagan philosophy and the curiosity that draws one into its grip. Indeed, we cannot underestimate Tertullian's influence on Augustine's view of the sinfulness of curiosity and its various manifestations (including an attraction to spectacles). By the same token, Tertullian could have provided a viable conduit for the transmission of insights derived from Apuleius (most notably the condemnation of magic and occult practices so prominent in the *Metamorphoses*).[93]

Augustine's own disdain of the magical arts and occultism dovetails with his admonition against the dangers of scientific investigation motivated by no more than a vain and curious desire to acquire novel experiences, not for any useful purpose, but merely for the sake of knowing them. For Augustine, the Manichaeans would always embody that species of *curiositas* which prompts an impious search for things beyond our proper ken. In Manichaeism, he found the concrete expression of that restless inquisitiveness so graphically captured by Apuleius' allegory of vain attempts to penetrate the "secrets" of nature.

Because the Manichaeans were thoroughgoing sensists, they confined their search for knowledge to the realm of corporeal images. But if they assumed that reality is disclosed through such images, then their cognitive gaze focused upon what is metaphysically impoverished. For this reason, they could not appreciate things in terms of the larger *ordo* of creation. By implication, they also failed to recognize the diversity and goodness of all things in relation to their Creator. Like the primal sins of carnal concupiscence and pride, then, curiosity confines the soul's attention to what is partial and fragmented, to the neglect of the whole.

But Augustine's critique of natural science demands qualification. He does not necessarily attack the scientific enterprise itself, or the expansion of our knowledge of the truth. Rather, his polemic is directed against those investigations whose goals are as unregulated as the lust which propels them. From Augustine's standpoint, such endeavors do not qualify as genuinely "scientific" (in a manner consistent with the classical meaning of *scientia* as knowledge), precisely because their objective is no more than the exhilaration of expanding one's intellectual horizons. When read from a twenty-first century perspective (and in light of the previous century's chronicle of global war, genocide, and nuclear proliferation), Augustine's critique becomes chillingly prescient of things to come. In one fell swoop, he lays bare the potential catastrophes of a science that can justify absolutely anything in the name of its own unfettered progress.

The *Confessiones* (like the works considered in the previous chapter), tightly integrates the moral and epistemological dimensions of *curiositas*. Augustine finds that his own curious attraction to images and phantasms leads him to the misuse of the will that constitutes iniquity. But the same curiosity that is capable of prompting a moral disorder in the soul also displaces it from its proper mid-rank between God and lesser things. From this standpoint, the concupiscence of the eyes carries significant metaphysical implications as well.

In assessing his own life, Augustine perceived that the cares (*curae*) and troubles (*negotiae*) the soul incurs by virtue of its temporal involvements are part and parcel of a larger, all-encompassing human *lapsus* from the tranquility and stability of eternity to the restlessness and instability of the temporal order. In this respect, Augustine's treatment of the sin of *curiositas* is inextricably bound up with the fallen soul motif that permeates (and indeed, undergirds) his analysis of the motives of iniquity. His source of this motif, and the diverse uses to which he puts it, found a highly likely inspiration in the *libri platonicorum*, and more specifically, in the Neoplatonic philosophy of Plotinus. I address the Plotinian heritage of Augustine's interpretation of *curiositas* (with a special attentiveness to its metaphysical connotations) in the following chapter.

## NOTES TO CHAPTER 5

1. *Confessiones* III,8(16): CC XXVII,35-36: *Haec sunt capita iniquitatis, quae pullulant principandi et spectandi et sentiendi libidine aut una aut duabus earum aut simul omnibus...*

2. *Confessiones* I,7(11).

3. *Confessiones* I,7(11).

4. *Confessiones* I,19(30): CC XXVII,17: *Istane est innocentia puerilis? Non est, domine, non est, oro te, deus meus. Nam haec ipsa sunt, quae a paedagogi et magistris, a nucibus et pilulis et passeribus, ad praefectos et reges, aurum, praedia, mancipia, haec ipsa omnino succedentibus maioribus aetatibus transeunt, sicuti ferrulis maiora supplicia succedunt.*

5. *Confessiones* I,10(16): CC XXVII,9: *amans in certaminibus superbas uictorias et scalpi aures meas falsis fabellis, quo prurirent ardentius, eadem curiositate magis magisque per oculos emicante in spectacula, ludos mairorum;*

6. *Confessiones* I,13(22): CC XXVII,12: *Peccamur ergo puer, eum illa inania istis utilioribus amore praeponebam. Iam uero unum et unum duo, duo et duo quattuor odiosa contio mihi erat et dulcissimum spectaculum uanitatis equus ligneus plenus armatus et Troiae incendium atque ipsius umbra Creusae.*

7. *Confessiones* II,1(1).

8. *Confessiones* II,1(1)-2(2). The language here represents a synthesis of insights drawn from Ecclesiasticus 10:9-14 (which depicts the proud man as "spewing forth" his innermost good) and Plotinus' *Ennead* III.7(45).11 (and its account of Soul's distention in time). Here, Augustine anticipates his own formal discussion of the soul's temporal distention in *Confessiones* XI. I address the Plotinian (and in broader terms, the Neoplatonic) heritage of Augustine's account of the temporalization of the soul (and the key role of *curiositas* in this movement) in the following chapter.

9. In *Confessiones* II,4(9), Augustine describes how he joined with friends in robbing a local pear orchard, not in order to eat the fruit, but merely to exult in their collective act of theft.

10. *Confessiones* II,4(9): CC XXVII,22: *Foeda erat, et amaui eam; non illud, ad quod deficiebam, sed defectum meum ipsum amaui...*

11. *Confessiones* III,1(1).

12. *Confessiones* II,5(10). In this context, Augustine reflects the eudaimonistic assumption that the will always moves toward ends it perceives as good (even if those ends are not objectively good). For support, he cites the case of Lucius Sergius Catiline (c. 108-62 B.C.), a cruel man who was still motivated by the goals to which his crimes were directed.

13. Cf., *De Beata Vita* IV,4; *De Ordine* II,8(25); *De libero arbitrio* I,11(22).

14. *Confessiones* II,6(13).

15. *Confessiones* II,6(13): CC XXVII,24: *Curiositas affectare uidetur studium scientiae, cum tu omnia summe noueris.* Augustine's characterization of the "masquerade" inherent in other sins follows in this vein (*Confessiones*

II,6[13]): ambition seeks honor and glory; the cruelty of the mighty desires to be feared; the caresses of the wanton seek love; ignorance and folly carry the deceptive names of "simplicity" and "innocence"; sloth seeks rest; luxury desires to be named "plenty" and "abundance"; prodigality pretends to be liberality; avarice desires many things; envy wishes excellence; anger seeks vengeance; fear watches for safety; sadness wastes away for what is lost.

16. *Confessiones* II,6(14): CC XXVII,24: *Peruerse te imitantur omnes, qui longe se a te faciunt et extollunt se aduersum te. Sed etiam sic te imitando indicant creatorem te esse omnis naturae et ideo non esse, quo a te omni modo recedatur. Quid ergo in illo furto ego dilexi et in quo dominum meum uel uitiose atque peruerse imitatus sum?* From Augustine's standpoint, the very use of the will in a morally defective manner constitutes an exercise in "deformed liberty," a feeble attempt at imitating Divine omnipotence (*Confessiones* II,6[14]).

17. *Confessiones* III,1(1).

18. *Confessiones* III,2(2): CC XXVII,27: *Quid est, quod ibi homo uult dolere eum spectat luctuosa et tragica, quae tamen pati ipse nollet? Et tamen pati uult ex eis dolorem spectator et dolor ipse est uoluptas eius. Quid est nisi mirabilis insania?*

19. *Confessiones* III,3(5): CC XXVII,29: *In quantas iniquitates distabui, et sacrilegam curiositatem secutus sum, et deserentem te deduceret me ad ima infida et circumuentoria obsequia daemoniorum, quibus immolabam facta mea mala, et in omnibus flagellabas me!*

20. *Confessiones* III,4(7).

21. *Confessiones* III,4(8).

22. Cf., *De Doctrina Christiana* II,40(60), where Augustine likens secular wisdom to the gold and silver vessels which the Israelites took with them out of Egypt. In Augustine's use of this metaphor, he stresses that truth should be sought wherever it is to be found, whether in Revelation or in Graeco-Roman thought (with the *proviso*, of course, that any conflicts between the two traditions must assume the primacy of the truth of Revelation over the findings of human reason).

23. Augustine's distinction between "use" (*uti*) and "enjoyment" (*frui*) is relevant here. (Cf., *De Doctrina Christiana* I,4[4], where Augustine defines this distinction in terms of love.) In Augustinian terms, the distinction provides a key criterion for the moral life, specifically in regard to our attitude toward created goods. For Augustine, only God should be enjoyed as an end in Himself; everything else should be used as a means to the realization of our final end of beatitude. (Humans, however, are an exception to this rule. Augustine would acknowledge that humans can be enjoyed, but in relation to their Creator, not as ends in themselves.)

24. *Confessiones* III,5(9).

25. For a discussion of Augustine's reliance upon images as a Manichaean, see my *Creatio ex nihilo* and the Theology of St. Augustine. The Anti-Manichaean

*Polemic and Beyond* (New York: Peter Lang Publishing, Inc., 1999), 138-145.

26. *Confessiones* III,7(12).

27. *Confessiones* IV,1(1).

28. *Confessiones* IV,10(15): CC XXVII, 48: *Eunt enim quo ibant, ut non sint, et conscindunt eam desideriis pestilentiosis, quoniam ipsa esse uult et requiescere amat in eis, quae amat. In illis autem non est ubi, quia non stant.*

29. *Confessiones* IV,11(17).

30. *Confessiones* IV,14(21).

31. Confessiones IV,16(29).

32. *Confessiones* V,3(4).

33. *Confessiones* V,3(4): CC XXVII,59: *Trucidant exaltationes suas sicut uolatilia et curiositates suas sicut pisces maris, quibus perambulant secretas semitas abyssi, et luxurias suas sicut pecora campi.* Cf., *Confessiones* XIII,21(30), where Augustine again personifies the triadic sins in the animalistic terms of the *De Genesi contra Manichaeos* I,23(40): "Keep yourselves clean from the monstruous savagery of pride, from sluggish delights of sensuality, and from the false name of knowledge, so that the wild beasts may be tamed, the cattle mastered, and the serpents rendered harmless. In allegory, the passions of the soul are such things, but haughty pride, lustful delight, and poisonous curiosity are motions of a dead soul" (CC XXVII,259: *Continete uos ab immani feritate superbiae, ab inerti uoluptate luxuriae et a fallaci nomine scientiae, ut sint bestiae mansuetae et pecora edomita et innoxii serpentes. Motus einim animae sunt isti in allegoria: sed fastus elationis et delectatio libidinis et uenenum curiositatis motus sunt animae mortuae.*)

34. *Confessiones* V,3(6).

35. *Confessiones* V,3(3): CC XXVII,58: *nec si illi curiosa peritia numerent stellas et harenam et dimetiantur sidereas plagas et uestigent uias astrorum.*

36. *Confessiones* V,3(5).

37. *Confessiones* V,10(9). This assumption extended to evil as well. Accordingly, the Manichaeans viewed evil as a substance that exists in opposition to the good.

38. *Confessiones* V,14(24); VI,4(6); VI,5(8).

39. *Confessiones* VI,6(9).

40. *Confessiones* VI,6(9).

41. *Confessiones* I,1(1).

42. Alypius converted to Christianity along with Augustine and became Bishop of Tagaste in 394/5.

43. *Confessiones* VI,7(8).

44. *Confessiones* VI,8(13): CC XXVII,82: *Nam quodam pugnae casu, cum clamor ingens totius populi uehementer eum pulsasset, curiositate uictus.*

45. *Confessiones* VI,8(13): CC XXVII,83: *Vt enim uidit illum sanguinem, immanitatem simul ebibit et non se auertit, sed fixit aspectum et hauriebat furias et nesciebat et delectabatur scelere certaminis et cruenta uoluptate inebriabatur.*

*Et non erat iam ille, qui uenerat, sed unus de turba, ad quam uenerat, et uerus eorum socius, a quibus adductus erat.*

46. *Confessiones* VI,12(22): CC XXVII,88: *ipse desiderare coniugium nequaquam uictus libidine talis uoluptatis, sed curiositatis.*

47. *Confessiones* VI,12(22): CC XXVII,88: *Stupebat enim liber ab illo uinculo animus seruitutem meam et stupendo ibat in experiendi cupidinem uenturus in ipsam experientiam atque inde fortasse lapsurus in eam quam stupebat seruitutem.*

48. *Confessiones* VI,11(20).

49. *Confessiones* VII,1(1).

50. *Confessiones* VII,1(1).

51. *Confessiones* VII,3(5).

52. *Confessiones* III,8(16).

53. *Confessiones* VII,8(12).

54. *Confessiones* VII,12(18).

55. *Confessiones* VII,12(18).

56. *Confessiones* VII,16(22): CC XXVII,106: *Et quaesiui, quid esset iniquitas, et non inueni substantiam, sed a summa substantia, te deo, detortae in infima uoluntatis peruersitatem proicientis intima sua et tumescentis foras.*

57. I address the Neoplatonic dimension of Augustine's interpretation of iniquity and the fallen soul theory it presupposes in the following chapter.

58. *Confessiones* VII,17(23).

59. *Confessiones* VIII,3(8): CC XXVII,118: *cum a summis caelorum usque ad ima terrarum, ab initio usque in finem saeculorum, ab angelo usque ad uermiculum, a motu primo usque ad extremum omnia genera bonorum.*

60. *Confessiones* VIII,5(10): CC XXVII,119: *Quippe ex uoluntate peruersa facta est libido, et dum seruitur libidini, facta est consuetudo, et dum consuetudini non resistitur, facta est necessitas. Quibus quasi ansulis sibimet innexis... tenebat me obstrictum dura seruitus.*

61. *Confessiones* VIII,5(10).

62. *Confessiones* X,1(1).

63. *Confessiones* X,2(2).

64. *Confessiones* X,32(48).

65. *Confessiones* X,8-25.

66. *Confessiones* X,8(12). Cf., *Confessiones* X,8(14), where Augustine describes the "vast court" of memory; *Confessiones* X,8(15), where he refers to an "inner chamber" of memory; X,40(65), where he refers to "spacious chambers filled with marvelous varieties of countless rich stores" and to "wide treasuries" of memory.

67. *Confessiones* X,30(41).

68. *Confessiones* X,30(41): CC XXVII,176: *Iubes certe, ut contineam a concupiscentia carnis et concupiscentia oculorum et ambitione saeculi.*

69. *Confessiones* X,31(44): CC XXVII,178: *Et cum salus sit causa edendi ac bibendi, adiungit se tamquam pedisequa periculosa iucunditas et...saepe*

*incertum fit, utrum adhuc necessaria corporis cura subsidium petat an uo-luptaria cupiditatis fallacia ministerium suppetat... ut obtentu salutis obum-bret negotium uoluptatis.*

70. *Confessiones* X,31(45).

71. *Confessiones* X,33(49): CC XXVII,181: *Voluptates aurium tenacius me implicauerant et subiugauerant...*

72. *Confessiones* X,33(49): CC XXVII,181: *Sed delectatio carnis meae...saepe me fallit, dum rationi sensus non ita comitatur...sed...etiam praecurrere ac ducere conatur.*

73. *Confessiones* X,33(50).

74. *Confessiones* X,33(50): CC XXVII,182: *Ita fluctuo inter periculum uo-luptatis et experimentum salubritatis.*

75. *Confessiones* X,34(51): CC XXVII,182: *Pulchras formas et uarias, nitidos et amoenos colores amant oculi.*

76. *Confessiones* X,34(53).

77. *Confessiones* X,34(53).

78. *Confessiones* X,34(53).

79. *Confessiones* X,35(54): CC XXVII,184: *Praeter enim concupiscentiam car-nis, quae inest in delectatione omnium sensuum et uoluptatum...inest animae per eosdem sensus corporis quaedam non oblectandi in carne, sed experiendi per carnem uana et curiosa cupiditas nomine cognitionis et scientiae palliata.*

80. *Confessiones* X,35(54): CC XXVII,184: *Quae quoniam in appetitu noscen-di est, oculi autem sunt ad noscendum in sensibus principes, concupiscentia oculorum pertinet.*

81. *Confessiones* X,35(54): CC XXVII,184: *oculorum uocatur, quia uidendi officium, in quo primatum oculi tenent, etiam ceteri sensus sibi de similitudine usurpant, cum aliquid cognitionis explorant.* In support of this interpreta-tion, Augustine highlights the role of the visual metaphor in our attempts to explain various aspects of sense experience. We say for example, "See how it sounds" or "See how it smells," or "See how it tastes," as if vision somehow encompasses all the other senses.

82. *Confessiones* X,35(55): CC XXVII,185: *Quid enim uoluptatis habet uidere in laniato cadauere quod exhorreas?* Augustine does not appear to consider this example in the abstract. It is highly suggestive of the gladiatorial com-bats which drew the blood lust of many of Augustine's contemporaries (including his close friend Alypius).

83. *Confessiones* X,35(55).

84. *Confessiones* X,35(55): CC XXVII,185: *Hinc ad perscrutanda naturae, quae praeter nos est, operta proceditur, quae scire nihil prodest et nihil aliud quam scire homines cupiunt.*

85. *Confessiones* X,35(55).

86. *Confessiones* X,35(56). In this connection, Augustine also emphasizes that he was never preoccupied with necromancy, that is, seeking answers "from the shades of the dead."

87. *Confessiones* X,35(57).
88. *Confessiones* X,37(60).
89. *Confessiones* X,40(65).
90. *Confessiones* X,40(65).
91. *Confessiones* X,42(67). Augustine draws here upon Eph. 2:2, referring to the "powers of this air" whose potent magic deceives the proud.
92. *Confessiones* X,41(66).
93. P.G. Walsh, "The Rights and Wrongs of Curiosity (Plutarch to Augustine)," *Greece & Rome*, 2nd Ser., Vol. 35, No. 1 (Apr., 1988), 82 suggests that "the *Confessions* of Augustine greatly gains in significance by being read in harness...with *The Golden Ass*." While Walsh contends that "it would be a clear exaggeration to claim that the *Confessions* is a coded version of *The Golden Ass*," he still maintains that "there is a strong case for arguing that Apuleius' novel exercised a strong influence on the composition of the *Confessions*."

# CHAPTER 6

## *CURIOSITAS* AND THE PLOTINIAN HYPOTHESIS

Augustine was a masterful psychologist, and some of his most profound psychological deliberations emerge in his discussions of the role of curiosity in his own spiritual odyssey. But as we have seen, his treatments of the sin of curiosity principally stress its impact upon the life of the soul, even as he defines this primal vice as a desire for experiential knowledge of the external world. In this respect, Augustine's understanding of curiosity as the "lust of the eyes" is bound up with an assumption of humanity's fallenness from a pre-lapsarian condition of Divine fellowship and an accompanying harmony of the order of creation as whole.

For Augustine, as we have seen, the sin of curiosity reflects a defective movement of the will in the context of our own existential situation. From this standpoint, Augustine's commentary on the moral hazards of the curious disposition amounts to a commentary on universal human experience. In broader terms, however, Augustine views curiosity as one of the key motives (along with pride and carnal concupiscence) for our initial alienation from God through the sin of Adam. But a consideration of the fallen soul theme in Augustine brings to the fore the closely related issue of his dependence upon Plotinian Neoplatonism in articulating the mainlines of his psychology, anthropology, and moral theory.

Any consideration of the link between the fall of the soul theme and a Plotinian influence in Augustine must address the body of writings of Robert J. O'Connell, S.J.[1] For our purposes, O'Connell's extended project assumes two important dimensions. On the one hand, he defended the hypothesis that whatever positive influence the early Augustine derived from the *'libri platonicorum'* had a distinctive

Plotinian inspiration.[2] On the other hand, he discerned in the *Enneads* the matrix within which Augustine developed his position on the origins of iniquity in terms of a triad of vices that he skillfully coordinated with the triple concupiscence of I Jn. 2:14-16.[3]

My own tests of O'Connell's hypothesis have focused specifically on the Plotinian heritage of Augustine's triadic interpretation of the motives of iniquity.[4] In this connection, my work explored O'Connell's argument that the notion of *tolma* (the prime motive for the soul's fall in Plotinus) offers something of a heuristic device for delineating the complexities of each of the triadic components.[5] In the present context, however, the Plotinian inspiration of Augustine's triadic schematization of iniquity offers a particularly illuminating touchstone for exploring the moral, epistemological, and metaphysical implications of *curiositas*. Once Augustine's wide-ranging discussions of this notion are viewed through the lens of the *Enneads*, its full significance comes into much sharper focus. This Plotinian "lens" is especially revealing in respect to its metaphysical import.

While Augustine could praise our deeply seated drive to know, he considers it heavily laden with a tendency to overstep its appropriate parameters or to distort our grasp of true reality. This does not mean that he wished to restrict our innate desire for knowledge, a desire implicit in the quest for happiness that ultimately leads us to God. But in Augustine's reckoning, the free-ranging character of cognitive appetite (spurred by curiosity and the inquisitive spirit it engenders) can easily exceed the norms of order and moderation.

## THE FALLEN SOUL HYPOTHESIS

Before addressing the Plotinian underpinnings of Augustine's interpretation(s) of *curiositas* (specifically in the writings composed from the Cassiciacum dialogues to the *Confessiones*), a preliminary issue must be addressed. Does a recognition of Plotinus' influence on this aspect of Augustine's thought commit one to the position that we are so many fallen souls? Any answer I offer here must be highly qualified. If curiosity is instrumental in prompting the soul's fall (in temporal or bodily terms), then we must define precisely how the notion of a "fall" is to be construed. This becomes rather pressing when we confront those later works (e.g., *De Genesi ad litteram*, *De Trinitate*, and

*De Civitate Dei*) that Augustine wrote *after* he supposedly abandoned the fallen soul motif on doctrinal grounds.

But while the issue of the soul's fall is most relevant to this investigation, it remains (in and of itself) of peripheral relevance to our major focus, namely, the expressions and roles of curiosity in Augustine. In point of fact, the extent to which Augustine remained committed to an understanding of human beings as fallen souls (or whether he rejected and eventually returned to that position) is a question that has generated much debate.[6] My overarching concern here, however, is not with Augustine's account of the soul's origin *per se* (that is, how or when it became conjoined to the body). My real interest lies in what he has to say about the soul's experience *now* (i.e., as it exists along with the body, in its composite status), and the impact of curiosity upon that existential condition. Accordingly, I wish to avoid the somewhat murky waters of debate surrounding the soul's origin in relation to the body, and confine my analysis to the dynamics of curiosity, one of the key motives for moral evil in Augustine's psychology. This, of course, is not to deny the links between curiosity and the fallen soul theme, and the plethora of interpretive problems generated by those links.

From this standpoint, I support the general thrust of O'Connell's interpretation of Augustine (from at least his earliest writings to the *Confessiones*), a period in which Augustine seems to have embraced the anthropological theory that we are fallen souls and articulated it in clear Plotinian terms. In O'Connell's succinct assessment of this position (formulated toward the end of his career), Augustine "thought of us as fallen souls, who…sinned by turning away from…our highest good…plunging downward into the sensible world of time, mortality, and restless bodily activity."[7] While O'Connell recognized Augustine's subsequent rejection of the individual soul's prenatal sin in its preexistence of the body (in the face of his appreciation of the implications of Rom. 9:9), he claimed that the mature Augustine upheld the thesis that we all sinned collectively in our common life with Adam.[8] In respect to the later Augustine (as reflected in his anti-Pelagian polemic), O'Connell thus contended that the notion of the soul's fall survived in a modified version.

In my estimation, however, the pivotal issue is not whether the later Augustine retained this notion of the soul's temporal and corporeal fall in a literal sense. For our purposes, what matters is whether he exhibited an ongoing fidelity to the language and imagery of Plotinus' mechanism of the soul's descent. Indeed, even if Augustine rejected and then readopted the fallen soul thesis in a modified version, we must still come to terms with the fact (as O'Connell ably showed) that he continued to speak of the soul in Plotinian terms (as if it were, in fact, fallen). But the determination of whether the later Augustine meant this in a literal or metaphorical sense is a question from which I largely prescind in this study.

This is precisely why I opt for the term "metaphysical" in referring to one of the dimensions of Augustine's treatment of curiosity (and in broader terms, the fall of the soul). Here, I implicitly distinguish "metaphysical" from "ontological": according to my interpretation, the latter term pertains to a literal descent of the soul into time and a particular body, and a transition from a spiritual to a composite existence; the former term, on the other hand, highlights the effects of sin on our way of being as finite creatures, as reflected in a radical disordering of our relationship to God and the hierarchy of creation.[9] This distinction, I believe, affords me the freedom to discuss Augustine's evolving interpretations of the soul's fall and its motives, without necessarily binding me to a literal understanding of its "descent" in the ontological sense that Plotinus espouses.

## A KEY PLOTINIAN TOUCHSTONE

On the basis of those works of Augustine that we considered in the previous two chapters, we might well wonder whether he developed one overall interpretation of curiosity (with diverse connotations), or several distinct interpretations of the term in his ongoing search for the motives for iniquity. If he did develop several interpretations (reflecting the role of *curiositas* on a moral, epistemological, and metaphysical level), to what extent do we discern some continuity or point of contact that links them together in a more unified manner? How, for example, does the notion of a prying inquisitiveness so prominent in Augustine's anti-Manichaean polemic relate to the notion of restlessness that dominates its discussion (in conjunction with pride) that comes to the fore in the sixth book of the *De Musica* and in the *Confessiones*? In my estimation, this is why an attunement to Augustine's sources is so crucial.

In a very real sense, the wide range of meanings inherent in Augustine's treatment of the lust of the eyes suggests an inspiration (or inspirations) rich enough to do justice to the multi-dimensional character of this notion in his writings. As the first part of this study has shown, Augustinian *curiositas* reflects the influence of any number of sources (e.g., Scripture, the patristic tradition, classical antique authors in both the Greek and Latin languages). In this respect, Augustine could have been influenced by specific sources on an individual basis. But in light of the impact of the *libri platonicorum* on his outlook, another possibility presents itself. The very fact that Augustine imbues *curiositas* with such a profound metaphysical import strongly suggests a Plotinian referent. O'Connell made a persuasive case for assuming that the ideal Plotinian counterpart for *curiositas* in Augustine is found in the *polupragmon*-language of *Ennead* III.7(45).11.[10] Let us test this hypothesis in greater detail.

## REVISITING *ENNEAD* III.7(45).11

Our test requires a reconsideration of the finepoints of *Ennead* III.7(45).11 and the crucial role of *polupragmon*-language in Plotinus' account of the hypostasis Soul's temporalization. In this passage, Plotinus describes the Soul (along with lower psychic principles) as turning from the contemplation, stability, and rest of the noetic realm to a lower world characterized by action, mutability, and turbulence. As we saw in Chapter 1 of this study, *Ennead* III.7(45).11 proceeds from a commentary on the "quiet life of eternity" existing in that contemplative mode of existence characterizing the intelligible world.[11] This commentary proceeds from Plotinus's rhetorical question to time as to how it came into being. Time's reply underscores the tension between the peace of contemplation and the action-oriented life inherent in temporality.

Before its generation, time relates, it was "at rest in eternity in real being."[12] But this noetic calm was disturbed by a "restlessly active" (*polupragmonos*) nature which sought self-governance and more than it already possessed.[13] That *polupragmatic* spirit, in turn, prompted the movement which is the earmark of temporal process. In Plotinus's rendering, "we made a long stretch of our journey and constructed time as an image of eternity."[14] The "unquiet power" that Plotinus describes here is not merely symptomatic of a sense of alienation with its present state. This dissatisfaction also gives way to an imitative creation, whereby time attempts to translate its vision of the intelligible world into a partial and fragmented mode of being consistent with its desire for the novelty of change.

But this transference only yields negative consequences for the life of Soul. Plotinus describes this downward *excursus* by means of the image of an "uncoiling" or "unraveling" seed which advances to a "weaker extension" of its original greatness, squandering itself in a distention of its powers.[15] The earlier *Ennead* III.8(30).8 applies a comparable image to the hypostasis *Nous*, the Principle of Intellect. Like the hypostasis Soul, *Nous* is motivated by a desire for more than it already possesses. Nous becomes the manifold, like someone "heavy" with drowsiness, "unrolling" itself in its desire to possess everything.

But any expansion on the part of *Nous* or Soul is merely a negative one, leading to a diminishing of their powers on the manifold (that is, sheer otherness in the case of *Nous*, or temporal distention in the case of Soul). In this connection, Plotinus's contrast between the "here" (i.e., the temporal world of our own experience) and the "There" (i.e., the higher intelligible realm) highlights the extent of the transition effected by Soul's restless disposition.

> Soul…making the world of sense in imitation of that other world, moving with a motion which is not that which exists There, but like it, and intending to be an image of it.[16]

Soul's crafting of time as a moving image of its eternal prototype carries a penal dimension. Plotinus depicts this imaging in terms of an enslavement of being to temporal limitations. The major temporal limitation, of course, is reflected in the quality of intellectual activity itself. The successiveness of temporality gives rise to a successiveness of thoughts, with "another thought coming after that which it had before."[17] Still, this fragmented mode of being constitutes but one aspect of Soul's entry into temporal process. In broader terms, it entails a "spreading out" (*diastasis*) of life in general, that is, Soul's life in "a movement of passage from one way of life to another."[18]

Soul's descent and temporalization not only encompasses the downward inclination of the hypostasis Soul itself, but the descent and embodiment of individual souls as well. In this regard, Plotinus's account of Soul's temporalization in *Ennead* III.7(45).11 must be interpreted in the wider context of his treatment of the descent of being from the One, beginning with *Nous* (the Intellectual Principle), as described in *Enneads* VI.9(9).5, III.8(30).8, and V.8(31).13. *Ennead* III.7(45).11, in fact, displays a clear kinship with the earlier *Ennead* V.1(10).1, which posits an act of *tolma* (that is, an audacity or self-will for otherness) as the motive for the fall of individual souls.

Implicit in souls' *tolma* is a desire for self-determination and primal differentiation. These desires find expression in the incursion into temporal process. Accordingly, both *Ennead* V.1(10).1 and *Ennead* III.7(45).11 link the descent of psychic principles with an orientation toward process, change, and movement. Strictly speaking, the hypostasis Soul's gravitation toward temporality (as depicted in *Ennead* III.7(45).11) entails the supervision of a lower order of reality. The *tolma* of individual souls, however, bind them directly to the bodies they govern.

These differences notwithstanding, both passages stress an inclination toward autonomy, in lieu of a participation in a higher contemplative mode of existence; each passage depicts temporal involvement as indicative of a declension in the life of Soul or individual souls; each describes temporal experience as a weakening or dissipation of psychic powers. In this respect, Plotinus's use of *polupragmon*-language also suggests a bold venturesomeness or rash curiosity inherent in *tolma*.[19] We find the suggestion of a fascination with what exceeds one's appropriate range of interests in *polupragmonos* and *tolma* alike.[20]

## THE IMAGERY OF ECCLESIASTICUS

Our analysis of Augustine's reliance upon Plotinus in formulating his interpretation(s) of *curiositas* must address the close relationship between *Enneads* III.7(45).11 and *Ennead* V.1(10).1 in explicating the dynamics of descent. Augustine's reading of Plotinus could have provided grounds for linking the account of Soul's distention in time in *Ennead* III.7(45).11) with the fall account of individual souls in *Ennead* V.1(10).1. Augustine's own account of the curious soul's attraction to temporal images reflects an interweaving of themes drawn from these two Plotinian sources. But it also reflects his creative adaptation of the connotations surrounding the *polupragmatic* and *tolmatic* drives. First and foremost, this adaptation is evident in Augustine's exegesis of a key scriptural text drawn from Ecclesiasticus.

*Ennead* III.7(45).11 provides a key motif that offered Augustine a fertile touchstone in the interests of his own scriptural exegesis. Plotinus's description of the hypostasis Soul as "uncoiling" to a "weaker extension" of its powers finds a scriptural counterpart in the language of Ecclesiasticus 10:9-14 and its depiction of the proud man's "swelling" beyond himself. As early as the *De Quantitate Animae*, in fact, Augustine discussed the soul's intellectual expansion into certain frivolous areas in disparaging terms as a "tumorous" growth. From Augustine's perspective, such an expansion of interests can only yield detrimental consequences, precisely because they dissipate the soul's powers on a multiplicity of cares. In this context, Augustine indicts those studies which focus on the things which are extraordinary rather than useful, and enlarge the soul in an abnormal manner.[21]

The significance of the *De Quantitate Animae's* "tumor" analogue reveals itself in Augustine's use of the "swelling" image of Ecclesiasticus in the *De Genesi contra Manichaeos* (II,9[12]), in discussing the proud soul's aversion from God and its expansive movement toward temporality. He uses this image in conjunction with a second one from Ecclesiasticus, which describes the proud soul as "casting away" or "spewing forth" its insides (*projecit intima sua*), thereby moving to that outer ontological limit where it stands away from God in "affect of mind."[22]

Plotinus provided a framework within which Augustine could discern a deeper metaphysical import in this scriptural commentary on the effects of pride, the "beginning of sin" (Eccl. 10:13).[23] According to Augustine's commentaries in the *De Genesi contra Manichaeos* (II,5[6]) and the *De Musica* (VI,16[53]), pride prompts a "standing apart from God" (*apostatare a Deo*). This estrangement coincides with a distention of the soul's innermost good (i.e., a "spewing forth") that is intensified by the manifold cares (*curae*) and busyness (*negotia*) of earthly existence. The depiction of the proud's soul "standing apart from God" finds a Plotinian referent in *Ennead* V.1(10).1, and its assertion that individual souls "stood away" at a great distance.

The fact that Augustine connects the soul's curiosity and pride so closely with a love of action lends further support to the supposition that he was influenced by *Enneads* III.7(45).11 and V.1(10).1, and that he discerned a conceptual linkage between these treatises. For

Augustine, the curious soul's love of acting on the body or upon the
bodily passions is rooted in the pride which expresses itself as a "general love of action."[24] Once again, Augustine found a viable Plotinian
counterpart for this dynamic interpretation of curiosity and pride
in the image of the Soul's "uncoiling" like a seed. This movement is
prompted by an "unquiet power" or "restlessly active" (*polupragmonos*)
nature that seeks the novelty of movement and change. Similar language, as we have already seen, is found in *Ennead* V.1(10).1, where
Plotinus roots the fall of individual souls in a *tolmatic* urge for self-actualization that finds its terminus in the world of temporal process.

For Augustine's purposes, Ecclesiasticus 10:9-14 offered a firm but
adaptable scriptural base that was highly amenable to a Christian
Neoplatonic reading in two important contexts. First, Augustine integrates the Plotinian understanding of Soul's temporalization with
the imagery of Ecclesiasticus in forging his own definition of time as a
"distention of the soul" (*distentio animi*).

> The innermost bowels of my soul (*intima viscera animae meae*)
> are torn asunder by tumult and change (*tumultuosis varietatitus*
> *dilaniantur*).[25]

Secondly, Augustine defines iniquity itself in terms of a willful movement from God toward lesser reality. This definition represents his
ultimate response to the question with which he struggled for so many
years: "Whence comes evil?".

> Iniquity is perversity of will, twisted away from God, and towards
> lower things, and casting away its innermost good, and swelling be-
> yond itself.[26]

## POLUPRAGMON-LANGUAGE AND CURIOSITAS

If Augustinian *curiositas* displays a diversity and ambiguity of meanings, such a conceptual instability may well tell us something about
its Plotinian inspiration. The very fertility of that term for Augustine
finds an intriguing parallel in *polupragmonos*, the term Plotinus uses to
express the turbulent spirit motivating Soul's downward movement in
*Ennead* III.7(45).11.

In the *De Genesi contra Manichaeos*, Augustine depicts the curious soul's worldly orientation as a desire to penetrate "deep and dark

questions of a temporal and an earthly nature."[27] In this context, he interprets the serpent's punishment to "eat earth" in a manner again suggestive of a Plotinian inspiration.[28] The soul beset with curiosity exhibits the same meddlesome tendency that we associate with *polupragmon*-language in Plotinus. But the serpent's condemnation to "eat earth" also amounts to a sentence to partake in the most inferior realities. This is the lot of the curious soul as well. It becomes as metaphysically impoverished as the images in which it finds its delight.

Once again, *Ennead* III.7(45).11 provides Augustine's template. In Plotinus's rendering, Soul's *polupragmatic* nature prompts a declination from the contemplative life to a time-bound one. When Augustine defines *curiositas* as a "natural enemy of peace," he aligns it squarely with the notion of restlessness inherent in *polupragmon*-language. This language, as we have seen, is not only prominent in Plotinus, but in the broader intellectual tradition in which Plotinus participated.

In Augustine's Plotinian adaptation, curiosity prompts the soul to expand its range of interests, but in a decidedly negative way. By assuming the "heavy burdens of daily cares," it is "spread thin," so to speak.[29] It distention incurs an unremitting cycle of busyness encompassing all the distractions and responsibilities of life in the world.[30] In keeping with this motif, Augustine describes the curious soul as turning to an "external good" when it is "eager to know the personal affairs of others, or whatever is none of its concern."[31]

Augustine's assimilation of Plotinian insights extends to the *De Vera Religione*, the pivotal text which fully unfurls the triad of pride, curiosity, and carnal concupiscence as an organizing principle of his moral theory. Augustine's cataloging of the infirmities proceeding from a "vain and perishable curiosity" (i.e., a "worship of phantasms," a subjection to temporal forms, a proliferation of sensations, and an expansion of corporeal needs) remind us of Plotinus' description of Soul suffering under a "weaker extension" of its powers.[32] Similarly, *Ennead* IV.8(6).4 depicts the fallen individual soul as a "partial thing, isolated, weakened, full of care, intent upon the fragment...buffeted about by a worldful of things." Augustine's *De Ordine* faithfully echoes this characterization of the distended soul's plight.

> The soul spreading out from itself is battered and worn out because the multitude does not permit it to find unity.[33]

For Augustine and Plotinus alike, the love of the world is a wearisome enterprise. In the paradoxical language of the *Confessiones*, it constitutes a "weariness without rest," an absorption in temporal cares that move the soul through "many a troubled twist and turn."[34]

## A PORPHYRIAN INFLUENCE?

Augustine's ongoing treatment of *curiositas* from his earliest writings to the *Confessiones* display some definite parallels with insights (and terminology) drawn from Plotinus' *Enneads*. These parallels lend support to O'Connell's overall hypothesis. As observed above, that hypothesis turns on the dual assumption that (a) the *libri platonicorum* offered Augustine a "distinctively Plotinian" inspiration; and (b) that the *Enneads* provided the matrix within which Augustine articulated his triadic interpretation of iniquity.

But were the writings that Augustine designates as the *"libri platonicorum"* necessarily limited to a Plotinian source alone? Various scholars have raised this question in proposing Plotinus' disciple/editor Porphyry as an alternate Neoplatonic inspiration for Augustine.[35] For his part, O'Connell seriously addressed the evidence in favor of a Porphyrian influence on Augustine's outlook. But he qualifies this acknowledgement by emphasizing the centrality of Plotinus in shaping Augustine's anthropological presuppositions.

> I do not mean to outlaw any possibility that Augustine read *any* Porphyry during these years; nor do I claim that such readings could not have had and did not have any discernible influence alongside and distinguishable from Plotinus' influence. My claim is both more modest and more precise: when it comes to understanding those aspects of Augustine's developing theory of man... (A.D. 386-391), the most rewarding procedure is that of considering the *Enneads* as the dominant Neo-Platonic influence on his thinking, so dominant that any competing influence from Porphyry can safely be ignored.[36]

For purposes of this study, of course, considerations of a possible Porphyrian background of Augustine's thought have a specific applicability to Augustine's interpretations of *curiositas*. In this context, we must consider the contribution of W. Theiler to this debate, as articulated in his work *Porphyrios und Augustin*.

According to Theiler, Augustine's reliance on Neoplatonic philosophy was confined to Porphyry alone. Moreover, Theiler argued that Augustine's moral triad of pride, curiosity, and carnal concupiscence was derived directly from Porphyry as well. He based this claim on Augustine's fully developed use of the triad in the *De Vera Religione* and the second book of the *De libero arbitrio*. For all practical purposes, then, Theiler contended that Augustine merely extracted the triad from a Porphyrian source.[37]

From O'Connell's perspective, Theiler's error (and by extension, the error of the Porphyrian hypothesis) proceeds from his apparent assumption that Augustine's formulation of a triadic understanding of iniquity (including his interpretations of curiosity) was the result of a mere appropriation of ideas from Porphyry, rather than any creative adaptation on Augustine's part.

> Since (Theiler claims) none of these themes is to be found in exactly the same connections or emphasized with equal intensity by Plotinus, Augustine must have found them, neatly packaged for him…in the writings of Porphyry. Augustine is given little if any credit for creative originality; his intellectual project is viewed as transmitting faithfully the riches of Porphyrian philosophy. It never seriously enters Theiler's mind that he might have found elements of such a synthesis…in Plotinus and subtly transposed them in forging is personal synthesis.[38]

The implications of Theiler's thesis for Augustine's understanding of the negative effects of curiosity are profound. For, if Augustine merely appropriated the triad from Porphyry, then his treatment of this notion should be fairly consistent. But as we have observed, Augustinian *curiositas* is anything but stable in its meanings and connotations. Indeed, its very conceptual richness point to a corresponding fertility in any Neoplatonic source on which Augustine would have drawn. In the final analysis, however, a rebuttal of Theiler's Porphyrian hypothesis cannot rest upon the deficiencies of his position alone. It must also be grounded upon a recognition of convincing conceptual and terminological parallels between Augustine and Plotinus.

## THE CASE FOR PLOTINUS

As we have observed, Augustine's early writings (up to and including the *Confessiones*) exhibit a skillful grafting of Plotinian insights onto scriptural themes and motifs. Plotinus closely linked his discussion of the hypothesis Soul's temporalization with the more particularized fall of individual souls which resulted in their embodiment. In this connection, *Enneads* III.7(45).11 and V.1(10).1 provide especially illuminating sources for Augustine's purposes. In both passages, Plotinus attributes the descending movement of psychic principles to an attraction to what is lower in the hierarchy of reality, or more precisely, with what is no more than a semblance of true reality. In Augustinian terms, this motif translated into an emphasis on the curious soul's absorption in vain, transitory images. Moreover, Augustine's exegesis of Ecclesiasticus 10:9-14 draws heavily on Plotinus' depiction of Soul's "uncoiling" to a "weaker extension" of its authentic Self. Such language provided an ideal idiom for describing the outward "swelling" prompted by pride, the beginning of all sin.

For Augustine, such a negative expansiveness (likened to a tumorous growth) encompasses the soul's unrestricted drive to know those things exceeding the parameters of virtue and usefulness. Accordingly, the proud soul which "swells beyond itself" squanders its innermost good on a plethora of dissipating cares and concerns. This is why an adequate grasp of the deeper metaphysical implications of *curiositas* in Augustine requires an appreciation of its affinities with pride (*superbia*). As we have consistently seen, Augustine treats *curiositas* as both an outgrowth of *superbia* (the primal sin in his triad of vices) and its natural accompaniment. While this linkage is most explicit in the sixth book of the *De Musica*, it is evident in Augustine's earlier writings as well.

Augustine's pairing of the sins of pride and curiosity finds an intriguing Plotinian precedent in the parallelism between *tolma* (the "original sin," so to speak, of individual souls) and the "restlessly active" (*polupragmonos*) nature instrumental in Soul's temporalization. This parallelism offers a convincing rationale for Augustine's assumption that temporal involvement amounts to a fall from a higher contemplative mode of being to one bound up with the change and fragmentation inherent in temporality. If pride precipitates a "standing apart" from God, curiosity only intensifies this "uncoiling" or "unraveling" of souls' powers. Augustine's notion of the soul's distention thus points to an assimilation of insights drawn from Ecclesiasticus and Plotinus alike.

In the final analysis, Plotinus' notion of Soul's *polupragmatic* character provides an effective heuristic device for penetrating the multi-dimensional character of *curiositas* in Augustine. The Plotinian tensions between contemplation and action, eternity and time, stability and rest carry over into Augustine's understanding of *curiositas* as an "enemy of peace," an inner turbulence that preoccupies the soul with worldly entanglements.

But if Augustine's understanding of human beings as "fallen souls" points to an inspiration derived from the *Enneads*, his indebtedness to Plotinus extends to other anthropological themes as well. While Augustine depicts the soul as "fallen," he never considers it entirely so. In the present life, the soul occupies a rather tenuous "mid-rank" which places it between God and corporeal natures in the hierarchy of created realities.[39] Augustine draws here upon Plotinus's depiction of the soul as occupying a mid-rank between the higher intelligible world and the material world of sense experience.[40]

In Plotinian terms, the soul situated in the middle of things has the capacity to direct its gaze toward what is higher in the universe of being or toward what is lower and unworthy of its abiding attention. In Augustine's Christianized version of this notion, the human will constitutes an "intermediate good," because it can adhere to the immutable Good common to all (i.e., God, the soul's *Summum Bonum*) or pursue finite mutable goods.[41] As defined by Augustine, *curiositas* is one of the prime motives in the soul's tendance toward the transitory things of this world. More specifically, *curiositas* constitutes that misuse of the will which is directed toward external goods, "when it is eager to know the personal affairs of others or whatever is none of its own business."[42]

In my estimation, then, we find additional grounds for recognizing a Plotinian dependence in Augustine's discussions of *curiositas* in his conception of the soul's mid-rank, his depiction of the human will as an intermediate good, and his penetrating analysis of the instability inherent in finite being.

As one of the major sources of *iniquitas*, *curiositas* assumes an important contributory role in the evil use of the will. But wherein does its evil lie? By its very nature, *curiositas* entails an epistemological significance in distorting the soul's vision of true reality. By arousing the soul's interest in things of a transitory, trivial, or contemptible nature, the sin of *curiositas* diverts its focus upon what is eternal, abiding, and conducive to the life of virtue.

From this standpoint, the depiction of the soul as "fallen" only tells us part of the story, so to speak, of Augustine's interpretations of *curiositas*. Our very creatureliness (and accompanying finitude) renders us vulnerable to the pull of the body, the senses, and our curious intellectual attraction to earthly things. Accordingly, an adequate grasp of the moral, epistemological, and metaphysical import of *curiositas* in Augustine's writings presupposes a attunement to his hierarchical conception of reality in which everything finds its appropriate place and role for the goodness of the whole. For humans, good order presupposes a governance by reason and the supervision of what is less excellent in the hierarchy of creation by what is more excellent. By its very nature, *curiositas* contributes to a disordering of priorities, whereby the soul confines its natural pursuit of true being to a milieu that is no more than a semblance of the really and truly real.

## ASSESSMENT OF PART II

The distinctiveness of curiosity as a member of Augustine's triad of vices is evident when we consider its relation to the other triadic members. In this connection, some questions must be addressed pertinent to the link between the triad, iniquity, and the notion of the soul's fall. In Augustine's adaptation of the Plotinian account of the soul's descent, pride (*superbia*) prompts the "standing apart from God" whereby the soul seeks self-mastery, opting for its own good. Pride constitutes the most fundamental expression of that evil will that posits lesser goods as objects of its devotion or love. For this reason, pride underlies the motivation for any defective use of the will whatsoever.

In Augustine's scheme of reality, pride assumes a significant structural role; this sin precipitates the moral and metaphysical disordering which undermines the soul's proper mid-rank between God and corporeal natures. Morally, it diverts the soul from a single-minded focus on God as the ultimate object of its love. Metaphysically, this shift in allegiance results in the soul's gravitation toward those very things which it should rightfully govern and use in pursuit of its final end of beatitude. But in more concrete terms, such moral and metaphysical disordering is tantamount to a disordering of priorities that violates what Augustine defines as the "rule of perfect religion" (i.e., to serve the creature rather than the Creator). In this way, finite things assume a preeminence in the soul's esteem over God, the eternal and immutable Good which can never be lost.

But in what sense can pride be designated as the "root" of Augustine's moral triad of primal vices? This question must be considered in conjunction with two others. First, if the soul's fallenness ultimately proceeds from pride (the "beginning of all sin," in scriptural terms), what is its relationship to the sins of curiosity (*curiositas*) and carnal concupiscence (*concupiscentia carnis*)? Secondly, are curiosity and carnal concupiscence effects or outgrowths of pride, or do they emerge independently, as alternate expressions of lust or unregulated desire? The thrust of Augustine's analysis casts pride in the role of the causal principle of curiosity and carnal concupiscence alike. In its absence, the soul would never have succumbed to those lusts of the "eyes" and "flesh," respectively.

Even if pride is the foundational sin, however, curiosity and carnal concupiscence are intimately bound up with the human alienation from God. While Augustine traces *iniquitas* principally to pride, curiosity and carnal concupiscence aid and abet this defective movement. From this perspective, curiosity can be characterized as something of the crucial linchpin of Augustine's moral triad of vices, incorporating elements of both pride and carnal concupiscence in its operation. On the one hand, curiosity exhibits a kinship with pride; like that root fault, it encompasses a vain pretense to knowledge of things beyond our ken (that is, those things beyond our grasp or matters which do not properly concern us). This relationship is particularly evident in Augustine's early discussions of the motives of the soul's fall and his characterizations of both pride and curiosity as instrumental in its focus on a particular sphere of interests, in lieu of a commitment to the Good common to all. Still, the essence of pride for Augustine lies in willfulness (suggestive of the dynamics of *tolma* in Plotinus' account of the descent of being from the One). Curiosity, however, assumes a more specific epistemological import, as that vice which incites the soul toward the acquisition of experiential knowledge.

For Augustine, the scope of curiosity is extremely wide-ranging, covering the entire field of temporal experience. Nothing is immune to the potential attraction of the curious disposition, from the sublime to the horrible, and everything lying between these extremes of cognitive interest. In this regard, curiosity also displays an overlapping of meanings with carnal concupiscence. Both sins entail a desire for finite goods; each species of lust requires the body and sense experience for its expression. But a crucial difference is also apparent. Curiosity prompts the mind (the highest part of the soul) toward the acquisition of knowledge through the instrumentality of the senses. Carnal concupiscence, however, has a more explicit link with the gratification of the senses and the desires of the flesh in general.

The very blurring of the distinction between the curious and the carnal dispositions may well account for the marked instability which *curiositas* assumes in Augustine's writings. But that instability is reflected in our own concrete experience as well. Things which we find intellectually interesting also yield pleasure in their very pursuit. This is particularly the case in visual experience. Vision itself can be a source of sensual delight; we take physical pleasure in what is seen and in the very act of seeing. But in broader terms, vision is paradigmatic of the mind's cognitive grasp of the temporal world. Augustine's identification of the sin of *curiositas* with the Johannine "lust of the eyes" (*concupiscentia oculorum*) underscores the connection between the desire to "take a look at" (i.e., to know about something) and the soul's increasing immersion in temporal involvements. For this reason, *curiositas* thereby "temporalizes" the soul. By its very nature, it is antithetical to the mind's contemplative focus upon immutable truths.

In Part III of this study, we consider Augustine's analysis of the dynamics and effects of the sin of *curiositas* in the crucible of human existence, and more specifically, in the context of Christian life. This analysis emerges against the background of his broader understanding of the order of creation. The order of creation as a whole establishes the standard for a moral order in which what is more perfect is ordained to govern and supervise what is less perfect in the hierarchy of finite being. On a human level, this arrangement presupposes a relationship of subordination and contingency, whereby the body depends upon reason, and reason ultimately depends upon God.

While Part III draws upon a range of writings, its principal focus lies in two major works that Augustine completed rather late in his career: the *De Trinitate* (Chapter 7) and the *De Civitate Dei* (Chapter 8). By the time he wrote them, Augustine had seriously modified his theory of the soul's origin in relation to the body. In so doing, he drastically revised his initial attitude toward Neoplatonism in the interests of his anthropological and psychological theories.

But this distancing from aspects of Plotinus's account of the soul's descent by no means diminished Augustine's allegiance to language and imagery drawn from the *Enneads* in coming to terms with the human defection from the Divine Goodness. This Neoplatonic dimension is crucial in Augustine's treatment of *curiositas* as a key component of the soul's fall. In point of fact, Augustine's triadic analysis of sin is closely aligned with his classic interpretation of iniquity as an aversion from God (the highest Good) toward lower, mutable goods. This definition reveals a careful grafting of Plotinian imagery and motifs onto scriptural teaching, or alternatively, an interpretation of Neoplatonic ideas within a Judeo-Christian framework.

But as Augustine internalized and creatively adapted a Plotinian outlook in the interests of his moral theory, epistemology, and metaphysics, he was also applying these philosophical insights to his interpretations of the triadic members of pride, curiosity, and carnal concupiscence. This accounts for his incorporation of such dichotomies as common/proper, whole/part, and immutable/mutable into his discussions of the sources of inquity. In the final analysis, however, Augustine's own life experience proved as important as Scripture and Neoplatonism in coming to terms with the origins of moral evil.

While Augustine's *Confessiones* certainly treat the triadic components on an individual basis (as exemplified in his examination of conscience in *Confessiones* X), we are also struck by their interplay in his spiritual journey. This interplay (i.e., of pride and curiosity, of curiosity and carnal concupiscence) must be addressed if we are to make sense of the diverse meanings and connotations of *curiositas* in the Augustinian *corpus* as a whole. Indeed, Augustine continually highlights the extent to which the curious "concupiscence of the eyes" is an outgrowth or accompaniment of the proud "ambition of the world". Likewise, he constantly affirms the linkage between the sin of curiosity and that broader "concupiscence of the flesh" which so decisively shapes the soul's range of appetites and affectivities.

As we will see, Augustine's analysis of the dynamics of *curiositas* follows a dual trajectory. On one level, he treats this sin in the context of human cognition and the mind's orientation toward images of a temporal and corporeal nature. In this respect, the blameworthiness of *curiositas* can be judged as a matter of the degree of the soul's immersion in the objects of its cognitive desire. But on this level, it is part and parcel of that lower function of the mind which places us in touch with the outer world and the needs of the body. On another level, Augustine depicts *curiositas* as instrumental in the soul's fall, and as symptomatic of its fallenness. Accordingly, the sin of *curiositas* figures prominently in Augustine's wholesale critique of pagan culture and its underlying value system. For Augustine, however, pagans by no means have a monopoly on this particular vice. Christians are likewise susceptible to the "lust of the eyes," the outgrowth of that fallenness which permeates the human condition.

### NOTES TO CHAPTER 6

1. For bibliographies of Robert J. O'Connell's writings, see Roland J. Teske, S.J., Ronnie J. Rombs, and Joseph T. Lienhard, S.J., "In Memory of Robert John O'Connell, S.J. 1925-1999. Tribute and Bibliography," *Augustinian Studies* 31:1 (2000): 49-57 (compiled by Rombs and Lienhard); and Ronnie J. Rombs, *Saint Augustine and the Fall of the Soul. Beyond O'Connell and His Critics* (Washington, D.C.: The Catholic University of America Press, 2006), 218-220.

2. Robert J. O'Connell, S.J., "*Confessions*, VII,ix,13-xxi,27," *Revue Études Augustiniennes* 19(1973): 99. A number of O'Connell's publications offer persuasive evidence for establishing the plausibility of this hypothesis: "*Ennead* VI,4-5 in the Work of St. Augustine," *Revue des Études Augustiniennes*(1963): 1-39; "The Plotinian Fall of the Soul in St. Augustine," *Traditio* 19(1963): 1-35; "The *Enneads* and St. Augustine's Image of Happiness," *Vigiliae Christianae* 17(1963): 129-164; "The Riddle of St. Augustine's *Confessions*: A Plotinian Key," *International Philosophical Quarterly* 4(1964): 327-372; *St. Augustine's Early Theory of Man, A.D., 386-391* (Cambridge, Mass.: The Belknap Press of Harvard University Press, 1968); "Pre-Existence in the Early Augustine," *Revue des Études Augustiniennes* 26(1980): 176-188; "Faith, Reason, and Ascent to Vision in St. Augustine," *Augustinian Studies* 11(1980). For criticisms of O'Connell's interpretation, see: Goulven Madec, A Note in *Revue des Études Augustiniennes* 11(1965): 372-375; "Une lecture de *Confessions* VII,ix,13-xxi,27," *Revue des Études Augustiniennes* 16(1970):79-137; Olivier DuRoy, *L'Intelligence de la Foi en la Trinité selon Saint Augustin*

(Paris, 1966); G.J.P. O'Daly, "Did St. Augustine Ever Believe in the Soul's Pre-Existence?," *Augustinian Studies* 5(1974): 227-235.

3. Robert J. O'Connell, S.J., *St. Augustine's Early Theory of Man, A.D. 386-391*, 4: "My exact contention here is that the *Enneads* provided the early Augustine with a comprehensive philosophic matrix, an intellectual frame. So promising did Plotinianism appear to him that it inspired a 'confidence' that all he deemed valid in the other influences shaping his mind could find a natural place within that matrix."

4. In this chapter, I draw upon and refine my own previous tests of this hypothesis, beginning with my dissertation: "Plotinian *Tolma* and the Fall of the Soul in the Early Philosophy of St. Augustine" (Fordham University, 1987); "St. Augustine's Treatment of *Superbia* and its Plotinian Heritage," *Augustinian Studies* XVIII(1987): 66-79; "*Curiositas* in the Early Philosophical Writings of Saint Augustine," *Augustinian Studies* XIX(1988): 111-119; "St. Augustine's Triadic Interpretation of Iniquity in the *Confessiones*," in *Collectanea Augustiniana* I (*Augustine, Second Founder of Faith*, ed. Joseph C. Schnaubelt, O.S.A. and Frederick Van Fleteren (New York: Peter Lang, 1989), 159-174; "'*Pondus meum amor meus*': The Significance of the 'Weight' Metaphor in St. Augustine's Early Philosophical Writings," *Augustinian Studies* XXI(1990): 163-176.

5. For O'Connell's explorations of this theme, see especially his *St. Augustine's Early Theory of Man, A.D., 386-391*; *St. Augustine's Confessions. The Odyssey of Soul* (Cambridge, Mass.: The Belknap Press of Harvard University Press, 1969), 135-144; *Art and the Christian Intelligence in St. Augustine* (Cambridge, Mass.: Harvard University Press, 1978), 70-83.

6. For an excellent survey and critical assessment of O'Connell's extended project, see Rombs' *Saint Augustine and the Fall of the Soul. Beyond O'Connell and His Critics*.

7. Robert J. O'Connell, S.J., "Augustinism: Locating the Center," in *Presbyter Factus Sum, Collectanea Augustiniana*, ed. Joseph T. Lienhard, S.J., Earl C. Muller, S.J., and Roland J. Teske, S.J. (New York: Peter Lang, 1993), 210.

8. According to O'Connell (*The Origin of the Soul in St. Augustine's Later Works* [New York: Fordham University Press, 1987], 16), the mature Augustine developed "a view of human beings as contemplative souls, plunged into the misery to which the painful 'mortality' of our present bodies clearly attests. For we must once have lived a 'common' life, not only 'in' Adam, but a life which makes us identical with Adam. We sinned in his sinning; his sin was truly ours..."

9. I make this distinction in response to a key aspect of the critical assessment of Robert O'Connell's extended project by Rombs (*St. Augustine and the Fall of the Soul. Beyond O'Connell and His Critics*), who uses the term "ontological" in characterizing the fallen soul thesis, and thereby, seems to assume that any reference to the fall motif in Augustine must presuppose the notions of the soul's descent into the corporeal and its preexistence

in Plotinian terms. He opts instead for an interpretation of the soul's fall in terms of a "psychology of sin" in addressing the position of the later Augustine. According to Rombs (p. 110), the later Augustine "limits his conception of the fall of the soul to the interior or psychological process of the soul when it sins…a psychology of sin without any causal relation to the coming-to-be of the world or to individual existence." Rombs thus links the "ontological/cosmogonic" dimension with the Plotinian mechanism of the soul's fall. By implication, then, its continuing presence in Augustine would amount to his tacit endorsement of the notion of the soul's fall in explicit Plotinian terms. My difficulty with this interpretation lies in the fact that the psychological dimension that Rombs isolates indeed reflects marked ontological and cosmogonic implications (e.g., a drastic disordering of our mid-rank status between God and corporeal natures, as revealed in an impairment of our capacity to love in a rightly ordered way). This is why I opt for the term "metaphysical": in my estimation, this term offers something of a middle ground between "ontological" and "psychological," permitting us to recognize the effects of the soul's fall on our way of being, without necessarily emphasizing the notion of a literal fall into the body conveyed by the term "ontological."

10. See O'Connell, *Art and the Christian Intelligence in St. Augustine*, 67-83. In this work (72), O'Connell succinctly stated his position in these terms: "…as analysis of Book Six will show, the atmosphere, central intuition, and method are all drawn principally from Plotinus' treatise, *Ennead* III,7… and the origin of… all man's symbolic activity is to be found…in the… soul's 'fallen' state." For my own discussions of this aspect of O'Connell's hypothesis, see my "*Curiositas* in the Early Philosophical Writings of Saint Augustine"; "St. Augustine's Triadic Interpretation of Iniquity in the *Confessiones*"; "Curiosity," in *Saint Augustine Through the Ages: An Encyclopedia* (Grand Rapids, Michigan: William B. Eerdmans, 1999), 259b-261a.

11. *Ennead* III.7(45).11, 3-5.

12. *Ennead* III.7(45).11, 3-5.

13. *Ennead* III.7(45).11, 14.

14. *Ennead* III.7(45).11, 19.

15. *Ennead* III.7(45).11, 23-27.

16. *Ennead* III.7(45).11, 27-34.

17. *Ennead* III.7(45).11, 36-39.

18. *Ennead* III.7(45).11, 42-45.

19. For an extended study of the role of *tolma* in Plotinus's *Enneads*, see my *Plotinian Tolma and the Descent of Being. An Exposition and Analysis* (New York: Peter Lang, 1993).

20. Cf., *Ennead* I.8(51).9. As we saw in Chapter 3, this notion of an indiscreet curiosity is also prominent in Philo Judaeus (*De Somniis* I,x,54), where it assumes the form of a daring inquisitiveness to determine what

is indeterminate. We likewise encounter it in the Hermeticist tradition, which links *tolma* with *periergia*-language in designating a prying curiosity into divine matters.

21. *De Quantitate Animae* 19(33).

22. *De Musica* VI,13(40).

23. I explore the Plotinian heritage of *superbia* in the early Augustine (with a specific focus upon the parallels between Plotinian *tolma* and *superbia* as the root of Augustine's moral triad) in "St. Augustine's treatment of *superbia* and its Plotinian Affinities," *Augustinian Studies* XVIII(1987): 66-79.

24. *De Musica* VI,13(39); VI,13(40).

25. *Confessiones* XI,29(39).

26. *Confessiones* VII,16(22).

27. *De Genesi contra Manichaeos* II,18(27).

28. *De Genesi contra Manichaeos* II,18(27).

29. *Contra Academicos* II,2(3).

30. *De Musica* VI,14(48).

31. *De libero arbitrio* II,19(53).

32. *De Vera Religione* 52(101); 38(69); 21(41).

33. *De Ordine* I,2(3).

34. *Confessiones* II,2(2); VI,6(9).

35. The following seminal studies argue in favor of a Porphyrian inspiration in Augustine: W. Theiler, *Porphyrios und Augustin* (Halle/Saale: Max Neimayer Verlag, 1933); J.J. O'Meara, *Porphyry's Philosophy from Oracles in Augustine* (Paris, 1959); F.E. Van Fleteren, "Authority and Reason, Faith and Understanding in the Thought of St. Augustine," *Augustinian Studies* 4 (1973): 33-72.

36. Robert J. O'Connell, S.J., *St. Augustine's Early Theory of Man, A.D., 386-391*, 25.

37. W. Theiler, *Porphyrios und Augustin*, 37: "Eine Triade von Begierden wird wiederholt genannt; di Namen lauten etwa 70 *libido-superbia-curiositas* und werden in den Bibelvers 1 Jn 2:16 hineingelegt *concupscentia carnis est et concupiscentia oculorum* (schon 40 darauf angesspielt et *ambitio saeculi*); warum Augustin die Triade nicht in der Reihenfolge des Bibelverses gibt, sondern so wie eben aufgezahlt (a b c) oder in der Wiederholung nach bekanntem antiken Gebrauch in Umkehrung (c b a) wird sich später erklären. Behandelt wird 72-83 das erste Glied der körperlichen Genusssucht, 84-93 das zweite Glied der Herrschsucht, 94-100 die falsche Sucht nach Erkenntnis. Und dann in wirbelndem Tanze begegnet die Dreiheit immer wieder bis zum Schlussprotreptikos 108, wo vom Nichstein noch einmal ein Aufstieg folgt bis hinauf zur Trinität, mit deren überschwenglichen Prädikation das Buch schliesst. Wir behaupten nun, dass auch diese Begierdentriade, deren gemeinsames Kennzeichen die Abkehr, ἀποστροφή, vom innern wahren vollen Sein ist, aus Porphyrios ubernommen ist—trotz des Bibelspruches, der wie Sap 11, 21, für die

Reihe οὐσία-εἶδος-τάξις nachträglich Augustin die begluckende Bezeugung der Gleichförmigkeit von *ratio* und *auctoritas* liefert (oben S. 34). Dass Porphyrios die einzelnen Glieder für sich immer wieder verwendet hat, berdarf kaum der Darlengung." Cf., *Porphyrios und Augustin*, 39: "Doch um auf Ausgangspunkt zuruckzukommen, genügt das Bisherige noch nicht, die Eigentümlichkeit gerade der triadischen Anordnung, für die ein Bibelzeugnis gennant worden ist, auf Porphyrios zurückzufuhren. Da is der Schritt zur Beobachtung wichtig, dass schon vor de v. rel. in arb. 2,53 die Triade ohne Bibelverse vorkommt." Theiler extends this claim to the triadic schematization of the *Confessiones* as well (*Porphyrios und Augustin*, 40): "Wir können nun zufügen, dass der Abstiegsweg von v. rel. mit dem Verweilen auf der Begierdentriade dem Rest des Konfessionenbuches entspricht. Etwas zugespitzt können wir es so bezeichnen: conf. 10 ist der Form der Beweisfuhrung nach die Neuauflage von v. rel. zweite Hälfte (von 52 an)."

38. Robert J. O'Connell, S.J., *St. Augustine's Early Theory of Man, A.D., 386-391*, 22. In this vein, O'Connell also critiques Theiler's focus on the *De Vera Religione* and the *De libero arbitrio* (II) as his principal referents in dealing with Augustine's use of *curiositas* in the context of his triad (*St. Augustine's Early Theory of Man, A.D., 386-391*, 174-175): "Having supposed that this final category was taken bodily from Porphyry, where it was presumably directed against the imagination and its works, Theiler must suppose a constancy in Augustine's use of it, which precludes the tentative work of adaptation that in point of fact characterizes the initial introduction of the category into his writings. Theiler's mistake…is partly accounted for by the fact that he starts his investigation of Augustine with the relatively systematized *De Vera Religione*, then somewhat blandly assures his readers that the earlier works present *ein ähnliches Bild* (*Porphryios*, p. 57). Partly, too his confidence reposes on the use of the triad in the second book of the *De Libero Arbitrio*, which he mistakenly assumes is prior to the *De Genesi Contra Manichaeos*, when it is…subsequent to it…"

39. *De Genesi contra Manichaeos* II,9(12).

40. *Ennead* V.3(49).3.

41. *De libero arbitrio* II,19(53).

42. *De libero arbitrio* II,19(53).

# PART III

# *CURIOSITAS* AND
# THE EARTHLY CITY

# CHAPTER 7

# IN *IMAGO DEI*

St. Augustine's *De Trinitate* places his discussions of the sin of *curiositas* on a bold new trajectory. At first glance, this might appear somewhat surprising. Why would a speculative treatise on the triune nature of God provide a basis for sounding out the depths of cognitive desire in the restless mind? Such a topic, however, is wholly consistent with the general thrust of this great speculative enterprise. Indeed, the *De Trinitate* is not about God alone. As Rowan Williams observes, "*De Trinitate* is more than simply a meditation on a particular doctrine; it is an integral theological anthropology…in which diverse doctrinal themes are woven together in an account of how human acting, desiring, and thinking come to participate in the action of God."[1]

In point of fact, Augustine's extended discourse on God's triunity is intimately bound up with his analysis of humans as images of God. So, if the *De Trinitate* makes a substantive contribution to Augustine's theory of the curious disposition, it does so in this anthropological context. More specifically, it delineates the psychological significance of curiosity in exploring the dynamics of human thought and the very parameters of our way of knowing.

But what does it mean to say that humans are "images" of God, or that we are created in God's own image? In Augustinian terms, such imaging must run to our very nature. This prompts an additional question. What, for Augustine, constitutes human nature? In keeping with his soul-centered anthropology, the image of God can only reside in the human mind, the highest part of the soul, and in broader terms, the highest part of our humanness. God's image is thus disclosed in that activity of the mind which directs it toward immaterial reality. But in being so directed, it not only comes to discern the nature of

God, but itself as well. From this standpoint, any attempt to know God on our part requires a grasp of our mind as an immaterial image of our Creator.[2]

Conversely, Augustine denies that the Divine image in us can be discovered through the agency of the body or through the sense experience which places us in touch with the external world. But the sheer inadequacy of bodily existence for this purpose does not reflect an epistemological limitation alone. More decisively, it says something about our very metaphysical constitution as embodied souls. In the final analysis, Augustine defines human nature in terms of the soul's immateriality. Accordingly, we discern the Divine reality (and the Divine image we bear) on the basis of the fundamental affinity between our souls (and cognitive life) and what is really and truly real. The soul grasps what is like unto it, despite its createdness. This is not to say, of course, that the finite mind can know God directly. Rather, it must resort to the images and analogues drawn from created things in discerning the Divine nature and its own status as image of God.

While Augustine upholds the soul's substantial unity, he diversifies its cognitive activities by means of a distinction between mind's higher and lower functions. The higher, sapiential function of mind allows for the contemplation of the eternal reasons of things, and ultimately, their Divine Ground. In this way, it also apprehends itself as an image of God. The lower, sciential function of mind entails the supervision of the body in its orientation to the outer world of temporal process and mutable corporeal images. On the one hand, mind's lower focus is part and parcel of the soul's functional structure. From this standpoint, it is good for the soul to oversee our bodily existence. On the other hand, however, the mind's involvement with external interests presents a moral pitfall.

For Augustine (as for all thinkers who endorse a Platonic or Neoplatonic perspective), an inordinate preoccupation with temporal and corporeal images can only obscure the mind's attunement to its own immateriality. In this respect, Augustine's dichotomies between "inner" and "outer," "within" and "without," or "higher" and "lower" are fully operative in his discussion of the soul's immersion in materialistic concerns. Such an absorption in an alien environment (that is, alien to the soul's immaterial nature) becomes morally culpable when it entails what Edmund Hill describes as "a disruption of the divinely appointed order by which man is under the dominion of God and exercises dominion of the world."[3] This disordering of the soul's commitments amounts to sin, the willful rejection of God's authority in favor of a voluntary submission to lesser things.

The *De Trinitate* presents its most probing chronicle of mind's *excursus* and its impact on the life of soul in Books X and XII. These books provide us with a veritable mother lode of information regarding the sin of *curiositas* as the blameworthy expression of the mind's sciential function. Each of these books, in fact, offers a rich conceptual vein of insights that illuminate the role of the curious disposition in the mind's flawed search for true knowledge. In Book X, Augustine describes how mind's entanglement with bodily existence results in a "self-forgetting" that encompasses a loss of a sense of its true nature, and by implication, its exalted status as image of God. An exclusive reliance on temporal and corporeal images thus diminishes its capacity to appreciate the difference between immaterial and material reality, between God and things finite.

In Book XII, Augustine inserts this tension between the mind's contemplative/sapiential function and its active/sciential function into the fall account of Genesis. In the personages of Adam and Eve, he finds historical representatives of these diverse (and potentially conflicting) dimensions of the soul's cognitive powers. By grounding the soul's functionality in a narrative on the plight of everyman, Augustine infuses his understanding of iniquity with a profound psychological significance. Sin in this primal sense constitutes a fall from mind's contemplation of eternal truths through a proud lust for domination, a carnal lust for sensual pleasure, or a curious lust for images and phantasms.[4]

## MEMORY, INTELLIGENCE, AND WILL (*DE TRINITATE* X)

*De Trinitate* X builds upon one of Augustine's key images of the Trinity in the human mind: memory (*memoria sui*), intelligence (*intelligentia*), and will (*voluntas*).

In this connection, memory is not to be construed as a recollection of things past, but in terms of the mind's self-knowledge or self-recognition. Herein lies a difficulty rooted in the mind's natural reliance upon images for the contents of its knowledge. What insures that its

understanding of self is authentic, and to what extent is this comprehension clouded by the deceptive input of sense experience? This
problem is not one confined to self-understanding alone. Our very
ability to know anything of the Divine nature requires us to transcend
the epistemological limitations of sense data, and thereby, to bridge
the gap between finite and infinite reality. In Augustinian terms,
self-knowledge (and the process of interiorization it entails) opens the
way to knowledge of God. Accordingly, theological anthropology is
intertwined with speculative theology on its most foundational level.

If the mind is able to recognize itself as God's image, it can only do
so in light of its contemplative focus on eternal truths.[5] Conversely, its
immersion in the images of lesser things (that is, those images grounded in temporality and derived from corporeal realities) severely undermines the perspicacity of its cognitive vision. In this regard, Augustine
posits an extremely close relationship between knowing and loving,
the expressions of mind and heart, respectively. Interestingly, he imparts a distinct epistemological connotation to love that sets it apart
from a frivolous curiosity into matters that are morally questionable
(at least from an Augustinian perspective).[6] More precisely, Augustine
contrasts the love of study (*amor studium*) with an inquisitive appetite
(*appetitus inveniendi*). While the former encompasses a sound devotion to learning that ultimately leads the mind to the contemplation of
God and eternal truths, the latter is the hallmark of mind's lower function when given free, unregulated rein over our range of affections.
This tension between studiousness and inquisitiveness must be considered on the basis of Augustine's ongoing exploration of cognition
in the *De Trinitate*, specifically as he defines the relationship between
knowledge and love.

Book IX already considered how knowledge engenders self-knowledge, and how knowing encompasses both knower and what is known.
This discussion proposed a more fundamental trinitarian image that
is propaedeutic to what we encounter in Book X: mind (*mens*), knowledge (*notitia*), and love (*amor*). In Book IX, Augustine recognizes a
substantive difference between self-knowledge and self-love. When
the mind knows itself, the mind is author of its knowing, as knower and known.[7] But while self-knowledge can be begotten by oneself,
self-love does not allow for such self-generation, even when the mind
loves itself. In coming to terms with this dilemma, Augustine embarks
upon an extended deliberation about the dynamics of knowledge.

At the outset, Augustine affirms the relationship between knowing as a revelatory act and knowing as a begetting or generation. These features of the cognitive process find their motive force in the simple desire or appetitiveness for knowledge.

> Knowledge is a kind of finding out what is said to be brought forth or brought to light…often preceded by a certain inquisitiveness that is going to rest in that end. Inquisitiveness is an appetite for finding out, which amounts to the same thing as 'bringing to light.' But things that are brought to light are…brought forth, which makes them similar to offspring.[8]

Here, the spirit of inquiry itself promotes that "coming to birth" which constitutes knowledge. Objectively speaking, things clearly exist without our knowing them or inquiring about them. For Augustine, however, the very passage through inquiry is instrumental in yielding knowledge, like something of an offspring in the mind of the knower.

> Now this appetite shown in inquiry proceeds from the inquirer, and it is left somewhat hanging in the air and does not rest assuaged in the end it is stretching out to, until what is being looked for has been found and is coupled with the inquirer.[9]

On the one hand, Augustine acknowledges a fundamental difference between the inquisitive appetite and the mind's natural love for the object of its knowledge. But by the same token, he recognizes a certain kinship between these diverse manifestations of will in the very desire to know. In this respect, Augustine treats inquisitiveness (that is, the desire to "find out") and the desire to know as correlative. More precisely, such an inquisitiveness is conducive to studiousness, that passionate desire to know encompassing the acquisition of sound learning in general.

> Parturition by the mind is preceded by a kind of appetite which prompts us to inquire and find out about what we want to know, and as a result knowledge itself is brought forth as offspring. The same appetite with which one longs open mouthed to know a thing becomes love of the thing known when it holds and embraces… knowledge, and joins it to its begetter.[10]

By Book X, then, Augustine had formulated an image of the Trinity comprising (a) the mind and its knowing; (b) its offspring, expressed by a word about itself; and (c) the mind's love for what it knows.[11] In this respect, Augustine draws a parallel between the mind's self-expression in a word and God the Father's begetting of the Son, the eternal Word. Just as the Father and the Son are united in love, the mind is conjoined with itself when it loves the object of its own knowing. In *De Trinitate* X, love assumes a central focus in Augustine's investigation of the scope of cognitive appetite. This investigation requires a contrast between that praiseworthy desire to know (found in studious people) with those counterfeit forays into the search for knowledge prompted by *curiositas*. Accordingly, Augustine's point of departure amounts to a critical question: what kind of love do the studious possess?[12]

By its very nature, the studious disposition represents a transitional state, whereby the mind desires a knowledge that it does not yet enjoy. Augustine readily discerns the paradox inherent in this desire. Indeed, studious individuals cannot completely lack the knowledge to which they aspire. If so, they could not love what they seek to grasp, wanting to know what they do not know.[13] Herein lies the difference between those who are studious and those who are merely curious. In Augustine's assessment, curious people exhibit a marked indeterminism in their search for knowledge, "carried away by the mere love of knowing unknown things for no known reason."[14] Still, the curious-minded reject the unknown as much as the studious-minded, since the very appetite for knowledge disdains its privation. In this sense, the love of knowing fosters a hatred of the unknown, and the desire for knowledge stands opposed to its lack, "since he would like nothing to be unknown and everything known."[15]

This position is wholly consistent with the thrust of Augustine's essentialist metaphysics and its assumption that mind and will are attuned to the really and truly real. In this instance, however, he simply wishes to stress that we cannot love the unknown in its own right.[16] But the question of the mind's desire to know itself introduces new challenges. For this reason, Augustine confronts a particularly acute probem: how can the mind (which is immediately present to itself) be its own object of knowledge?[17] Augustine discerns a serious obstacle to such self-reflection that is rooted in a tendency toward a forgetfulness of one's own mind. This anesthetizing to the reality of our innermost self proceeds from an excessive care for those material things which become impressed upon our memory and imagination.[18]

From Augustine's standpoint, images (and their accompanying phantasms) distract us to such an extent that we "lose ourselves" in the vain objects of our attention. In this way, the mind's inborn passion for self-knowledge is only frustrated. But if self-knowledge is stifled, so is self-love. "What," Augustine asks, "is it loving…since it does not yet know itself and no one can love what he does not know?"[19] In keeping with his commitment to the spirit of Hellenic rationalism, Augustine could readily discern in the Delphic injunction "Know thyself!" a command which carries the force of obligation. Indeed, the mind's quest for self-knowledge is nothing less than a moral duty rooted in its own essence.

> Why then is the mind commanded to know itself? I believe it means that it should think about itself and live according to its nature…it should want to be placed according to its nature.[20]

Augustine's words also reveal a residual attachment to Stoic ethics that now shapes and defines his emphasis on the importance of self-knowledge. In this respect, living "according to nature" establishes the standard for maintaining the soul's mid-rank between what is above it and what is below it in the hierarchy of reality, extending from the immutable and incorruptible Godhead to mutable and corruptible corporeal natures.

> Under him it should be subject to and over all that it should be in control of; under him it should be ruled by, over all that it ought to rule. In fact many of the things it does show that it has twisted its desires the wrong way round as though it had forgotten itself.[21]

The mind that fails to maintain its crucial middle station (which subordinates it to God and places it above lower things) plunges into that disordering of priorities that is the mark of sinfulness. Augustine's classic definition of *inquitas* as a perversity of will is fully operative in his discussion of the moral dimension of intellectual pursuits.[22] In this context, misplaced desires give rise to a forgetfulness of self, that is, a forfeiting of the soul's true nature in favor of an inferior mode of existence. Augustine's language here assumes a marked Plotinian tone. We are reminded of Plotinus's depiction of the fallen soul as an alien or exile from its native land, drawn into a condition of moral disorder and strife as a result of its concupiscential drives. This theme is most notable in *Ennead* V.1(10).1 (the *locus classicus* of Plotinus's account of the fall of individual souls), which likens lapsed souls to a child taken from home at an early age, who forgets its rank and dignity, wholly ignorant of its origins. More explicitly, Augustine evokes Plotinus's image of Soul's temporalization (prompted by its *polupragmatic* spirit) as an overextension to a "weaker greatness" of its power.

> It turns away from him and slithers and slides down into less and less which is imagined to be more and more; it can find satisfaction neither in itself nor in anything else as it gets further away from him who alone can satisfy it.[23]

While Augustine's remarks are applicable to primal sin in general, they have a specific relevance to the sin of *curiositas*, the lust of the eyes. He tips his hand in this direction, in fact, in his description of the errant mind's "slithering" and "sliding" downward. Such language immediately reminds us of the *De Genesi contra Manichaeos's* identification of the sin of curiosity with the serpent of Scripture, the animal that crawls on the ground and "eats earth," consuming the basest of things. Similarly, the curious mind "feasts" on the images and phantasms of inferior reality, and in so doing, abdicates its identity as image of God.

> Greedy to acquire knowledge of all sorts from things outside it-self...it loses its carefree sense of security, and thinks of itself all the less the more secure it is in its sense that it cannot lose itself.[24]

The tension between the mind's curious appetite for temporal and corporeal images and its contemplative gaze upon eternal truth underscores the instability and contingency of human existence. Accordingly, the mind's conflicting intellectual drives reflect the radical contingency of rational creatures in both a metaphysical and a moral sense. In Augustinian terms, our metaphysical contingency proceeds from the sheer fact of our creation from nothing; moral contingency proceeds from our fallenness and an ongoing susceptibility to sin.

Paradoxically, Augustine defines the evil will inherent in sin as a distorted expression of the soul's love. In this respect, he discerns a serious pitfall in the very love of knowing rooted in our rational nature. Once again, Augustine exhibits a Plotinian mindset. In *Ennead* IV.3(27).12, Plotinus describes how souls discern their images in bodies and gravitate toward material embodiment, entranced by the possibilities for an actualization of their powers. In Augustine's interpretation of this motif, our very concern for lesser things attaches us to them in a servitude to these objects of our affection, as if "glued" to them by manifold *curae*.

> Such is the force of love that when the mind has been thinking
> about things with love for a long time and has got stuck to them
> with the glue of care, it drags them along with itself even when it
> returns after a fashion to thinking about itself. Now these things
> are bodies which it has fallen in love with outside itself through
> the senses of the flesh and got involved with through a kind of long
> familiarity.[25]

The fact that the mind turns to things of a material, bodily nature is
significant. Because mind is immaterial in nature, it can never internalize such realities. In Augustine's diagnosis of this malaise, the mind
has but one recourse: it must preoccupy itself with the very images
"made in itself out of itself."[26] Yet, mind cannot succumb completely
to the influence of images, even in response to its own curious inclinations. By virtue of its immateriality, it is able to maintain its distance
from these objects of its making. At its highest level, mind functions
as a rational intelligence which remains free in its capacity for critical
judgments.[27] But mind can become so engrossed with these semblances of the really real that it loses sight of its authentic nature, placing
itself on a par with bodily beings.[28] In this way, it conforms itself to
lesser things, not only in epistemological terms, but more drastically,
in the degree of its loving attachment to them.

> It is…in the things that it thinks about with love, and it has got
> used to loving sensible…bodily things; so it is unable to be in itself
> without their images… it cannot make itself out among the images
> of the things it has perceived with the senses…all stuck astonish-
> ingly fast together with the glue of love.[29]

But what is this misplaced love, if not a loss of the mind's sense of itself? In response to this forgetting of our very nature, Augustine advises what amounts to an *anamnesis*, that is, a recollection that brings to
the fore of our consciousness what we truly are as persons. Augustine's
repeated use of the "adhesion" (or more graphically the "gluing") metaphor is illuminating. We are reminded of his description of the soul's
love as a "cleaving" (*inhaerere*) in *De libero arbitrio* (II,19,52-53). In the
*De Trinitate*, Augustine stresses that the mind has the potential to become one with what it loves. Thus, he contrasts the mind's coalescence
with material images with its love of self. In this context, however,
self-love does not point to any vain egoism. Rather, it refers to the
mind's recognition of its ontological difference from corporeal natures.

Once again, self-love and self-knowing are well-nigh synonymous for Augustine.

> Let the mind then recognize itself and not go looking for itself as if it were absent, but rather turn on to itself the interest of its will, which had it straying about through other things, and think about itself. In this way it will see that there never was a time when it did not love itself, when it did not know itself.[30]

## CURIOSITAS AND SCIENTIA (DE TRINITATE XII)

In *De Trinitate* XII, Augustine treats the diverse expressions of the soul's love in light of a psychological model which posits two functions of the mind. A higher function entails the contemplation of eternal truths, while a lower one assumes a distinct orientation toward the supervision of temporal matters and corporeal needs.[31] But does the mind's dual function undermine its substantial unity? In responding to this challenge, Augustine stresses the crucial point of intersection between the inner and the outer dimensions of the human being. In point of fact, references to the "outer man" are broad in scope, encompassing everything we share in common with animals. Augustine, however, stresses that the "outer man" is not confined to the body alone, but pertains to the whole living being in its relation to the external world through the faculty of sensation.[32] This position is consistent with Augustine's indictment of the mind's reliance on images. When the mind retains the images of things in its memory, it draws on the data derived from the "outer man" in formulating its judgments. But the mind by no means abdicates its rationality by virtue of its reliance upon the input of the senses. Indeed, the mind's orientation to the external world reflects one of its major functions.

By the same token, however, the mind's external orientation opens it to the moral pitfalls that Augustine discussed so extensively in *De Trinitate* X. From this standpoint, our very preoccupation with the temporal and corporeal spheres threatens the rationality which runs to the mind's own nature.

> While that part of us...occupied with the performance of bodily and temporal actions...is indeed rational, still it has so to say been led off from that rational substance of our minds by which we cling from underneath to the intelligible and unchanging truth,

and deputed to the task of dealing with and controlling these lower matters.[33]

This statement underscores the extent to which Augustine has absorbed a Neoplatonic model of the soul/body relationship. In this respect, his delineation of the mind's "higher" and "lower" functions (attending to the "inner" and "outer" man, respectively) is wholly consistent with Plotinus's depiction of the soul as occupying the middle ground between the noetic world of pure intelligibility (i.e., what is "above" it) and the material world encompassing bodily existence (i.e., what lies "below" it).

Plotinus anticipates Augustine's attribution to the soul the ability to oscillate from a contemplative focus on the "higher" life of thought to an attachment to what is "lower" in the hierarchy of reality (that is, the changing images of sense experience). In Plotinian terms, sound moral living coincides with a commitment to intellectual pursuits and the cultivation of the intellectual virtues. Accordingly, Plotinus affirms that when "good people are in this state their life is increased… not spilt out into perception, but gathered together in one in itself."[34] Augustine follows suit: in its stewardship of the body, the mind directs its attention toward what is beneath it in power and esteem. One unified mind thus assumes a fragmented character, seemingly at odds with itself in its conflicting loves. "Something rational of ours is assigned the duty of this work," Augustine contends, "not…divorced from the mind in breach of unity, but…derived from it in helpful partnership."[35] Augustine likens this partnership to the conjugal union between Adam and Eve (Gen. 2:24): in God's decree that *they shall be two in one flesh*, he finds scriptural support for his notion of a duality in one mind.[36]

Although the mind's dual function does not impinge upon its internal unity, it does pose a problem for Augustine's search for a trinitarian image in the very operation of mental and volitional life. If an image of the Trinity resides within us, it must be found in the nature of the mind as a whole, that is, in the mind as undivided.[37] But Augustine cautions that this presupposes the cessation of the mind's focus on temporal activity. He denies, however, that we may discover the trinitarian image on that lower psychic level. If we have a claim to the status of "images of God," it must be rooted in the higher aspect of the mind concerned exclusively with the contemplation of things eternal.[38]

Augustine's exploration of the functionality of the human mind provides his segue for an exegesis of I Cor. 11:7: *A man…is the image and glory of God, but woman is the glory of man.* On the basis of this Pauline prescription, Augustine comes to terms with the overarching issue regarding our standing as images of God, as well as an important ancillary one. Does Paul mean to attribute the Divine image to man alone, to the exclusion of woman? Augustine's attempt to answer this question provides the impetus to his penetrating exploration of the dynamics of human thought. In so doing, he revisits one of his perennial exegetical interests—the fall account of Genesis.

As already observed, the sexual union of Adam and Eve serves as Augustine's symbol of the mind's substantial unity. At this juncture, he expands upon this typology. The fall narrative of Genesis provides Augustine's framework for analyzing the mind's *excursus* into the temporal and corporeal realm. In this exegetical context, Adam's eating of the forbidden fruit represents the mind's downward movement by which "he may slide too much into outer things by making unrestrained advances."[39] In the process, the mind forfeits its abiding commitment to eternal verities in pursuit of something alien to its nature.

In keeping with the presuppositions (and biases) inherent in the intellectual tradition in which he shares, Augustine identifies the higher, rational part of the mind with Adam; the lower, sense-oriented part of the mind finds its symbol in Eve. This motif is ideal for Augustine's purposes, highlighting as it does a hierarchical ordering which places reason and rationality in an administrative capacity over the non-rational dimension of human nature. By virtue of this supervision, however, mind incurs an active role which can too easily degenerate into an over-excessive involvement with what is beneath it in the hierarchy of creation.

First and foremost, Augustine discerns the sin of pride in the soul's love of its own power and its choice of a good which is partial and private to itself over what is common to all.[40] This proud "standing apart" bespeaks an avaricious desire for more than it already possessed in its commitment to the totality of things.

> By the apostasy of pride…it strives to grab something more than the whole and to govern it by its own laws; and because there is nothing more than the whole it is thrust back into anxiety over a part, and so by being greedy for more it gets less.[41]

The soul's proud appropriation of the novelties of the manifold carries a double culpability: *first*, its option for self-determination goes against the grain of universal Divine law, the law that orders all things for the realization of their good; *secondly*, the soul downgrades its efficacy (specifically in regard to its mental life) by entwining itself with corporeal reality.

By relying on the body (even as it retains its incorporeality), the soul treats what is partial as if it were the whole. But pride is reinforced by a curiosity that seeks experience through the senses, along with a conceit in its powers and a carnal delight in bodily pleasures.[42] The very proliferation of the mind's range of cares only weakens and dissipates the very faculties it seeks to enlarge. Accordingly, Augustine sharply contrasts a vain privatizing of the soul's commitments with an unselfish love of the higher truths common to all, "possessed in a chaste embrace without…limitations or envy."[43]

As we saw in Chapter 4 of this study, the tensions between the common (*commune*) and the proper (*proprium*), between participation in the whole and a grasping after the part, figure prominently in Augustine's deliberations on the origins of iniquity. The overall language and motifs operative in this discussion bespeak a Neoplatonic inspiration suggestive of Plotinus's psychological treatises. In this vein, *Ennead* IV.8(6).4's depiction of the plight of individual souls offers a philosophical touchstone for Augustine's extended statement on the "particularization" of the mind and intellectual life in *De Trinitate* XII. Plotinus describes how souls defect from a noetic realm that is free of trouble, like kings who remain aloof from practical concerns; how they descend from the universal to become partial and self-centered; how they desert from their supervision of the totality in a weariness for otherness, tending toward bodies of their own; and how this downward tendance leaves them isolated, enervated, and laden with burdensome cares.[44]

Augustine is faithful to these Plotinian sentiments. But in this context, the fall is not defined in terms of soul's embodiment, but as a radical shift in its cognitive, volitional, and affective focus. By relying upon the input of the bodily senses (and investing its good in bodily existence), the soul internalizes deceptive images to such an extent that it loses sight of the things of God, those external truths most akin to its immateriality. Augustine delineates this tendency by means of the triadic components of curiosity, pride, and carnality, respectively.

> When the soul, greedy for experience or for superiority or for the
> pleasure of physical contact, does something to obtain the things...
> sensed through the body to the extent of setting its end and its prop-
> er good in them, then...it drags the deceptive semblances of bodily
> things inside...until it cannot even think of anything divine...in its
> private avarice...loaded with error and in its private prodigality...
> emptied of strength.[45]

In keeping with the exegetical thrust of his deliberations, Augustine
reintroduces the serpent imagery he put to such good use in the early
*De Genesi contra Manichaeos*. Such imagery serves several purposes.
On the one hand, the serpent's slithering movement provides an excellent contrast to that single-minded devotion to truth characteristic of
the well-ordered soul. On the other hand, the serpent symbolizes the
debasement of the fallen soul, immersed in an alien milieu beneath its
dignity as image of God.

> The careless glide little by little along the slippery path of failure,
> and beginning from a distorted appetite for being like God they end
> up by becoming like beasts.[46]

In strict epistemological terms, "the slippery path" to which Augustine
alludes encompasses *scientia*, the knowledge derived from the experience of mutable temporal realities which stands opposed to *sapientia*,
the wisdom which remains stable and abiding.[47] When assessed in
light of the fall account of Genesis, the soul's attraction to experiential
knowledge calls to mind Eve's temptation to eat the fruit of the tree
planted in the middle of paradise, whose fruit promises to open her
eyes and render her like gods, *who know what is good and what is bad*
(Gen. 3:3-5).

## CURIOSITAS AND MIND'S SCIENTIAL FUNCTION

Augustine's exploration of God's triune nature prompts his incisive
analysis of the role of *curiositas* in our orientation to the world at large.
This orientation is rooted in our very constitution as embodied souls.
But our embodied status underscores the dual character of our cognitive activities. Augustine's structuring of the mind along such functional lines, however, lends itself to something of an ambiguity. On the one
hand, he recognizes the necessity of the mind's supervision of bodily
existence and the focus on images (both temporal and corporeal) that

such supervision necessarily entails. Still, the mind's very attentiveness to such images opens the soul to the possibility of moral error.

While Augustine perceives the influence of each of the three primal vices (i.e., pride, curiosity, and carnal concupiscence in an excessive preoccupation with images (and their phantasms), he imparts a special significance to *curiositas* in the mind's outward (or in metaphysical terms, "downward") orientation. In *De Trinitate* X, *curiositas* assumes a prominent role in Augustine's investigation of the mind's search for self-knowledge.

For him, as we have seen, the drive to know is correlative with the love for knowledge. Augustine's contrast between the studious-minded and the curious-minded highlights the tension between the love of genuine knowledge and the mere appetite for worldly experience. While the studious seek a knowledge of God and eternal truths, the curious appetite stimulates a restless pursuit of vain images. By the same token, Augustine discerns a pronounced affinity between the love of knowledge and inquisitiveness. Each disposition displays an attraction to the objects of its attentive gaze; each considers the unknown something to be overcome. So, the distinction between these dispositions ultimately lies in divergent levels of commitment to knowledge.

As Part I of this study demonstrated (specifically, Chapter 2, above), *curiositas* carries the connotation of a half-hearted, fickle interest in intellectual pursuits that fall short of the steadfast love of truth found in authentic knowledge. But this is merely one aspect of the blameworthiness of the curious appetite. We must also consider the objects of its attention. If the mind's higher contemplative function is naturally oriented toward what is immutable and abiding, its lower active function (which opens it to *curiositas*) is intimately bound up with mutable, transitory realities. This latter orientation amounts to a forgetfulness; absorption in images undermines self-awareness and an attunement to the inner life. In Augustinian terms, *curiositas* poses a formidable obstacle to knowledge, since one cannot really "know" transitory images. For Augustine, *curiositas* plunges the soul into a downward spiral that promotes a wholly distorted sense of truth. But an unregulated interest in images even obscures the mind's sense of its own nature. By loving itself, the mind becomes one (as knower) with what is immaterial. In fixing its cognitive gaze upon images, however, it becomes "glued" to them, bound up with what it can never completely internalize.

*De Trinitate* XII expands upon Augustine's functional analysis of the dynamics of the soul's love. These diverse functions presuppose a hierarchical relationship whereby the mind's sciential role is subordinate to its sapiential one. We can neither deny the fact of our embodiment, nor the sciential function that supervises bodily existence. This function is properly ordered when it attends to its appropriate task of overseeing the outer dimension of the human being. But there is a rather fine line between this external orientation and the kind of reliance upon images and phantasms which amounts to an abdication of the mind's own integrity.

## CURIOSITAS AND THE FALLEN SOUL

In Adam and Eve, as we have seen, Augustine discerns scriptural symbols of the union of these diverse functions in one mind. But Adam and Eve also figure prominently in Augustine's reliance upon the fall account of Genesis in depicting the mind's "outward" (epistemologically speaking) or "downward" (metaphysically speaking) sciential focus. In this connection, *De Trinitate* XII,3(13) is particularly noteworthy for its explicit use of "fall" terminology. As noted above, this passage characterizes Adam's sin as that movement "by which he may slide too much into outer things by making unrestrained advances" (*immoderato progressu nimis in exteriora prolabitur*). While we might well adhere to Edmund Hill's somewhat figurative translation of the verb *prolabor* as "to slide" or "to slip," its more literal meaning of "to fall down" cannot be overlooked here. From this standpoint, Augustine's choice of language is highly suggestive of a return to his early understanding of the soul's fall into bodily existence and temporality.

But by the same token, Augustine's discussion of the soul's *lapsus* in *De Trinitate* XII does not immediately rule out alternative interpretations concerning its origin. Robert J. O'Connell acknowledged as much, contending that this work "sheds very little direct light on the question of the origin of our souls, beyond this clear affirmation that the sin of Adam must be considered our sin as well."[48] In this regard, O'Connell focused upon Augustine's dichotomy between what is common to all (*commune*) and what is private or "proper" (*proprium*) to the individual soul alone.

"Is he suggesting, or toying at least with the possibility," O'Connell asked, "that we may all have enjoyed a 'common' life—and committed a 'common' sin—before entering upon this life that each of us recognizes as his or her 'very own'?"[49] He succinctly framed his answer in these terms:

> Bodily, temporally, and historically, we are individuals distinct from our historical father, Adam, each of us living our own "proper" life; but as souls, our identity mysteriously transcends those obvious limitations. The obscure mystery surrounding the origin of our souls permits Augustine to read such texts as Romans 5:12 the way he did, at least for a time: that "in" Adam all of us sinned, fell from "justice" and its attendant "bliss."[50]

While O'Connell saw the Augustine of the *De Trinitate* as having lessened the gulf between the soul's pre-lapsarian and post-lapsarian conditions, he still perceived a marked continuity between the early and the later Augustine in this vein.

> Having placed its delight in "bodily forms and motions"…the fallen soul can become increasingly enmeshed in the network of its sensible images and phantasms, and thus plunge even more deeply into the kinds of activities inspired by pride, concupiscence, and curiosity, the very same triadic sin…to which he attributed the soul's "fall" in his early works and in the *Confessions*.[51]

This interpretation, however, is challenged by Rombs, who discerns in the *De Trinitate* a "fundamental break with Augustine's earlier conception," so that even if he crafts a Plotinian theory of the soul's fall, that theory amounts to a "psychology of sin where our moral lapse has broken our proper *relation* both to the world and to God."[52] Rombs' observation has a special applicability to the role of *curiositas* in the *De Trinitate*'s account of the soul's fall. Are the triadic components (including *curiositas*) the cause of the soul's entry into bodies and temporality, or are they the outgrowths of that lapse? In Augustine's writings, we find grounds for responding in the affirmative to both options.

As stated in Chapter 6, my major concern does not lie in the *mechanism* of the soul's fall, but in the existential impact of its fallenness. In point of fact, we can become so engrossed with the question of the soul's origin that we lose sight of the implications of its embodiment. A major implication is its subservience to the promptings of *curiositas*, the *concupiscentia oculorum* which draws it into increasing

entanglements in worldly cares. In *De Trinitate* X and XII, Augustine
offers a penetrating analysis of our cognitive life when directed toward
the world of sense experience. In this respect, he links the soul's *lapsus* with conscious awareness, "overweighted with a sort of self-heavi-
ness...heaved out of happiness...having squandered and lost its
strength."[53] Augustine's imagery could not be more Plotinian in its
evocation of the language of *Ennead* III.8(30).8:

> Beginning as one it did not stay as it began, but became many, as if
> heavy, and unrolled itself, because it wanted to possess everything.[54]

If read through this Plotinian prism, Augustine's metaphor of the
"heaviness" of consciousness dovetails nicely with his notion of the
soul's "weight" (*pondus*), the motive force drawing it to the objects of
its loves and affections.[55] In practical terms, the downward gaze of reason (i.e., in its function as *scientia*) is bound up with restless activity.
In this respect, *scientia* finds its Plotinian counterpart in the *polupragmon*-language of *Ennead* III.7(45).11, with its connotations of a busyness about temporal matters.

By the same token, any such *lapsus* on the soul's part cannot be confined to intellectual life alone. When the mind's active orientation is
conjoined with a carnal appetite for personal gratification, it opens the
way to sin in both thought and deed. In this connection, Augustine
interprets the temptation generated by the carnal (animal) sense in
terms of the serpent's enticement of Eve to eat the forbidden fruit.
Accordingly, he again appeals to the figure of Adam and Eve as symbols of the mind's diverse functions.

From this exegetical standpoint, the mere entertaining of temptation (symbolized by the serpent's deception of Eve) is consummated
by the bodily enjoyment of mutable things as its own private goods
(symbolized by Adam's eating of the fruit along with Eve).[56] In the
final analysis, however, the mind cannot will to sin unless reason lends
its assent, and thereby, enslaves the mind to non-rational instincts.
Augustine recognizes the limitations of his own typology in this context. While Adam and Eve constitute distinct individuals in their own
right, the respective functions of the mind that they symbolize are
grounded in the unity of the individual human being.

> This...is one person, one human being, and the whole of him will be
> condemned unless these things that are...sins of thought alone...
> are forgiven by the grace of the mediator.[57]

In its broadest terms, Augustine's exegesis of the fall account of Genesis in the *De Trinitate* represents a commentary on the mind of everyman. From his perspective, however, this methodology in no way undermines the historical truth (founded on Divine authority) regarding Adam and Eve as the first parents of the human race.[58] But we must not overlook the fact that Augustine's preoccupation with their temptation and sin is driven by his struggle with the meaning of I Cor. 11:7: *A man is the image and glory of God, but woman is the glory of man.* Accordingly, he seeks to answer the question as to "why the apostle attributes the image of God to the man and not the woman as well."[59]

Augustine concludes that Paul's emphasis on sexual differentiation highlights the human mind's possession of two functions, even as it retains its unity. This position signals a rather marked break with certain representatives of the patristic tradition, most notably Ambrose of Milan.[60] In this respect, Augustine rejects the claim that Eve symbolizes the bodily senses; he instead finds the scriptural symbol of the senses (which we share with irrational animals) in the figure of the serpent.[61] The fact that the serpent is identified with such traits as cunning and duplicity make it the ideal representative of mind on its most pronounced sciential level. At that level, it is completely engrossed with images and phantasms, those spurious claimants to the really and truly real.

A final qualification is in order here. While I acknowledge the psychological import of Augustine's analysis of the soul's *lapsus*, I feel that he is offering far more than just a "psychology of sin" (to use Rombs' phrase). As I stressed in Chapter 6 (above), I favor something of a middle way between the positions of O'Connell (who leaves open the possibility that the later Augustine was still committed to an ontological understanding of the soul's fall) and Rombs (who attributes a psychological/moral import to Augustine's prominent use of fall language). If Augustine develops a "psychology of sin," then, I believe he does so with a sensitivity to its profound metaphysical implications as well. These implications comprise a clouding of reasoning, a weakening of the will, and a general disordering of our mid-rank status which subordinates us to God and places us "above" corporeal natures. In existential terms, our "fallenness" encompasses our ongoing suceptibility to the pull of pride, curiosity, and carnal concupiscence. But because the *De Trinitate* focuses so explicitly upon our cognitive life, it places a special emphasis upon the sin of *curiositas*, the outgrowth of the mind's sciential function.

Our examination of Augustine's delineation of the mind's functions in the *De Trinitate* opens the way to our consideration (in Chapter 8) of another dichotomy in his outlook that has a direct bearing on Christian life in the temporal realm. This dichotomy emerges in the *De Civitate Dei*. In that great commentary on the ebb and flow of human history, Augustine draws a distinction between the heavenly and the earthly cities. In analyzing the character of the earthly city, he provides a widespread critique of pagan culture. A major focus of this critique is an indictment of the role of demonology in pagan religious practice. For Augustine, the curious lust for futile knowledge provides a major feature of the attraction to demons, along with the occultism and magical arts associated with their invocation.

## NOTES TO CHAPTER 7

1. Allan D. Fitzgerald, O.S.A., ed., *Augustine through the Ages. An Encyclopedia* (Grand Rapids, Michigan/Cambridge, U.K.: William B. Eerdmans Publishing Company, 1999), 846b, s.v. "De Trinitate," by Rowan Williams.

2. Allan D. Fitzgerald, O.S.A., ed., *Augustine through the Ages. An Encyclopedia* (Grand Rapids, Michigan/Cambridge, U.K.: William B. Eerdmans Publishing Company, 1999), 563b, s.v. "Mind," by Wayne B. Hankey: "Knowing God and knowing ourselves are indissolubly united. Knowing God depends upon coming to understand that mind is immaterial and that it is image of the trinitarian God…common to God and the human, the infinite medium in which they meet."

3. Edmund Hill, O.P., Foreward to his translation of St. Augustine's *De Trinitate* in *The Works of Saint Augustine. A Translation for the 21st Century* (Brooklyn, New York: New City Press, 1991), 262.

4. The fact that Augustine speaks in terms of a *lapsus* in the *De Trinitate* is readily evident. The difficulty, however, lies in determining how this *lapsus* is to be construed, especially in light of Augustine's evolving theories of the soul's origin in relation to bodily existence. I address this issue toward the conclusion of this chapter, revisiting the diverse responses of Robert J. O'Connell and Ronnie Rombs.

5. Etienne Gilson, *The Christian Philosophy of Saint Augustine*, trans. L.E.M. Lynch (New York: Random House, 1960), 221.

6. Augustine's Christian Neoplatonic perspective dictates that he adopt a critical attitude toward things that rank on the lower end of the scale of created reality, especially when our interest in these things exceeds the norms of due moderation.

7. *De Trinitate* IX,3(18). All subsequent references to the *De Trinitate* in this chapter are designated as "**DT**".

8. **DT** IX,3(18): CC L (SL), 309,50-310,55: *notitia iam inuentum est quod partum ule repertum dicitur, quod saepe praecedit inquisitio eo fine quietura. Nam inquisitio est appetitus inueniendi, quod idem ualet si dicas reperiendi. Quae autem reperiuntur quasi pariuntur, unde proli similia sunt.*

9. **DT** IX,3(18): CC L (SL), 310,58-61: *Porro appetitus ille qui est in quaerendo procedit a quaerente et pendet quodam modo, neque requiescit fine quo intenditur nisi id quod quaeritur inuentum quaerenti copuletur.*

10. **DT** IX,3(18): CC L (SL), 310,69-75: *Partum ergo mentis antecedit appetitus quidam quo id quod nosse uolumus quaerendo et inueniendo nascitur proles ipsa notitia, ac per hoc appetitus ille quo concipitur pariturque notitia partus et proles recte dici non potest. Idemque appetitus quo inhiatur rei cognoscendae fit amor cognitae dum tenet atque amplectitur…notitiam gignentique coniungit.*

11. **DT** IX,3(18). Cf., I Jn. 5:8.

12. **DT** X,1(1).

13. **DT** X,1(3): CC L (SL), 314,110-111: *non est amor eius rei quam nescit sed eius quam scit propter quam uult scire quod nescit.*

14. **DT** X,1(3): CC L (SL), 314,111-315,114: *Aut si tam curiosus est ut non propter aliquam notam causam sed solo amore rapiatur incognita sciendi, discernendus quidem est ab studiosi nomine iste curiosus;*

15. **DT** X,1(3): CC L (SL),315,114-116: *sed nec ipse amat in incognita, immo congruentius dicitur, 'odit incognita,' quae nulla esse uult dum uult omnia cognita.*

16. **DT** X,1(3).

17. **DT** X,2(5).

18. **DT** X,2(5).

19. **DT** X,2[3](5): CC L (SL),317,1-2: *Quid ergo amat mens cum ardenter se ipsam quae rit ut nouerit dum incognita sibi est?*

20. **DT** X,5(7): CC L (SL),320,1-3: *Vtquid ergo ei praeceptum est ut se ipsa cognoscat? Credo ut se cogitet et secundum naturam suam uiuat, id est ut secundum suam naturam ordinari appetat…*

21. **DT** X,5(7): CC L (SL),320,3-6: *sub eo scilicet cui subdenda est, supra ea quibus praeponenda est; sub illo a quo regi debet, supra ea quae regere debet. Multa enim per cupiditatem prauam tamquam sui sit oblita sic agit.*

22. Cf., *Confessiones* VII,16(22): CC XXVII,106: *Et quaesiui, quid esset iniquitas, et non inueni substantiam, sed a summa substantia, te deo, detortae in infima uoluntatis peruersitatem proicientis intima sua et tumescentis foras.*

23. **DT** X,5(7): CC L (SL),320,10-12: *mouerturque et labitur in minus et minus quod putatur amplius et amplius quia nec ipsa sibi nec ei quidquam sufficit recendenti ab illo qui solus sufficit.*

24. **DT** X,5(7): CC L (SL),321,15-19: *atque ita cupiditate adquirendi notitias ex his quae foris sunt...perdit securitatem, tantoque se ipsam minus cogitat quanto magis secura est quod se non possit amittere.*

25. **DT** X,5(7): CC L (SL),321,24-28: *tanta uis est amoris ut ea quae cum amore diu cogitauerit eisque curae glutino inhaeserit attrahat secum etiam cum ad se cogitandum quodam modo redit. Et quia illa corpora sunt quae foris per sensus carnis adamauit eorumque diurturna quodam familiaritate implicata est...*

26. **DT** X,5(7): CC L (SL),321, 30-31: *imagines eorum conuoluit et rapit factas in semetipsa de semetipsa.*

27. **DT** X,5(7).

28. **DT** X,3(8).

29. **DT** X,3(11): CC L (SL),324,4-9: *Sed quia in his est quae cum amore cogitat, sensibilibus autem, id est corporalibus, cum amore assuefacta est, non ualet sine imaginibus eorum esse in semetipsa...rerum sensarum imagines secernere a se non potest ut se solam uideat; cohaeserunt einim mirabiliter glutino amoris.*

30. **DT** X,3(11): CC L (SL),325,22-25: *Cognoscat ergo semetipsam, nec quasi absentem se quaerat, sed intentione uoluntatis qua per alia uagabatur statuat in se ipsa et se cogitet. Ita uidebit quod numquam se non amauerit, numquam nescierit...*

31. **DT** XII,1(1).

32. **DT** XII,1(1).

33. **DT** XII,1(3): CC L (SL),357,1-6: *Illud uero nostrum quod in actione corporalium atque temporalium tractandorum... rationale est quidem, sed ex illa rationali nostrae mentis substantia qua subhaeremus intelligibili atque incommutabili ueritati tamquam ductum et inferioribus tractandis gubernandisque deputatum est.*

34. *Ennead* I.4(46).10.

35. **DT** XII,1(3): CC L (SL),358,12-14: *Et ideo quiddam rationale nostrum non ad unitatis diuortium separatum sed in auxilium societatis quasi deriuatum in sui operis dispertitur officio.*

36. **DT** XII,1(3).

37. **DT** XII,1(4).

38. **DT** XII,1(4).

39. **DT** XII,3(13): CC L (SL), 368,6: *immoderato progressu nimis in exteriora prolabitur...*

40. **DT** XII,3(14). Cf., *De libero arbitrio* II,16(41)-20(54).

41. **DT** XII,3(14: CC L (SL),368,2-8: *apostatica illa <u>superbia</u> quod <u>initium peccati</u> dicitur, cum in uniuersitate creaturae deum rectorem secuta legibus eius optime gubernari potuisset, plus aliquid uniuerso appetens atque id sua lege*

*gubernare molita, quia nihil est amplius uniuersitate, in curam partilem trudi-tur et sic aliquid amplius concupiscendo minuitur...*

42. DT XII,3(14): CC L (SL),369,15-16: *curiose corporalia ac temporalia per corporis sensus quaerit...*

43. DT XII,3(15): CC L (SL),369,1-4: *Cum ergo bona uoluntate ad interiora ac superiora percipienda quae non pruiatim sed communiter ab omnibus qui talia diligunt sine ulla angustia uel inuidia casto possidentur amplexu uel sibi uel aliis consulit...*

44. *Ennead* IV.8(6).4,1-22.

45. DT XII,3(15): CC L (SL),369,10-17: *Cum uero propter adipiscenda ea quae per corpus sentiuntur propter experiendi uel excellendi uel contrectandi cupiditatem ut in his finem boni sui ponat aliquid agit...et corporearum rerum fallacia simulacra introrsus rapiens et uana meditatione componens ut ei nec diuinum aliquid nisi tale uideatur, priuatim auara fetatur erroribus et priua-tim prodiga inanitur uiribus.*

46. DT XII,3(16): CC L (SL),370,2-4: *sic lubricus deficiendi motus neglegentes minutatim occupat, et incipiens a peruerso appetitu similitudinis dei peruenit ad similitudinem pecorum.*

47. DT XII,3(16): CC L (SL),370,16-19: *Cum enim neglecta caritate sapi-entiae quae semper eodem modo manet concupiscitur* scientia *ex mutabilium temporaliumque experimento,* inflat *non* aedificat; Cf., DT XII,3(17): CC L (SL),371,27-30: *Nunc de illa parte rationis ad quam pertinet scientia, id est cognitio rerum temporalium atque mutabilium nauandis uitae huius actioni-bus necessaria...*

48. Robert J. O'Connell, S.J., *The Origin of the Soul in St. Augustine's Later Works* (New York: Fordham University Press, 1987), 280.

49. Robert J. O'Connell, S.J., *The Origin of the Soul in St. Augustine's Later Works*, 281.

50. Robert J. O'Connell, S.J., *The Origin of the Soul in St. Augustine's Later Works*, 279.

51. Robert J. O'Connell, S.J., *The Origin of the Soul in St. Augustine's Later Works*, 261. O'Connell later (278) characterizes Augustine's ongoing com-mitment to the fallen soul theme along these lines:"...in the deeper reaches of Augustine's thought and affect, man remains much more a soul 'using' a body, a contemplative soul with so slack a relationship to the body, its senses, imagination, feelings, and involvement in the temporal world of ac-tion, that Augustine can still employ a language of 'fall' to warn us against 'immoderate' immersion in any of those incarnate activities."

52. Ronnie J. Rombs, *Saint Augustine and the Fall of the Soul. Beyond O'Connell and His Critics* (Washington, D.C.: The Catholic University of America Press, 2006), 161-162.

53. DT XII,3(16): CC L (SL),370,19-371,24: *ita praegrauatus animus quasi pondere suo a beatitudine expellitur, et per illud suae medietatis experimen-tum...effusis ac perditis uiribus...*

54. *Ennead* III.8(30).8,32-34. As we saw in Chapter 6 of this study, this particular text also provides a compelling Plotinian referent for Augustine's exegesis of Eccli. 10:9-14 and the "swelling" imagery which he applies to the proud man who "spews forth" his innermost good on a multiplicity of lower things.

55. Cf., *Genesi contra Manichaeos* II,22(34), for an example of Augustine's creative adaptation of the Aristotelian teaching (in the interests of his moral theory) that each body tends toward its natural locus. For a more extended discussion of the role of the *pondus* theme in Augustine, see my "'Pondus meum amor meus': The Significance of the 'Weight' Metaphor in St. Augustine's Early Philosophical Writings," *Augustinian Studies* XXI (1990): 163-176.

56. **DT** XII,3(17): CC L (SL),371,17-372,23: *Cum ergo huic intentioni mentis quae in rebus temporalibus et corporalibus propter actionis officium ratiocinandi uiuacitate uersatur carnalis ille sensus uel animalis ingerit quandam inlecebram fruendi se, id est tamquam bono quodam priuato et proprio non tamquam publico atque communi quod est incommutabile bonum, tunc uelut serpens alloquitur feminam. Huic autem inlecebrae consentire de ligno prohibito manducare est.*

57. **DT** XII,3(18): CC L (SL),373,52-56: *Haec quippe una persona est, unus homo est, totusque damnabitur nisi haec quae...solius cogitationis sentiuntur esse peccata per mediatoris gratiam remittantur.*

58. **DT** XII,3(19).

59. **DT** XII,3(19): CC L (SL),373,64-67: *apostolus imaginem dei uiro tantum tribuendo non etiam feminae...*

60. Cf., *De Noe et Arca* 92.

61. **DT** XII,3(20).

# CHAPTER 8

# THE *CURIOSITAS* OF PAGANS

Like the *De Trinitate*, the *De Civitate Dei* initially seems an unlikely source for Augustine's deliberations on the significance of *curiositas*. In point of fact, however, the *De Civitate Dei* offers a veritable treasure trove of references to *curiositas*, specifically (but not exclusively) in regard to its moral dimension. This great work (composed by Augustine on a sporadic basis over some twelve years) constitutes an ambitious Christian *apologia* against pagan charges that Christianity had undermined the integrity of the Roman Empire. In responding to these charges, Augustine crafted an elaborate critique of pagan thought, with a special focus on the falsity of its teachings. The sin of *curiositas* assumes a prominent role in this polemical context. Augustine specifically discerns a crucial link between the primal vice of *curiositas* and the demonology operative in pagan religious practices. As he affirms in *Sermo* 112A, "all prying, inquisitive people throw themselves" on the evil one, since "unlawful curiosity represents a pestilential poverty of truth."[1]

Accordingly, Augustine's critique of paganism rests upon a broader condemnation of the religious edifice on which it rested (and which, in turn, generated its cults and devotions). His wide-ranging acquaintance with the literary, philosophical, and theological currents of late antiquity provided abundant information concerning the technical aspects of pagan observance, including its propitiatory rites. Later Platonists such as Apuleius and Porphyry offered particularly illuminating referents for exploring the lengths to which pagan religion could go under the influence of an illicit curiosity. In the *De Civitate Dei*, then, the sin of *curiositas* encompasses the whole panoply of demonic lure, including superstition, occultism, magical arts, divination, and astrology. This chapter explores these diverse connotations of the term in connection with Augustine's critique of pagan religion and its cultural support system.

## THE LURE OF *SPECTACULI*

Augustine's moral deliberations reveal a special concern with the corrosive effects of spectacles. In this connection, we find him working within a patristic tradition that highlighted the dangers accompanying *spectaculi* of all kinds.[2] By their very nature, *spectaculi* assume a visual significance. For this reason, Augustine's condemnation of spectacles displays a compelling link with the Johannine "lust of the eyes" (*concupiscentia oculorum*) that he explicitly defines as the sin of *curiositas*. As his probing examination of conscience in the *Confessiones* discloses, Augustine was highly suspicious of "allurements of the eyes," whether they focused upon theatrical performances, gladiatorial contests, or pagan religious devotions (along with the erotic exhibitions these rites often incorporated). The *De Civitate Dei's* anti-pagan critique follows in this vein.

In *De Civitate Dei* I, Augustine's condemnation of *spectaculi* is not so much directed at their content as at their origin. "The facts," Augustine informs us, are that "these disgusting spectacles of frivolous immorality," were not instituted by humans but on the orders of the gods themselves.[3] Here, he specifically refers to the pagan belief that the gods initiated theatrical productions for the purpose of their own honor, in order to neutralize the devastating effects of a plague (c. 364-363 B.C.). From Augustine's standpoint, however, the physical impact of that plague (which ran its natural course) was superseded by a "far more serious pestilence" which undermined the health of the mind.[4] The extent to which this moral disease infected the Roman spirit becomes a dominant theme in Augustine's ensuing polemic. In this context, however, Augustine by no means adopts the disinterested tone of the detached social critic or cultural commentator. Indeed, his analysis not only reveals an acquaintance with the subject matter under scrutiny, but a susceptibility to its attractions as well.

## THE INFLUENCE OF DEMONS

"When I was a young man," Augustine admits, "I used to go to sacrilegious shows and entertainments," in which he "thoroughly enjoyed the most degrading spectacles put on in honour of gods and goddesses."[5] Here, he discerns a culpability on the part of humans and divinities alike. On the one hand, he attributes the gathering of the spectators (himself included) to the enticement of curiosity.[6] On the other hand, he attributes the blame directly to the gods' failure to prevent the decline in popular morality, by virtue of their inability to provide sound moral guidance to their adherents.[7]

From Augustine's standpoint, the divinities' moral *agnosis* was tantamount to a tacit endorsement of the most obscene exhibitions, all for the sake of their own self-aggrandizement. In the public's fondness for such performances, Augustine perceives a demonic influence encompassing the inner and outer dimensions of human nature. While such practices were detrimental to bodily existence (and the world that people inhabit), they posed the greatest danger to the mind, the "ruler of the flesh" which should rightfully govern our corporeal nature.[8]

Augustine's tracing of the progress of demonic influence thus runs parallel to his hierarchical understanding of human nature. In this scheme, the body is subordinate to the soul, and the soul in turn to the mind, the highest level of the soul constituting the center of our rational capacity and free will. Accordingly, the "evil spirit drives men's minds to wickedness by a secret compulsion," goading them toward iniquity.[9]

In Augustine's experience, of course, one of the most salient expressions of this compulsion is the "lust of the eyes" (*concupiscentia oculorum*), which not only opens people to enticing visual spectacles, but to the allurements of worldly experience in general. The lure of what is visually appealing is merely one expression of a more wide-ranging gravitation toward the world at large.

> There were crowds converging from all directions… and we watched the acted shows with the closest interest.[10]

## CURIOSITAS AND SUPERSTITION

A major component of Augustine's anti-pagan polemic is a challenge to the uncritical assumption that devotion to the gods guaranteed the well being of the state, including an ongoing reign of peace. He specifically cites the case of Numa Pampilius (successor to Romulus), who supposedly secured a long period of tranquility by earning divine favor through the institution of religious rites.[11] For Augustine, the ultimate test of this theory is not provided by Numa's rule itself. Rather, it must be based on what followed Numa's establishment of the rites. Augustine argues that there was no more than a year of peace from Rome's founding to the age of Augustus.[12] So much for the claim that the gods whose protection the rites promised actually safeguarded the city. Augustine suggests that Numa would have been worthy of praise for achieving peace if he had devoted himself to a search for the true God, instead of succumbing to the effects of a "pernicious curiosity."[13]

But how is the meaning of *curiositas* to be construed in this context? In the *De Civitate Dei*, the term is all but synonymous with *superstitio*. This link, however, is by no means readily apparent, at least not on the surface of Augustine's critique. Only a deeper analysis of the import of *superstitio* reveals the intriguing parallels with the religious connotations surrounding *curiositas*. Granted, *superstitio* (derived from *superstare*, i.e., "to stand upon or over") has a more pronounced religious significance. On its most basic level, the term refers to an irrational awe in the face of what is unknown or veiled in mystery. In this respect, the psychological dimension of *superstitio* cannot be overlooked.

But if *superstitio* can prompt an attitude of awe or reverence, it is because it proceeds from a condition of fear or ignorance on the part of its subject. This is precisely where *superstitio* displays an overlapping of meanings with *curiositas*. Both terms are highly suggestive of an excessive concern that finds expression in an extravagant devotion or punctiliousness of observance. Such connotations, as we have seen, are earmarks of the notion of *curiositas* (or its adjectival variant *curiosus*) in its manifold appearances in classical literature, philosophy, and theology. In *superstitio*, these connotations assume the added import of the idolatrous observances associated with pagan religion (in the minds of Christians, at least).

Augustine roots his analysis of pagan superstition in pronouncements from prominent pagan intellectuals. For Cicero, the use of images diverts human reason from genuine scientific knowledge, in pursuit of goods produced by the human imagination.[14] Cicero classifies these false notions as superstition, in contrast to the religious piety of his own Stoic-inspired teaching. But in Cicero's distinction between superstition and religion, Augustine finds a failed attempt to extricate authentic ancestral worship from the vain reliance upon images. Augustine, in contrast, perceives evidence of the worshiping of images in the very origins of Roman history. Cicero himself was by no means free of ambiguity on this front.

> For all the eloquence with which he strives to… free himself from the charge, he did hold that those institutions should be treated with reverence.[15]

The polymath Varro exhibts a similar inconsistency, exhorting a conformity to established devotions, even as he adopts the stance of the critical theologian.[16] Varro, in effect, tries to reconcile his deeply ingrained scepticism with a desire to respect customs long enshrined in civic life.

> If he had been founding the city at the beginning, he would have consecrated the gods and their names according to the rule of Nature. But he asserts that he is bound…to encourage the common people to honour the gods.[17]

According to Augustine, Varro taught that the Romans worshiped the gods for nearly two hundred years without recourse to vain images.[18] For Varro, continuance of that trend would have permitted a more refined mode of worship, without the errors and irreverence that image worship inspired. In support of this theory, he cites the example of the Jews. But Augustine laments that someone as close to the truth as Varro failed to acknowledge the one true God responsible for imparting the very blessings that intercession to so many Roman gods could not yield.[19] From Augustine's standpoint, the Jews' happiness would have persisted if they had not succumbed to the polytheistic worship of strange gods and idols. Their defection, he proposes, was rooted in their seduction by the impious *curiositas* of the magical arts.[20] In his reckoning, then, the corrosive effects of superstition (spurred by a curious attraction to what is novel or occult) were by no means confined to the pagan world. Indeed, even the people of the Law were susceptible to its negative influence.

## CURIOSITAS AND THE EARTHLY CITY

Augustine's attribution of a "pernicious curiosity" to the Roman state reflects his disposition toward the secular sphere in general. His moral expectations regarding the *saeculum* assume a rather pragmatic character. Pagan and Christian societies alike are only as virtuous as life in the temporal sphere allows. In the aftermath of the Christianization of the Roman Empire, Christians were required to forge a new relationship with the world at large.

In Augustinian terms, God alone possesses power over the destiny of human kingdoms and empires. While God grants happiness to the good alone in the Heavenly Kingdom, He grants earthly kingdoms to the good and bad alike, "according to His pleasure."[21] Augustine thus assumes that God granted dominion to Rome as He willed, just as He extended sovereignty to the Assyrians, Persians, and Hebrews. But what is true of temporal sovereignties is equally true of individual human leaders. The same God Who granted power to Marius, Gaius Caesar, Augustus, Nero, the Vespasians, and Domitian also extended it to the Christian Emperor Constantine.[22] Like every other human being, an earthly ruler is finite and fallen. For this very reason, Christian identity alone does not insure the moral perfection of any sovereign.

By the same token, Augustine still draws a significant line between those who worship God and those in the grip of demons. God's bestowal of great gifts upon Constantine had the educative purpose of showing that the attainment of earthly kingdoms need not require demonic supplications.[23] Augustine likewise commends Theodosius for not falling into "sacrilegious and illicit curiosity."[24] By virtue of their allegiance to the true God, Constantine and Theodosius thus reveal a proper ordering of priorities; both recognized the ultimate source of their own power. In contrast, Julian the Apostate distorted his great personal gifts by a "sacrilegious and abominable curiosity" through which he invested his trust in counterfeit oracles of superstition.[25]

## THE CURIOSITAS OF OCCULTISM

In the *De Civitate Dei* VII, Augustine revisits the historical personage Numa Pampilius, who achieved great acclaim for supposedly securing a long peace by recourse to demonic worship. At this juncture, however, Augustine focuses specifically upon the secrecy surrounding the varieties of pagan occultism introduced by Numa and other founders of Rome. Occultism encompasses such diverse practices as magic, alchemy, astrology, necromancy, hydromancy, and divination. Augustine closely links these esoteric features of Roman religion with the *curiositas* which draws humans into the grip of vain *superstitio*.

Once again, Varro provides a veritable encyclopedia for Augustine's polemical purposes. On the basis of a quote from Varro's *Liber de cultu deorum*, he recounts a strange tale.

> A man named Terentius had a farm near the Janiculum. His ploughman was driving his plough near the tomb of Numa Pampilius when he turned up the books of that author which dealt with the reasons for the established ceremonies of religion.[26]

According to this account, the writings were subsequently examined by the Roman Senate. But it was agreed that their contents should be burnt, rather than shared with the populace. In Augustine's interpretation of these events, secrecy and curiosity assume two dimensions. On the one hand, he charges that Numa himself acquired this information through an *illicita curiositas*, which impelled him to investigate demonic teachings.[27] On the other hand, however, he contends that the Senate had this material destroyed (rather than reburied) out of fear that this same *curiositas* would motivate people to learn the rationale for those forms of worship.[28] From Augustine's standpoint, the upshot of this action is clear: the Roman establishment found it more desirable to keep its people in ignorance than reveal the truth of their own ancestral religion.

## APULEIUS AND PORPHYRY

The *De Civitate Dei* provides ample evidence that Augustine was firmly in touch with late antique sources defining *curiositas* as a morally dangerous trait. His critique of these sources, however, was itself imbued with that same suspicion toward excessive inquisitiveness that these pagan writings convey. From this standpoint, Augustine himself was clearly influenced by the very intellectual milieu that the *De Civitate Dei* subjects to some of its most scathing criticism. His detailed discussions of later *Platonici* (Apuleius and Porphyry) provide cases in point, specifically in regard to magic and theurgy, and the extent to which these practices were instrumental in arousing a curiosity in demonic rites.

In a very real sense, Augustine's references to "pernicious" or "illicit" *curiositas* throughout the *De Civitate Dei* exhibit a marked Apuleian legacy. Apuleius of Madaura, in fact, was a major source of Augustine's knowledge of pagan demonology and its influence on Roman religion. As Chapter 3 of this study disclosed, Apuleius represents one of the most important late antique commentators on the evils of excessive curiosity. In *De Civitate Dei* XVIII, Augustine explicitly refers to Apuleius' *The Golden Ass* (alternately entitled the *Metamorphoses*), in connection with his examination of pagan accounts depicting the transformation of humans into animals.[29] In the present context, however, Augustine simply highlights the outlandishness of these tales.[30] "Stories of this kind," he stresses, "are either untrue or at least so extraordinary…we are justified in withholding credence."[31] Indeed, Apuleius offers a critical touchstone for coming to terms with that unregulated desire for knowledge that constitutes the root fault of the curious disposition.

But by the same token, the Augustine of the *De Civitate Dei* exhibits something of an ambiguity in his attitude to Apuleius. On one level, Augustine draws upon Apuleius' writings (most notably, the *De Deo Socratis*) for evidence of pagan attitudes toward their own religious tradition. But underlying this critique, we find him implicitly incorporating Apuleian sentiments into his overall indictment of human forays into such forbidden realms as magic and theurgy. What, precisely, does Augustine derive from Apuleius in this vein? First and foremost, Apuleius draws an intriguing parallel between the inner life of humans and demons.

> Apuleius the Platonist…treats of the character of the demons, and says that they are liable to the same emotional disturbances as human beings.[32]

Augustine's chief concern here lies in the demons' intellectual life, rather than in their passions alone. He finds a reference to intellectual pursuits in the very origins of the term "demon," derived from *daemones*, which Plato links with the ego or *nous*, and to which he imparts the connotations of "knowing" or "wisdom" (*Cratylus* 398b).[33] Demonic knowledge can only be malignant, since it exhibits an arrogance

antithetical to the love of God.[34] More specifically, Augustine views
that brand of knowledge (for all its pretensions) as devoid of any claim
to Christian charity.

> Without charity, knowledge exalts man to an arrogance which is
> nothing but…emptiness.[35]

Augustine's emphasis on the inflationary character of demonic knowledge calls to mind his exegesis of Ecclesiasticus 10:9-14 and its image
of the proud man's outward distention upon the cares of the temporal
manifold.[36] When read against the background of *De Trinitate* X and
XII, Augustine depicts the knowledge of demons as the veritable paradigm of the human mind's lower, sciential orientation. The upshot of
this orientation is that the mind can become so engrossed in temporal
endeavors that it abdicates its contemplative focus on higher truths
(and ultimately, God). In this way, curiosity works closely in conjunction with pride. Accordingly, Augustine characterizes the arrogance of
demons as a vain attempt to reserve for themselves the honors and
service rightfully reserved for God alone.[37]

By extension, Augustine cites a lack of humility in those who aspire
to imitate the demons. "They resemble the demons in arrogance," he
charges, "but not in knowledge."[38] Accordingly, he contrasts the vain
attempts to know on the part of demons with the angelic disposition
toward material and temporal affairs. From Augustine's standpoint,
the crucial difference lies in the respective attitudes of demons and
angels toward what is lower in the hierarchy of creation as a whole.

> The good angels hold cheap all the knowledge of material and tem-
> poral matters, which inflates the demons with pride.[39]

This stance on the part of the angels is wholly consistent with a recognition of the ordering of creation, and the proper relation between the
created world and God. In keeping with Augustine's vision of *ordo*, a
knowledge of mutable things is only possible if one appreciates them
in light of their first causes in the Divine Word.

> It is one thing to conjecture temporal matters from temporal evi-
> dence, mutable things from mutable evidence, and then to interfere
> in events in a temporal and mutable fashion…a very different thing
> to foresee the changes of the temporal order in the eternal and un-
> changing laws of God.[40]

But how is this demonic tendency to manipulate the order of nature reflected in human activities? Once again, Augustine reflects the influence of Apuleius, albeit for critical purposes. In Apuleius' *Metamorphoses* (i.e., *The Golden Ass* to which Augustine refers at *De Civitate Dei* XVIII,18), we recall, the narrator confesses to his susceptibility to an excessive curiosity with magic. This inquisitiveness not only led to his transformation into a beast, but subjected him to all the vicissitudes accompanying the pursuit of forbidden knowledge. In this vein, Augustine attributes the vice of *curiositas* directly to magical practitioners. This indictment of magic is closely aligned with a condemnation of theurgy, that brand of the magical arts rooted in the *Chaldaean Oracles* and later endorsed by the Neoplatonic philosophers Porphyry and Iamblichus.[41]

In actuality, Augustine's attitude toward Porphyry (A.D. c. 234-c.301) is as ambivalent as his attitude toward other representatives of Graeco-Roman thought. By virtue of his own indebtedness to the Neoplatonic tradition, Augustine considered Porphyry the Neoplatonic thinker whose search for a "universal way of salvation" placed him close to Christianity (despite his own vehement opposition to Christian teaching).[42] But Augustine likewise viewed Porphyry in highly critical terms in light of Porphyry's endorsement of theurgy (even as he recognized its dangers). The reason for Porphyry's inconsistency regarding these practices clearly puzzles Augustine.

> You return to them again and again; your only object...to give the appearance of being an expert in those matters...and to ingratiate yourself with those who hanker after such illicit practices, or else to arouse a curious interest in them.[43]

It is interesting to observe Augustine's use of *curiositas*-language in this context. While *curiositas* encompasses a fascination with these activities, it also covers (as we have seen above) a superstitious preoccupation with idolatrous observances. Augustine's imaginary appeal to the long deceased Porphyry reflects this fertility of meaning.

> Do you still doubt that they are malignant demons? Or is it perhaps that you pretend ignorance for fear of offending the theurgists, who have taken advantage of your superstition to seduce you into accepting the pernicious nonsense of their teaching as if it were a great benefit?[44]

From Augustine's standpoint, then, the practitioners of theurgy only exploit people's innate curiosity in order to deceive them into accepting their demonic rites. If Porphyry fails to renounce such practices (for all his supposed allegiance to Platonism), then he incurs a culpability as well.

> You did not get this doctrine from Plato. It was your Chaldaean teachers who persuaded you to bring human weakness up into the exalted heights of the universe…so that your gods might be able to give supernatural revelations to the theurgists.[45]

Augustine's remarks point to a certain evolution in Porphyry's attitude toward theurgy. His initial disdain of magic and its accompanying superstitions (in a spirit of fidelity to his teacher Plotinus) gave way to a partial receptivity to theurgy under the influence of the *Chaldaean Oracles*. While he continued to maintain a critical perspective toward these practices, he linked them with a "universal way" to purification and salvation for the spiritual soul.[46] In this respect, Porphyry reveals what Augustine perceives as an irreconcilable tension.

> One can observe him…wavering between a superstition which amounts to the sin of blasphemy, and a philosophical standpoint.[47]

Augustine seizes upon this ambiguity in Porphyry in the interests of his indictment of the evils inherent in the magical arts. From his perspective, however, the appellation people impart to these arts (whether it be "magic," "sorcery," or the more lofty designation of "theurgy") is a moot point. Whatever the title, these practices are all governed by "the rules of criminal superstition" (i.e., *curiositas*) in service of demonic rites.[48] In the broader context of Augustine's anti-pagan polemic, magic and theurgy represent no more than pretenses to legitimate avenues to knowledge, and ultimately, the attainment of wisdom. In this regard, he sharply distinguishes the worship of demons (and human imitations of their dispositions) from the salutary influence of true religion.[49] In this respect, the miracles achieved by a simple faith in the one true God only highlight the folly of all the deceitful manifestations of the magical arts.[49]

Augustine's distinction between demonic worship and true religion assumes a special significance for a Neoplatonist like Porphyry. Any dabbling on Porphyry's part with the magical arts (even when ennobled as "theurgy" in support of the higher soul's purification) is ultimately rooted in an even greater flaw he shared with other Neoplatonists, including Plotinus: the pride which prevented his acceptance of the Incarnation and the grace which Christ offers those who believe. These sentiments are poignantly expressed in Augustine's *Confessions* (at the end of the same book in which he celebrates the impact of the *libri platonicorum* upon his outlook):

> All this those writings of the Platonists do not have. Their pages do not have this face of piety, the tears of confession, your sacrifice, a troubled spirit, a contrite and a humbled heart.[50]

But the errors of the Neoplatonists only reflect a more pervasive alienation from truth which characterizes the sinfulness of humanity as a whole. Augustine's anti-pagan polemic highlights the extent to which sin permeates the human condition. In the context of his socio-political theory, this sinful state encompasses the entire secular sphere (that is, the earthly city). But how is the earthly city distinguished from the Heavenly City, the City of God? Ultimately, these realms are defined in terms of the quality of their collective loves.

> The earthly city was created by self-love reaching the point of contempt for God, the Heavenly City by the love of God carried as far as contempt of self. Consequently, in the earthly city its wise men who live by men's standards have pursued the goods of the body or of their own mind, or of both.[51]

Augustine's understanding of this solidarity of sinners provides something of a template for his critique of pagan culture, and more specifically, for his emphasis on the sin of *curiositas* as a stimulus for various aspects of its religious observance. But what constitutes the "sinfulness of humanity" in the *De Civitate Dei*? This question prompts us to reconsider the theme of the "fallen soul" in Augustine's interpretation of the scope and extent of *iniquitas*, the ultimate source of moral evil.

## CURIOSITAS AND FALLENNESS IN THE
## DE CIVITATE DEI

Augustine's most explicit treatment of the origin of sin is found in *De Civitate Dei* XIII and XIV. These books articulate his mature position regarding the soul's *lapsus*: if sinners stand in solidarity with each other, their corporate guilt proceeds from their common identity in Adam.

> The whole human race was in the first man, and it was to pass from him through the woman into his progeny, when the married pair had received the divine sentence of condemnation. And it was not man as first made, but what man became after his sin and punishment, that was thus begotten, as far as concerns the origin of sin and death.[52]

In Augustinian terms, the contrast between "man as first made" and "what man became after sin and punishment" has a direct bearing on the classic problem of evil. By means of this distinction, Augustine alleviates God (as supreme Creator of all natures) from responsibility for sin and its devastating effects. Accordingly, "what man became after sin and punishment" pertains to the moral culpability of rational natures created in God's image, but capable of deviating from the good through the exercise of free will.

But where does the evil use of the will originate? In broad metaphysical terms, Augustine roots the tendency to moral wrongdoing (even before Adam's sin) in the very fact of creation *ex nihilo* and the sheer finitude of our creatureliness.[53] In moral terms, however, this fallibility proceeds from our collective union as Adam's progeny.

> Man was willingly perverted and justly condemned, and so begot perverted and condemned offspring. For we were all in that one man, seeing that we all were that one man who fell into sin through the woman who was made from him before the first sin.[54]

Augustine's language here is unmistakably clear. Just as he distinguishes human nature *as created* from human nature *in sin* (that is, our pre-lapsarian and post-lapsarian condition, respectively), he distinguishes human nature in its seminal state (when we were one with Adam) from our embodied mode of existence embracing "forms individually created and assigned to us...to live in them as individuals."[55] For Augustine, the initial *lapsus* of Adam precipitated a moral upheaval in the order of creation amounting to an endless death.

> From the misuse of free will there started a chain of disasters: mankind is led from that original perversion, a kind of corruption at the root, right up to the disaster of the second death, which has no end.[56]

In Augustine's depiction of human nature before and after sin, O'Connell discerned a "doubling" of Adam's mind/body constitution and the spiritual/corporeal paradise he inhabited.[57] On the basis of his Neoplatonic reading of the *De Civitate Dei*, O'Connell saw evidence of Augustine's commitment to the Plotinian notion of a higher transtemporal/transindividual human. In keeping with this interpretation, O'Connell further perceived a theory of a common fall of humanity from contemplative union with God (with Adam representing the fullness of human nature in which we all share).[58]

But these two levels of humanness (the contemplative and the incarnate) point to a dual level of sinning: *first*, the "external" or "outward" sin of Adam's disobedience perpetrated in the embodied existence proper to him alone; *secondly*, that initial defection from God prompted by pride in the contemplative life of our common humanity.[59] In Augustinian terms, then, the historical commission of sin on Adam's part was preceded by an evil will which opened the way to a radical alienation from Divine fellowship.

> It was in secret that the first human beings began to be evil; and the result was that they slipped into open disobedience. For they would not have arrived at the evil act if an evil will had not preceded it. Now, could anything but pride have been the start of the evil will? For 'pride is the start of every kind of sin' (Eccl. 10,13). And what is pride except a longing for a perverse kind of exaltation?[60]

If humans share in Adam's guilt, it can only proceed from our common identity in Adam's sin on a transindividual level. In this respect, the *De Civitate Dei* offers a means of redefining the meaning of the "fallenness" of souls. According to Rombs, the Augustine of the *De Civitate Dei* period (the "later" Augustine) defended the doctrine of Adam's sin in the Pauline sense of "derivation" from Adam.[61] From this standpoint, primal sin is not necessarily linked with embodiment *per se*. Rather, it lies in the will's aversion from God in favor of those goods proper to itself alone.[62] For Rombs, this amounts to a recasting of the Plotinian understanding of the soul's fall from a strict ontological interpretation to a metaphorical one, whereby "fallenness" is construed in terms of a moral lapse or "psychology of sin."[63]

But however we interpret Augustine's meaning in this context, the fact remains that the fall motif takes on a rather prominent role in the *De Civitate Dei's* discussions of the origins of sin. Indeed, Augustine's depiction of the will as "falling away from its true being" bespeaks an ongoing commitment to the Plotinian understanding of the soul/body relationship, along with its dichotomies between the common and the proper, the whole and the part, the contemplative and the active, the higher and the lower.

> Only a nature created out of nothing could have been distorted by a fault. Consequently, although the will derives its existence, as a nature, from its creation by God, its falling away from its true being is due to its creation out of nothing.[64]

So, whether Augustine embraces an ontological or moral/psychological theory of the soul's fallenness is not the pivotal issue for the present purposes. Rather, my concern here lies in his analysis of the soul's sin in the concrete circumstances of human existence, at "ground level," so to speak. As I affirmed in Chapter 6 and 7 (above), I adopt a position somewhat intermediate to the positions of O'Connell and Rombs.

While I recognize (*pace* O'Connell) the marked Plotinian character of Augustine's conception of psychic fallenness, I situate this theory (*pace* Rombs) firmly in the soul's existential experience as embodied. From my perspective, however, Augustine's treatment of the soul's fall encompasses more than a moral/psychological dimension. In keeping with his theory of the soul's mid-rank status between God and corporeal natures, it assumes marked metaphysical implications relevant to the quality of the soul's very being. For Augustine, sin disrupts the soul's mid-rank and proper ordering which places it in submission to Divine authority and in governance of what lies beneath rational natures in the hierarchy of creation as a whole. In this respect, the evil will cuts across the lines of any distinction between "higher" (contemplative) and "lower" (embodied) psychic levels.

In Augustinian terms, the sin of Adam finds its most salient expression in pride, the paradigmatic use of the evil will. But in Augustine's reckoning, pride does not work in complete isolation. Rather, it is tightly conjoined with the other triadic components of curiosity and carnal concupiscence. Accordingly, Augustine interprets the range of human sins in terms of St. Paul's moral category of the "works of the flesh."[65] Such deeds are not restricted to sensual indulgence alone, but also embrace "faults of the mind," proceeding from the deepest recesses of human motivation.[66]

Joseph Torchia Restless Mind

Any exercise of the evil will encompasses an intellectual element of intentionality. But Augustine's reference to "faults of the mind" has a special applicability to the sin of *curiositas*, the triadic vice rooted in an unregulated cognitive desire. In this connection, his reference to sorcery as an example of one of these "faults of the mind" (along with devotion to idols, enmity, quarrelsomeness, jealousy, animosity, party intrigue, and envy) acquires a marked significance in relation to his critique of pagan culture and its religious practices. As we have seen, Augustine's anti-pagan polemic draws heavily upon *curiositas*-language in describing the attraction to various aspects of the magical arts (including sorcery and theurgy).

In a very real sense, the *curiositas* of pagans is the *curiositas* of everyman who inhabits the earthly city. From Augustine's perspective, that encompasses us all. For him, this species of lust exerts a powerful influence in shaping the value system of those already alienated from God by virtue of Adam's primordial defection. But this alienation is only intensified in the absence of the moral guidance of true religion and its devotion to the one God. By extension, pagan *curiositas* reveals the capacity of fallen humanity to attach itself to the most bizarre and outlandish religious practices, ostensibly for the good of the state. In this regard, the excessive care inherent in *curiositas* assumes a whole new dimension in the context of demonic worship. This brand of care (with its various cognitive and emotional connotations) prompts a superstitious reverence or awe before what are no more than malignant powers oriented toward the destruction of human societies. The very drawing power of *curiositas* allows it to cloud the minds of those who unwittingly submit themselves to such a distorted religious perspective.

## NOTES TO CHAPTER 8

1. *Sermo* 112A: MA I,256: *Intelligitur iste princeps daemoniorum diabolus, in qualm irruunt omnes curiosi: omnis enim curiositas illicita pestilens inopia est veritatis.*
2. For further discussion of Augustine's early attraction to shows, see *Confessiones* I,10(16); III,2. For precedents in patristic discussions regarding the evils of *spectaculi*, see Novatian's *De spectaculis* (which rejects the viewing of public performances), a work which found inspiration in

Augustine's North African forerunner, Tertullian (whose own *De spectac-ulis* indicts public games, athletic events, and gladiatorial combats).

3. *De Civitate Dei* I,32. All subsequent references to the *De Civitate Dei* in this chapter are designated as "**DCD**". I am indebted in this chapter to Gerard O'Daly's *Augustine's City of God. A Reader's Guide* (Oxford: Oxford University Press, 2009) for its excellent treatment of those aspects of the work dealing with Augustine's anti-pagan polemic.

4. **DCD** I,32. At **DCD** I,31, Augustine refers to the efforts of Scipio Nasica Corculum (155 B.C.) to induce the Senate to forego the building of a stone theater, so as to protect the populace from the infiltration of Hellenic cor-ruption into the Roman character. But Augustine bemoans the fact that the same individual failed to banish the spectacles (and by implication, the authority of the demons) from Rome.

5. **DCD** II,4.

6. **DCD** II,4: CC (SL) XLVII,37,29-31: *Quaesi inlecta curiositate adesse potu-it circumfusa, saltem? offensa castitate debuit abire confusa.*

7. **DCD** II,4. Here, Augustine refers specifically to the annual festival of Berecynthia's purification, which he seems to link with the cult of the Heavenly Virgin. Cf., **DCD** II,26, for Augustine's reference to the rites surrounding the devotion of the Heavenly Virgin.

8. **DCD** II,6.

9. **DCD** II,26.

10. **DCD** II,26.

11. **DCD** III,9.

12. **DCD** III,9. Periods of peace were marked by the closing of the gates of the temple of Janus.

13. **DCD** III,9: CC (SL) XLVII,70,6: *perniciosissima curiositate neglecta Deum…*

14. **DCD** IV,30. More precisely, Cicero depicts (*On the Nature of the Gods* II,28,70) the Stoic philosopher Quintus Lucilius Balbus as participating in this discussion and expressing these sentiments.

15. **DCD** IV,30.

16. Marcus Terentius Varro (116-27 B.C.), an extremely prolific writer (who provided a veritable encyclopedia for Augustine's purposes), was an Academic philosopher who renounced the New Academy's scepticism.

17. **DCD** IV,31.

18. **DCD** IV,31.

19. **DCD** IV,34.

20. **DCD** IV,34: CC (SL) XLVII,127,24-26: *Et si non in eum peccassent, im-pia curiositate tamquam magicis artibus seducti ad alienos deos et ad idola defluendo.*

21. **DCD** V,21.

22. **DCD** V,21.

23. **DCD** V,25.

24. **DCD** V,26: CC (SL) XLVII,161,10-11: *hic in angustiis curarum suarum non est lapsus ad curiositates sacrilegas atque inlicitas...*

25. **DCD** V,21: CC (SL) XLVII,157,23-24: *cuius egregiam indolem decepit amore dominandi sacrilega et detestanda curiositas.*

26. Augustine quotes Varro at **DCD** VII,34.

27. **DCD** VII,34: CC (SL) XLVII,214,21-23: *que Numam Pampilium curiositate inlicita ad ea daemonum peruenisse secreta, quae ipse quidem scriberet, ut haberet unde legendo commoneretur;*

28. **DCD** VII,34: CC (SL) XLVII,214,29-215,37: *Senatus autem cum religiones formidaret damnare maiorum et ideo Numae adsentiri cogeretur, illos tamen libros tam perniciosos esse iudicauit, ut nec obrui rursus iuberet, ne humana curiositas multo uehementius rem iam proditam quaereret, sed flammis aboleri nefanda monumenta, ut, quia iam necesse esse existimabant sacra illa facere, tolerabilius erraretur causis eorum ignoratis, quam cognitis ciuitas turbaretur.*

29. **DCD** XVIII,17-18.

30. Cf., **DCD** XVI,8, where Augustine discusses accounts in pagan history regarding certain monstrous races of humans, "taken from books of 'curiosities,' as we may call them" (CC[SL] XLVIII,508,18: *ex libris deprompta uelut curiosioris historiae*). In this context, Augustine uses *curiositas*-language in reference to what is perceived as unusual, and therefore, conducive to drawing humans to scrutinize these things (however monstrous or bizarre), simply for the sake of the fascination itself. In contemporary usage, a "curiosity" might be viewed in more innocuous terms, as something which is simply interesting, with no claim to intellectual depth or profundity.

31. **DCD** XVIII,18.

32. **DCD** VIII,16.

33. **DCD** IX,20.

34. **DCD** IX,19.

35. **DCD** IX,20.

36. Cf., *De Genesi contra Manichaeos* II,6; *De Musica* VI,13(40).

37. **DCD** IX,20.

38. **DCD** IX,20.

39. **DCD** IX,22.

40. **DCD** IX,22. Augustine, however, also affirms (**DCD** IX,22) that the demons possess a greater knowledge of the future than do humans, "by their greater acquaintance with certain signs which are hidden from us."

41. According to Anne D.R. Sheppard ("Theurgy," Simon Hornblower and Antony Spawforth, eds., *The Oxford Classical Dictionary*, 3rd Ed. Revised [Oxford: Oxford University Press, 2003], 1512a-b), theurgy "was a form of pagan religious magic associated with the Chaldaean Oracles and taken up by the later Neoplatonists...from rain-making and cures to animating

statues of the gods ...based on a theory of cosmic sympathy...to promote union of the human soul with the divine."

42. Cf., **DCD** X,23-32. For Augustine's attitude toward Porphyry, see Frederick Van Fleteren, "Porphyry," in *Augustine Through the Ages. An Encyclopedia* (Grand Rapids, Michigan/Cambridge, UK: William B. Eerdmans Publishing Company, 1999), 661b-662a. According to Gerard O'Daly (*Augustine's City of God. A Reader's Guide*, 259), "Porphyry is an essential source for Augustine's views on higher, philosophically influenced attitudes to the afterlife and preparation for it."

43. **DCD** X,28: CC (SL) XLVII,303,12-14: *nisi ut talium quoque rerum quasi peritus appareas et placeas inlicitarum artium curiosus, uel ad eas facias ipse curiosos.* When Augustine describes these practices as "illicit," he does not mean it in moral terms alone. In point of fact, legislation prohibiting magical practices was present from the earliest days of the Roman Empire, with a resurgence of these restrictions in his own era. H.S. Versnel ("Magic," in *The Oxford Classical Dictionary*, 3rd Ed. Revised, 910a) describes this trend in the fourth century in these terms: "In this period, ...magic was practically identified with *prava religio* ('bad religion') and *superstitio* ('superstition'), which together, served as conveniently comprehensive (and vague) classificatory terms to discredit social, political, and/or religious opponents." Versnel's observation regarding the identification of "bad religion" with *superstitio* is consistent with Augustine's treatment of these notions.

44. **DCD** X,26: CC (SL) XLVII,301,31-34: *Adhuc dubitas haec maligna esse daemonia, uel te fingis fortasse nescire, dum non uis theurgos offendere, a quibus curiositate deceptus ista perniciosa et insana pro magno beneficio didicisti?*

45. **DCD** X,27.

46. For clarification of Porphyry's evolving disposition toward theurgy (from his critical stance as a disciple of Plotinus to his receptiveness to such practices by virtue of his influence by the Chaldaean Oracles), see Robert Dodaro, O.S.A., "Theurgy," *Augustine Through the Ages*, 827b. According to Dodaro, the "universal way" was a means "by which the majority of people, unable to sustain the rigors of contemplation without ritual, could achieve at least partial moral and spiritual purification." Garth Fowden (*The Egyptian Hermes. A historical approach to the late pagan mind* [Cambridge, UK: Cambridge University Press, 1986], 131) offers this assessment of Porphyry's apparent inconsistency on the subject of theurgy (an inconsistency which Augustine is quick to highlight in the interests of his own polemic): "Porphyry...was the first major philosopher to take the *Oracula Chaldaica* seriously, yet he never espoused them whole-heartedly. There is nothing strange, especially in a pupil of Plotinus, in the sharp distinction Porphyry makes in his *De abstinentia* between the unclean magician...and the divine man...pure both without and within. It is striking... to find Porphyry attacking theurgy in his *Epistola ad Anebonem*...on the

grounds of its irreconcilability with the fundamentally intellectual character of Greek philosophy, but conceding, in the *De regressu animae*, that it was a possible means of purifying the spiritual soul."

47. **DCD** X,9: CC (SL) XLVII,282,16-18: *ut uideas eum inter uitium sacrilegae curiositatis et philosophiae professionem sententiis alternantibus fluctuare.*

48. **DCD** X,9: CC (SL) XLVII,281,3-7: *Fiebant autem simplici fide atque fiducia pietatis, non incantationibus et carminibus nefariae curiositatis arte compositis, quam uel magian uel detestabiliore nomine goetian uel honorabiliore theurgian uocant...*

49. **DCD** X,9. At **DCD** X,27: CC (SL) XLVII,302,35-37, Augustine contrasts a reliance on Christ with the errors of self-reliance or a reliance upon superstition: *Quem tu quoque utinam cognouisses eique te potius quam uel tuae uirtuti, quae humana, fragilis* et infirma est, uel perniciosissimae curiositati *sanandum tutius commisisses.*

50. *Confessiones* VII,21(27). Augustine also assumes a critical attitude toward the Plotinian school regarding an interest in magic on the part of some of its members in *Ep.* 118,5(33): "...the school of Plotinus flourished at Rome, and had as disciples many extremely shrewd and clever men but some of them were led astray by an attraction for the practices of magic..." (CSEL XXXIII, Pars 2, 697: *sed aliqui eorum magicarum atrium curiostate deprauati sunt*).

51. **DCD** XIV,28: CC (SL) XLVII,451,1-3; 12-14: *terrenam scilicet amor sui usque ad contemptum Dei, caelestem uero amor Dei usque ad contemptum sui. Ideoque in illa sapientes eius secundum hominem uiuentes aut corporis aut animi sui bona aut utriusque sectati sunt...*

52. **DCD** XIII,3: CC (SL) XLVII,22-27: *In primo igitur homine per feminam in progeniem transiturum uniuersum genus humanum fuit, quando illa coniugum copula diuinam sententiam suae damnationis excepit; et quod homo factus est, non cum crearetur, sed cum peccaret et puniretur, hoc genuit, quantum quidem adtinet ad peccati et mortis originem.*

53. I explore this theme in greater detail in my article "Creation, Finitude, and the Mutable Will: Augustine on the Origin of Moral Evil," *Irish Theological Quarterly* 71(2006), 63: "For Augustine, things created from nothing are characterized by a mutability that sets them apart from the immutability of the Divine nature. In rational creatures, this mutability manifests itself in the defective use of the will, the basis of moral evil and the source of their corruptibility. As the expression of the bad will, moral evil is rooted not in created reality as such, but in the tendency toward non-being that harkens back to creation *ex nihilo*."

54. **DCD** XIII,14: CC (SL) XLVII,395,2-5: *sed sponte deprauatus iusteque damnatus deprauatos damnatosque generauit. Omnes enim fuimus in illo uno, quando omnes fuimus ille unus, qui per feminam lapsus est in peccatum, quae de illo facta est ante peccatum.*

55. **DCD** XIII,14: CC (SL) XLVII,395,6-7: *singullatim creata et distributa forma, in qua singuli uiueremus;*

56. **DCD** XIII,14: CC (SL) XLVII,395,10-396,13: *Ac per hoc a liberi arbitrii malo usu series calamitatis huius exorta est, quae humanum genus origine deprauata, uelut radice corrupta, usque ad secundae mortis exitium, quae non habet finem...*

57. Robert, J. O'Connell, S.J., *The Origin of the Soul in St. Augustine's Later Works* (New York: Fordham University Press, 1987), 318: "In line with his mature theory, this doubling would imply that, *qua* embodied, Adam was an historical individual living his own proper life and, therefore, an individual distinct from any and all of his descendants. But *qua* contemplative soul, dwelling on the luminous heights of this "spiritual" paradise, this incarnate Adam could simultaneously be what Plotinus would describe as... contemplative Soul."

58. Robert J. O'Connell, S.J., *The Origin of the Soul in St. Augustine's Later Works*, 318: "This would permit him to be the totality of "human nature" in which we all once commonly participated; as such, "his" fall from the spiritual paradise of contemplative union with God could indeed be "our" common fall, as well."

59. Robert J. O'Connell, S.J., *The Origin of the Soul in St. Augustine's Later Works*, 318: "That fall...was due to a "hidden" sin of pride which ...must in some real...sense have preceded its expression in the "outward" act of disobedience Adam committed as incarnate individual in the "corporeal" paradise."

60. **DCD** XIV,13: CC (SL) XLVII,434, 1-6: *In occulto autem mali esse coeperunt, ut in apertam inoboedientiam laberentur. Non enim ad malum opus perueniretur, nisi praecessisset uoluntas mala. Porro malae uoluntatis initium quae potuit esse nisi superbia? <u>Initium</u> enim <u>omnis peccati superbia est</u>. Quid est autem superbia nisi peruersae celsitudinis appetitus?*

61. Ronnie J. Rombs, *Saint Augustine and the Fall of the Soul. Beyond O'Connell and His Critics* (Washington, D.C.: The Catholic University of America Press, 2006), 188: "Augustine's thought in regard to the soul's origin has undergone substantial development: given that he will now defend the doctrine of original sin only in the Pauline terms of derivation from Adam, the question of the origin of the soul ceases to possess the theological significance it once held for him. In other words, since Augustine's interest in the fallen soul theory was always limited to the theory's capacity to explain the current anthropological situation, and since he now demonstrates that such a situation can be explained only in terms of Paul's schema of derivation from Adam, the question of the origin of the soul has no significant theological role to play. The question of the soul's origin can be safely set aside; the later Augustine can remain agnostic about the soul's origin without theological compromise."

62. Ronnie J. Rombs, *Saint Augustine and the Fall of the Soul. Beyond O'Connell and His Critics*, 199: "Unity is a matter of harmony of will; it is not ontological. Unity and alienation are understood in terms of proximity of will, not by corporeity nor by ontological separation or individuation... individuation and corporeity have nothing to do with sin. Rather, our unity or separation, our blessedness or fallenness, is based upon the orientation of our will."

63. Referring to **DCD** XIV,13, Rombs (*Saint Augustine and the Fall of the Soul. Beyond O'Connell and His Critics*, 204) asserts: "Man did not fall away to the extent of losing all being; but when he had turned towards himself his being was less real than when he adhered to him who exists in a supreme degree." In this vein, Rombs further contends (204) that the abandonment of "God for oneself is not a movement toward individuation or ontological separation but a moral lapse of the will; the effect is characterized by psychological or inner separation." By the same token, Rombs' interpretation of "fallenness" has a bearing on his interpretation of our relation to Adam. In this respect, as we have seen, Rombs (197; 199) holds that our Adamic unity is not to be understood in ontological terms, but in terms of a *societas* that anticipates our perfection as spiritual bodies joined in a fellowship of peace and beatitude.

64. **DCD** XIV,13: CC (SL) XLVII,434,23-26: *Sed uitio deprauari nisi ex nihilo facta natura non posset. Ac per hoc ut natura sit, ex eo habet quod a Deo facta est; ut autem ab eo quod est deficiat, ex hoc quod de nihilo facta est.*

65. Gal. 5:19-21: "Now the works of the flesh are obvious: immorality, impurity, licentiousness, idolatry, sorcery, hatreds, rivalry, jealousy, outbursts of fury, acts of selfishness, dissensions, factions, occasions of envy, drinking bouts, orgies, and the like."

66. **DCD** XIV,2.

# CHAPTER 9

# THE *CURIOSITAS* OF
# CHRISTIANS

A ugustine's socio-political theory is marked by a stark realism. Because he accepts the world on its own terms, he never envisions anything remotely resembling a utopia emerging from the earthly city. Nor does he expect a greater level of perfection from human societies than our creaturely finitude can achieve. The major reason for this pessimism (aside from psychological factors touching upon his own disposition or temperament) lies in his theological conviction in the pervasiveness of sin in every facet of our lives. Peter Brown describes this aspect of the Augustinian perspective (with a special focus upon Augustine's preoccupation with the intellectual life):

> Augustine's view of the Fall of mankind determined his attitude to society. Fallen men had come to need restraint. Even man's greatest achievements had been made possible only by a 'strait jacket' of unremitting harshness. Augustine was a great intellect, with a healthy respect for the achievements of human reason. Yet he was obsessed by the difficulties of thought, and by the long, coercive processes, reaching back into the horrors of his own schooldays, that had made this intellectual activity possible.[1]

As the preceding chapter has shown, Augustine perceives the impact of sin as especially pronounced in a pagan world deprived of any acquaintance with the teachings of Christ. But he by no means considered the Christian community as immune to its degenerative effects. Indeed, he has much to say to his fellow Christians about their own susceptibility to vice in all its forms, including *curiositas*, the lust of the eyes. These statements emerge largely in Augustine's scriptural exegesis, in his sermons, and in other pastorally oriented writings.

This pastoral dimension cannot be overlooked in our study of the diverse contexts in which Augustine discusses the sin of curiosity. His entry into religious life, his subsequent consecration as a bishop, and his increasing apostolic care for his flock exerted an incalculable influence upon his outlook.[2] This is equally the case in his ongoing exploration of the dynamics of sin, including the curiosity that most people today view as an expression of a vigorous intellectual life. In this respect, Augustine's counsels regarding curiosity must be appreciated in the pastoral context in which they were articulated.

## CHRISTIAN LIFE IN THE *SAECULUM*

The fact that Augustine was gifted with formidable intellectual gifts and a fertile imagination is beyond doubt. But by the same token, he was fully attuned to the extent to which these faculties could be dissipated on the manifold cares (*curae*) and busyness (*negotiae*) of temporal existence. His conversion (both in intellectual and moral terms) by no means rendered him oblivious to the curiosity which drove him so relentlessly in his past life. After his conversion, he could draw upon this experience in the interests of his fellow Christians. In keeping with his ecclesiology of the two cities, Augustine recognized the complexity of life in the *saeculum*. A Christian *societas* still immersed in the influences of pagan culture was vulnerable to all the temptations that the *De Civitate Dei* so painstakingly catalogues.

In Augustinian terms, the Church constitutes a "mixed body" (*corpus permixtum*) of saints and sinners, or more precisely, aspiring saints and actual sinners. As the Church proceeds on its pilgrimage through the world, "many reprobates are mingled…with the good…collected…in the dragnet of the Gospel."[3] By virtue of this commingling, Christians must come to grips with their status as resident aliens in a morally hazardous realm. The *saeculum* (or alternately the *mundus*) provides the broad setting for Augustine's pastoral admonitions concerning the lust of the eyes (*concupiscentia oculorum*) in all its forms.

## CHRISTIANS AMONG PAGANS

From the earliest days of the Church, Christians viewed themselves as the continuance and perfection of God's call to the people of Israel, set apart from other nations for the implementation of His redemptive plan. This perception of distinctness and exclusivity (which encompassed a desire to rise above the things of a passing world) was particularly pronounced during times of persecution. In that violent era, Christians found a sense of solidarity in their common allegiance to Christ and the proclamation of the Gospel message. But in the aftermath of the Christianization of the Empire, the lines separating "us" from "them," or true believers from pagans became increasingly blurred.[4]

On the one hand, the ability to identify oneself as a Christian by no means provided an inviolable safeguard against the encroachments of the world at large. The lingering sentiments of pagan religion coupled with the residual presence of occultism and superstition, opened Christians to a vast array of opportunities to succumb to the "lust of the eyes." On the other hand, however, threats to Christian identity now emerged within the ranks of the Church itself. Accordingly, the distinction between pagan and Christian found a parallel in the distinction between orthodoxy and heresy.

In this pluralistic and increasingly fragmented milieu, then, Christians confronted both internal and external threats to their unity. In one of his earliest exercises in catechetical instruction, Augustine outlines these dangers, with a special emphasis on the diverse manifestations of diabolical influence:

> He is bold enough not only to tempt Christian people through the instrumentality of those who hate the Christian name…and still fondly desire to do service to idols and the curious rites of evil spirits, but…he also attempts the same through the agency of persons severed from the unity of the Church.[5]

The fact that Catholic Christians were required to maintain an uneasy coexistence with pagans and Christian heretics alike is evident in the sense of urgency inherent in Augustine's exhortation. The mixing of immoral practices with moral living, of the impious with the pious, of reprobates with the good, stands at the forefront of his catechetical concerns.

You will have to witness many drunkards, covetous men, deceivers, gamesters, adulterers, fornicators, men who bind upon their persons sacrilegious charms, and others given up to sorcerers and astrologers, and diviners practised in all kinds of impious arts.[6]

In this context, the "impious arts" to which Augustine refers provides a catch-all phrase for those wide-ranging expressions of *curiositas* that the pagan world celebrated, from magic to superstitious practices of all kinds. The challenge for Augustine as pastor, however, lay in the fact that his congregation was immersed in an environment whose value system was largely at odds with a Christian one. Accordingly, we find him lamenting that "those…crowds which fill the theatres on the festal days of the pagans also fill the churches on the festal days of the Christians."[7] For him, such exposure would inevitably promote imitation on the part of Christians. This danger was particularly acute in regard to public spectacles. "The world promises superfluous, even damnable spectacles to our curiosity," Augustine asserts.[8]

As we have observed in the preceding chapter, the term *spectaculi* embraces any number of popular observances. Literally, the term pertains to what is seen on a wide scale, accessible to a public audience. Metaphorically, however, it assumes a close connection with the Johannine "lust of the eyes" that Augustine linked with the sin of *curiositas*, the unregulated desire for experiential knowledge. The *Confessiones'* account of Alypius' attraction to the circus and gladiatorial exhibitions provides a memorable illustration of the temptations inherent in such *spectaculi*. In Augustine's reminiscence, Alypius fell prey to the enticements of a *curiositas* powerful enough to move his will toward what he so strongly resisted. "He was no longer the man who entered there," Augustine acknowledges, "but only one of the crowd that he had joined."[9]

We have already explored (Chapter 4, above) the prolonged creative process whereby Augustine coordinated the sin of *curiositas* with the *concupiscentia oculorum* of I Jn. 2:16. In the present context, however, it is worthwhile to consider Augustine's detailed exegesis of that particular text. This exegesis provides a crucial referent for his understanding of the relevance of the sin of *curiositas* for Christian living in the crucible of the secular world.

## FOR LOVE OF THE 'WORLD'

Augustine's commentary on I Jn. 2:16 has a direct applicability to those struggling with the moral challenges posed by immersion in the temporal realm. For him, in fact, "dwelling in the world" assumes the connotation of a loving attachment.[10] From this standpoint, affections shape the moral quality of human existence, defining one's relationship with God and neighbor alike. In Augustinian terms, then, those who love the world are designated as "the world," a collective term which embraces everyone in the grip of the *saeculum*.[11]

In keeping with the New Testament dictum that our heart is where our treasure lies (Mt. 6:21), Augustine links the soul's range of loves with an existential commitment that situates us in the hierarchy of creation, either oriented to the higher things of God or toward lower corporeal pleasures. The inclination toward worldly concerns finds expression in the "triple lust" of I Jn. 2:16: the concupiscence of the flesh, the concupiscence of the eyes, and secular ambition.

But Augustine is quick to stress that this scriptural text by no means prohibits the use of our sensory faculties as the embodied beings we are. It merely counsels against an *inordinate* fondness for corporeal and temporal delights. In this respect, Augustine employs his distinction between use (*uti*) and enjoyment (*frui*) in establishing the soul's proper disposition toward created realities in general.[12] This distinction differentiates what we should love (i.e., "enjoy") for its own sake from what we "use" as a means to a greater end.

> Let there be a limit, in respect of the Creator, so that these things do not shackle you by your love… so that you may not love for enjoyment what you ought to love for use.[13]

Augustine's words here remind us of his earlier injunction (in *De Moribus Ecclesiae Catholicae et de Moribus Manichaeorum* I,21,39) that we should not look upon material goods as desirable in and of themselves, but that we should utilize them with "the moderation of a user rather than the passion of a lover." In the present context, the "limit" to which Augustine refers pertains to the very parameters of our human nature, in a manner consistent with the requirements of one's life and duties.

By the time that he composed his exegesis of St. John's first epistle (c. 406/7), of course, Augustine had already coordinated the "triple lust" of I Jn. 2:16 with the primal vices of carnal lust, curiosity, and pride, respectively. In Augustine's reckoning, each of these lusts prompts the soul's movement toward some aspect of worldly experience. Conversely, the soul beset with these vices becomes as worldly as the objects of its love.

The all-encompassing character of sin is exemplified by curiosity. By equating curiosity with the Johannine "lust of the eyes," Augustine highlights the experiential focus of cognitive desire in all its forms. At this juncture of his spiritual journey, however, Augustine is especially concerned with the openness of Christians to this particular temptation, specifically in relation to the culture they inhabit.

> He calls all curiosity the desire of the eyes. Now how widely does curiosity extend? This in shows, in theaters, in the rites of the devil, in magical arts, in sorceries, this is curiosity. Sometimes it tempts even the servants of God so that they wish …to work a miracle, to test whether God listens to them in regard to miracles. It is curiosity. This is the desire of the eyes. It is not of the Father.[14]

The curious desire of Christians to test the efficacy of their own faith finds a scriptural touchstone in the account of Christ's temptations (Mt. 4:6). In the devil's suggestions that Christ cast Himself over the parapet of the Temple, he discerns a tempting by the lust of the eyes to witness His miraculous deliverance from harm. "He resisted the temptation," Augustine contends, "for if He had worked a miracle, He would only seem…to have yielded or…worked it out of curiosity."[16]

If Christians seek to imitate the pattern of Christ's life, they can also look to Him for guidance in the face of temptation. Augustine's implicit message to his readers is clear and unequivocal: Christian identity is not affirmed on the basis of what caters to fickle preoccupations of curiosity (those wondrous or unusual occurrences which arouse the eyes' lust), but in something far more substantial.

> Woe to you if your name has not been written in heaven. Do I say woe to you if you have not raised the dead…if you have not walked on the sea…if you have not driven out demons?[17]

For Augustine, love of the world and love of God are mutually exclusive commitments. This uncompromising stance reflects a Christian Neoplatonic perspective which distinguishes a changing temporal realm of corporeal (and hence, corruptible) natures from an

immutable, eternal mode of being in which we participate through the
life of the soul.

> If love of the world is there, love of God will not be there. Hold
> fast…to the love of God, that, as God is eternal, so…you may abide
> in eternity.[18]

Augustine considers the vice of curiosity one of the major ways of
"loving the world," to the neglect of God and eternal truths. But this
amounts to saying that *curiositas* (like sin in general) cannot be an expression of genuine love. Rather, it manifests an unrestrained desire
that draws the soul farther and farther from its Creator. Still, we can
discern two closely related dimensions inherent in *curiositas*.

In epistemological terms, the desire to know temporal affairs in
acquiring worldly experience is consistent with the mind's lower sciential function. But this sciential function (which is instrumental
in the knowing process of embodied souls) assumes a moral significance as well, when the mind "enjoys" the objects of its attention as
ends in themselves. The degree to which they appropriate and become
one with these things mirrors the depth of human fallenness. The
Christians to whom Augustine appeals as pastor gathered knowledge
of the external world in the same manner as every other human being. But morally speaking, their experiential field is also coextensive
with that of a fallen humanity. In this respect, there is a clear difference between grasping the outer world in a purely cognitive sense and
"fastening" oneself to it in a loving manner. When Augustine warns
his audience of the moral hazards of curiosity, he is addressing this
affective dimension. Indeed, the Christian vocation to a supernatural
destiny beyond this life raises the bar of moral striving to a higher
plane than that of pagans.[19]

## THE 'EYE-OPENING' CHARACTER OF SIN

St. John's first epistle provided Augustine with a fertile visual metaphor for the sin of *curiositas* and its world-oriented character. Once
he identified *curiositas* with the Johannine "lust of the eyes," he found
a means of linking the human craving for knowledge with the love of
worldly experience. Ever faithful to classical epistemological presuppositions, Augustine considers the eyes as representative of the five
senses, and vision paradigmatic of sense experience in general.

> The reason…these senses are…presented with reference to the eyes,
> the whole represented by the part, is that among the five senses the
> eyes have first place.[20]

In scriptural terms, however, this ocular motif harkens back to Gen.
3:6-7 and its reference to the "opening of the eyes" of Adam and Eve after succumbing to the serpent's temptation. Genesis offered Augustine
additional biblical support for the connection between the human
desire to know and the broadening of one's cognitive perspective expressed by means of the image of "seeing." His commentary on Gen.
3:6-7 sheds further light on his understanding of the implications of
the sin of *curiositas* in abetting the alienation of humans from God.

In Genesis, the disclosure that Adam and Eve's eyes were opened is
correlative with the serpent's promise that "your eyes will be open" once
they eat the fruit of the tree of knowledge of good and evil. Augustine
stresses that this revelatory experience does not imply that they were
physically blind to the world prior to sin.

> When they were created…their eyes were not closed…blind in the
> gardens of delights…in danger of unwittingly touching the forbid-
> den tree and…picking…the…fruit.[21]

If the post-lapsarian Adam and Eve can now "see," it must be in a
new way, from an alternate cognitive perspective. In Augustine's assessment, "they were opened to see and recognize what they had not
formerly noticed."[22]

The fact that they first perceive their nakedness after their transgression is significant in this context. Their very awareness of their
own physicality (with the sense of shame accompanying that awareness) underscores an inner transformation proceeding from a radically
changed relationship with God.

> As soon…as they violated the precept, they were completely naked,
> interiorly deserted by the grace which they had offended by pride
> and arrogant love of their own independence. Casting their eyes on
> their bodies, they felt a movement of concupiscence which they had
> not known.[23]

As the foregoing quote indicates, Augustine posits carnal concupiscence as a consequence of separation from God through disobedience.
Natural bodies destined for a spiritual condition become mortal "bodies of death."[24] Adam and Eve begin to regard each other exclusively

in corporeal terms, dominated by concupiscential desire. But as the quote also affirms, Augustine imputes the prime incentive for this act of defection to pride, the scriptural "beginning of all sin" (Eccl. 10:9-14). In this regard, however, pride works closely in conjunction with curiosity, the third component of Augustine's moral triad.

> When curiosity was stirred up and made bold to transgress a commandment, it was eager to experience the unknown, to see what would follow from touching what was forbidden, finding delight in taking a dangerous sort of liberty by bursting the bonds of prohibition.[25]

By virtue of its kinship with pride, curiosity presupposes an audacity to disobey the Divine command. The three motives that Augustine attributes to the curious disposition display clear affinities with the connotations surrounding *curiositas* (and its Greek counterparts *periergia* and *polupragmosune*) in the classical tradition: *first*, *curiositas* coincides with an eagerness to experience what is not known; *secondly*, it encompasses a venturesomeness to explore the forbidden; *third*, it takes pleasure in a rash quest for autonomy that Augustine characterizes as a "dangerous...liberty."[26] This flawed grasp at independence is evocative of the notion of a "deformed liberty" which Augustine imputes to his theft of pairs in the *Confessiones* (II,4,9), that is, a desire to do wrong for no other reason than the sheer exhilaration derived from exercising one's will. In the case of Adam and Eve, their curiosity for knowledge is the outgrowth of a more radical desire to explore the consequences of their own rebelliousness. In this way, *curiositas* reinforces the *superbia* that prompts a "standing apart from God" (*apostatare a Deo*) and a choice of the good proper to oneself alone over a commitment to the Good common to all.[27]

Augustine's pastoral concerns prompt him to alert Christians to maintain a proper disposition toward the world and its goods. But he does not condemn worldly experience in a blanket fashion. For him, the crucial consideration lies in an awareness of our priorities, according to the dictates of *ordo* and what he defines as the "rule of perfect religion."[28] This critical stance has a direct bearing on his attitude toward the objects of intellectual fascination, from aspects of the natural world to doctrinal matters. In this respect, his indictment of Manichaeism offers an important segue for analyzing the limits of human reasoning and defining the proper relationship between faith and reason.

## THE LURE OF MANICHAEISM

The Manichaean religion provided Augustine with an ideal foil for highlighting the dangers of preoccupying oneself exclusively with images. In both epistemological and metaphysical terms, the Manichaeans confined their understanding of the really and truly real to what we grasp on the basis of temporal and corporeal images and their phantasms. Their interpretation of what exists was inextricably bound up with what and how we know. Despite their fantastic teaching (based on an elaborate cosmogony structured by means of a radical dualism), they promised their adherents a genuinely rational approach to reality as a whole (including the Divine nature).[29]

Augustine's own embracing of Manichaeism (from the ages of 19 to 28) attests to its persuasiveness, not merely for simple believers, but to those with the kind of critical acumen that he himself possessed.[30] Wherein lay the attraction? Augustine attributes its drawing power to the curiosity which he describes as the outgrowth of an untutored mind.[31] But the very susceptibility to its pull reflects an inordinate preoccupation with the mutable realities disclosed by sense experience. In broader moral terms, curiosity (along with its triadic partners) subjects one to the domination of the world at large.

> By sinful pleasures...vanity, and baneful curiosity...the world can obtain the mastery over us. That is to say, these things of the world, by their deadly delight, enslave the lovers of things transitory.[32]

From Augustine's standpoint, Manichaeism promotes this very enslavement to the world and transitory goods by focusing on a corruptible universe to the exclusion of incorporeal reality. In this polemical vein, the Manichaeans command their following by exploiting a curiosity for what is novel, unusual, or extraordinary that finds a special appeal among those lacking a solid grounding in the faith. By promoting an intellectual interest in the world and its workings, Manichaeism could only divert the unwary from the contemplation of higher truths. In this regard, Augustine draws a sharp contrast between those who find an "empty joy in ever curious satisfactions" and those who "soar upwards in spirit to things divine, having no concern for temporal goods."[33] In the final analysis, the Manichaeans did not deliver on their exorbitant truth-claims, precisely because they had no substantive knowledge to offer.[34]

## THE HABIT OF PIOUS INQUIRY

At the heart of Augustine's anti-Manichaean polemic, we encounter an epistemological conviction in the character of genuine knowledge as justified true belief. The Manichaeans firmly believed in their own teachings and presented elaborate justifications in defending them. But Augustine continually stresses that those teachings were not grounded upon true reality. By the same token, the search for knowledge itself must be guided by proper motivations that define the nature of sound intellectual inquiry.

Augustine perceives a vast gulf between those who plunge recklessly into rash opinions and those who "cultivate in the Church the pious habit of inquiry" which brings believers to a deeper spiritual grasp of scriptural figures and parables.[35] In a brilliant turning of the tables on his opponents (and former co-religionists), he lauds anthropomorphic depictions of God by those Christian believers the Manichaeans derided as naive and simplistic. From Augustine's perspective, depictions of God in human terms assume a higher respectability than Manichaean portrayals of the Father of Light as a boundless, extended material mass.[36] In his reckoning, such theological anthropomorphism can open the way to a more refined understanding of the Divine nature.

Because Manichaeism aroused the curiosity of its followers in natural processes, it stifled the mind's attunement to the higher truths that Augustine deemed so essential to the life of faith. His sentiments here are unmistakably autobiographical, and heavily conditioned by his pastoral concerns. For he warns against the lure of the same religion that he himself had found so compelling in his youth (albeit to his later regret). In this respect, he implicitly alludes to his own passage from a crude materialism which rendered even God corruptible (and vulnerable to the encroachments of evil) to an appreciation of the multi-layered meanings of Scripture under the influence of Ambrose's allegorical method of exegesis.[37]

Augustine skillfully integrates his critique of the spurious teachings of the Manichaeans with a more general indictment of pretenses to learning that is evocative of Stoic sentiments. We saw in Chapter 2 of this study how classical Latin authors like Seneca and Quintilian derided what they viewed as superfluous interests, at least in relation to what really matters to us as rational beings. Augustine follows suit, endorsing the Stoic tendency to reject any desire to know that exceeds the parameters of what is useful.

But what constitutes "usefulness" in Christian terms? The answer to this question presupposes a sense of the Christian *telos*. In contrast to pagans, Christians are not absorbed in this-worldly concerns alone. Their sights are (or should be) set on a supernatural destiny. This is why Augustine encourages his hearers to order their intellectual priorities enroute to this final end. It also accounts for his condemnation of false claimants to knowledge who are more concerned with the appearance of learning than with essential truth.

> You think of nothing else day and night but of being praised...for your studies and your learning. I have always thought this a dangerous tendency even in those whose aim is sure and upright, but I see it proved in you.[38]

In practical Christian terms, learning must ultimately be subordinated to the quest for truth and a commitment to the life of service. Augustine finds the paradigm for a sound attitude toward intellectual pursuits in the example of Christ. Jesus' humility stands in direct opposition to that "ignorant knowledge...which makes us take pleasure in knowing what Anaximenes, Anaxagoras, Pythagoras, and Democritus thought for the sake of appearing learned...far removed from learning and erudition."[39] But Augustine also draws on his own pastoral example. In *Ep.* 118 (to Dioscorus, c. 410/11), he defers a response to certain questions by citing his own busyness in a variety of time-consuming tasks. In this respect, he contrasts the *curae* inherent in Dioscurus' vain *curiositas* with the *curae* of his demanding episcopacy.

> I should like to tear you from...your delightful inquiries, and set you down among my cares, so that you might learn not to be vainly curious, or not to...impose the task of feeding and nourishing your curiosity on those who have as one of their most pressing duties to curb and restrain the curious.[40]

## IN DEFENSE OF BELIEF

As a Christian philosopher, Augustine was committed to the complementarity of faith and reason. But in a manner consistent with that long tradition of "faith seeking understanding" (*fides quaerens intellectum*) which he so greatly shaped, he also considered human reason as subordinate to faith in the truths of Divine Revelation. As one commentator describes this position, "faith sets the agenda for the philosophical endeavor."[41] For this reason, Augustine by no means considered belief as something to be overcome in the interests of intellectual maturation.

What the Manichaeans would deride as the trait of the simple-minded, Augustine saw as an indispensable component in the process of knowing the truth. This is not to say that he endorsed a blind faith based upon an uncritical acceptance of scriptural teachings. In Augustinian terms, faith rests on the immutable *rationes* that ultimately proceed from the Divine intelligence.

For our purposes, Augustine's *De Utilitate Credendi* (A.D. 391) provides an illuminating document for examining his understanding of the proper motivation for intellectual inquiry. As the title of this work affirms, Augustine viewed Christian belief as a "useful" endeavor, precisely because it contributes to the realization of our final end of beatitude. But if Christians desire to know the truths of faith, how should this desire find expression? In addressing this issue, Augustine distinguishes two dispositions toward the subject matter of such theological inquiry: the curious (*curiosus*) and the studious (*studiosus*). While these dispositions can overlap in human experience, they also reveal radically different orientations toward the pursuit of knowledge. What, then, separates those who are "studious" from those who are merely "curious?"

> Each is moved by an intense desire to know, still, the curious man inquires into things which have no reference to him at all, while the studious man …investigates what concerns himself.[42]

We could not find a closer approximation to the meaning of *polupragmosune* in its many appearances in the classical Greek tradition. For Augustine, the distinguishing factors between *studiosus* and *curiosus* lie in the degree of concern (or more specifically, "care"), and the norms governing the appropriate focus of a given investigation. From this standpoint, an "intense desire to know" does not necessarily guarantee the moral and epistemological soundness of such inquiry.

An illustration is in order here. Augustine presents the scenario of a visitor in a foreign land who inquires about the condition of the relatives of everyone he happens to meet. Can that inquirer really be called "studious?" If someone merits that particular distinction, it is only because of a commitment to the life of the mind, the highest part of our rational nature.

> While every studious soul does...wish to know those matters which refer to himself...not everyone who does this should be called studious, but rather he who with utmost zeal seeks that which tends to the liberal cultivation and enrichment of the mind.[43]

Strictly speaking, then, Augustine perceives a significant difference between those who merely happen to study and those who are genuinely studious. Once again, the influence of Stoicism (or at least, Augustine's kinship with Stoic themes) is apparent. A pedantic adherence to detail may be all-consuming. But Augustine (like certain Stoics we have considered) does not perceive any necessary connection between that kind of "care" and a zeal for truth. A similar qualification applies to evaluations of curious people. Someone can be "all ears" regarding a tantalizing story, exhibiting enough interest to appear deeply concerned about its content (even if, objectively speaking, it does not concern him at all). But Augustine still would not automatically designate that person as *curiosus*.

> If anyone should listen willingly to a tale which would be of no value to him at all...one relating to matters of no concern to him, and did this in no offensive way nor often, but very rarely and moderately...would he seem to you to be curious? I think not, but in listening willingly he would surely seem to have some care for that matter.[44]

From this standpoint, we might view the *curiosus*-type as the negative counterpart of the *studiosus*-type. While the latter pursues true knowledge according to the dictates of usefulness and moderation, the former is motivated by an unrestricted passion to know, just for the sake of knowing. For all its precision, however, Augustine's discussion of the difference between *studiosus* and *curiosus* is no mere academic exercise. It has a direct bearing on his defense of the right of Christians to believe. For, just as he distinguishes between (a) those who study and those who are studious, and (b) those who are concerned and those who are curious, he likewise contrasts (c) those who believe from those who are credulous.

True belief does not amount to the credulity that one expects of naive and simplistic people. In the context of the *De Utilitate Credendi*, the crucial question amounts to this: *in religious matters, can we be justified in believing before knowing?* Augustine not only affirms that justification; he also challenges the hyper-rationalist claim that one should not believe anything without knowledge. Belief is nothing less than the necessary propaedeutic for understanding.

> What can be a more healthful way than first to become fitted for the reception of truth by believing those things which have been divinely appointed for preparing and cultivating the mind in advance?[46]

If Augustine stresses the necessity of belief, he does not confine this prescription to those unable to grasp the underlying reasons by which we understand. He even extends it to the most intellectually astute, lest they succumb to the danger of over-hasty or erroneous judgments. In this respect, belief (or knowledge, for that matter) cannot be grounded solely upon an intense or passionate concern. It must proceed from a *proper* concern, as reflected in an attitude of mind which subordinates itself to the guidance of a higher authority.

> Unless he first believes that he will arrive at the [goal] which he has set for himself, and shows the mind of a suppliant, obeying certain…necessary precepts…purging himself by a certain way of life, he will not in any other way attain to…pure truth.[47]

Any knowledge of God and related matters must be rooted in a willingness to recognize our own contingency at every stage of the knowing process. In this way, Augustine aligns himself with the thrust of Christian Socratism and its conviction that knowing begins with a recognition of what we do not or cannot know. "For, whatever kind of excellent ability they may have," Augustine contends, "unless God is present, they creep along the ground."[48]

One who qualifies as *studiosus*, then, encompasses everything that the *curiosus* individual lacks. As described in the *De Utilitate Credendi*, the *curiosus*-type displays all the earmarks of the "busybody" so memorably profiled by Plutarch in his treatise of the same name (see Chapter 1, above): meddlesome, prying, intrusive to the neglect of moderation, order, and propriety. Augustine, in his turn, emphasizes the great disparity between a search for Divine knowledge motivated by a rash inquisitiveness and one which acknowledges our creaturely dependence. The studious individual, in contrast, is willing to believe those things beyond our grasp, which simply cannot be demonstrated by means of positive reasoning alone.[49]

In speaking to his fellow Christians, Augustine seeks to harmonize the restless mind with a restless heart that only finds its fulfillment in God, its *Summum Bonum*. This amounts to a harmonization of the inclinations of intellect and will, reasoning and desire in the search for truth. As Augustine's own life experience affirms, curiosity may well initiate the quest of the human spirit for its final end. But such cognitive desire must be accompanied by a capacity to wonder—not simply at material complexity, but at the larger *ordo* which provides for the fittingness of all things for the realization of the good.

## ASSESSMENT OF PART III

Augustine was unequivocal in his affirmation of the fundamental goodness of creation. By the same token, however, his writings disclose a certain suspicion toward the transitory world of sense experience. Whether this ambivalence represents a lingering attachment to the Manichaean sentiments he so vehemently rejected is a matter of ongoing conjecture and debate. But his commitment to a Neoplatonic outlook (shortly after his break with Manichaeism) could only contribute to any wariness he already entertained regarding the material realm. From a metaphysical, epistemological, and moral standpoint, Augustine exhibits a marked preference for what is stable and immutable over the change and variation inherent in corporeal reality. This stance shapes his socio-political theory as well, along with his general attitude toward life in the earthly city.

If there is a dominant moral pitfall which Augustine discerns in the *saeculum*, it lies in curiosity. This is not to downplay or underestimate the moral importance he attributes to the sins of pride and carnal concupiscence. For Augustine, the lusts of domination and the flesh are instrumental in shaping the value systems of human societies. But if pride and carnality abet the soul's movement from God for self-aggrandizement and self-gratification, curiosity is that expression of lust encompassing the life of the mind. In this respect, curiosity provides

the stimulus for the mind's unregulated quest for experiential knowledge and an immersion in worldly concerns.

Augustine's *De Trinitate* develops a penetrating structural analysis
of cognitive activity in which the sin of *curiositas* assumes a pivotal
role. In *De Trinitate* X and XII, he skillfully integrates his psychological deliberations with his commentary on the fall account of *Genesis*.
Although Augustine stresses the mind's substantial unity, its functional structure suggests a duality running to its very nature. While the
mind's higher function engages in a contemplation of eternal verities
(and ultimately, God), its lower sciential function is oriented toward a
supervision of the body. In the context of Augustine's exegesis, Adam
and Eve represent the higher and lower functions of the mind, respectively. The fall itself constitutes a *lapsus* from a contemplative to an
active mode of being in which the mind forfeits its recognition of itself as God's image. As symbolic of the mind's contemplative function,
Adam exemplifies the love of genuine learning. Eve, on the other hand,
reflects the inquisitive spirit which seeks to "find out" for no reason
other than the desire to know.

In the *De Trinitate*, the fall is not a matter of embodiment *per se*;
it encompasses a shift in cognitive focus and the range of the soul's
loves. Drawing upon the scriptural image of the earth-bound serpent
(condemned to "eat earth," that is, to consume what is lowest on the
scale of creation), Augustine likens the mind's gravitation to images to
a "slithering" or "sliding" (the negative counterpart of a single-minded
devotion to truth). Becoming one with the objects of its desire, the
mind abdicates its sovereignty over the body and undermines its mid-
rank status between God and corporeal natures.

By giving itself over to what is alien to its own immateriality, the
mind becomes alienated from itself, as well as from God. In keeping
with two key Plotinian motifs that he creatively adapts in the interests
of his moral theory, the sin of *curiositas* coincides with (a) a privatizing
of the soul's concerns in the temporal sphere; and (b) an option for
delights proper to itself alone in lieu of a commitment to those truths
common to all. But the sheer fact of human embodiment generates a
tension in Augustine's exploration of the blameworthy character of
*curiositas*.

As embodied beings, we rely upon sense experience in order to come
to terms with the external environment. Still, the mind's necessary
governance of bodily existence can give way to an excessive absorption

in sense images. Life in the world can easily blur the distinction between the mind's attentiveness to bodily existence on the one hand, and an inordinate preoccupation with temporal and corporeal cares on the other. Mind's own sciential function becomes morally culpable through its submission to the dictates of *curiositas*.

Augustine's analysis of the mind's sciential function provides the framework within which he explores the dynamics of *curiositas* at work among the inhabitants of the earthly city. The fact that pagans and Christians alike succumb to this vice attests to the universal fallenness of humanity. In religious terms, Augustine viewed pagans and Christians as worlds apart. But he also recognized their sharing in the common fact of Adam's fall. From this standpoint, Christians are as susceptible to the lure of *curiositas* as their pagan contemporaries.

In the *De Civitate Dei*, Augustine's extended anti-pagan polemic fully exploits the diverse meanings which had accrued to the notion of *curiositas* throughout the classical tradition. For his critical purposes, *curiositas* encompasses a wide range of connotations revolving around pagan religious observances, from magical practices to various forms of superstition. In a culture given to public spectacles of all kinds, Augustine found ample illustrations of the lust of the eyes. These manifold cases demonstrate the extent to which "pernicious curiosity" was woven into the fabric of life in the earthly city.

Augustine's indictment of pagan *curiositas* assumes a personal tone rooted in his own past participation in some of the very spectacles he condemns. This sharing in aspects of pagan culture involved his intellectual pursuits as well. In this regard, Augustine reflects the influence of some of the same sources he critiques. He polemicizes against magic and theurgy in a manner inspired by thinkers like Apuleius and Porphyry (even as he challenges their teachings on doctrinal grounds). In this connection, he views the knowledge of demons as paradigmatic of arrogant attempts to seize the Divine prerogative.

On the human side, the attempt to imitate the demonic quest for knowledge proceeds from a vain curiosity, an outgrowth of the sciential function of the mind at its farthest remove from things Divine. In contrast to the demons' inflation with pride in their intellectual prowess, true knowledge requires a spirit of humility modeled on the example of Christ. In epistemological terms, the imitation of Christ on the part of humans amounts to a recognition of the limits of the human capacity to know.

As depicted by Augustine, paganism exemplifies the moral vacuity of the earthly city. But Christians themselves bore the influence of a pervasive pagan culture which touched every aspect of their lives. In Augustinian terms, the "world" encompasses this broader social and religious milieu in which the Church's members found themselves intermingled with hostile non-believers, morally lapsed Christians, and Christian heretics. *Curiositas* provides a salient expression of the love of the world. But as a way of loving (or more precisely, lusting for) the world, *curiositas* is very much a matter of *how we love*. This is why Augustine's distinction between "use" and "enjoyment" (*uti/frui*) is so crucial in his overall analysis of the soul's relationship with the world and its goods.

As already observed, the mind's sciential function necessarily entails a concern with the outer world of sense experience and secular affairs. But this interest assumes a morally blameworthy character on the basis of the soul's (or more specifically, the mind's) affections. For this reason, the *uti/frui* distinction serves as a key criterion for evaluating the mind's absorption in the world. From Augustine's perspective, the measure of sin lies in whether one loves as ends in themselves those things that should be used in pursuit of our ultimate end as rational beings created in God's image.

In the metaphorical language of the *De Trinitate*, the curious mind binds or "glues" itself to those things which are no more than the means to our fulfillment. In this respect, Augustine coordinates his understanding of *curiositas* as the "lust of the eyes" with the "opening of the eyes" of Adam and Eve. By succumbing to the temptation to override the limits of their creaturely capacity to know, Adam and Eve expand their range of cognitive "vision" over a broader experiential plane. In eating of the tree of knowledge, they "see" the world from a thoroughly creaturely perspective, with a focus upon what is proper to themselves, rather than upon the Good common to all.

In the context of Augustine's exegesis of this fall account, curiosity assumes the character of a venturesome audacity (reminiscent of Plotinian *tolma*). By implication, *curiositas* presupposes a heightened sense of freedom, in defiance of Divine authority. The curious mind seeks to "find out" whatever it wishes without restriction of any kind. From a contemporary vantage point, such a trait is considered a wholly praiseworthy one, the mark of a vigorous intellect. But from

Augustine's perspective, it by no means guarantees a commitment to genuine knowledge.

In Augustine's own journey, the Manichaean experience provided the most salient example of his susceptibility to the pull of *curiositas*. Accordingly, his anti-Manichaean polemic provides the basis of his interpretation of the appropriate means of pursuing Christian wisdom in its fullest sense. In opposition to vain *curiositas*, Augustine promotes the "pious habit of inquiry." This is not some cloistered approach to truth requiring a complete withdrawal from the outer world. But it does demand an adherence to the same norms that facilitate the attainment of human happiness. Like moral living, the quest for knowledge cannot be a haphazard affair, dependent upon the fickle whims of the curious disposition. If our happiness has a supernatural end, then human knowledge on every level must be guided by truths which transcend the natural world. From this standpoint, curiosity no more allows for knowledge than carnal lust alone sustains a loving commitment to another person.

The distinction between the curious and the studious dispositions that emerges in the *De Trinitate* figures prominently in Augustine's defense of the usefulness of belief. Belief points to a recognition that there are things beyond our immediate grasp worthy of serious and prolonged investigation. In and of itself, however, curiosity renders the search for knowledge too facile an endeavor. In contrast to modern and contemporary outlooks, Augustine proceeds from the premise that curiosity really undermines the desire to know by generating the illusion that knowledge is merely "there for the taking," so to speak. Those motivated by studiousness, on the other hand, are attuned to the hidden depth of the created order.

In the face of the mystery of creation, the only viable response is one of a humble sense of wonder at what God has wrought. Accordingly, Augustine raises the bar of intellectual striving to another metaphysical plane. While curiosity confines the range of human inquiry to the realm of sense experience, studiousness places us on a trajectory toward the infinite, the ultimate goal of that "pious habit of inquiry" that Augustine sought to inculcate in his fellow Christians.

Only after we link Augustine's conception of studiousness with the notion of wonder so crucial to the intellectual enterprise, can we begin to grasp the wisdom inherent in his condemnation of *curiositas* as a lustful vice. In the context of his Christian Neoplatonism, *curiositas* focuses on the parts of creation; studiousness cultivates a sense of the whole of things and the grand *ordo* which lends meaning and intelligibility to those components. But two critical questions must now be considered. *Is Augustine's interpretation of human knowledge (and the means of attaining it) antithetical to a healthy scientific approach to the natural world? Moreover, should limits ever be placed on our scientific investigations in the interest of the common good?*

Both of these questions touch upon the role of moral values in science. I address this topic in the concluding chapter, with an assessment of what Augustine can say to a contemporary audience about the scope and extent of human inquiry, specifically in the context of scientific research. It may well be that Augustine's relevance concerning these issues reflects something of a "delayed reaction effect," that is only fully discernible in a time far removed from his own.

## NOTES TO CHAPTER 9

1. Peter Brown, *Augustine of Hippo* (Berkeley and Los Angeles: University of California Press, 2000), 234.
2. This transformation is evident in Augustine's evolving attitude toward Stoicism, especially its ideal of the self-sufficiency of the sage. Augustine's pastoral experience coincided with a rejection of Stoic autarchy and an increasing emphasis on our need for the assistance of Divine grace.
3. *De Civitate Dei* XVIII,49: CC XLVIII (SL), 647, 5-6: *multi reprobi miscentur bonis et utrique tamquam in sagenam euangelicam colliguntur.* In the *Enarrationes in Psalmos* 8,13 (CC XXXVIII [SL], 57), Augustine describes the integration of sinners with the good and holy in triadic terms, on the basis of the scriptural identification of carnal concupiscence with beasts of pleasure, pride with the birds of the air, and curiosity with the fish of the sea (*sed insuper et pecora uoluptatis, et uolucres superbiae, et pisces curiositatis*).
4. Peter Brown (*Augustine of Hippo*, 243) describes the complexity of the situation in this way: "The congregations who heard Augustine preach were not exceptionally sinful. Rather, they were firmly rooted in long-established attitudes, in ways of life and ideas, to which Christianity was peripheral. Among such men, the all-demanding message of Augustine merely suffered the fate of a river flowing into a complex system of irrigation: it lost its power, in the minds of its hearers, by meeting innumerable little ditches, by being broken up into a network of neat little compartments. Even the religious imagination...was rigidly comparmented. There

were two worlds: this world and the next. Each was governed by its own
rulers. The pagan gods...were almost impossible to banish: for they were
not the classical Olympians, they were faceless 'powers'. These 'powers' had
increasingly come to pour into the gap that had widened between the daily
concerns of a man... and a Supreme God."

5. *De catechizandis rudibus* 25(48).

6. *De catechizandis rudibus* 25(48).

7. *De catechizandis rudibus* 25(48).

8. *s.* 284(5): PL XXXVIII,1291: *Promittit mundus superfluas vel damnabiles
curiositates.*

9. *Confessiones* VI,8(13).

10. *In Epistolam Joannis ad Parthos*, Tr. 2(12).

11. *In Epistolam Joannis ad Parthos*, Tr. 2(12): PL XXXV, 1996: *Omnes enim
dilectores mundi...mundus vocantur.*

12. For some of Augustine's key formulations of this distinction, see his *De
Doctrina Christiana* I,4(4), 11(25); *De Trinitate* X,10(13); 11(17); *De
Civitate Dei* XI,25; *De diversis quaestionibus* 30.

13. *In Epistolam Joannis ad Parthos*, Tr. 2(12).

14. *In Epistolam Joannis ad Parthos*, Tr. 2(13): PL XXXV, 1996: *Et desiderium
oculorum: desiderium oculorum dicit omnem curiositatem. Jam quam late pa-
tet curiositas? Ipsa in spectaculis, in theatris, in sacramentis diaboli, in magicis
artibuds, in maleficiis ipsa est curiositas. Aliquando tentat etiam servos Dei, ut
velint quasi miraculum facere, tentare utrum exaudiat illos Deus in miraculis;
curiositas est, hoc est desiderium oculorum; non est a Patre.* A.H.M. Jones
(*The Later Roman Empire* 284-602, Vol. 2 [Baltimore, MD: The Johns
Hopkins University Press, 1990], 962) offers the following assessment
of a cultural milieu in which Christians found themselves in such close
promixity to pagan religious and occultist practices: "It is evident that the
religion of the age was riddled with superstition. The common man had
always believed in magic and divination, and astrology, owing to its pseu-
do-scientific character, was often accepted by the most enlightened. All
these practices...were criminal offences in the law of the Principate, but
they were...widespread and often openly tolerated. Christians naturally
regarded magic and divination as sinful, since they involved the invocation
of pagan gods or demons, but they believed in their efficacy. Astrology
they endeavoured to discredit on rational grounds...but it is doubtful
whether their arguments had much effect on popular belief."

15. *In Epistolam Joannis ad Parthos*, Tr. 2,14(1).

16. *In Epistolam Joannis ad Parthos*, Tr. 2,14(3): PL XXXV, 1997: *Ille restitit
tentatori: si enim faceret miraculum, non videretur nisi aut cessisse, aut curiositate fecisse.*

17. *In Epistolam Joannis ad Parthos*, Tr. 2,13. Cf., *In Ioannis Evangelium
Tractatus* CXXIV, Tr. 50(14). Augustine extends this flawed motive
even to those who directly witnessed Christ's working of miracles. In his

exegesis of Jn. 11:55-12:11 (*In Ioannis Evangelium Tractatus* CXXIV, Tr. 50,14), he argues that those who came to see the risen Lazarus did so out of sheer curiosity, rather than out of love.

18. *In Epistolam Joannis ad Parthos*, Tr. 2,14(5).

19. But consider the contention of A.H.M. Jones (*The Later Roman Empire 284-602*, Vol. 2, 979), who proposes an alternate interpretation of early Christian morality: "It is strange that during a period when Christianity... came to embrace practically all the citizens of the empire, the general standards of conduct should have remained in general static and in some respects have sunk. If the moral code taught by the church was not notably higher than that of pagan philosophy, it was preached with far more vigour to a far wider audience, and was backed by the sanction of eternal punishment in the next world. One reason for the church's failure may have been that it set its standards too high, and...when ...it became mingled with the world, its demands became intolerable."

20. *s.* 112,6(7).

21. *De Genesi ad Litteram* XI,31(40).

22. *De Genesi ad Litteram*, XI,31(41).

23. *De Genesi ad Litteram* XI,31(41): CSEL XXVIII, Sect. III, Pars 1, 365,19-24: *mox ergo ut praeceptum transgressi sunt intrinsecus gratia deserente omnino nudati, quam typho quodam et superbo amore suae potestatis offenderant, in sua membra oculos iniecerunt eaque motu eo, quem non nouerant, concupiuerunt.*

24. *De Genesi ad Litteram* XI,31(40). In the *De Genesi ad Litteram*, Augustine distinguishes between a natural body and a spiritual body to be attained at the resurrection, in a manner consistent with the teaching of I Cor. 15:44. Cf., *De Genesi ad Litteram* VI,19(30); IX,3(6); 10(17).

25. *De Genesi ad Litteram* XI,31(41): CSEL XXVIII, Sect. III, Pars 1, 365,10-15: *ubi enim ad transgrediendum praeceptum audax curiositas mota est, auida experiri latentia, quidnam tacto uetito sequeretur, et noxia libertate habenas prohibitionis rumpere delectata.*

26. This interplay of curiosity and audacity point to a Plotinian influence that finds its source in the notion of *tolma*, the audacious drive toward otherness that also carries the connotation of a venturesomeness to explore lower levels of reality. This theme is evident in *Ennead* V.1(10).1 (the *locus classicus* of Plotinus' discussion of the *tolma* of individual souls) and *Ennead* IV.4(27).12, where Plotinus attributes a narcissism to souls whose self-love he likens to "seeing" their own images in the corporeal natures into which they descend (drawing upon the myth of Narcissus).

27. Cf., *De Genesi contra Manichaeos* II,5(6); *De Musica* VI,13(40).

28. Cf., *De Vera Religione* 10(19), for Augustine's classic formulation of the "rule of perfect religion": "Do not serve the creature rather than the Creator or become vain in our thoughts."

29. This feature of Manichaeism was probably a key factor in Augustine's gravitation toward the religion (and his movement away from the conservatism of North African Christianity).

30. But by the same token, Augustine's association with Manichaeism was a rocky one, punctuated by growing scepticism and increasing disenchantment (culminating in his encounter with the Manichaean bishop Faustus, as recounted in *Confessiones* V, 6-7).

31. *De agone christiano* 4(4): PL XL, 293: *ut cum respondere non potuerit, traducetor ab eis per curiositatem; quia omnis anima indocta curiosa est. Qui autem fidem catholicam bene didicit, et bonis moribus et vera pietate munitus est, quamvis eorum haeresim nesciat, respondet illis tamen.*

32. *De agone christiano* 6(6): PL XL, 294: *Quia per illicitas delectationes suas et pompas et perniciosam curiositatem nobis dominari potest hic mundus, id est, ea quae in hoc mundo perniciosa delectatione colligant amatores rerum temporalium.*

33. *De agone christiano* 12(13).

34. *De diversis quaestionibus* 68,1.

35. *Contra Epistolam Manichaei Quam Vocant Fundamentum* 23(25).

36. Augustine's refutation of the radical dualism of Mani's *Fundamental Epistle* (in his *Contra Epistolam Manichaei Quam Vocant Fundamentum*) challenges the Manichaean imposition of boundaries on the Divine nature, and the corresponding depiction of God in corporeal terms. For an extended discussion of this refutation, see my *Creatio ex nihilo and the Theology of Saint Augustine. The Anti-Manichaean Polemic and Beyond* (New York: Peter Lang Publishing Inc., 1999), Chapter 3, pp. 135-163.

37. Certainly, Augustine's absorption of the Neoplatonic metaphysics (especially its theory of incorporeal reality), was also instrumental in his refutation of Manichaean dualism. Cf., *s.* 51,5(6), where Augustine draws on the lesson of his own experience: "I am speaking to you as one who was myself caught out once upon a time, when as a lad I wanted to tackle the divine scriptures with the techniques of clever disputation before bringing to them the spirit of earnest inquiry."

38. *Ep.* 118,1(4). Cf., *Confessiones* I,18(29), where Augustine discusses an excessive preoccupation with grammatical rules, to the extent that some consider the mispronunciation of Latin terms a more grievous offense than a sin against charity.

39. *Ep.* 118,4(23).

40. *Ep.* 118,1(1): CSEL XXXIII, Pars II, 665,11-15: *ego te autem uellem abripere de medio deliciosarum iniquisitionum tuarum et constipare inter curas meas, ut uel disceres non esse inaniter curiosus uel curiositatem tuam cibandum atque nutriendam inponere non auderes eis, quorum inter curas uel maxima cura est reprimere ac refrenare curiosos.* Drawing upon the Gospel *ethos* articulated by Christ, Augustine (*s.* 14,6: PL XXXVIII,114) also views material wealth (along with its attendant cares) as an impediment to

Christian living: *Attendite curas divitum, et comparate securitati pauperum.*
*Sed audiat dives iste, ut non superbe sapiat, neque speret in incerto divitiarum.*

41. Frederick Van Fleteren, "*De Utilitate Credendi*," in *Augustine Through the Ages. An Encyclopedia* (Grand Rapids, Michigan/Cambridge, UK: William B. Eerdmans Publishing Company, 1999), 861a-862b.

42. *De Utilitate Credendi* 9(22): PL XLII,80: *quod quamvis uterque agatur magna cupiditate noscendi, curiosus tamen ea requirit quae nihil ad se attinent; studiosus autem contra, quae ad sese attinent requirit.*

43. *De Utilitate Credendi* 9(22): PL XLII,80: *quod omnis quidem studiosus ea nosse vult quae ad se pertinent, non tamen omnis qui id agit studiosus vocandus est; sed is qui ea quae ad animum nutriendum liberaliter atque ornandum pertinent, impensissime requirit.*

44. *De Utilitate Credendi* 9(22): PL XLII,80: *si quis fabellam libenter audiret, nihil sibi omnino profuturam, id est, rerum ad se non pertinentium; neque id odiose atque crebro, sed rarissime ac modestissime... videreturne tibi curiosus? Non opinor: sed certe habens illius rei curam, quam libenter audiret, profecto videretur.*

45. One might object, of course, to this contention on the grounds that *any* intellectual pursuit is self-justifying, even if its value is not immediately evident. Are not some of the greatest scientific discoveries and advances outgrowths of seemingly trivial observations or the most commonplace experiences? Augustine would not, I think, deny this. But by the same token, he would no doubt still take pains to distinguish those matters which arouse our interest on the basis of some passing fancy and those which prompt (and merit) a deep commitment on our part as rational beings.

46. *De Utilitate Credendi* 10(24).

47. *De Utilitate Credendi* 10(24). Cf., *De Utilitate Credendi* 3(9), where Augustine specifies the proper method to be followed in discerning the senses of Scripture, "studiously and faithfully, not turbidly and rashly."

48. *De Utilitate Credendi* 10(24).

49. Augustine (*De Utilitate Credendi* 10,24) cites the example of friendship in illustrating how certain fulfilling aspects of human life must be accepted on the basis of belief alone, since they do not allow for any rational demonstration. Can we demand "proof" of others' motives before accepting their offer of friendship? Augustine's position here calls to mind that of William James in his essay "The Will to Believe" (in John Hick, ed., *Classical and Contemporary Readings in the Philosophy of Religion*, 3rd ed. [Englewood Cliffs, N.J.: Prentice Hall, 1990], 208): "A social organism of any sort whatever... is what it is because each member proceeds to his own duty with a trust that the other members will simultaneously do theirs. Whenever a desired result is achieved by the cooperation of many... its existence as a fact is a pure consequence of the precursive faith in one another of those immediately concerned. There are, then, cases where a fact cannot come at all unless a preliminary faith exists in its coming."

# CONCLUSION

# AUGUSTINE, *CURIOSITAS*, AND SCIENTIFIC VALUES

A reading of the previous six chapters might well justify the assumption that Augustine's attitude toward curiosity was a decidedly negative one. The fact that he defines it as a morally disordered love or lust could easily confirm this assumption. But that definition, as we have seen, must be understood in the context of his overall theological and psychological outlook, along with its Platonic, Neoplatonic, and Stoic criteria of genuine knowledge. Still, what appears cogent from an Augustinian perspective might well raise eyebrows in current intellectual circles. Indeed, the thought-world we inhabit is fairly unanimous in its conviction that curiosity is an essential component of scientific research and discovery.

For many of our contemporaries, "science" is inseparable from the curiosity that drives its practitioners. By the same token, most people consider an aversion to curiosity tantamount to an attack on science itself. It is not surprising, then, that Augustine provides such a convenient target for those who champion the pursuit of empirical knowledge in all its forms. As Carl Sagan scathingly charged, the end of Augustine's life coincided with nothing less than the onset of the Dark Ages.[1]

But does Augustine's interpretation of *curiositas* as a primal vice (the Johannine "lust of the eyes" abetting human fallenness) necessarily imply a corresponding hostility toward the scientific enterprise (at least as that phrase is now understood)? In broader terms, did his condemnation of *curiositas* impede the growth of western science? In this concluding chapter, I defend Augustine in the following terms: far from assuming the role of an opponent of science, Augustine can be viewed as a significant (albeit highly critical) ally in its search for truth.

Arguably, however, Augustine's relevance for science can only be appreciated in the aftermath of the great scientific and technological explosions of the past 150 years or so. His indictment of attempts "to penetrate nature's secrets" acquire a prophetic quality in the face of the threats posed by nuclear energy disasters, acid rain, toxic waste, global warming, and the wholesale destruction of the ecosystem. In Augustinian terms, the danger does not lie in scientific activity *per se*. Rather, it proceeds from the widespread tendency to regard it in a value-neutral manner. Does scientific curiosity justify the expansion of knowledge in any way whatsoever? In my estimation, the fact that so many people would respond in the affirmative to this question attests to the need for a continual reassessment of science's moral relevance. Augustine, I think, can provide a cogent, much needed voice in a world which takes for granted things like the mapping of the genome, genetic engineering and screening, cloning, stem cell research, artificial life-support technology, and increasingly ambitious attempts at organ harvesting. This voice needs to be heard, precisely because such advances have a tremendous impact upon how we understand what it means to be human and the value we impart to human beings.

## AUGUSTINE ON 'SCIENTIA'

At the outset, we must reconsider Augustine's key statement regarding the morality of natural science, as articulated in the first book of the *De Moribus Ecclesiae et de Moribus Manichaeorum*. If any compelling evidence can be found for his supposed negativity toward scientific endeavors, it lies in that probing critique of Manichaean materialism and sensism. In this polemical context, Augustine explicitly equates *scientia* with "certain corporeal images conceived by the mind."[2] In keeping with the dictates of his epistemology, an absorption in images does not qualify as knowledge at all. Stated in other terms, *scientia* at best represents a spurious claim to knowing. And because it rests upon mere semblances of reality, Augustine cautions that the contents of *scientia* should not be objects of any curious attraction on our part.[3]

But what constitutes true knowledge for Augustine? The question is crucial because it touches upon the tension that Augustine perceives between the mind's contemplative and sciential functions. The mind's sciential function encompasses a "downward" focus upon a mutable world of corruptible things that distract us from our proper contemplative gaze upon God and eternal truths.

The critical thrust of the *De Moribus*, then, is directed against those oblivious to the immateriality and immutability of the Divine nature. Because of this metaphysical blindspot, they "busy themselves with intense and eager curiosity exploring that universal mass of matter we call the world."[4]

But it would be erroneous to assume that Augustine's remarks reveal an outright attack on natural science. If this endeavor poses a problem for him, it really proceeds from the fact that it is conducive to a materialist mentality, whereby one is "deceived into thinking that matter alone exists."[5] What applies to Augustine's Manichaean adversaries is equally applicable to any tendency to define knowledge (i.e., in its literal sense of *scientia*) exclusively in empiricist terms. When read from a contemporary vantage point, Augustine's words issue a challenge to reductionist attempts to define everything (including theological concepts) on the basis of what is accessible through sense experience. For him, the very desire for this "vain sort of knowledge" is antithetical to the mind's wish to "keep itself chaste for God."[6] In this connection, Augustine's attribution of the adjective "vain" to "knowledge" carries a dual connotation. On the one hand, knowledge that is vain is proud, failing to acknowledge the Divine transcendence; on the other hand, vain knowledge is epistemologically and metaphysically impoverished, grounded upon what are no more than empty images.

There is no question that science is extremely adept at dealing with facts and quantifiable data. But scientists must also be able to think in terms of systems, levels of organization, and greater wholes. Augustine's internalization of the Neoplatonic metaphysics attuned him to the totality of things in which we all participate. Because he distinguishes between material and immaterial reality, he discerns something more than what presents itself to us on the level of sense experience. Accordingly, he denies that reason can rest content with the appearances of things alone, no matter how pleasing or alluring they are to the senses. Ultimately, it seeks unchanging principles without which things could not be designated as "good" or "beautiful" at all.

> Reason advanced to the province of the eyes. Scanning the earth and the heavens, it realized that nothing pleased it but beauty; and in beauty, design; and in design, dimensions; and in dimensions,

number...and nothing which eyes beheld could in any way be compared to what the mind alone discerned.[7]

## AUGUSTINE'S THEOCENTRISM

As we have observed in the course of this study, Augustine interprets *curiositas* in terms of the full panoply of cognitive desire. But *curiositas* assumes an especially prominent role in arousing our interest in the outer world of the senses. For Augustine, the wide-ranging, unregulated character of *curiositas* must be tempered by moderation, lest it dissipate our intellectual focus over a manifold of cares and concerns. While curiosity might spur the quest for knowledge, it can never consummate it, in the absence of an abiding commitment to truth.

> If anyone dares rashly and without due order of the branches of learning to rush to the knowing of these things, he becomes, not a man of study, but...cares; not a man of learning but...credulity; not a man of discretion, but...ready to discredit everything.[8]

Augustine's contrasts (i.e., between study and cares; between learning and credulity; between discretion and a hyper-scepticism) highlight the pitfalls of the over-hasty "rush to knowing" motivated by *curiositas*.[9] An intellectualist by temperament, Augustine could only abhor the seeming frivolousness inherent in the curious disposition. In Augustinian terms, any serious inquiry worthy of the name must subordinate the content of sense experience to higher principles of meaning which the mind alone can grasp.

> What is there in us that searches out many things beyond the reach of the senses...grasped by the beckoning of the senses themselves?[10]

It would be erroneous to measure Augustine's comprehension of natural science on the basis of criteria we take for granted, in the aftermath of several scientific revolutions. In point of fact, his intellectual concerns were almost exclusively theological in orientation. By the same token, this theocentric focus was conducive to a downgrading of empirical investigation. As Augustine acknowledged, "I desire to have knowledge of God and the soul...of nothing else whatsoever."[11]

This theocentrism is wholly consistent with Augustine's epistemological presuppositions. By and large, he exhibits a preference for immutable truths accessible to reasoning over anything we derive from a changing world of sense experience. In this respect, his journey to God paralleled his search for a firm foundation of certitude immune to the encroachments of doubt.[12] God is the ultimate standard against which the validity of all knowledge must be evaluated. In Philip Ball's assessment of Augustine's epistemological agenda, "knowledge of the transcendent realm of God is…the only real knowledge worth having."[13]

Still, Augustine was no radical dualist. Regardless of his devaluation of the sense realm, he exalted creation in its totality as exceedingly good. While his theocentrist emphasis diminished his interest in the natural world, he by no means rejects investigations of nature outright. But he was careful to approach them in light of his conception of the hierarchical ordering of creation in relation to its Creator. Augustine's ongoing endorsement of the liberal arts attests to his recognition of their usefulness in attaining a knowledge of things Divine. Yet the study of nature is only a means to our final end of beatitude; it is not an end in itself. According to Ball, "Augustine believed that, as God's reason has rendered the world intelligible, this order can be discovered by the use of mathematics, geometry and astronomy…literature, poetry…musics…as a route to divine truth."[14] By virtue of his commitment to the efficacy of human reason (with the assistance of Divine Illumination), Augustine thus provides an important conduit for the transmission of the rationalist emphasis of modern science.[15] Likewise, his recognition of the intelligibility of creation was instrumental in promoting the causal analysis that is a hallmark of the scientific method.

## THE ORDER OF CREATION

The history of ideas displays a remarkable interweaving of insights drawn from diverse areas of human thought. A striking example of this conceptual crossbreeding is found in the relationship between the rise of modern science and the Christian doctrine of creation *ex nihilo*. If the world reveals the creative role of God, then it merits intense study, not merely as an object of inquisitiveness, but as a rich manifestation of Divine power, goodness, and providence. In his *Christian Theology and Natural Science*, E.L. Mascall has persuasively demonstrated the extent to which an affirmation of the createdness of things provided the basis of the philosophy of nature that supported the empirical side of modern science.

> A world…created by the Christian God will be both contingent and orderly. It will embody regularities and patterns, since its Maker is rational, but the particular regularities and patterns…can be discovered only by examination. The world, as Christian theism conceives it, is thus an ideal field for the application of the scientific method, with its twin techniques of observation and experiment.[16]

As a Christian thinker, Augustine upheld the doctrine of creation *ex nihilo* in its most unequivocal terms. His affirmation of the absolute power and transcendence of God is correlative with his recognition of the radical contingency of creatures. For humans, however, this contingency not only assumes a metaphysical connotation (to the extent that we depend upon God for our very being), but a moral one as well (since our capacity to do good reflects our continual dependence upon Divine grace). This is why his theodicy is so closely aligned with his theology of creation and its affirmation of a highly structured *ordo* in which all things find their appropriate place.

## A QUESTION OF VALUES

Augustine's view of the natural world as "created" invests it with a special dignity proceeding from its causal connection with God. But even those who recognize the fact of "createdness" might well downplay the value of certain things, relegating them to the status of "mere creatures," unworthy of even a semblance of respect. How might Augustine respond? For him, the rich mosaic of reality other than God underscores the fact that all things are deemed good in relation to the greater whole in which they participate.

What applies to creation pertains to its scientific investigation and manipulation as well. Augustine could never consider science a value-neutral endeavor. Such a position, however, flies in the face of the pervasive contemporary conviction that science and ethics are mutually exclusive. As one commentator succinctly affirms, "'scientific morality' is widely regarded as an oxymoron."[17] By and large, those who empty science of any value content do so because they assume that values lack the factual objectivity which science requires.

But can science and morality be so neatly demarcated without undermining both spheres? In my estimation, such a demarcation presupposes that science has no relation to assessments of the human good (at least not in any intrinsic sense of the word "good"). If science is considered value-neutral or value-free, then no limits can justifiably be imposed upon it. In response to this dilemma, some argue that science is unavoidably bound up with moral considerations. Douglas Allchin, for one, perceives the very tasks of science as value-laden, on both an epistemic and a socio-cultural level. According to Allchin, values touch science in three significant ways.

> First, there are…epistemic values, which guide scientific research itself. Second, the scientific enterprise is always embedded in some particular culture and its values enter science through its individual practioners, whether deliberately or not…Finally, values emerge from science, both as a product and process and may be distributed more broadly in the culture or society.[18]

Allchin's remarks highlight the mutual, give-and-take relationship between scientific activity and the human communities which provide its support systems and ultimate beneficiaries (or victims). The embeddedness of science in culture and the influence of a given culture's values on scientists is evident against the background of the history of science itself. The reciprocal impact of science upon culture (especially in transforming existing values), however, might not be so readily apparent. But this does not diminish the fact that science is inextricably bound up with the promotion of (or detraction from) the human good in countless ways. Whether scientists wish to shoulder this moral burden or not, there is much to Allchin's contention that "the researcher is an ethical agent responsible for the consequences of his or her actions, good or bad."[19]

Allchin's emphasis on epistemic values is particularly important, since it takes us into the heart of the scientific enterprise. If science is true to its root meaning (*scientia*), is not its defining activity morally relevant? The critical question here, however, concerns the rationale for this relevance. In this respect, we observe a trend to define scientific values in terms of the very tasks that scientists themselves perform. This approach was endorsed by Jacob Bronowski, who wished to develop "an ethic for science which derives directly from its activity."[20] For Bronowski, such an ethic encompasses those factors which allow science to flourish, in a manner consistent with its pursuit of empirical facts.

> As originality and independence are private needs for the existence of a science, so dissent and freedom are its public needs. No one can be a scientist…if he does not have independence of observation and thought. But if…science is to become effective as a public practice… it must protect independence. The safeguards which it must offer are potent: free inquiry, free thought, free speech, tolerance.[21]

But as laudable as these values are, we must still inquire about their end. For his part, Bronowski places truth at the veritable center of scientific activity. More precisely, he stipulates that science must possess "the habit of truth" in its most dynamic sense.[22] Yet if he defines the value of science on the basis of its fidelity to truth, that truth is legitimized by standards internal to science itself. But this merely suggests that science is a self-justifying endeavor that should be promoted for its own sake in an indiscriminate manner.

While Augustine would undoubtedly share Bronowski's commitment to the truth-value of science, he would part company with him on a fundamental point. In Augustinian terms, the value of science cannot be grounded solely upon what scientists actually do or attempt to do. Rather, it must conform to standards transcending the boundaries of scientific research and development. By extension, scientific values cannot be determined by the dictates of scientific endeavors alone. Rather, those endeavors must be subject to the oversight of a higher set of moral norms.

## CRAFTING AN AUGUSTINIAN ETHIC

One who recognizes that science requires the same moral guidance as any other human endeavor does not automatically become an opponent of scientific progress. From my standpoint, this observation is directly applicable to Augustine. If one were to develop an "Augustinian ethic" guiding scientific inquiry, what shape would it assume? In what follows, I attempt just this, drawing upon certain aspects of Augustine's moral theory that exhibit a clear relevance for assessing the method and implications of scientific investigation.

The mainlines of the ethic I craft here is broad enough in scope to encompass a variety of scientific activities and the moral dilemmas they might generate. What I offer is something of a skeletal framework which the reader can flesh out in a practical, applied context as he or she wishes. Moreover, this ethic is highly tentative in its selection of themes. I propose, in fact, but five themes (in the form of criteria) for purposes of discussion: (1) the common/proper criterion; (2) the use/enjoyment criterion; (3) the transcendentals of created being criterion; (4) the goodness of the whole criterion; (5) the moral relevance criterion.[23]

At the outset, it is interesting to observe that these same themes (and the principles we derive from them) are implicit in Augustine's critique of *curiositas*. That critical stance, as we have seen, finds a special focus in what Augustine designates as the "sciential" function of the mind, when it opens itself to the pull of the outer world of sense experience. For this reason, my proposed ethic also draws upon insights prominent in his discussions of the moral pitfalls inherent in the curious disposition. As we have observed, these discussions must be appreciated against the backdrop of his theory of reality as an orderly whole.

## 1. The Common/Proper Criterion

Augustine's distinction between the common (*commune*) and the proper (*proprium*) is a crucial component of his evolving understanding of iniquity. By virtue of this distinction, Augustine defines sin as a forfeiture of the supreme Good common to all (which can never lost against our will) for the goods proper to oneself alone or a private sphere of interests. By extension, the *commune/proprium* distinction provides an ideal means of delineating the morality of scientific pursuits on two levels: *first*, in regard to the motives of scientists in conducting their investigations; *secondly*, in respect to the impact of their labors on society. Scientists need not be ethicists in any formal sense to recognize their obligation to contribute to the long-term good of humanity. This sense of social responsibility is antithetical to the assumption that the scientist is a morally autonomous agent, whose work (as significant or beneficial as it may be) is all that matters.

Augustine would not shrink from affirming the inviolable dignity of the human person, even if such an affirmation imposes limits on the scope of research and experimentation. Such an imposition does not seek to undermine the freedom of scientists to do their work. From this perspective, science becomes a highly humanistic enterprise, because every phase of its activity is infused with value considerations. Whether a scientist embraces the religious conviction that we are "created in God's image" or not, a commitment to the incommensurable value and integrity of human life is crucial if science is to live up to its lofty aspiration to be "a force...and...disinterested power for good."[24] This requirement, it seems, must also encompass the curiosity that prompts scientists to open new horizons of inquiry or expand the knowledge we already possess in bold new ways.

For minds dominated by *curiositas*, however, the value dimension of science can all too easily be overshadowed by the sheer exhilaration of exploring what is novel, unusual, or simply intellectually interesting, regardless of its potential effects. In this respect, the common/proper criterion is wholly consistent with the ideals of Christian stewardship.[25] By its very nature, "stewardship" implies a custodial care of something to which one has been entrusted, but which one does not fully possess as a private possession or personal dominion. We do not "own" the natural world and its goods because we cannot; those goods are common to all as the effects of God's creative presence. In contemporary terms, this conviction has a special relevance to the negative impact of violations of the environment upon the quality of human life, or more precisely, the good of persons.

## 2. The Use/Enjoyment Criterion

A scientific ethic that recognizes the good of the whole person (encompassing our physical and spiritual dimensions) cannot view human beings as so many means to ends conducive to scientific progress. In Augustine's moral theory, we find another criterion tailor-made for addressing this very feature of scientific valuation. Augustine distinguishes those goods which we should rightfully "use" (*uti*) enroute to our final end of beatitude from that highest Good (i.e., God) that we "enjoy" (*frui*) for its own sake, as an end in itself.[26] This distinction, in effect, provides Augustine's standard for determinations of what is virtuous and what is morally blameworthy. If virtue consists in a right ordering of the soul's affections, vice constitutes a use of what should be enjoyed, and an enjoyment of what should be used.[27] In its broadest terms, the *uti/frui* distinction is a foundational feature of Augustine's moral theory, defining as it does the dynamics of rightly ordered love in every context of decision-making.

In Augustinian terms, what we should use encompasses the entire range of finite goods. This would certainly include the good of knowledge, along with the knowledge we derive from scientific investigation. But this wide interpretation of the "useful" must be qualified, lest it imply that we approach created goods in a purely consequentialist manner. This is particularly the case in regard to our fellow human beings. Augustine, in fact, would refrain from saying that we should use others as mere means to our ultimate end. More precisely, he counsels us to enjoy them, but in relation to God.[28]

What, then, is the scope of "use" in a scientific context? In order to answer this question, we must be attuned to the goal of a given activity. Indeed, the "useful" is always measured in relation to what contributes to the realization of human fulfillment, in a manner consistent with our supernatural destiny. In this respect, considerations of the "useful" can never be separated from a commitment to the human good in its fullest sense, that is, the good of the person. Scientific pursuits motivated by curiosity are certainly not antithetical to the promotion of the human good. But Augustine would object to attempts to justify each and every scientific pursuit solely for the sake of curiosity, especially for frivolous or reckless purposes, or when human dignity is compromised. In his examination of conscience in the *Confessiones*, we recall his cataloging of the negative consequences of an unregulated desire to know, exceeding the limits of usefulness.

> Because of this morbid curiosity…men proceed to search out the secrets of nature, things beyond our end, to know which profits us nothing, and of which men desire nothing but the knowing.[29]

For anyone committed to the unrestricted freedom of scientific investigation, such words can only be construed as an attack on the expansion of human knowledge and its enormous benefits. For Augustine, however, intellectual endeavors (including those of a scientific nature) must be appreciated in terms of a right ordering. If Augustine speaks of a "perverse science," it is because he has a standard for evaluating what constitutes "rightly ordered science".[30] A science that observes the norms of proper order can never forfeit its concern with the good of humans in the most objective terms. This imposes a responsibility on the scientific practitioner to cultivate a sense of priorities rooted in a steadfast commitment to the promotion of human dignity. From this standpoint, the importance of scientific pursuits for useful ends is but one side of the proverbial coin. So also, the scientist must not absolutize these pursuits as ends in themselves, for the sheer thrill of knowing.

## 3. *The Transcendentals of Created Being Criterion*

But what about the relation of science to the objects of its investigation (or research subjects), including human ones? As we have already observed, Augustine's conviction in the createdness of things endows them with a special status as effects of God's creative activity. I say "special status" here in a qualified way. From a theistic perspective, everything (from the highest to the lowest in the scheme of reality) in some way reflects the goodness and majesty of its Creator. In this connection, Augustine's notion of the transcendentals of created being provide another criterion for purposes of scientific valuation.

The transcendentals in question pertain to the overarching principles inherent in the natures of things. Augustine's metaphysics presupposes that God is creatively responsible for what contributes to each thing's completion. Accordingly, he assumes that every nature possesses an appropriate measure (*modus*), form (*forma*), and order (*ordo*).[31] In this triad, "measure" refers to limit or unity; "form" pertains to an overall structure or appearance; "order" designates a locus in the hierarchy of creation. Because Augustine approaches created reality in hierarchical terms, he affirms that some things are superior to others, to the extent that they are better measured, formed, and ordered. Conversely, he defines moral evil (i.e., the evil we freely choose to do) as a displacement of a nature, that is, an undermining of something's measure, form, and order.

On the basis of this "transcendental" criterion, we can establish moral parameters for scientific research, specifically (but not exclusively) regarding living things (including, human beings). A recognition of the measure, form, and order of a given reality is tantamount to a recognition of the integrity of its being.[32] Since the scope of scientific activity involving living things is extremely broad, however, we must also understand "integrity" in hierarchical terms. From this standpoint, the integrity of human life can never be overlooked or violated. But even lower life forms possess an appropriate definiteness, structure, and position of their own. In the words of Eugene TeSelle, "every thing…has its 'allotted' measure of space and time, giving it a privileged sphere…which constitutes the substratum of any subsequent formation or deformation, rectitude or perversity."[33]

This criterion does not seek to "tie the hands" of scientists in carrying out the necessary tasks normally performed in any laboratory. But it does affirm that there are objective standards (grounded in the natures of things) for determining the moral limits of experimentation. Despite postmodernist charges of "specieism," an Augustinian ethic of scientific activity would not hesitate to impart a higher moral standing to human beings than to animals (including higher primates) and the environment.[34] But by the same token, it would never consider animals or the environment as constituting just so much "raw material" at the ready disposal of scientific investigation, to be manipulated in any way whatsoever for its own ends. To do so would negate the fundamental integrity that all things possess, by virtue of the sheer fact of their existence.

## 4. The Goodness of the Whole Criterion

Augustine was firm in his belief that everything for which God is creatively responsible is fundamentally good. But individual things must be appreciated in their relation to a well-defined hierarchical scheme in which lesser things are subordinated to the governance of more excellent ones. "Terrestrial things are subject to celestial," Augustine writes, "and their time circuits join together in harmonious succession for a poem of the universe."[35] Even the defects we discern in creatures by no means mar this arrangement. For this reason, Augustine could extol the inherent goodness of even the least of things, "since all things together are better than the higher things alone."[36]

Augustine's affirmation of the goodness of the whole is one of the foundational principles of his theodicy (along with an interpretation of evil in negative terms as a privation or corruption of the good). Evil as we experience it at "ground level" is a matter of perspective, reflecting our limited vision of the perfection of the greater whole to which the parts contribute. As already observed, Augustine emphasizes the integrity of created being. But integrity on an individual level proceeds from participation in a harmonious system. In and of themselves, certain creatures might well appear defective and even insignificant in the grand scheme of things. But as participants in a universal order, they acquire a dignity of their own.

> From the heights of heaven down to the depths of the earth, from the beginning to the end of time, from the angel even to the worm, from the first movement up to the last, you seated, each in its proper place, all varieties of good things and all your just works, and caused them to be each in its proper season.[37]

An Augustinian-inspired ethic would encourage scientists to cultivate an appreciation of something they can so easily miss in the course of their specialized investigations: the marvelous interconnectedness of things.

This is consistent with a cosmic vision grounded upon a teleological conviction in the ordering of reality for the realization of the good. We discern a distinct aesthetic dimension in this perspective: universal order provides for a fittingness of parts exhibiting varying degrees of goodness, truth, and beauty. In a world given to an increasing compartmentalizing of knowledge, it would do scientists well to think in such holistic terms. This does not mean to suggest that they should embrace the outlook of metaphysicians. But it does seek to inculcate a sensitivity to the greater "whole" (whether it be a solar system or an ecosystem) in which a given scientific investigation unfolds. In this respect, an Augustinian ethic envisions a moral cosmos requiring a right relationship between scientists and the subject matter of their research.

## 5. The Moral Relevance Criterion

It almost goes without saying that if Augustine affirms the goodness of the whole of creation, then no aspect of creation is morally irrelevant or morally neutral. This is why the attempt to reduce things to mere "curiosities" is such an egregious error with potentially devastating consequences for people and nature alike. It is appropriate, then, to round out this "profile" of an Augustinian ethic of science with a moral criterion presupposed in the four criteria already considered. Indeed, a commitment to the common good (*criterion* #1) and the right use of things (*criterion* #2), a respect for the integrity of created being (*criterion* #3), and a recognition of the goodness of the whole of things (*criterion* #4) implicitly endorses the moral relevance (criterion #5) of everything which exists as well.

Augustine's unequivocal affirmation that everything has a moral significance carries the corollary that nothing is morally insignificant. But in order to grasp the full import of this criterion for Augustine, we must address the critique of Stoicism from which it emerged. Augustine challenged the Stoic claim that anything connected with bodily existence (including health) is classified as "morally indifferent". Since such things or concerns have no effect upon our rationality (as the Stoics contend), they are assumed to lack any moral import at all. More precisely, the Stoics hold that "morally indifferent things" (*adiaphora*) either exceed reason's power to govern or do not attract or repel the will.[38] While the Stoics define the human good in terms of what contributes to our rationality and being, Augustine contends that creatures are not only fundamentally good but morally valuable as well.[39]

If all things are deemed morally relevant simply by virtue of their createdness, then their scientific investigation cannot be divorced from a sense of moral obligation on the part of investigators. From this standpoint, things *matter*, not merely for utilitarian purposes, but because they possess an inherent value of their own. An Augustinian ethic thus demands a degree of respect for the natural world and for all living things, in keeping with their relation to a universal order. In this conceptual framework, stewardship must always take precedence over any commitment to the harnessing, control, and domination of nature. By the same token, the desire for knowledge itself must always be balanced by an abiding commitment to truth.

## AUGUSTINE'S LEGACY

Far from stifling the scientific enterprise, Augustine ennobles it by broadening the scope of intellectual inquiry to include the full panoply of creation, along with the causes ultimately responsible for its grandeur. This is why humans cannot rest content with the objects of curiosity alone. In that case, our commitment to truth would be as transitory as the desire that motivates it from moment to moment. In point of fact, however, there is good brand of curiosity and a superficial one. In this writer's estimation, good curiosity really amounts to wonder in the classical sense of the term. I suspect, then, that when our contemporaries sing the praises of the curious mind as the impetus to scientific progress, they are really referring to a penetrating sense of wonder.

This is not a matter of semantical hairsplitting on my part. I believe it touches upon something crucial about the nature of knowing. If we equate wonder with curiosity (or more drastically, lose a sense of wonder altogether), we seriously dilute the passionate commitment to truth that has stimulated the most significant scientific advances. Curiosity undoubtedly arouses our interest in a variety of things. But wonder presupposes that deeper vision that not only fastens upon what is immediately present, but allows us to imagine untold possibilities for the future. As Shaw memorably said, "Some see things as they are and ask 'Why?' I dream of things that never were and say "Why not?'"

Augustine's ultimate goal was the harmonization of the urgings of the restless mind with a restless heart that only finds fulfillment in God, its *Summum Bonum*. This amounts to a conjoining of the inclinations of mind and will, reasoning and desire, in the interests of truth. As Augustine's own experience affirmed, curiosity is instrumental in this life-long quest. But such wide-ranging desire must still be enlivened by a capacity to marvel, not simply at the sheer complexity of nature, but at the overarching order which makes it intelligible. This order provides that fittingness of things which renders them not only good, but *very good* before their Creator's loving gaze.

## NOTES TO CONCLUSION

1. I refer here to the Sagan quote cited at the very beginning of this study (see Preface).
2. *De Moribus* I,21(38): PL 32,1327: *Est item aliud quod de corporibus per imaginationes quasdam concipit anima, et eam vocat rerum scientiam.*
3. *De Moribus* I,21(38).
4. *De Moribus* I,21(38): PL 32,1327: *si universam istam corporis molem, quam mundum nuncupamus, curiosissime intentissimeque perquirant.*
5. *De Moribus* I,21(38): PL 32,1327-1328: *Tali enim amore plerumque decipitur, ut ut nihil putet esse, nisi corpus;*
6. *De Moribus* I,21(38): PL 32, 1327: *Reprimat igitur se anima ab hujusmodi vanae cognitionis cupiditate, si se castam Deo servare disposuit.*
7. *De Ordine* II,15(42).

8. *De Ordine* II,5(17).

9. Cf., Augustine's critique of this error of scientific method seems to anticipate Sir Francis Bacon's "Idols of the Theatre" and its critique of the tendency of "empirical philosophy" to base its conclusions upon a few circumscribed, vague observations.

10. *De Ordine* I,8(26).

11. *Soliloquia* I,2(11).

12. Cf., *Confessiones* VI,4(6), where Augustine admitted his own need for a sense of certitude in theological matters: "I wished to be made as certain of things I could not see, as I was certain that seven and three make ten…I wanted other things to be known with the same certainty, whether bodily things…not present to my senses, or spiritual things…" Also see A.C. Crombie, *Augustine to Galileo. The History of Science A.D. 400-1650* (Melbourne, London, Toronto: William Heinemann Ltd., 1957), 5: "The chief aim of Augustine was to find a certain basis for knowledge and this he found in the conception of eternal forms or ideas…."

13. Philip Ball, *Universe of Stone. A Biography of Chartres Cathedral* (New York: HarperCollins Publishers, 2008), 80.

14. Philip Ball, *Universe of Stone. A Biography of Chartres Cathedral*, 81.

15. A.C. Crombie, *Augustine to Galileo. The History of Science A.D. 400-1650*, 391-392.

16. E.L. Mascall, *Christian Theology and Natural Science* (London, New York, Toronto: Longmans, Green and Co., 1957), 132.

17. Ernest Partridge, "On 'Scientific Morality'," *The Online Gadfly* (gadfly.igc.org/pomo.scimoral.htm), 2.

18. Douglas Allchin, "Values in Science: An Educational Perspective," *Science & Education* (1999): 1-2.

19. Douglas Allchin, "Values in Science: An Educational Perspective," 3.

20. Jacob Bronowski, *Science and Human Values* (New York: Harper and Row, Publishers, 1965), 62.

21. Jacob Bronowski, *Science and Human Values*, 61-62.

22. Jacob Bronowski, *Science and Human Values*, 60.

23. This list brings to the fore an important hermeneutical consideration. I am cognizant that the very criteria I propose reflect my own presuppositions (a) about the character of an Augustinian ethic of science; and (b) about which moral principles drawn from Augustine's writings are relevant to its formulation. Clearly, different readers will discern different areas of scientific relevance for the criteria discussed. In the present context, I do not provide any explicit applications of these criteria. But I suggest two areas of scientific activity which offer potentially fruitful fields for ethical analysis from an Augustinian perspective, namely, genetic engineering and ecology.

24. Richard Holmes, *The Age of Wonder* (New York: Vintage Books, 2008), 371, referring to the vision of Sir Humphrey Davy (1778-1829): "The

gratification of the love of knowledge is delightful to every refined mind; but a much higher motive is offered in indulging it, when that knowledge is felt to be practical power, and when that power may be applied to lessen the miseries or increase the comforts of our fellow creatures" (*Collected Works*, Volume 6, 4).

25. Cf., I Cor. 4:1-2: *Thus should one regard us: as servants of Christ and stewards of the mysteries of God. Now it is of course required of stewards that they be found trustworthy.*

26. *De Civitate Dei* I,4(4).

27. *De diversis quaestionibus* LXXXIII,30.

28. *De Civitate Dei* I,33(36-37).

29. *Confessiones* X,35(55).

30. At *Confessiones* X,35(55), Augustine also posits *curiositas* as the motive when things are investigated by "magic arts" and "perverse science".

31. Augustine's writings present variations on this triad (although the transcendental "order" is a constant): measure, number, and order; unity, number, and order; unity, species, and order. For Augustine's uses of the triad, see *De Natura Boni* 3; *De Vera Religione* 7,13; *De Moribus* II,6(8); *De Civitate Dei* XIX,13.

32. In this context, I use the term "integrity" in a loose sense to highlight the fact that everthing (to the extent that is exists) possesses an internal unity which enables it to endure and thrive as the thing it is.

33. Eugene TeSelle, *Augustine the Theologian* (New York: Herder and Herder, 1970), 119.

34. I interpret "specieism" (as understood by postmodernists like Peter Singer) in the following terms: the unjustifiable exaltation of the human species over animal species on the assumption that human beings possess a privileged status (based on their rationality or creation in God's image) which renders their rights preeminent (regardless of their cognitive capacity), at the expense of non-human species. According to Singer (*Unsanctifying Human Life*, ed. Helga Kuhse [Malden, Mass.: Blackwell, 2002], 228), "the doctrine of the sanctity of human life, as it is normally understood, has at its core a discrimination on the basis of species and nothing else."

35. *De Musica* VI,11(29).

36. *Confessiones* VII,13(19).

37. *Confessiones* VIII,3(8).

38. *De Civitate Dei* XIX,4.

39. *De Civitate Dei* XIX, 4. I provide a more extended treatment of this aspect of Augustine's Stoic critique in "St. Augustine's Critique of the *Adiaphora*: A Key Component of His Rebuttal of Stoic Ethics," *Studia Moralia* 38 (2000): 165-195.

# EPILOGUE

## AUGUSTINE IN A NEW VOICE

When we assess Augustine's significance as a philosopher and theologian, we are considering far more than the achievement of a single thinker. Augustine generated an all-embracing perspective that casts a long shadow over Western thought. Whether one endorses or opposes this perspective, its long-range impact must still be acknowledged. This is certainly true of Augustine's conception of curiosity. It is difficult to trace the history of this notion without coming to terms with his contribution to its development, from the early Middle Ages to the present. As we have seen, however, his own interpretation of cognitive appetite itself bore the imprint of diverse influences rooted in the pagan, scriptural, and patristic traditions. He skillfully channeled these influences in the interests of a distinctive Christian Neoplatonic understanding of knowledge and its parameters. But in so doing, he bequeathed to subsequent thinkers a certain ambivalence toward the very craving for new knowledge, depending upon the context in which it finds expression.

In this writer's estimation, the most enduring effect of Augustine's designation of curiosity as a vice lies in a persistent trepidation about unrestricted forays into intellectual endeavors, particularly in the scientific domain. The admonition that "curiosity kills the cat" is no empty platitude, but underscores a genuine reluctance to penetrate the unknown (with the implicit suggestion that we might well discover things better left alone). Such an uneasiness is not exclusive to the religious sphere, with its censure of vain pretensions to knowledge beyond our ken. It also looms large in secular circles, even after curiosity was elevated to the status of a virtue, with the rise of modern science and its rejection of a teleological, theocentrist world-view.

Can we find a better illustration of the tension accompanying this paradigm-shift than in Marlowe's *Dr. Faustus*, the tale of a tragic hero willing to forfeit his own soul for the sake of unlimited knowledge? Faustus personifies that same desire to "penetrate nature's secrets" that Augustine perceived as a major outgrowth of the curious "lust of the eyes." But Faustus also exemplifies the plight of modernity, disenchanted with the old ways of knowing on the one hand, but uncertain about how to use its new found knowledge on the other. For Faustus, the acquisition of occult knowledge is intimately connected with the drive for power.

> These metaphysics of magicians and necromantic books are heavenly. Lines, circles, signs, letters, and characters— Ay, these are those that Faustus most desires. O, what a world of profit and delight, of power, of honor, of omnipotence, is promised to the studious artisan![1]

In the absence of a supernatural frame of reference, Faustus is cast adrift; left to his own devices, his quest is stifled by pathetic attempts at asserting his sense of autonomy. His experience thus falsifies any uncritical credence in the Baconian dictum that "knowledge is power." Neither his ability to do as he pleases nor his unrestricted desire for knowledge provide guarantees of lasting happiness.

In a very real sense, Faustus reflects the Renaissance exuberance for the experimental method and the prospect of new worlds of man's own making. But the sweeping technological transformations of the ensuing centuries only served to sober this initial confidence in the efficacy of scientific knowledge. The Industrial Revolution (and its accompanying exaltation of reasoning) coincided with renewed warnings about the reckless manipulation of nature and the veritable "monsters" it might unleash. In a memorable passage from her novel *Frankenstein*, Mary Shelley depicted the appetitiveness inherent in the "enticements of science" in these terms:

> In other studies you go as far as others have gone before you, and there is nothing more to know; but in a scientific pursuit there is continual food for discovery and wonder. Whence, I often asked myself, did the principle of life proceed? It was a bold question, and one which has ever been considered as a mystery; yet with how many things are we upon the brink of becoming acquainted, if cowardice or carelessness did not restrain our enquiries.[2]

We recall Augustine's indictment (issued over a millennium earlier) of investigations prompted by a "certain vain and curious desire, cloaked over with the title knowledge and science," whereby people "search out the secrets of nature, things beyond our end."[3] In Dr. Frankenstein's case, the "enticements of science" lead to a heretofore forbidden realm of scientific discovery—the fabrication of human life itself. For all of his idealism (and the compelling qualities of his Creature), the experiment results in unspeakable tragedy. Nineteenth century poets echoed this wariness about the penalties of tampering with nature. For Wordsworth,

> Our meddling intellect
> Mis-shapes the beauteous forms of things:-
> We murder to dissect.[4]

And Keats, bemoaning the triumph of "cold" reasoning, predicts how

> Philosophy will clip an Angel's wings,
> Conquer all mysteries by rule and line,
> Empty the haunted air, and...
> Unweave a rainbow...[5]

Prophetic words indeed, anticipating the pervasiveness of science in every aspect of human existence.

Robert Oppenheimer's response to the first atomic detonation (quoting the *Bhagavad-Gita*) provides a haunting commentary on the negative side of great technological advances: "Now I am become Death, the destroyer of worlds."[6] The late twentieth century, in fact, witnessed an increasing scepticism toward the Enlightenment ideal of knowledge and the very notion of progress. In a contemporary setting, Augustine's critical stance toward natural science can find a surprisingly receptive audience. That audience comprises those thinkers who have taken the "hermeneutical turn," charging that calculative, ratiocinative knowledge might not disclose the full truth of things, especially the truth of what it means to be human. Stated in other terms, is scientific discourse normative for discourse in general? In a postmodernist vein, this concern is well expressed by Richard Rorty:

> The fear of science, of "scientism," of naturalism, of self-objectivation, of being turned by too much knowledge into a thing rather than a person, is the fear that...there will be objectively true or false answers to every question we ask... This is frightening because it

cuts off the possibility of something new under the sun, of human life as poetic.[7]

It is something of an irony that one of the most prominent twentieth century exponents of Augustine's critique of the "lust of the eyes" would come to distance himself from the Christian intellectual tradition altogether.[8] In the existential analytic of Martin Heidegger (1889-1976), we find an intriguing recasting of Augustine's treatment of curiosity. Heidegger allows Augustine to speak to us in a new voice, in a manner attuned to the exigencies of life in a world dominated by the ever expanding reach of technology. In so doing, he reveals a fresh relevance for Augustine's understanding of the implications of cognitive desire, especially in relation to scientific investigation.

In Heidegger's monumental *Being and Time* (1927), curiosity assumes a prominent role in his probing assessment of the "fallenness" of Dasein. Embedded in this discussion, we encounter an extended quote from Augustine's examination of his ongoing susceptibility to the sin of curiosity, that is, *concupiscentia oculorum* (*Confessiones* X,35). But this gloss must be considered against the background of an earlier one that emerges in Heidegger's "Augustine and Neoplatonism" (1921), part of a lecture course on religious phenomenology which lays the groundwork for key aspects of *Being and Time*.[9]

At the outset, a qualification is in order. The pivotal question, it seems, it not whether Heidegger discovered these elements in Augustine, or whether he interpreted Augustine by means of his existential analytic. In John Caputo's reckoning, the real issue is how such elements "emerged from the creative interaction of the young philosopher...with the ageless beauty and power of the *Confessions*."[10] Let us consider the results of that interactive process.

## HEIDEGGER'S AUGUSTINE LECTURES

In "Augustine and Neoplatonism," Heidegger identifies genuine Christian experience with life as factually realized.[11] In this way, he strives to liberate religion from the metaphysical presuppositions (in Augustine's case, Neoplatonic metaphysics) that have obscured the facticity of experience under the veneer of representational thinking. From Heidegger's perspective, this epistemological model has decisively shaped Western metaphysics from ancient times onward. He thus sets himself to the ambitious task of retrieving the problematic of facticity from its metaphysical encrustation. Accordingly, Heidegger attempts to isolate Augustine's account of authentic religious experience (with its attunement to conflicting desires and temptations) from an alien conceptual overlay. By the same token, however, Heidegger's commentary on Augustine's treatment of concupiscence freely incorporates salient images prominent in the Neoplatonic depiction of the soul's temporal distention. But he puts them to new use in his investigation of *curare* as the mark of factical life.

In the Augustinian tension between continence and concupiscence, Heidegger discerns a deeper conflict between a condition of unity and one given over to multiplicity, that is, between being "gathered together" and being dispersed in the manifold.

> The *"in multa defluere"* [scattered, dissolution into the many] is an oriented being-pulled by and in *delectatio*; the life of the world in its manifold significance…appeals to us.[12]

From this standpoint, Augustine's examination of conscience in *Confessiones* X becomes a reaction against the dispersion inherent in human existence. This is the essence of *curare*, the "being concerned" that Heidegger posits at the heart of facticity. By its very nature, the state of "being concerned" promotes an instability, fluctuating between the poles of fear (*timere*) and desire (*desiderare*). For this reason, *curare* must be understood in relational terms.

> The *multum* is the manifold, the many significances in which I live. These significances are sometimes *prospera* (supportive, conducive, appealing…carrying over and supporting in the direction of significance), at other times *adversa* (impeding, countering that for which I strive).[13]

Far too many commentators have construed this part of the *Confessiones* as no more than an excessive (and even scrupulous) exercise in self-criticism.[14] For Heidegger, however, the motive which drives Augustine is first and foremost a search for God.

> One views the considerations…too easily as mere hair-splitting reflections of a pedantic "moralizer"; or one gets lost in isolated, surprising psychological analyses. In both cases, one has lost the real direction of understanding.[15]

Such a misunderstanding extends to Augustine's interpretation of concupiscence as well. For Heidegger, Augustine does far more than catalogue the varieties of the concupiscential drive. In Heidegger's analysis, the "triple concupiscence" becomes "three directions of the *defluere*, of the possibility of defluxion and the danger."[16] But wherein lies the danger? It can only proceed from the same world into which the self is inexorably drawn.[17]

As Augustinian commentator, Heidegger is faithful to Augustine's own order of procedure. In keeping with this order, the discussion of *concupiscentia oculorum* (the second form of *tentatio*) in *Confessiones* X,35 is preceded by a consideration of the pleasure of "these eyes of my flesh" (*Confessiones* X,34,51). This methodology is crucial, since Augustine's treatment of curious lust relies so heavily on vision as a metaphor for knowing.

Augustine's exploration of the dynamics of visual pleasure opens the way for his discussion of the epistemological dimension of "seeing." In this respect, Heidegger characterizes "seeing" in its most general terms as a mere "dealing with" sense objects, rather than as a genuine concern with the quest for happiness. Heidegger focuses specifically upon "the artists and followers of external beauty" for whom "what is significant is experienced...suffices for itself, by itself, and by its continuation."[18] Once again, he plays upon the tension between a commitment to authentic selfhood grounded in facticity and the loss of self in the manifold.

> They do not preserve the security and liveliness of the enactment of concern and...engagement for themselves...but they dissipate it and spend it easily in an amusing slackness and a delightful laziness. It is no longer at their disposal for an authentic decision. They fail while giving themselves...a borrowed significance and posture as the enjoyers and connoisseurs of these things, pretending to be familiar and intimate with the meaning of the world and the secrets of life.[19]

Absorption in visual delights focuses one upon the immediacy of experience—not in any penetrating way, but simply for the sake of pleasure. Yet such enjoyment does not yield contentment. This is why one needs to *impose meaning* on the world enjoyed, neglecting possibilities of commitment in favor of one's own version of the real.

One is not content with mere enjoyment and connoisseurship, but
at the same time one adds a great world-view theory...."deepening,"
in order to achieve an even greater expansion by calling upon the
deepening.[20]

As a metaphor for knowing in general, vision is intimately linked with
that "different form" of temptation delineated in *Confessiones* X,35(55).
The "lust of the eyes" (*concupiscentia oculorum*) is distinct from the desire for visual pleasure or the pleasure we derive from sense experience
in general, "being entertained by something...dealing with the content
of what becomes accessible through the senses."[21] In this respect, sen-
suous pleasure *in the flesh* is different from experiencing *through the
flesh* when we take pleasure in the desire to know.

It is the appetite of *looking-about-oneself* (not of dealing with) in the
various regions and fields ...curiosity as the greedy desire for the
new [Neugier].[22]

Heidegger exploits the literal meaning of *Neugier* in accenting what
is central to the curious appetite: an avarice for the novel that can justify any investigation whatsoever for the sake of knowledge. Because
the mere "looking-about" does not entail any "dealing-with," it deprives
one of a genuine commitment to knowing.[23] The attraction here lies
in the sheer novelty, not the content. Such lust masquerades under the
deceptive titles of *knowledge* and *science*, "assuming the cover of profundity and...the absolute cultural necessity of special achievements."[24]

Heidegger (echoing Augustine) is clearly struck by how curiosity
(in contrast to carnal concupiscence) takes delight even in what is contrary to the sensually pleasing, "out of lust for knowing—not for the
trouble they bring."[25] If the monstrous or grotesque does not disturb
the curious mind, it is because it can so easily detach itself from such
experiences.

Even that which does not yield positive enlightenment to the worldly, factical enjoyment, even the opposite of that, is intended, because
the intention...renders the content of the What accessible in such a
way that it cannot trouble it, and keeps it at bay.[26]

From an Augustinian perspective, the curious appetite assumes
manifold expressions, from magic to mysticism to theosophy. In
Heidegger's commentary on Augustine, even God becomes "a factor in
human experiments," required to respond to "an inquisitive, pompous,

and pseudo-prophetic...curious looking-about-oneself."²⁷ But this amounts to carving out an interpretation of God in our own image, making Him "dance to our tune," so to speak. By reducing God to another "knowable" (the outgrowth of theorization rather than submission to His objectivity), we lose any sense of the Divine mystery.

For Heidegger, however, the paradigmatic example of this "looking-about-oneself" is found in what Augustine designates as *perversa scientia*, the veritable *finis delectationis* which forfeits "any criticism about its own sense of enactment."²⁸ This amounts to saying that curiosity carries an enabling power that legitimizes every intellectual pursuit in the name of its own lascivious desire. "In curiosity," Heidegger asserts, "everything is in principle accessible, without restraint."²⁹

By glibly relegating everything to so many items of information, curiosity confines the knowable to what meets our immediate gaze. The internet age offers countless examples of the intellectual dissipation that follows from the fundamental human "need to know" all things. Once "knowledge" is equated with what is readily accessible at the touch of our fingertips, wherein lies its mystery? The very rapidity with which we now acquire information about every conceivable subject lends itself to a trivialization of knowing itself. More radically, the conjoining of curiosity with the assumption that science is a self-justifying enterprise generates the illusion that everything is indeed possible. Who would dare stifle scientific progress, especially when science presents itself as enhancing the human good? Since the cognitive appetite is so wide-ranging, however, it cannot tolerate any restrictions to its scope of investigation. Just as familiarity breeds contempt, curiosity easily empties things of their profundity and depth.

Heidegger's Augustine lectures exhibit a penetrating religious sensibility, rooted in the anti-metaphysical stance of the Protestant Christianity exemplified by figures like Luther and Kierkegaard. His treatment of the negative aspects of curiosity assume a direct relevance for coming to terms with the ongoing struggle inherent in human existence against those competing desires which draw the soul from God and divert its attention to the world at large. In this respect, Heidegger incorporates the Neoplatonic distinction (even as he disavows the Neoplatonic metaphysics appropriated by Augustine) between "dispersion" (i.e., into the world) and "gathering together" (i.e., in relation to God). In this respect, curiosity introduces an instability into Christian experience. The *cura* (*Bekummerung*) of the Augustine lectures is intimately linked with an inner turbulence. Even if the language changes in *Being and Time* (*Bekummerung* becomes *Sorge*), the sentiments of the earlier work are operative in the later. As Caputo observes, "the central claim of the existential analytic, that the Being of *Dasein* is care (*Sorge*), derives almost directly from the Augustine lectures."[30]

## CURIOSITY IN *BEING AND TIME*

In *Being and Time*, Heidegger explores the structures of factical experience, but in a manner transcending a Judeo-Christian or Greek metaphysical perspective. If *The Phenomenology of Religious Experience* is infused with a sense of the reality and challenges of the cross, *Being and Time* offers a highly formalized analysis of humans in their most stark existential terms. Factical existence encompasses our being as "being-in-the-world" (*Dasein*). Accordingly, "care" (*Sorge*) provides something of an organizing principle for addressing the scope of our encounters with the larger world.[31] This means that *Dasein's* being is inextricably connected with the being of others and an encounter with others. Indeed, the very being of *Dasein* is care.[32] *Dasein* exists in the world to the extent that it is being as engaged with things; being-in-the-world is always correlative with being-with-others.[33] For this reason, an analysis of the existential status of *Dasein* cannot be divorced from a consideration of its relation to a public "They," and the dangers such involvement poses to *Dasein's* authenticity.

Inauthenticity, in fact, is an unavoidable implication of *Dasein's* everydayness, that is, its absorption in the exigencies of life that anesthetize it to its possibilities for self-actualization.[34] Inauthenticity reduces us to so many "things" lost in the anonymity of the "They."

> In these characters of Being...everyday Being-among-one-another...averageness, leveling down, publicness ...lies that 'constancy' of *Dasein* which is closest to us. This "constancy" pertains not to the enduring Being-present-at-hand of something, but rather to Dasein's kind of Being as Being-with. In these modes one's way of Being is that of inauthenticity and failure to stand by one's Self.[35]

This tendency toward inauthenticity amounts to a "fallenness". But "fallenness" here is not to be construed in terms of some ontological declension from a higher to a lower metaphysical plane.

> There is revealed a basic kind of Being which belongs to every-dayness; we call this the "falling" of *Dasein*. This term does not express any negative evaluation, but is used to signify that *Dasein* is proximally... alongside the 'world' of its concern. This "absorption in..." has mostly the character of Being-lost in the publicness of the "they."[36]

Heideggerian "fallenness," then, is principally rooted in a failure to recognize the meaning of Being and its possibilities. This touches upon a central theme of *Being and Time*, namely, Heidegger's claim that the Western intellectual tradition has contributed to an obscuring of what it means to be, precisely because it has been so preoccupied with the being of things. The oblivion into which Being has fallen is tantamount to a "forgetfulness." But as one commentator points out, the "forgetfulness of Being" assumes a dual connotation for Heidegger: *first*, a "forgetfulness" of our own grasp of Being in an everyday context; *secondly*, the historical "forgetfulness of Being" as a result of its encrustation in the metaphysical tradition itself.[37] The need for a retrieval of the primal experience of what it means to be (as it emerged at the well-springs of Western metaphysics) finds a counterpart in the search for authenticity in the face of the fallennesss/inauthenticity accompanying participation in the public arena of life.

But how does inauthenticity manifest itself? Heidegger posits three phenomena, or more precisely, "symptoms," proceeding from *Dasein's* loss of self in the "They": idle talk (*Gerede*), curiosity (*Neugier*), and ambiguity (*Zweideutigkeit*).[38] These three symptoms, however, are closely interrelated. This is a crucial consideration for our purposes, since the existential implications of curiosity can only be properly appreciated in relation to idle talk and ambiguity. What immediately stands out is the sheer ordinariness of these marks of fallenness. Indeed, it is their very rootedness in such commonplace experiences that renders them so threatening to *Dasein's* authenticity.

If inauthenticity constitutes a mode of existence, then such a counterfeit version of Being emerges in the way we express it through idle talk, in the way we "see" the world through curiosity, and in the ambiguous way our sense of self is distorted by everyday forms of speaking and "seeing" reality.[39] In each case, we discern a special relationship to the world and those inhabiting it.

> Idle talk discloses to *Dasein* a Being toward its world, towards Others, and towards itself...in a mode of groundless floating.

Curiosity discloses everything and anything, yet in such a way that Being…is everywhere and nowhere. Ambiguity hides nothing from Dasein's understanding, but only in order that Being-in-the-world should be suppressed in this uprooted "everywhere and nowhere."[40]

By the same token, each of these existential symptoms of inauthenticity find an authentic counterpart. Idle talk stands in polar tension with discourse, curiosity with understanding, and ambiguity with self-disclosure. The line between idle talk and discourse is a rather fine one. Both phenomena rely upon language, the vehicle of communication. But while idle talk allows for communication, the level of intelligibility it yields reflects *Dasein* in its most average everydayness. Idle talk certainly expresses something. But what it expresses is not concerned with comprehension, only with absorbing what is said in a superficial way.

> Idle talk is the possibility of understanding everything without previously making the thing one's own. If this were done, idle talk would founder; and it already guards against such a danger. Idle talk is something which anyone can rake up; it not only releases one from the task of genuinely understanding, but develops an undifferentiated kind of intelligibility, for which nothing is closed off any longer.[41]

Idle talk impedes the very disclosure of truth that discourse seeks. According to Heidegger, this does not necessarily imply an intention to deceive. In point of fact, idle talk lacks what is necessary to engage in "consciously passing off something as something else."[42] Heidegger's assertion that "nothing is closed off any longer" in idle talk provides a link with the wide-ranging character of curiosity, the second symptom of inauthenticity. Idle talk and curiosity both exhibit a groundlessness which resists any commitment to genuine possibilities of Being, whether through speech or in the desire to know. In broad terms, Heidegger's treatment of curiosity provides a commentary on the traditional interpretation of knowing in terms of the visual metaphor. More specifically, he finds his inspiration for the equation of knowing with seeing in Augustine's examination of the persistence of the *concupiscentia oculorum* (*Conf.* X,35). On the basis of that extended quote, he frames a question: "Which existential state of *Dasein* will become intelligible in the phenomenon of curiosity?"[42] Once again, he anchors his analysis in *Dasein's* everydayness:

We designate this tendency by the term "curiosity" [Neugier], which...is not confined to seeing, but expresses the tendency towards a peculiar way of letting the world be encountered by us in perception.[43]

Curiosity, then, reflects that tendency which is part and parcel of *Dasein's* mode of existence—the tendency toward "seeing." In this context, Heidegger interprets Aristotle's teaching (*Meta.* A I,980 a 21) that "all men desire by nature to know" as a desire "to see," construing *eidenai* in its most literal sense. But he does not confine this analysis to cognition alone. For him, the "desire" specified by Aristotle indicates that "care (*Sorge*) for seeing that is essential for man's Being."[44] This points to *Dasein's* fundamental orientation toward absorption in worldly concerns.

Being-in-the-world is proximally absorbed in the world of concern. This concern is guided by circumspection, which discovers the ready-to-hand and preserves it as thus discovered.[45]

But "seeing" can be construed in purely perceptual terms or in a more penetrating way. If curiosity encompasses the former way of "seeing," the latter constitutes a "beholding," which discloses truth. As Heidegger asserts, "primordial and genuine truth lies in pure beholding."[46] By virtue of the care inherent in curiosity, however, one is not concerned with the world as it is, but merely as it appears.

Dasein lets itself be carried along solely by the looks of the world; in this kind of Being, it concerns itself with becoming rid of itself as Being-in-the-world and rid of its Being alongside that which, in the closest everyday manner, is ready-to-hand.[47]

Heidegger discerns a freedom in curiosity that promotes a special type of concern. In and of itself, concern has a specific focus—a task to be done or goal to be accomplished. But if curiosity is concerned with seeing, it is "just in order to see."[48] This is why it takes refuge in novelty and the incessant movement from one novel thing to another.

In this kind of seeing, that which is an issue for care does not lie in grasping something and being knowingly in the truth; it lies rather in its possibilities of abandoning itself to the world...characterized by a specific way of *not tarrying* alongside what is closest.[49]

When one loses oneself in novelty, one need not come to grips with the ultimate questions confronting human existence. Such a mindset has no time for that leisure that is conducive to deeper thinking. Curiosity thus becomes a means of evading the very authenticity it appears to seek. What it does, in fact, seek is incessant restlessness and the stimulation it draws from novel experience. Heidegger's language here is evocative of Plotinus' depiction of the *polupragmatic* nature of Soul (*Ennead* III.7[45].11) that exerted so great an influence on Augustine's linking of curiosity with the "cares" and "busyness" of temporality.

Heideggerian curiosity is the antithesis of wonder (*thaumazein*), that capacity for marveling at things. But this carries a risk: marveling at things might lead us "to the point of not understanding."[50] This is not to say, of course, that curiosity seeks genuine understanding. Rather, its concern lies in a pseudo-understanding that conveys the illusion of knowing, in a wholly superficial way. In this connection, Heidegger posits three constitutive components of curiosity. First, curiosity consists in the phenomenon of not tarrying. Curiosity simply cannot tarry, by virtue of the restless spirit which drives it. Secondly, curiosity prompts a distractedness by new possibilities. What else can the curious mind be but distracted, when it disavows any real commitment to understanding or even risking the inability to understand? By virtue of this free-floating character, curiosity assumes a third constituent: the phenomenon of *never dwelling anywhere*. In the context of *Dasein's* everydayness, the curious mind finds no dwelling place.

> Curiosity is everywhere and nowhere. This mode of Being-in-the-world reveals a new kind of Being of everyday Dasein…in which Dasein is constantly uprooting itself.[51]

Because it is "everywhere and nowhere," curiosity is bound up with idle talk. One everyday mode of Being supports the other. Idle talk defines the scope of curiosity, even dictating what must be read and seen.[52] But such distortions of discourse (through idle talk) and seeing (through curiosity) also presuppose ambiguity, the final symptom of *Dasein's* inauthenticity. When nothing is excluded from investigation and everything can be understood (or more precisely, appears understandable), how does one discern what constitutes true understanding?

> Idle talk and curiosity take care in their ambiguity to ensure that what is genuinely and newly created is out of date as soon as it emerges before the public. Dasein is always ambiguously 'there'… in that public disclosedness of Being-with-one-another where the

loudest idle talk and the most ingenious curiosity keep 'things moving', where, in an everyday manner, everything…is happening.
This ambiguity is always tossing to curiosity that which it seeks;
and it gives idle talk the semblance of having everything decided in
it.[53]

In *Being and Time*, curiosity (along with idle talk and ambiguity) is
an unavoidable implication of *Dasein's* everydayness. Heidegger shares
Augustine's assumption that immersion in temporal affairs is not only
prompted by, but conducive to a spirit of restlessness. For both, curiosity plunges one into a ceaseless search for the stimulation derived from
new experiences. But this drive (which is deeply rooted in the active
life) can easily lead to a distorted vision of knowledge and understanding. For Augustine, curiosity is closely connected with the soul's gravitation toward time and the manifold *curae* that reflect a fragmented
mode of being. Heidegger adapts this model of the fall motif (in both
his Augustine lectures and in *Being and Time*) in linking curiosity with
a tendency toward *defluxion* and a corresponding loss of self in the
manifold of dissipating concerns.

Heidegger, in fact, perceives a special relationship between curiosity and the "specific temporality of falling."[54] This is why his existential analysis presupposes a recognition of *Dasein's* temporality and
the historicity which attaches to its identity. If the Being of *Dasein* is
care, then the very significance of care is grounded upon an ecstatic
temporality in which *Dasein* is coming-towards-itself (in projection),
coming-back-to-itself (in thrownness), and making things present
(by concern).[55] Among the three symptoms of *Dasein's* inauthenticity,
curiosity is most relevant to temporality, fluctuating between what is
present-at-hand, what is continually anticipated, and what no longer
compels its interest.

> As this making-present…curiosity has an ecstatic unity with a cor-
> responding future and a corresponding having been.
> The craving for the new is…a way of proceeding towards some-
> thing not yet seen…but in its craving…desires such a possibiity as
> something… actual.[56]

## HEIDEGGER AND AUGUSTINE IN CONVERSATION

In the contexts of their own times, Heidegger and Augustine are powerful cultural critics. Each thinker offers unsettling admonitions to cultures under the alluring spell of curiosity and the fickle commitment to knowledge it inspires. For Augustine, succumbing to the vice of curiosity amounts to an absorption in the images and phantasms of the really and truly real. This accounts for his suspicion of natural science and what he perceives as its restricted version of truth. If curiosity qualifies as a "sin" for Heidegger, it is one which is endemic to Being-in-the-world. Heideggerian curiosity bespeaks the inauthenticity that is part and parcel of *Dasein's* everydayness.

Heidegger translates Augustine's understanding of the "lust of the eyes" into a contemporary framework in which an absorption in virtual reality assumes an all-pervasive character: from media to entertainment to the cyber-revolution which shapes so many of our presuppositions about what it means to learn, to know, and to understand. In all of these ways, we confront the prospect of losing touch with what we are about on the most fundamental level as human beings, that is, beings with the capacity to know more than the mere being of things. In that case, we stand to lose any sense of what will ultimately satisfy the cravings of the restless mind and heart.

But why do thinkers so far removed historically and ideologically find curiosity so problematic? Historically speaking, Augustine's reasons for his polemical attitude are more understandable, in view of the deeply rooted suspicion of cognitive desire in the classical tradition. But as a twentieth century philosopher, Heidegger's critique of curiosity is somewhat puzzling, in the aftermath of its exaltation as the stimulus toward scientific knowledge from the Renaissance period onward.

If Augustine and Heidegger find an elusive common ground, however, it not only lies in their emphasis upon the pitfalls inherent in curiosity. It also lies in their attitudes about the means to truth. This is not to say that their interpretations of truth are one and the same. Augustine endorses the classical correspondence theory of truth as an adequation or conformity of the intellect to immutable standards accessible to reason under the guidance of a higher Divine Light. In this respect, Augustine construes truth as the *id quod est*, that which truly exists.[57] This is precisely the interpretation of truth that Heidegger rejects. For Heidegger, truth is revelatory rather than representational, as a disclosure of what lies concealed.

> Considered with respect to truth as disclosedness, concealment is...
> undisclosedness and...untruth.[58]

Such divergent interpretations of truth notwithstanding, Augustine and Heidegger appeal to a higher order of understanding which transcends the kind of knowing which finds its paradigm in scientific investigation. Augustine, we recall, distinguished the higher contemplative function of the intellect from its active (sciential) focus on a changing, temporal world.

Heidegger, in turn, draws a distinction between a meditative mode of thinking and a calculative one.[59] The former allows for an encounter with Being, without relying upon the representational mediation of concepts; the latter focuses upon beings, seeking the quantitative precision that is the hallmark of the "hard" sciences.

For Heidegger, curiosity is implicit in the preoccupation with calculative thinking that defines truth in terms of the truth of things, rather than the disclosedness of Being. By virtue of its instability and wide-ranging character, curiosity distorts our cognitive vision, and by implication, our very conception as to what constitutes thinking and knowing.

> We conceive of thinking on the model of scientific knowledge and
> its research projects...by the... successful achievements of *praxis*...
> but the deed of thinking is neither theoretical nor practical.[60]

When Heidegger denies that thinking is a matter of *theoria* or *praxis*, he is not claiming that it has no role in such endeavors. Rather, he affirms something vital about the nature of thinking that Augustine could readily endorse: genuine thinking must seek a truth that goes beyond the surface appearances of things. From this standpoint, Augustine's critique of the natural science of his own day might be viewed as anticipating Heidegger's rejection of the scientific way of knowing as paradigmatic of knowing in general.

In respect to the goals and direction of his philosophical outlook, Heidegger (particularly in his later works) could not be more removed from Augustine's theocentric vision of reality. For Augustine, humans are not merely beings-toward-death, but rational embodied spirits that find their ultimate fulfillment in a supernatural end. By the same token, however, Heidegger's analysis of *Dasein's* curiosity reveals an attunement to the existentialist implications of Augustine's own attitude toward the "lust of the eyes." On one level, Heidegger renders Augustine's critiques of *curiositas* cogent to a 21st century audience. But Heidegger also enables us to appreciate the contemporary relevance of what *Augustine himself* has to say about the impact of cognitive appetite, in personal and cultural terms. If Heidegger allows Augustine to speak in a "new voice," then, it is very much a voice for our time.

## A VOICE FOR OUR TIME

Whether we interpret Augustine from a Heideggerian perspective, or Heidegger from an Augustinian one, we discern in them a mutual conviction that knowledge requires a more pronounced existential commitment on our part than anything *mere* curiosity can inspire. But if this is the case, what sustains the defining human drive to know—not just as a means to an end, but for its own sake? It can only proceed from the experience of wonder which Plato designated as the veritable beginning of the love of wisdom.[61] Now, one might easily assume that curiosity and wonder are synonymous, and people often conflate the meanings of these terms. But to do so overlooks a crucial dimension of the mind's cognitive capacity. Strictly speaking, wonder presupposes an intuition of the mystery inherent in the world around us. While curiosity finds its ideal metaphor in "seeing" (the Johannine "lust of the eyes"), wonder is best depicted in terms of a "beholding"—not simply seeing, but *seeing intently*, with a spirit of reverential awe for what is apprehended.

In point of fact, many of our contemporaries (particularly in the scientific community) might cringe at the suggestion that the pursuit of knowledge should be accompanied by a sense of reverence, awe, or mystery. Are not such notions better left to the realm of religion or mysticism? But at a time when we confront the prospect that all things are potentially knowable, we stand in serious danger of losing the very incentive which sustains this search. This is accompanied by a risk that some may not wish to confront: that there are things which exceed our comprehension and resist our efforts to understand them in a definitive, exhaustive way. This point is affirmed by Brian Green in his own quest for the ultimate theory of the universe.

> The astonishment at our ability to understand the universe…is eas-
> ily lost sight of…maybe there is a limit to comprehensibility…that
> after reaching the deepest possible level of understanding science
> can offer, there will…be aspects of the universe that remain unex-
> plained…that certain features of the universe are the way they are
> because of happenstance, accident, or divine choice. The success of
> the scientific method…has encouraged us to think that…we can
> unravel nature's mysteries. But hitting the absolute limit of scientific
> explanation…would be a singular event, one for which past experi-
> ences could not prepare us.[62]

Only a recognition of the mystery of nature allows for an expansion of our intellectual horizons into heretofore uncharted areas of inves-tigation. As Richard Feynman puts it, "with more knowledge comes deeper, more wonderful mystery, luring one to penetrate deeper still… with pleasure and confidence…to find unimagined strangeness lead-ing to more wonderful questions and mysteries…"[63] Curiosity, to be sure, can promote an intense preoccupation with things. But from Augustine's perspective, curiosity never allows for an appreciation of things in relation to the *whole*, that vast totality encompassing material and immaterial reality alike. For this reason, Augustine (anticipating Heidegger) perceives curiosity as an impediment to genuine knowl-edge. In Augustine's assessment, "we marvel less at things we can fully grasp."[64] Augustine by no means derides attempts to apply our reason-ing to difficult matters. It is *facile reasoning* he rejects.[65] But because the objects of wonder simply do not allow for easy comprehension, they are never susceptible to superficial attempts to know them.

In actuality, Augustine does not explicitly contrast curiosity with wonder. For him, the positive counterpart to the curious disposition lies in studiousness. As we saw in Chapter 9, Augustine's distinction between the "curious" and the "studious" in the *De Utilitate Credendi* underscores an important facet of his conception of the human search for knowledge and truth. In his estimation, the studious are sincere in pursuing these ends because they are willing to submit themselves to the arduous process that their acquisition demands. By the same token, they are not content with what immediately meets our cognitive gaze. For Augustine, the very mystery inherent in created being (mysteri-ous because it always eludes our complete grasp) mitigates against the unregulated character of *curiositas*. This mystery by no means poses an obstacle to the learned. Instead, it offers them a unique advantage.

> This is...the usefulness of the hidden works of God, lest they be despised because common and cease to be wonderful because comprehended.[66]

A perusal of our Western heritage quickly discloses the great disparity between what is considered a viable avenue of intellectual inquiry and what is not, between a laudable sense of wonder in profound truths and a casual interest in trivial matters. We do, in fact, actively impose parameters upon our cognitive appetites in the interests of focus, purposefulness, or sheer practicality. In their absence, a mind dominated by curiosity would be given to much intellectual "wheel-spinning." The challenge lies in maintaining a healthy balance between sound epistemological standards and the roles of creativity, spontaneity, and even playfulness in our investigations.

But any thinker who assumes a critical stance toward curiosity is liable to incur widespread suspicion and even contempt in a contemporary setting. Why is this the case? Chiefly, because we tend to view curiosity as one of the distinguishing characteristics of *homo sapiens*, a deeply cherished trait which we consider indispensable to the expansion of our intellectual horizons and the progress of the human species. These sentiments are succinctly but powerfully expressed by John Steinbeck:

> And this I believe: that the free, exploring mind of the individual human is the most valuable thing in the world. And this I would fight for: the freedom of the mind to take any direction it wishes, undirected.[67]

I think that Augustine himself would readily agree with these words, but only to a point. While he would celebrate the mind's God-given freedom to "take any direction it wishes," he would object to the claim that this direction should go completely "undirected." For Augustine, the mind's desire to know can never be divorced from those higher values which are as relevant to intellectual inquiry as to any other aspect of human existence. In Augustinian terms, we must remember, "freedom" (the ability to choose) can only be perfected by "liberty" (the capacity to choose rightly, in a manner consistent with the promotion and realization of the human good). From Augustine's standpoint, unregulated cognitive desire (no matter how stimulating) leads nowhere.

It is as ineffectual (and potentially destructive) as the "deformed liberty" that he found at the root of that act of adolescent vandalism which came to define his understanding of inquiry.[68]

Yet, Augustine does not represent such a lone voice when we realize how discriminating people can be about the parameters of knowledge and what is considered "legitimate academic inquiry." Despite the fact that Western culture extols curiosity as the stimulus to discovery and scientific progress, academe still looks somewhat askance at an excessive absorption in what are generally characterized as "curiosities." How seriously, for example, would the academy view forays into areas like ESP research, speculation about extraterrestrial life, or theories of a lost Atlantean civilization? My question does not seek to undermine people's right to investigate such matters or the integrity of their inquiries.[69] But if intellectual endeavors are to gain credibility, those engaged in them must offer more convincing justification than the claim "How intriguing!" or "How fascinating!" Serious intellectual endeavors, it would appear, must offer (or at least attempt to offer) new embodiments of knowledge. In other words, we generally assume that our inquisitiveness must be directed toward something more substantive than the sheer thrill of exploring what is strange or unusual.

This is precisely where Augustine can speak to us in a compelling way. Does research of any kind provide its own justification, without any consideration of its purpose? Moreover, does curiosity require constraint when it infringes upon the interests of the common good? Viewed from this perspective, Augustine's discussions of curiosity assume a fresh relevance, particularly in connection with the justifiable limits of scientific inquiry.

Augustine was fully cognizant of the complexity of the natural world and wholly receptive to its rich diversity. In the *Contra Julianum*, he cites his own ability to catalogue "a thousand things" that move "incomprehensibly as though through deserted wildernesses, acting contrary to nature."[70] Paradoxically, such incomprehensibility provides a powerful heuristic stimulus. Nature presents untold anomalies that draw us into deeper and deeper levels of investigation. Viewed through the lens of an inquiring faith, creation displays a brilliant luminosity attesting to the presence of its Creator.

The difference between curiosity and wonder is a glaring one. Curiosity undoubtedly prompts many intriguing questions. But only wonder renders us bold enough to raise the "Why?" question. This question does not focus exclusively on specific problems or individual things and their behavior. It concerns nothing less than the Ground of Being and the ultimate purpose of reality as a whole. Ultimately, I believe, the difference between curiosity and wonder reveals itself in the intellectual zeal that wonder inspires, whatever the cost. Augustine identifies this zeal with studiousness. But studiousness entails more than a scholastic bent. It encompasses an orientation of mind and heart that can never remain content with superficial inquiry dictated by shifting tastes or popular trends. In moral terms, this tendance presupposes the discipline to moderate cognitive desire in a manner conducive to in-depth investigation on every level. This requires a willingness to go to the heart of the matter, expending oneself in pursuit of a truth that might always elude our complete grasp. For those so committed, that quest promises to be the most exhilarating (and humbling) of endeavors.

### NOTES TO EPILOGUE

1. Christopher Marlowe, *Dr. Faustus*, Act I, 79-85 (Indianapolis/Cambridge: Hackett Publishing Company Inc., 2005).
2. Mary Shelley, *Frankenstein* (Boston: Boston Books of St. Martin's Press, 1992), 53. The novel must be appreciated against the background of the nineteenth century Vitalism debate, with its unsettling contention that electricity could be used for the purpose of reanimating dead bodies.
3. *Confessiones* X,35(55).
4. William Wordsworth, *The Tables Turned.*
5. John Keats, *Lamia*, Part II, 235-237.
6. Robert Oppenheimer, as quoted in Richard Rhodes, *The Making of the Atomic Bomb* (New York/London/Toronto/ Sydney/Singapore: Simon and Shuster, 1986), 676. Rhodes, in turn, credits the quote to Len Giovannitti and Fred Freed, *The Decision to Drop the Bomb* (Coward-McCann, 1965), 197.
7. Richard Rorty, *Philosophy and the Mirror of Nature* (Princeton, New Jersey: Princeton University Press, 1979), 388-389.
8. Heidegger's evolving attitude toward Christianity (from his rearing as a Catholic, to his break with Catholicism in 1919, to his movement toward Protestantism, to his complete break with Christianity [coinciding with his drift toward National Socialism] after 1928, to his request for a Catholic funeral Mass) is well charted in John Caputo's "Heidegger and

theology," in *The Cambridge Companion to Heidegger*, edited by Charles Guignon (Cambridge, UK: Cambridge University Press, 1993), 270-288.

9. At that time, Heidegger held the position of Privatdozent at the University of Freiburg.

10. John Caputo, "Heidegger, Martin," in *Augustine Through the Ages. An Encyclopedia* (Grand Rapids, Michigan and Cambridge, UK: William B. Eerdmans Publishing Company, 1999), 421a.

11. John Caputo, "Heidegger, Martin," in *Augustine Through the Ages. An Encyclopedia*, 421b; J.L. Mehta, *The Way and the Vision* (Honolulu: The University Press of Hawaii, 1976), 11.

12. *Phenomenology of Religious Life* 152. (Subsequent citations are designated as "**PRL**," followed by the page number of the edition listed in the Bibliography.)

13. PRL 153.

14. In Augustine's examination of conscience in *Confessiones* X, he focuses upon such perceived faults as the enjoyment of food and drink (X,31,44), the "delights of the ear" (X,33,49) accompanying the pleasure of listening to liturgical music, and the delight in being praised (X,37,61), even for good acts.

15. PRL, 155.

16. PRL 156.

17. PRL 156.

18. PRL 163.

19. PRL 164.

20. PRL 164.

21. PRL 166.

22. PRL 166. Cf., the comments of Theodore Kisiel, *The Genesis of Heidegger's Being and Time* (Berkeley/Los Angeles/London: University of California Press, 1993), 211-212: "[Curiosity] is ultimately not related to the content of knowledge, but to the sheer actualizing of cognizance. It is swept along by the sheer dynamics of cognition, but without its substance. If sensuality "goes about" absorbed in enjoyment, curiosity "looks about" absorbed in that very activity of spectacle...not in the content of the environing world."

23. PRL 166.

24. PRL 166. Heidegger's link of cognitive appetite with a sense of the "cultural necessity" of certain scientific developments is one which we can readily appreciate, at a time when a dazzling array of new gadgetry (especially in the computer industry) can generate the perception of urgent need on the part of consumers for things they never suspected they needed at all.

25. PRL 166.

26. PRL 166-167.

27. PRL 166-167.

28. PRL 167.

29. PRL 169.

30. John Caputo, "Heidegger, Martin," in *Augustine Through the Ages. An Encyclopedia*, 421b.

31. Dorothea Frede, "The question of being: Heidegger's project," in *The Cambridge Companion to Heidegger*, edited by Charles Guignon (Cambridge, UK: Cambridge University Press, 1993), 63: "We project ourselves, our whole existence, into the world and understand ourselves as well as everything in the world in terms of the possibilities within the design or 'projection' that we make of ourselves."

32. *Being and Time* I.6, sec. 41, 237. (Subsequent citations of *Being and Time* are designated as "**BT**," followed by the page number of the edition listed in the Bibliography.)

33. Paul Gorner, *Heidegger's Being and Time. An Introduction* (Cambridge, UK: Cambridge University Press, 2007), 4-5.

34. Thomas Langan, *The Meaning of Heidegger. A Critical Study of an Existentialist Phenomenology* (New York and London: Columbia University Press, 1959), 22-23.

35. **BT** I.4, sec. 27, 166.

36. Dorothea Frede, "The question of being: Heidegger's project," 57.

37. Dorothea Frede, "The question of being: Heidegger's project," 57-60.

38. I draw the term "symptoms" from Robert F. Schwartz, "Born to Fail? Aristotle and Heidegger on Akratic Action," *Prolegomena* (Summer, 2001), 5, who describes the features of *Dasein's* inauthentic state (both ontically and ontologically) in this manner.

39. Michael Gelven, *A Commentary on Heidegger's Being and Time*, Revised Edition (De Kalb, Illinois: Northern Illinois University Press, 1989), 109.

40. **BT** I.5, sec. 38, 221.

41. **BT** I.5, sec. 35, 213.

42. **BT** I.5, sec. 36, 216.

43. **BT** I.5, sec. 36, 214.

44. **BT** I.5, sec. 36, 215.

45. **BT** I.5, sec. 36, 216.

46. **BT** I.5, sec. 36, 215.

47. **BT** I.5, sec. 36, 216.

48. **BT** I.5, sec. 36, 216.

49. **BT** I.5, sec. 36, 216.

50. **BT** I.5, sec. 36, 216.

51. **BT** I.5, sec. 36, 216.

52. **BT** I.5, sec. 36, 217.

53. **BT** I.5, sec. 37, 218-219.

54. **BT** II.4, sec. 68(c), 397.

55. Paul Gorner, *Heidegger's Being and Time. An Introduction*, 10.

56. **BT** II.4, sec. 68(c), 397-398.

57. Cf., *Soliloquia* I,15(27).

58. "On the Essence of Truth," *Basic Writings*, 132. (Subsequent citations of selections from this anthology [listed in the Bibliography] are designated as "**BW**," followed by the page number of the edition.) This interpretation of truth is a prominent feature of Heidegger's later essays. In "The Origin of the Work of Art" (**BW**, 176), he asserts that "the unconcealedness of beings…is never a merely existent state, but a happening…(truth) is neither an attribute of factual things…nor one of propositions." In "The Question Concerning Technology" (**BW**, 307) he speaks of "the unconcealment in which everything that is shows itself at any given time." In "The End of Philosophy and the Task of Thinking" (**BW**, 387), he describes "unconcealment" as "the opening which first grants Being and thinking and their presencing to and for each other…the place of stillness from which alone the possibility of…being and thinking…can arise at all." In connection with this way of understanding of truth, Caputo (*The Mystical Element in Heidegger's Thought* [Athens, Ohio: Ohio University Press, 1978], 263) describes what he perceives as a salient trend in the later Heidegger: "I believe that the central thrust of his later writings consists in calling us back to this forgotten and withdrawn world, calling us back out of the technological world in which we are systematically divested of our humanity and robbed of our worth. The technical world threatens to consume us, and Heidegger's writings are a summons to find a new possibility in the midst of an all too present and suffocating actuality."

59. Mary-Jane Rubenstein (*Strange Wonder. The Closure of Metaphysics and the Opening of Awe* [New York: Columbia University Press, 2008], 27) comments upon this distinction, with a special focus on Heidegger's affinities with Augustine in this vein: "Of course, it must be granted that calculative-representational thinking "works": it gets airplanes into the sky, medicine into our veins, and food on the table…Heidegger concedes as much. Sounding like Augustine in his fourth-century critique of the astronomers, Heidegger does not deny the effectiveness of calculation. But just as Augustine's astronomers fail to acknowledge the source of their wisdom, calculative-representative thought forgets that "adequation" is only one kind of truth—one particular form of unconcealment."

60. "Letter on Humanism," **BW**, 240.

61. Plato, *Theaetetus* 155d: "…wonder is the feeling of a philosopher and philosophy begins in wonder."

62. Brian Green, *The Elegant Universe* (New York: Vintage Books, 2000), 385.

63. Richard Feynman, "The Value of Science" in *The Pleasure of Finding Things Out: The Best Short Works of Richard P. Feynman*, edited by Jeffrey Robbins (Cambridge, Mass.: Perseus Books, 1999), 144.

64. *Contra Julianum* VI,7(17): PL XL, 832: *quae minus solet mirari quod potuerit comprehendere.* Cf., the observation of Basil Willey (*The Seventeenth Century Background* [New York: Columbia University Press, 1967], 5):

"An explained thing, except for very resolute thinkers, is almost inevitably 'explained away'. Speaking generally, it may be said that the demand for explanation is due to the desire to be rid of mystery."

65. *Contra Julianum* VI,7(17).

66. *Contra Julianum* VI,7(17): PL XL,832: *Et revera haec est utilitas occultorum operum Dei; ne prompta vilescant, ne comprehensa mira esse desistant.* In support of this argument, Augustine quotes Eccl. 11:5: "...*you know not the works of God Who is the maker of all.*"

67. John Steinbeck, *East of Eden*, Part I, Ch. 13.

68. I refer here to the "theft of pears" episode recounted in the *Confessiones* (II, 4-8).

69. In citing these topics for illustrative purposes, my concern lies in public perceptions of their intellectual credibility and their acceptability by the academic community at large. It is not my intention to disparage those engaged in such investigations or to call into question their worth or worthiness as subjects of inquiry. When we consider the ebb and flow of intellectual history, it is striking how subject matter viewed as "occult," "offbeat," or "on the margin" in one era can be viewed as "cutting edge" or "groundbreaking" in another. The histories of fields like chemistry and psychology provide cases in point.

70. *Contra Julianum* VI,7(17).

# BIBLIOGRAPHIES

## PRIMARY SOURCES

### A. Greek and Latin Texts

*Corpus Christianorum*. Series Latina. Volume XXIX; XXVII; XXXII; XXXVIII; XLVII; XLVIII; L; L(a). Turnholti: Typographi Brepols Editores Pontifici 1954, 1955; 1968; 1978; 1981.

*Corpus Scriptorum Ecclesiasticorum Latinorum*. Sancti Aurelii Augustini. Volume XXVIII, Sect. III, Pars 1 [1894]; XXXIII, Pars II [1895]. Pragae, Vindobonae, Lipsiae.

Migne, J.P. *Patrologiae Cursus Completus. Patrologiae Graecae*. Volume 7; 8; 10; 11; 16; 20; 25; 26; 31; 32; 33; 36; 37; 44; 47; 58; 59; 62; 67. Paris, 1841,ff.

Migne, J.P. *Patrologiae Cursus Completus. Patrologiae Latinae*. Volume 1; 2; 5; 14; 32; 34; 35; 38; 40; 42. Paris, 1841,ff.

### B. Translations

References to translations from *The Loeb Classical Library* (Cambridge, Mass.: Harvard University Press; London: William Heinemann Ltd.) will be designated as "Loeb," followed by the year of publication. References to translations drawn from the *Ante-Nicene Fathers* and *Nicene and Post Nicene Fathers* (Edinburgh: T. & T. Clark; Grand Rapids, Michigan: William B. Eerdmanns) are designated as **AN** and **NPNF**, respectively, followed by the volume number, translator(s), and year of publication. Translations drawn from *The Fathers of the Church* are designated as **FC**, followed by the volume number, translator's name, and place/date of publication. Translations from the *Ancient Christian Writers* series are listed as **ACW**.

Aeschines. *The Oratory of Classical Greece*, Volume 3. Trans. Chris Cary. Austin: University of Texas Press, 2000.

Ambrose. *Hexameron*. **FC** 42. Trans. John J. Savage. New York: Fathers of the Church, Inc., 1961.

Annaeus Seneca (Lucius, "The Younger"). *De Ira*. Trans. John W. Basore. Loeb, 1970.

―――. *Epistulae Morales ad Lucilium*. Trans. Richard M. Gummere. Loeb, 1953.

Apuleius. *The Golden Ass*. Trans. P.G. Walsh. Clarendon Press, 1994.

Aristophanes. *Acharnians, Birds, Plutus*. Trans. Jeffrey Henderson. Loeb, 1998, 2000, 2002.

―――. *The Ecclesiazusae*. Trans. Benjamin Bickley Rogers. Loeb, 1931.

Aristotle. *Politics*. Trans. H. Rackham. Loeb, 1959.

―――. *On Respiration*. Trans. W.S. Hett. Loeb, 1995.

―――. *On Rhetoric*. Trans. John Henry Freese. Loeb, 1959.

Arnobius. *Against the Heathen*. **AN** VI. Trans. H. Bryce and H. Campbell, 1997.

Athanasius. *Select Works and Letters*. **NPN** (2nd s.) IV. Trans. A. Robertson, 1998.

Augustine of Hippo. *De agone christiano*. **FC** 2. Trans. Robert P. Russell, O.S.A. New York: CIMA Publishing Co., Inc., 1947.

―――. *Confessiones*. Trans. John K. Ryan (with Introduction and Notes). Garden City, New York: Image Books, 1960.

―――. *Contra Epistolam Manichaei Quam Vocant Fundamentum*. **NPNF** 4, ser. 1. Trans. Richard Stothert. Peabody, Mass.: Hendrickson Publishers, Inc., 1994.

―――. *Contra Julianum*. **FC** 35. Trans. Matthew A. Schumacher. New York: Fathers of the Church, Inc., 1957.

―――. *De catechizandis rudibus*. **NPNF** 3, ser. 1. Trans. S.D.F. Salmond. Peabody, Mass.: Hendrickson Publishers, Inc., 1994.

―――. *De Civitate Dei*. Trans. Henry Bettenson. Edited David Knowles. Harmondsworth, Middlesex: Penguin Books Ltd., 1972.

―――. *De diversis quaestionibus octoginta tribus liber I*. Trans. David L. Mosher. Washington, D.C.: The Catholic University of America Press, 1982.

———. *Epistulae.* **FC** 18. Trans. Sister Wilfred Parsons. New York: Fathers of the Church, Inc., 1953.

———. *De Genesi ad Litteram.* **ACW** 42. Volume II. Trans. John Hammond Taylor, S.J. New York, N.Y./Ramsey, N.J.: Newman Press, 1982.

———. *De Genesi contra Manichaeos.* **FC** 84. Trans. Roland J. Teske, S.J. Washington, D.C.: The Catholic University of America Press, 1991.

———. *De libero arbitrio.* **FC** 59. Trans. Robert P. Russell, O.S.A. Washington, D.C.: The Catholic University of America Press, 1968.

———. *De Moribus Ecclesiase Catholica et de Moribus Manichaeorum.* **FC** 56. Trans. Donald A. Gallagher and Idella Gallagher. Washington, D.C.: The Catholic University of America Press, 1966.

———. *De Trinitate.* Trans. Edmund Hill, O.P. *The Works of Saint Augustine.* A Translation for the 21st Century. Brooklyn, New York: New City Press, 1991.

———. *De Utilitate Credendi.* **FC** 2b. Trans. Luanne Meagher, O.S.B. New York: CIMA Publishing Co., Inc., 1947.

———. *De Vera Religione.* Trans. J.H.S. Burleigh. Chicago: Henry Regnery Company, 1959.

———. *Enarrationes in Psalmos.* **NPNF** 8. Trans. A. Cleveland Coxe. Peabody, Mass.: Henrickson Publishers, Inc., 1994.

———. *In Epistolam Joannis ad Parthos.* **FC** 92. Trans. John W. Rettig. Washington, D.C.: The Catholic University of America Press, 1995.

———. *In Ioannis Evangelium Tractatus CXXIV.* **FC** 88. Trans. John W. Rettig. Washington, D.C.: The Catholic University of America Press, 1993.

———. *Sermones.* Trans. Edmund Hill, O.P. *The Works of St. Augustine,* III, III/4. Brooklyn, New York: New City Press, 1991, 1992.

———. *The Writings of Saint Augustine.* **FC** 1. *De Beata Vita.* Trans. Ludwig Schopp; *Contra Academicos.* Trans. Denis J. Kavanagh; *De Ordine.* Trans. Robert P. Russell, O.S.A.; *Soliloquia.* Trans. Thomas F. Gilligan. New York: CIMA Publishing Col, Inc., 1948.

———. *The Writings of Saint Augustine.* **FC** 2. *De Quantitate Animae. Trans. John J. McMahon; De Musica.* Trans. Robert C. Taliaferro. New York: CIMA Publishing Co., 1947.

Basil of Caesarea. *Ascetical Works.* **FC** 9. Trans. M. Wagner. New York: Fathers of the Church, Inc., 1950.

———. *Letters.* **NPN** (2nd s.) VIII. Trans. B. Jackson, 1996.

Breton, Lancelot C.L. *The Septuagint with Apocrypha Greek and English*. Grand Rapids, Michigan: Zondervan Publishing House, 1982.

Catullus (Gaius Valerius). *Carmina*. Trans. Francis Warre Cornish. Loeb, 1988.

Cicero (Marcus Tullius). *De Finibus Bonorum et Malorum*. Trans. H. Rackham. Loeb, 1961.

———. *De Natura Deorum*. Trans. H. Rackham. Loeb, 1951.

———. *Epistulae ad Atticum*. Trans. E.O. Winstedt. Loeb, 1953, 1956.

———. *Epistulae ad Familiares*. Trans. D.R. Shackleton Bailey. Loeb, 2001.

———. *Oratio pro Flacco*. Trans. C. MacDonald. Loeb, 1977.

———. *Oratio pro Sestio*. Trans. R. Gardner. Loeb, 1966.

———. *Tusculan Disputations*. Trans. J.E. King. Loeb, 1950.

Clement of Alexandria. *Christ the Educator (Pedagogus)*. **FC** 23. Trans. Simon P. Wood. New York: Fathers of the Church, Inc., 1954.

———. *The Exhortation to the Greeks (Protrepticus)*. Trans. G.W. Butterworth. Loeb, 1960.

———. *Stromateis*. **FC** 85. Trans. John Ferguson. Washington, D.C.: The Catholic University of American Press, 1991.

———. **AN** IV. Trans. William Wilson, 1871.

Copenhaver, Brian P. *Hermetica. The Greek Corpus Hermeticum and the Latin Asclepius* in a new English translation, with Notes and Introduction. Cambridge, UK: Cambridge University Press, 2000.

Demosthenes. *Against Zenothemis*. Trans. A.J. Murray. Loeb, 1958.

———. *Against Aristogeiton*. Trans. J.H. Vince. Loeb, 1956.

Dionysius of Halicarnassus. *Selected Works*. Trans. Stephen Usher. Loeb, 1974.

Epictetus. *Discourses of Arrianus*. Trans. W.A. Oldfather. Loeb, 1966.

Eusebius. *The Ecclesiastical History*, Vol. I. Trans. Kirsopp Lake. Loeb, 1965.

———. Vol. II. Trans. J.E.L. Oulton. Loeb, 1964.

———. *Life of Constantine*. **NPN** (2nd s.) I. Trans. E.C. Richardson, 1997.

Gregory Nazianzen. *Orations, Sermons, and Letters*. **NPN** (2nd s.) VII. Trans. Charles Gordon Browne and James Edward Swallow, 1996.

Gregory Thaumaturgus. *The Oration and Panegyric Addressed to Origen*. **AN** VI. Trans. S.D.F. Salmond, 1997.

Heidegger, Martin. *Basic Writings*. Edited by David Farrell Krell. New York/ Hagerstown/San Francisco/London: Harper & Row, Publishers, 1977.

———. *Being and Time*. Trans. John Macquarrie and Edward Robinson. New York and Evanston: Harper and Row, Publishers, 1962.

———. *The Phenomenology of Religious Life*. Trans. Matthias Fritsch and Jennifer Anna Gosetti-Ferencei. Bloomington and Indianapolis: Indiana University Press, 2004.

Herodotus. *Historiae*. Trans. A.D. Godley. Loeb, 1960; 1971.

Hippocrates. *Decorum* and *Precepts*. Trans. W.H.S Jones. Loeb, 1923; 1962.

Hippolytus of Rome. *The Refutation of All Heresies*. AN V. Trans. J.H. MacMahon, 1995.

Horace (Quintus Horatius Flaccus). *Epodes*. Trans. Niall Rudd. Loeb, 2004.

Irenaeus. *Against Heresies*. AN I. Trans. A. Roberts, 1996.

Isocrates. *Orationes*. Trans. George Norlin. Loeb, 1961; 1962.

John Chrysostum. *Homilies on the Gospel of John*. NPN (1st s.) XIV. Trans. Philip Schaff, 1996.

———. *Homilies on Gospel of St. Matthew*. NPN X (1st s.) X. Trans. George Prevost, 1998.

———. *Homilies on Timothy*. NPN (1st s.). XIII. Trans. Philip Schaff, 1994.

Julian. *Works*. Trans. Wilmer Cave Wright. Loeb, 1913; 1959.

Justin Martyr. *Writings*. FC 1. Trans. Thomas B. Falls. New York: Christian Heritage, Inc., 1948.

Libanus. *Orationes*. Trans. A.F. Norman. Loeb, 1977.

Lucian. *Works*. Trans. A.M. Harmon. Loeb, 1913; 1915; 1961.

Menander. *Samia*. Trans. Francis G. Allinson. Loeb, 1930.

Minucius Felix. *Octavius*. AN IV. Trans. R.E. Wallis, 1994.

*New American Bible*. New York and Oxford: Oxford University Press, 1990.

Nock, A.D. and Festugière, A.J. *Corpus Hermeticum*: Tome I, *Traités* I-XII, 3rd ed. Paris: Belles Lettres, 1972. Tome II, *Traités* XIII-XVIII, *Asclepius*, 1973. Tome III, *Fragments extraits de Stobée* I-XXII, 1972. Tome IV, *Fragments extraits de Stobée* XXIII-XXIX, Fragments divers, 1972; 1st ed., 1946-54.

Pausanias. *Description of Greece*. Trans. W.H.S. Jones. Loeb, 1935.

Philo Judaeus. *Legum Allegoria; De opificio mundi; De Agricultura; De Ebrietate; De Sobrietate; De Migratione Abrahami; De Congressu Quaerendae Eruditionis Gratia; De Fuga et Inventione; De somniis; De Mutatione*

*Nominum; De Specialibus Legibus*. Trans. F.H. Colson and G.W. Whittaker. Loeb, 1958; 1960; 1962, 1994; 1996; 2001.

———. *De Vita Mosis; De Abrahamo; Quod Omnis Probis*. Trans. F.H. Colson. Loeb, 1958, 1994.

Plato. *Apology*. Trans. Harold North Fowler. Loeb, 1995.

———. *Gorgias, Laws*. Trans. R.G. Bury. Loeb, 1961.

———. *Republic*. Trans. Paul Shorey. Loeb, 1946.

———. *Statesman*. Trans. Harold N. Fowler. Loeb, 1962.

Plautus (Titus Maccius). *The Aulularia (The Pot of Gold)*. Prepared by Gilbert Lowall and Betty Nye Quinn. White Plains, N.Y.: Longmans Inc., 1988.

Plotinus. *Enneads*. Trans. A.H. Armstrong. Loeb, 1967; 1984; 1988; 1989; 1995.

Plutarch of Chaeronea. *Lives*. Trans. Bernadotte Perrin. Loeb, 1919.

———. *Moralia*. Trans. W.C. Helmbold. Loeb, 1957.

Polybius. *Historiae*. Trans. W.R. Paton. Loeb, 1925; 1960; 1972; 1979.

Quintilian (Marcus Fabius). *Institutiones Oratoriae*. Loeb, 1958, 1959.

Salaminius Hermias Sozomenus. *The Ecclesiastical History*. **NPN** (2nd s.) II. Trans. C.D. Hartranft, 1997.

Suetonius (Gaius). *Augustus*. Trans. J.C. Rolfe. Loeb, 1989.

———. *Vespasian*. Trans. J.C. Rolfe. Loeb, 1997.

Tatian. *Oratio ad Graecos and Fragments*. Trans. Molly Whittaker. Oxford: Clarendon Press, 1982.

Terence (Publius Terentius Afer). *Eunuchus*. Trans. John Sargeaunt. Loeb, 1959.

Tertullian. **AN** III. *The Apology* and *On Idolatry*. Trans. S. Thelwall; *Ad Nationes* and *The Prescription Against Heretics*. Trans. Peter Holmes, 1997.

———.*On the Apparel of Women*. **AN** IV. Trans. S. Thelwall, 1994.

*The Vulgate Bible*. Volume 1. *The Pentateuch*. Douay-Rheims Translation. Edited by Swift Edgar. Cambridge, Massachusetts; London: Harvard University Press, 2010.

Theophrastus. *Characters*. Trans. J.M. Edmonds. Loeb, 1946.

Thucydides. *The Peloponnesian War*. Trans. Rex Warner. Harmondsworth, Middlesex, England: Penguin Books, 1975.

Varro (Marcus Terentius). *De Lingua Latina*. Trans. Roland G. Kent. Loeb, 1938.

————. *De Re Rustica*. Trans. William Davis Hooper. Loeb, 1960.

Xenophon. *Anabasis*. Trans. Carleton L. Brownson. Loeb, 1998.

————. *Memorabilia*. Trans. E.C. Marchant. Loeb, 1992.

## SECONDARY SOURCES

Allchin, Douglas. "Values in Science: An Educational Perspective," *Science and Education* (1999): 1-12.

Assmann, Jan. "*Periergia*: Egyptian reactions to Greek Curiosity," in Erich S. Gruen (ed.), *Cultural Borrowings and Ethnic Appropriations in Antiquity*. Stuttgart: Franz Steiner Verlag, 2005, 37-49.

Ball, Philip. *Universe of Stone. A Biography of Chartres Cathedral*. New York: HarperCollins Publishers, 2008.

Blumenberg, Hans. "Augustins Anteil an der Geschichte des Begriffs der theoretischen Neugierde," *Revue Études Augustiniennes* 7 (1961): 35-70.

————. "*Curiositas* und *Veritas*. Zur Ideengeschichte van Augustin, *Confessiones* X,35," *Studia Patristica* VI (Berlin, 1962), 294-302.

————. *Der Prozess der theoretischen Neugierde*. Frankfurt am Main: Suhrkamp Taschenbuch Verlag, 1980.

Broeck, Roelof van den. "Gnosticism and Hermetism in Antiquity: Two Roads to Salvation," *Gnosis and Hermeticism from Antiquity to Modern Times*. Edited by Roelof van den Broeck and Wouter J. Hanegraaf. Albany, NY: State University of New York Press, 1998, 1-20.

Brown, Peter. *Augustine of Hippo*. Berkeley and Los Angeles: University of California Press, 2000.

Bronowski, Jacob. *Science and Human Values*. New York: Harper and Row, Publishers, 1965.

Cabassut, André. "*Curiosité*," *Dictionnaire de Spiritualité*, Tome II, pt. 2. Paris: Beauchesne, 1953, 2654b-2661a.

Caputo, John. "Heidegger, Martin," *Augustine Through the Ages. An Encyclopedia*. Grand Rapids, Michigan/ Cambridge, UK: William B. Eerdmans, 1999, 421a-422a.

————. *The Mystical Element in Heidegger's Thought*. Athens, Ohio: Ohio University Press, 1978.

Chadwick, Henry. "Philo," Part II, Chapter 8 of *The Cambridge History of Later Greek and Early Medieval Philosophy*. Edited by A.H. Armstrong. Cambridge, UK: Cambridge University Press, 1967, 135-137.

Crombie, A.C. *Augustine to Galileo. The History of Science A.D. 400-1650.* Melbourne/London/Toronto: William Heinemann Ltd., 1957.

Daston, Lorraine (and Katharine Park). *Wonders and the Order of Nature 1150-1750.* New York: Zone Books, 1998.

Decret, F. *Mani et la tradition manicheen.* Paris: Éditions du Seuil, 1974.

Dodaro, Robert, O.S.A. "Theurgy," *Augustine Through the Ages. An Encyclopedia.* Edited by Allan D. Fitzgerald, O.S.A. Grand Rapids, Michigan and Cambridge, UK: William B. Eerdmans Publishing Company, 1999, 827a-828b.

DuRoy, Olivier. *L'Intelligence De La Foi en La Trinité Selon Saint Augustin. Genèse De Sa Theologie Trinitaire Jusqu'en 391.* Paris: Études Augustiniennes, 1966.

Ehrenberg, Victor."Polypragmosyne: A Study in Greek Politics," *The Journal of Hellenic Studies* 67 (1947): 46-67.

Feynman, Richard. "The Value of Science" in *The Pleasure of Finding Things Out: The Best Short Works of Richard P. Feynman.* Edited by Jeffrey Robbins. Cambridge, Mass.: Perseus Books, 1999.

Foster, M.B. "The Christian Doctrine of Creation and the Rise of Modern Natural Science," *Mind* (N.S.), 43, No. 172 (October, 1934): 446-468.

Fowden, Garth. *The Egyptian Hermes. A historical approach to the late pagan mind.* Cambridge, UK: Cambridge University Press, 1986.

Frede, Dorothea."The question of being: Heidegger's project," *The Cambridge Companion to Heidegger.* Edited by Charles Guignon. Cambridge, UK: Cambridge University Press, 1993, 42-69.

Gelven, Michael. *A Commentary on Heidegger's Being and Time.* Revised Edition. De Kalb, Illinois: Northern Illinois University Press, 1989.

Gilson, Etienne. *The Christian Philosophy of Saint Augustine.* Translated by L.E.M. Lynch. New York: Random House, 1960.

Gorner, Paul. *Heidegger's Being and Time. An Introduction.* Cambridge, UK: Cambridge University Press, 2007.

Green, Brian. *The Elegant Universe.* New York: Vintage Books, 2000.

Hankey, Wayne."Mind," *Augustine Through the Ages. An Encyclopedia.* Edited by Allan D. Fitzgerald, O.S.A. Grand Rapids, Michigan/Cambridge, UK: William B. Eerdmans Publishing Company, 1999, 363b-367b.

Harrison, Peter. "Curiosity, Forbidden Knowledge, and the Reformation of Natural Philosophy in Early-Modern England," *Isis* 92 (2001): 265-290.

Holmes, Richard. *The Age of Wonder.* New York: Vintage Books, 2008.

James, William. "The Will to Believe," *Classical and Contemporary Readings in the Philosophy of Religion.* Edited by John Hick. Englewood Cliffs, N.J.: Prentice Hall, 1990.

Joly, Robert. "*Curiositas*," *L'Antiquité Classique* 30 (1961): 33-44.

———. "Notes Sur La Conversion D'Augustin," *L'Antiquité Classique* 35 (1966): 217-221.

Jones, A.H.M. *The Later Roman Empire 284-602.* Volume 2. Baltimore, MD: The Johns Hopkins University Press, 1990.

Junghanns, Paul. "Die Erzählungstechnik von Apuleius' Metamorphosen und ihrer Vorlagen," *Philologus*, Supplementband XXIV, Heft 1 (1932).

Kenny, Neil. *Curiosity in Early Modern Europe Word Histories.* Weisbaden: Harrassowitz Verlag, 1998.

Kisiel, Theodore. *The Genesis of Heidegger's Being and Time.* Berkeley/Los Angeles/London: University of California Press, 1993.

Labhardt, André. "*Curiositas.* Notes sur histoire d'un mot et d'une notion," *Museum Helveticum* 17 (1960): 206-224.

Lancel, S. "*Curiositas* et preoccupations spirituelles chez Apulee," *Revue de l'histoire des religions* 160 (1961): 25-46.

Langan, Thomas. *The Meaning of Heidegger. A Critical Study of an Existentialist Phenomenology.* New York and London: Columbia University Press, 1959.

Lieu, S. *Manichaeism in the Later Roman Empire and Medieval China.* Manchester, NH: Manchester University Press, 1985.

MacKay, L.A. "The Sin of the Golden Ass," *Arion* 4(1965): 474-480.

Marrou, Henri-Irénée. *Saint Augustin et La Fin De La Culture Antique.* Paris: Boccard, 1958.

Mascall, E.L. *Christian Theology and Natural Science.* London/New York/ Toronto: Longmans, Green and Co., 1957.

Mason, H.L. "*Fabula Graecanica*: Apuleius and His Greek Sources," in *Aspects of Apuleius' Golden Ass.* A Collection of original papers edited by B.L. Hijmans Jr. and R.Th. van der Paardt. Groningen: Bouma's Boekhuis B.V., 1978, 1-15.

Mehta, J.L. *The Way and the Vision.* Honolulu: The University Press of Hawaii, 1976.

Mette, Hans Joachim. "*Curiositas*," Festschrift Bruno Schnell. München: C.H. Beck'sche Verlagsbuchhandlung, 1956, 227-235.

Newhauser, Richard. "Towards a History of Human Curiosity: A Prolegomenon to its Medieval Phase," *Deutsche Vierteljahrsschrift für Literaturwissenschaft und Geistesgeschichte* 56 (1982): 559-575.

O'Connell, Robert J. (S.J.). *Art and the Christian Intelligence in St. Augustine.* Cambridge, Mass.: Harvard University Press, 1978.

―――. "Augustinism: Locating the Center," *Presbyter Factus Sum, Collectanea Augustiniana.* Edited by Joseph T. Lienhard, S.J., Earl C. Muller, S.J., and Roland J. Teske, S.J. New York: Peter Lang, 1991, 209-233.

―――. *St. Augustine's Confessions. The Odyssey of Soul.* Cambridge, Mass.: The Belknap Press of Harvard University Press, 1969.

―――. *St. Augustine's Early Theory of Man A.D. 386-391.* Cambridge, Mass.: The Belknap Press of Harvard University Press, 1968.

―――. *The Origin of the Soul in St. Augustine's Later Works.* New York: Fordham University Press, 1987.

O'Daly, Gerard. *Augustine's City of God. A Reader's Guide.* Oxford: Oxford University Press, 2009.

Penwill, J.L. "Slavish Pleasures and Profitless Curiosity: Fall and Redemption in Apuleius' *Metamorphoses*," *Ramus: critical studies in Greek and Roman literature* IV (1975): 49-83.

Perry, Ben Edwin. *The Ancient Romances. A Literary-Historical Account of Their Origins.* Berkeley and Los Angeles: University of California Press, 1967.

Peters, Edward. "The Desire to Know the Secrets of the World," *Journal of the History of Ideas* 62.4 (2001): 593-610.

Procopé, John. "Hermetism," *Routledge Encyclopedia of Philosophy*, Volume 4. Edited by Edward Craig. London and New York: Routledge, 1998, 395b-397a.

Reale, Giovanni. *A History of Ancient Philosophy*, Part IV. The Schools of the Imperial Age. Edited and Translated from the 5th Italian Edition by John R. Catan. Albany: State University of New York Press, 1990.

Rombs, Ronnie J. *Saint Augustine and the Fall of the Soul. Beyond O'Connell and His Critics.* Washington, D.C.: The Catholic University of America Press, 2006.

Rorty, Richard. *Philosophy and the Mirror of Nature.* Princeton, New Jersey: Princeton University Press, 1979.

Rubenstein, Mary-Jane. *Strange Wonder. The Closure of Metaphysics and the Opening of Awe.* New York: Columbia University Press, 2008.

Rüdiger, Horst. "*Curiositas* und Magie. Apuleius und Lucius als literarische Archetypen der Faust-Gestalt," in *Wort und Text*. Festschrift für Fritz Schalk. Herausgegeben von H. Meier und Hans Schommodau. Frankfurt am Main: Vittorio Klostermann, 1963, 57-82.

Sagan, Carl. *The Dragons of Eden. Speculations on the Evolution of Human Intelligence.* New York: Random House, 1977.

Sandy, G. "Knowledge and Curiosity in Apuleius' Metamorphoses," *Latomus. Revue D'Etudes Latines* 31,1(1972): 179-183.

Schlam, Carl C. "The Curiosity of the Golden Ass," *The Classical Journal* 64, no. 1 (Oct. 1968): 120-125.

Schwartz, Robert F. "Born to Fail? Aristotle and Heidegger on Akratic Action," *Prolegomena* (Summer, 2001): 1-16.

Scobie, Alexander. *Apuleius Metamorphoses (Asinus Aureus* I). A Commentary. Meisenheim am Glan: Verlag Anton Hain, 1975.

————. *Aspects of the Ancient Romance and its Heritage.* Essays on Apuleius, Petronius, and the Greek Romances. Meisenheim am Glan: Verlag Anton Hain, 1969.

Shattuck, Roger. *Forbidden Knowledge.* New York: St. Martin's Press, 1996.

Sheppard, Anne D.R. "Theurgy," *The Oxford Classical Dictionary*, 3rd Edition. Revised. Simon Hornblower and Antony Spawforth, eds. Oxford: Oxford University Press, 2003, 1512a-b.

TeSelle, Eugene. *Augustine the Theologian.* New York: Herder and Herder, 1970.

Theiler, Willy. *Porphyrios und Augustin.* Halle: Max Niemeyer Verlag, 1933.

Torchia, N. Joseph (O.P.). *Creatio ex nihilo and The Theology of St. Augustine. The Anti-Manichaean Polemic and Beyond.* New York: Peter Lang Publishers, Inc., 1999.

————. "Creation, Finitude, and the Mutable Will: Augustine on the Origin of Moral Evil," *Irish Theological Quarterly* 71 (2006): 47-66.

————. "*Curiositas* in the Early Philosophical Writings of Saint Augustine," *Augustinian Studies* XI (1988): 111-119.

————. "Curiosity," *Saint Augustine through the Ages: An Encyclopedia.* Edited by Allan D. Fitzgerald, O.S.A. Grand Rapids, Michigan/ Cambridge, UK: William B. Eerdmans, 1999): 259b-261a.

————. *Plotinian Tolma and the Descent of Being. An Exposition and Analysis.* New York: Peter Lang, 1993.

———. "Plotinian *Tolma* and the Fall of the Soul in the Early Philosophy of Saint Augustine," *Dissertation Abstracts International* 48, issue #4 (1987), Fordham University.

———. "'*Pondus meum amor meus*': The Significance of the Weight Metaphor in St. Augustine's Early Philosophical Writings," *Augustinian Studies* XXI (1990): 163-176.

———. "St. Augustine's Critique of the *Adiaphora*: A Key Component of His Rebuttal of Stoic Ethics," *Studia Moralia* 38 (2000): 165-195.

———. "St. Augustine's Treatment of *Superbia* and its Plotinian Heritage," *Augustinian Studies* XVIII (1987): 66-79.

———. "St. Augustine's Triadic Interpretation of Iniquity in the *Confessiones*," *Augustine, Second Founder of Faith. Collectanea Augustiniana*. Edited. Joseph C. Schnaubelt, O.S.A. and Frederick Van Fleteren. New York: Peter Lang, 1989, 159-174.

———. "Stoics, Stoicism," in *Saint Augustine Through the Ages: An Encyclopedia*. Allan D. Fitzgerald, O.S.A., General Editor. Grand Rapids, Michigan: William B. Eerdmans, 1999: 816b-820a.

———. "The *Commune/Proprium* Distinction in Saint Augustine's Moral Theory," *Studia Patristica* XXII: 356-363.

———. "The Significance of *Ordo* in St. Augustine's Moral Theory," *Collectanea Augustiniana* III. New York: Peter Lang Publishing, Inc., 1991, 321-335.

———. "The Significance of the Moral Concept of Virtue in Saint Augustine's Ethics," *The Modern Schoolman* LXVIII (November, 1990): 1-17.

Van Fleteren, Frederick. "Porphyry," *Augustine Through the Ages. An Encyclopedia*. Edited by Allan D. Fitzgerald, O.S.A. Grand Rapids, Michigan/ Cambridge, UK: William B. Eerdmans Publishing Company, 1999, 661b-662a.

———. "*De Utilitate Credendi*," *Augustine Through the Ages. An Encyclopedia*. Grand Rapids, Michigan/Cambridge, UK: William B. Eerdmans Publishing Company, 1999, 861a-862b.

Versnel, H.S. "Magic," *The Oxford Classical Dictionary*, 3rd Edition. Revised. Simon Hornblower and Antony Spawforth, eds. Oxford: Oxford University Press, 2003, 908b-910a.

Walsh, P.G. "The Rights and Wrongs of Curiosity (Plutarch to Augustine)," *Greece and Rome*, 2nd Ser., Vol. 35, No. 1 (Apr., 1988), 73-85.

Willey, Basil. *The Seventeenth Century Background.* New York: Columbia University Press, 1967.

Williams, Rowan. *"De Trinitate,"* *Augustine Through the Ages. An Encyclopedia.* Edited by Allan D. Fitzgerald, O.S.A. Grand Rapids, Michigan/Cambridge, UK: William B. Eerdmans Publishing Company, 1999, 845a-851a.

Wlosok, Antonie. "Zur Einheit der Metamorphosen des Apuleius," *Philogogus* 113(1969): 68-84.

Wolfson, Harry A. "Philo Judaeus," *The Encyclopedia of Philosophy,* Volume 6. New York: Macmillan Publishing Company, Inc. & The Free Press; London: Collier Macmillan Publishers, 1972, 151b-155b.

Yates, Frances A. "Hermeticism," *The Encyclopedia of Philosophy,* Volume 3. New York and London: Macmillan Publishing Company & The Free Press, 1972, 489b-490b.

# NAME INDEX

## A

Allchin, Douglas, 253

Ambrose of Milan, 82

Apuleius, 51; 53-58; 79; 81; 98; 140; 199; 205-206; 208; 238

Aristophanes, 45, n. 17; 45, n. 20, n. 21

Aristotle, 34-35; 42

Arrianus, 44, n. 14; 44, n. 15; 45, n. 21

Athanasius, 78

St. Augustine (of Hippo), allegorical method of exegesis 127; Alypius 127-129; Ambrose 134; anti-Manichaean polemic 100; Aristotle's *Categories* 126; Cicero's *Hortensius* 124; critique of natural science 110-111; 140; ecclesiology 222-224; examination of conscience (*Conf.* X) 132-138; 166; Manichaean experience 230; 240; *peregrinatio* motif 119ff.; studiousness 282; theft of pears episode 122; theocentrism 250-251

## B

Bacon, Sir Francis, 263, n. 9

Bronowski, Jacob, 253-254

Brown, Peter, 221

## C

Catullus, 51

Chadwick, Henry, 70; 73

Cicero (Marcus Tullius), 27; 50-51; 53; 124; 202-203; 215, n. 14

Clement of Alexandria, 79

## D

Davy, Sir Humphrey, 263-264, n. 24

Demosthenes, 45, n. 19

Dionysius of Halicarnassus, 44, n. 14

## E

Ehrenberg, Viktor, 32

Epictetus, 29

Eusebius, 79

## F

Fowden, Garth, 75

## G

Gregory of Nyssa, 78

## H

Heidegger, Martin, 23; 268ff.; ambiguity (*Zweideutigkeit*) 274; 277-278; Augustine Lectures 268-273; *Being and Time* 273-278; "being concerned" 269; care as *Bekummerung* 272; as *Sorge* 273; 276; curiosity (*Neugier*) 272; 274-278; *Dasein* and everydayness 273; 275-276; 278; 279; and fallenness 273-274; and forgetfulness of Being 274; and inauthenticity 273; and *Sorge* 273; temporality and historicity 278; defluxion 278; idle talk (*Gerede*) 274-276; thinking as meditative and calculative 280; wonder 277

Hermes Trismegistus, 74

.

# SUBJECT INDEX

## A

Adam, 190; 211-214; 228; 239; as symbol of mind's contemplative function 186

Adam and Eve, 66-67; as dual symbols of mind's functions 185; 192-193

*amor studium*, 178

*anamnesis*, 183

astrology, 18

Augustinian anthropology, 175-177; inner man/outer man 184

Augustinian psychology, 10-11

## C

Cappodocians, 78

Christian anthropology, 9; 13, n. 4

Christian Socratism, 235

Church, as a "mixed body" (*corpus permixtum*) 222

cognitive appetite, 11

*commune/proprium* distinction, 108-109; 117-118, n. 79; 187; 190; 255-256;

contemplative/sciential functions of the mind, 177; 185ff.; 237

Cupid and Psyche, 54-56

*cupiditas*, 97, 98, 100

*creatio ex nihilo*, 13, n. 3; 211; 251-252

*curae*, 182

*curiositas*, I Jn. 2:14-16, 95-96; 100; 104-106; 109; 120; 224-227; in Apuleius 53-58; Augustine's

*peregrinatio* 138-141; and carnal concupiscence (*concupiscentia carnis*) 165; "lust of the eyes" (*concupiscentia oculorum*) 16; 58; 65; 95; 105-106; 109; 135-136; 149; 165; 167; 182; 191; 200-201; 224; 239; 247; 270-271; 275; critique of pagan culture 199ff.; and *curae* 97-98; 104; 111; 127; demonic influence 201; desire for knowledge 139; desire for novel experience 140; desire for signs for God 137; desire for spectacles 107; disordering of the soul's priorities 163; etymology 27-28; 49-53; exploration of material world 100; fall of the soul theme (Augustine) 190-194; 210-214; fascination with temporal affairs 106; "heavy burdens of daily cares" 158; *illecebra oculorum* 15; as illicit 206; "impious acts" 224; source of iniquity 162; 164; *curiositas*-language in Latin patristic writing 80-81; love of acting on bodily passions 104; love of knowledge 189; love of vain knowledge 104; 111; love of operating on bodies 104; love of the world 227; 239; magical arts 203; 208-209; mind's sciential function 177; 184-190; 237-238; misuse of the will 162; moral triad ("triple concupiscence") 95ff.; 100-102; "morbid curiosity" 136; "natural enemy of peace" 104; 158; 162; occultism 204-205; Porphyry 159-160; pretense to knowledge 123; pretense to desire for knowledge 123; pride 105;